THE WHOLE WORLD CATALOG

THE WHOLE WORLD CATALOG

Delphine C. Lyons

Quadrangle / The New York Times Book Co.

Library of Congress Catalog Card Number: 73-79934
International Standard Book Number: 0-8129-0388-9

Interior design by Jerry Lieberman
Production by Planned Production

This book is a revised edition of *The Armchair Shopper's Guide: Mail Order Bargains Around the World,* An Essandess Special Edition.

CONTENTS

THE WHOLE WORLD CATALOG

INTRODUCTION

I'd like to begin by thanking my readers for all the letters I received in response to the first edition of *The Armchair Shopper* and my *Family Circle* articles on ordering by mail from abroad. Although I was unable to answer them personally, I have tried to incorporate as many of your suggestions as I could into this new edition. I'm afraid I still don't have the staff (in fact, I don't have a staff) to answer letters individually; however, I'm always glad to hear from you about your experiences with mail-order shopping, and what you might like to see included in future revisions of the book. I'm also always glad to hear of new sources, although, again, I am unable to acknowledge the information.

Acting upon your ideas, I have greatly expanded the book, particularly my coverage of crafts, needlework, the occult, and natural foods. I have continued to try to balance my emphasis equally between tools—seeds, paint, fabrics—and possessions—sweaters, china, watches—and to appeal to all degrees of affluence as well as a wide variety of tastes. You may discern a bias in favor of smaller firms and cottage crafts. The reason I don't describe the large, well-advertised firms in as much detail is not that I believe they necessarily offer inferior products or service, but that I believe you are more likely to have heard of them; or, if not, that the large and splendid catalogs which they put out will tell you all about them.

By and large, I have not included the numerous firms that don't seem to specialize in anything, but offer a little of this and a little of that . . . unless they happen to include items that I haven't found available elsewhere, in which case I've categorized them according to those items. Some firms fall into more than one category. Whenever that has happened, I have either repeated all the pertinent information whenever the firm is referred to or have given a cross reference to the original entry, depending on which seemed more convenient. A word of warning: some of the firms described here are exclusively mail-order houses and don't have shops, so don't drop in on them before you've received the catalogs and found out whether or not you'll be welcome.

I should explain at the outset that, although most of the firms described know that they're going to be included, there are a few to whom it may come as a happy (I trust) surprise. In order to compile this book, I got in touch with—or tried to get in touch with—over 5000 firms. Since, as I've already mentioned, I work alone—with occasional part-time help only at moments of crisis—I did this mainly by first sending away for the catalogs. If they seemed interesting, I would send a form letter to the various firms, telling them about *The Whole World Catalog,* and asking for their cooperation. In a few cases, when a catalog sounded very promising (and time was growing short), I sent the form letter without sending for the catalog first. Although the form letter stated clearly that it would be impossible for me to reply individually, some firms ignored this, insisting that I give them personal attention before they would cooperate. Others, although I had also stated explicitly that there would be no charges to those firms I decided to include, were sure that this was some cunning advertising ploy . . . or that, at the very least, I expected a commission.

A very few small firms wrote and said they were afraid they wouldn't be able to cope with the volume of catalog requests my book might engender, and those I did omit. Don't misunderstand me. Many firms were very helpful, and these form the bulk of the sources described in the following pages.

Anyhow, as my deadline drew near, and there were still firms I hadn't had a chance to get in touch with, I decided that, if a catalog I approved of was advertised in the media as free, or available for a specific sum, and I received it on those terms, then I was entitled by virtue of freedom of the press, etc., to disseminate this information in the public interest. And I decided also that, if a firm that doesn't advertise will send its catalogs to me—writing as everywoman and not as the perpetrator of *The Whole World Catalog*—free of charge, I was entitled to assume that they would democratically do the same for anyone who requested it, especially when the catalogs state explicitly, "Give us the names of your friends and we will send them our catalogs, too." Where a catalog was unusually elaborate, I did make a further effort to find out whether the firm wanted to make a token charge for it. If I got no answer, I took that to mean it was free.

I deduce from the amount of my mail not related to *The Whole World Catalog* which has definitely disappeared that a certain number of the letters that I sent out probably never reached their destinations; and that very likely some catalogs I wrote for and failed to receive may have actually been sent to me. The reason I'm telling you all this is so that you'll understand why some firms may be surprised to hear from you; and, also, why you may not receive a certain percentage of the catalogs you send for.

There shouldn't be too many surprised firms, because all those listed will be notified when the book appears; and, now that they know the purity of my intentions, they can tell me if they want to make any changes for the next edition. I repeat that there is no advertising of any sort involved in the book. Nobody pays—or can pay—to get in. I choose the firms that seem as if they would be most interesting either to the general public or to me. So far as is possible, I have made a point of not becoming personally acquainted with the personnel of the firms included in, or considered for, the book, since I feel it makes for greater objectivity. By the way, this seems like a good place to thank those firms which were kind enough to send me samples of their wares, and to apologize for not always having been able to acknowledge them. Naturally I have not allowed the samples to influence me in any way, except, of course, in evaluating those particular items. I must admit, however, that if I did get poisoned by some edible it would cause me to look upon the parent firm with a jaundiced eye. Objectivity has its limits.

Since my readers seem to want it, I have included a larger proportion of foreign mail-order houses than before. It's true that, although it is much easier to shop by mail from stateside sources, there are many advantages to ordering from abroad. You will be able to get a good many items that are unobtainable here, and you may be able to get items made to order at the same prices that you would have to pay for ready-to-wear here. You may also find broader ranges of certain commonly imported items than are usually available in the United States. Collectors, hobbyists, and craftsmen will be able to find some things that are difficult to get here because they are not in popular demand.

You will, of course, find *some* bargains. It isn't always easy for me to tell you whether or not an item is a bargain, because so much depends on where you do your shopping. If you live in New York, say, and buy at the elegant Fifth Avenue and East Side stores, you'll find a lot more bargains in these pages than if you patronize discount houses and scrounge around Orchard and Canal Streets.

You can be reasonably sure that most luxury items that are regularly imported, like perfumes, china, and glass, will be less costly in the countries of origin, no matter how high prices are there otherwise; although when it comes to china and glass you'll need to spend a lot of money before the saving in cost will compensate for the expenses of postage, packing, and insurance (unless you're buying very expensive stuff). Prices in the Orient, except for Japan, and wherever else labor is cheap, are generally lower than they are here.

But if it's a bargain you're after, be sure to compare prices carefully. Many things are cheaper in the United States than they are elsewhere; in fact, there are actually some European products that are cheaper here than in their places of origin, as one Swedish manufacturer of needlecraft supplies pointed out to me. In addition, the United States has developed a promising little handicraft industry of its own. We're starting to have cottage crafts, too, although our entrepreneurs will never be able to compete with the 80¢ per day wage scale cited to me by a Taiwan businessman as the reason he could keep prices so low.

Moreover, the products offered by the numerous American Indian houses that you'll find described here are as beautiful and exotic as the native crafts of other countries . . . and are, incidentally, much in demand there. Many of the U.S. firms listed in this book do a brisk mail-order trade with customers from overseas, so we must have something that they don't have; and, now that our dollar has been devalued, we can offer some very attractive bargains of our own. Most of the American firms mentioned in these pages will ship to Canada and Mexico, as well as overseas.

With very few exceptions, I have included only firms that offer catalogs with price lists, because I feel that it's unfair to both shops and customers to list sources that are unwilling to give me some idea of what they stock and the approximate price range. I use firms that omit price lists when sending me their catalogs only when there are no firms in the same category that are less cagey, when they appear to offer something extra special, or when they are what I call "piggy-back" firms; i.e., the ones that have no brochure but say, "We will give you 50 percent off the list price of Royal Ruritanian China." Even if they don't have a catalog, Royal Ruritania does.

When I quote prices, they are only approximations, to give you an idea of the relative costs of the items. By the time you read this, inflation and the devaluation of the dollar are bound to have pushed prices way up, both at home and abroad. Items that are available as this book is written may not be available by the time it is published, so *never send away for an item without sending for the catalog first.* And don't expect to get exactly the same catalogs and brochures that I have described here; they will change as new printings are made.

Not all the firms listed are strictly retail. Some are wholesalers or profess to be (sometimes it's just a come-on) who have set relatively low minimums; others are wholesalers who will sell sample orders to prospective customers without being too fussy about who these customers are. As one overseas dealer wrote me when I asked if he sold to retail customers, "After all, we have no control over who orders samples."

For some reason not unconnected with the fact that I can't speak any language but English fluently, you'll find that a disproportionate number of the foreign firms I write about happen to be in England or Ireland or in former British possessions. This means that the catalogs will, of course, be in English. Most of the catalogs from other countries will be in English, too. Wherever they aren't, I have indicated what language they are in. I've discovered that you don't necessarily have to know the language to order from a well-illustrated catalog full of familiar merchandise, but you may need a dictionary. Where a catalog gives prices in American dollars, I so indicate. If I don't say anything it means either that the catalog prices are in the country's own currency, or I forgot to put it in. Most of the firms seem able to correspond in English, although communication can break down under involved questioning.

Chapter 1

HOW TO ORDER

I've headed the information in this section Chapter I instead of making it part of the Introduction because I gathered from the letters I received in response to *The Armchair Shopper's Guide* that many of you didn't read the Introduction—which warned you against many of the difficulties you encountered and answered many of the questions you asked. It is important that you know all the things in this chapter before you send away for anything by mail. As a matter of fact, if you skipped the Introduction, it would be a good idea if you went back and took a look at it.

When you start writing for catalogs, you'll find that some firms ask a token sum to cover the cost of postage. (If you think a dollar is more than a token sum, take note of the current airmail rates.) Other firms prefer to absorb the costs and send out their catalogs free of charge, which doesn't mean that their merchandise is less expensive than the merchandise in the catalogs for which a charge is made; sometimes it's just the opposite. Free catalogs may be available only as long as the supply lasts. In most cases there will be another printing, but it may take many, many months, sometimes almost a year, before you receive a copy (or you may get a card saying that there is now a charge for the catalog).

If there's a huge demand for some of the catalogs for which there is a charge, you may also have to wait a long time because there's no way a firm can predict how many copies will be needed. After my previous book and my magazine pieces appeared, I found that hundreds of thousands of people might write to one mail-order house and only a few thousand to another. So, if you want to order by mail, the watchword is patience. You'll have to be patient in waiting for the catalog, and sometimes you may even have to be patient in waiting for the merchandise, especially if it's from overseas.

When there's a charge for a catalog, most firms prefer coin; however, some will accept stamps. If I don't put "coin only," it means the firms will accept stamps, however reluctantly. That applies only to U.S. firms, of course. A lot of my readers seem to be unaware of the fact that stamps are valueless outside the country of origin, except to philatelists. If a U.S. firm asks for a self-addressed stamped envelope

(which will be abbreviated in the text to SAE), always send a long one. "Refundable" (abbreviated "ref.") means that you will get your money back when you place an order (which may have to reach a certain minimum).

Wherever possible, I've tried to get the foreign firms to give their catalog charges in IRCs (International Reply Coupons), which you can buy at any post office. You can, of course, use these even when they're not specified, but remember that, although they cost you 22¢, they're worth only 15¢ because all they do is cover the cost of a first-class airmail letter. It is also possible to send coins to foreign countries (it's comforting to know that American cash is still acceptable almost anywhere); and I've sent coins and even dollar bills to the British Isles and other countries in Western Europe, and the money has always arrived safely. However, I don't recommend it; you follow my example at your own risk. As far as the rest of the world is concerned, even *I* wouldn't risk sending cash. To some countries, like India, you may even have to register a letter containing a check. If a catalog costs a dollar or more, I'd suggest a personal check (you should add 50¢ or so for conversion, but that's up to your conscience) or an International Money Order, fees for which start at 45¢. Several firms have asked me to tell you to seal the envelope carefully, as otherwise the enclosures may be pilfered.

When it comes to paying for the merchandise you must do whatever the firm requests. A few overseas firms will accept certain American charge cards, and some will take personal checks. However, many insist on a certified bank check or a money order. Some American firms also refuse to take personal checks. Others, both foreign and domestic, will, provided that you're willing to wait until the check clears before your merchandise is shipped.

You can save time by writing for catalogs from abroad via airmail because it can take several months for even first-class seamail to reach Africa, the Orient, or the Antipodes. Around Christmas it can take several months for mail from the United States to reach even Western Europe, and vice versa. You'll note that many overseas firms give estimates in their catalogs about how long it will take the merchandise to reach you. These estimates are always overly optimistic.

Once you send away for a catalog, you may find yourself on the company's permanent mailing list and continue to receive catalogs. Be sure that you order from the current issue. I admit that's sometimes difficult to do, since many firms don't mark their catalogs with any identifying date or number—which has given me considerable trouble in compiling this book (mail-order firms please take notice). In any case, don't order from a catalog that's over a year old before checking with the firm to make sure they still carry that item at the same price.

If you should buy from overseas, or even from out of state, you will not, of course, be charged sales tax. However, if you buy from a mail-order house that has a branch or a retail store in your state, you will usually be charged the tax, even though you have ordered your merchandise from another state and had it sent from there. Therefore, if the costs are the same, it will naturally save you money to order an item from a firm that has no branches.

Whether you're buying from local or foreign firms, always keep in mind the fact that the catalog price of the item isn't the amount you actually pay. When shipping expenses aren't included in the listed price, they become part of your cost. If I don't specifically say that shipping expenses are included, you must assume that they are additional. If you are ordering something that must be shipped by freight, try to find out what the cost will be before you place an order. In the case of something inexpensive, freight charges can come to more than the cost of the item. (For some items, as, for example, an antique, it may still be worth it, but take this into consideration first; don't just let the item be billed express collect or you may have a nasty surprise.)

In the case of small packages, many firms will tell you that they deliver via United Parcel (or some other service), and must have your street address, or they will be unable to deliver—which is fair enough. Others charge you postage then go ahead and send it by United Parcel. (Wherever I am aware of such a practice, I do not list the firm.) If you live in an urban area and have a post office box, watch out! United Parcel cannot deliver a package to your box. What they will do is mail a card there, telling you that they have a parcel which they will hold for a specified number of days. With the mails the way they are, you may receive the card long after the deadline, especially if you have rented a box because you sometimes are away for days at a time and want your mail held.

In that case, your parcel will be returned to the sender, who, in my experience, will make absolutely no effort to redeliver it to you. (If you think I speak out of bitter experience, you're absolutely right.) You will have to go to all of the trouble of writing a letter before they will deign to mail your parcel, and sometimes they won't even do that.

If you have a post office box and want to receive packages there, I have found that the following procedure works. I write on the order blank, in very large letters (red would be good): TO BE DELIVERED BY PARCEL POST ONLY. UPS (OR WHATEVER) NOT ACCEPTED. And I write on the check: "Merchandise to be delivered by Parcel Post only." By cashing the check, the firm implicitly agrees to *mail* you your merchandise. Therefore, if they don't want to send your order by mail, they must return your check immediately. I know—and, I'm sure, so do most other post office box holders—that United Parcel is often faster than the mails. However, there are considerations other than speed involved.

One of the best reasons for ordering from outside the United States is that you will automatically receive a small parcel by mail. An outsize parcel poses another problem. How large outsize is depends on the country involved; each one seems to have different regulations, which often are outlined in the firms' brochures. Sometimes I suspect that it is not the country that prohibits the mailing of a parcel over a certain weight or size, as claimed; it's the firm itself that doesn't want to be bothered. Be that as it may, really large parcels must be shipped by freight. On the whole, I don't recommend your buying goods from overseas that are so bulky that they must be sent by freight because this is not only expensive in itself, but may involve the services of a customs broker. This can come to an outrageous sum, unless you have ordered something so costly as to make the cost of a broker pale into insignificance. Airfreight is less complicated, I believe, if there's an airfield near you and you can collect the parcel yourself and fill out all necessary forms; but it is, of course, considerably more expensive than seafreight. The only time I would suggest that you order large items to be shipped from overseas via surface carrier is when the firm you are buying from will undertake to make all arrangements and can quote you all the charges in advance, or can recommend a carrier who will.

I've deliberately excluded foreign furniture houses from this book so far as I could, because I think ordering furniture from abroad is much too complicated and risky. For one thing, I advise my readers not to order merchandise unless it is returnable (and, if a catalog doesn't specifically state that the merchandise may be returned, to write and make sure it is before they order). You'll find there's plenty of red tape involved should you need to return something small; with furniture, it could become a nightmare. I'm warning you, because some of the firms I describe do include furniture as part of their lines.

If you buy items from abroad, you must also include duty as part of your cost. It's impossible to figure out duties precisely in advance, since they're laid on with what seems to be an erratic hand. However, here is a list of approximate duties on the most popular items:

TYPICAL RATES OF DUTY

ANTIQUES, produced at least 100 years before date of entry	no duty
BINOCULARS	
prism	20%
opera and field glasses	8.5%
CAMERAS	6.0-7.5%
camera lenses	12.5%
CANDY	5.0-7.0%
CHESS SETS	10.0%
CHINA	
bone	17.5%
nonbone, other than tableware	22.5%
nonbone tableware (in 77-piece sets)	
valued under $10.00 per set	10¢ doz., 48%
valued from $10.00 to $24.00	10¢ doz., 55%
valued from $24.00 to $56.00	10¢ doz., 55%
valued over $56.00 per set	5¢ doz., 18%
CLOCKS	75¢ to $1.12, 16%
CLOTHING	
with embroidery or ornamentation	2.0-42.5%
without embroidery or ornamentation	
cotton, knit	21%
cotton, other	7-21%
linen	7.5%
manmade, knit	25¢ lb., 32.5%
manmade, other	25¢ lb., 27.5%
silk, knit	10.0%
silk, other	16.0%
wool, knit	37.5¢ lb., 20.0-32%
wool, other	25 to 37.5¢ lb., 21%
sweaters, woolen, valued over $5.00 per lb.	37.5¢ lb., 20%
EARTHENWARE tableware (in 77-piece sets)	
valued under $3.30 per set	5¢ doz., 14%
valued from $3.30 to $12.00	10¢ doz., 21%
valued over $12.00	5¢ doz., 10.5%
GLASS TABLEWARE	
valued not over $1.00 each	22.5-50%
IVORY MANUFACTURES, except beads	6%
JADE	
unset, for use in jewelry	2.5%
other	21.0%
JEWELRY	
precious metal or stone	
silver, chief value, not	
over $18.00 per doz.	27.5%
other	12.0%
stones, but but not set	free-5%
beads, imitation precious or semi-precious	7-13.0%
beads, ivory	10.0%

LEATHER	
handbags	10.5%
shoes	2.5-20.0%
other	4.0-14.0%
MUSICAL INSTRUMENTS	
music boxes	8.0%
woodwinds, except bagpipes	7.5%
bagpipes	no duty
PEARLS	
loose or temporarily strung, without clasp	
genuine	no duty
cultured	2.5%
imitation	20.0%
strung, with clasp	12.0-21.0%
PERFUME	8¢ lb., 7.5%
RADIOS	
transistor	10.4%
other	6.0%
SHELL, manufactures of	8.5%
STERLING FLATWARE AND TABLEWARE	8.5-12.5%
TAPE RECORDERS	5.5-7.5%
TOYS AND DOLLS	12.5%
WATCHES	6.0-13.0%
WOODEN ITEMS	8.0%

This list is intended only to give you a general idea. Rates change frequently and don't always apply to specific items within the broad categories. Moreover, higher rates of duty apply on goods produced in Comunist China. In addition, when the post office delivers a package on which duty is to be collected, there is an additional fee of 70¢.

If you write to the Office of Information and Publication, Bureau of Customs, Department of the Treasury, Washington, D.C. 20226, they will send you a booklet called "Rates of Duty for Popular Tourist Items," which will give you the most up to date rates and instruction on where to get information on items not covered. Along with it, they'll send you a booklet called "Know Before You Go," to tell you what items cannot be brought into the United States under any circumstances, and another, "U.S. Customs Trademark Information," that tells you which trademarked articles may be brought into the United States only in limited quantities or may not be brought in at all. (That isn't as bad as it sounds; all you have to do is remove the trademark and they may be brought in without restriction.)

So far as I can determine, all the houses included in the following pages are firms of good standing, with excellent references. However, this book is intended to serve as a guide and not as an endorsement. In describing a firm, I am just telling you about its merchandise and services. I can offer no guarantees. And, although all the information given here is correct to the best of my knowledge at the time of writing, I cannot be responsible for any errors.

Chapter 2

CLOTHES

When you're ordering clothes, be sure that you know your size; and make sure, also, that the firm you're writing to uses standard sizes. What always infuriates me is the kind of store that offers clothes in *small, medium,* and *large,* without specifying exactly what they mean. (I've seen large applied to everything from a size 14 to a size 20.) Since I assume that American clothes will, as a rule, be readily available to you at your local stores, at prices no higher than by mail, in most cases (and, all things being equal, it's better to be able to try clothes on before you buy them), you'll find the emphasis in this chapter and the two that follow to be on overseas houses except for specialties . . . and bargains.

If you're ordering clothes from abroad, you'll find that some of the foreign mail-order houses that cater to Americans offer what purport to be American sizes. Sometimes they are; sometimes they don't seem to be the sizes of any country. Some firms offer only European sizes, which are wholly different from ours. Watch out for the English sizes; they *look* like ours, but they're actually quite different. In any case, it's wise to send your own measurements when you order, as insurance. It's also a good idea, when you order clothes from abroad—particularly major items, like coats and suits—to ask to see swatches of the fabric before you commit yourself.

A. GENERAL

The big American mail-order houses all have large selections of clothes, and their main advantage is that they have huge stocks in a wide range of sizes, and you're fairly well assured of getting your size in each of the colors offered (if you write at the beginning of the season, anyway). The clothes they offer are in the inexpensive to moderate price range, although you will find an increasing number of items in the higher price ranges.

In general, most of them will send you free catalogs the first time, although they tend to get peeved and take you off their list if you don't order a certain amount of merchandise. Some send partial catalogs containing a selection of merchandise they're pushing, and will let you have their big catalog only if you buy a certain amount from the small one—but they won't come out frankly and make a charge the way most of the European catalogs do. One or two will be reluctant to send you a catalog unless you take out a charge account. If you *want* a charge account, fine; but don't let yourself be pressured by steam-roller tactics into getting one. There seems no reason why they should prefer charge to cash customers, unless they figure that, by taking out a charge, you'll be tempted to go in over your head.

Anyhow, addresses are: **MONTGOMERY WARD AND CO.,** WW, 619 West Chicago Ave., Chicago, Ill. 60607 (they're the most coöperative); **SEARS, ROE-BUCK AND CO.,** WW, Philadelphia, Pa. 19132 (they can be pretty snotty); **SPIEGEL, INC.,** WW, 1061 West 35 St., Chicago, Ill. 60609 (their merchandise certificates often turn up as prizes on TV game shows); **J. C. PENNEY,** WW, Milwaukee, Wis. 53201; and **ALDEN'S,** WW, Chicago, Ill. 60607.

In general, you'll find the overseas houses more gracious about distributing their catalogs. (Of course, as I've said, most do charge, but I personally would prefer to pay rather than take out a charge account or buy merchandise I don't want.) Perhaps the best known of the mail-order houses on the continent is the German firm **QUELLE.** Although they're located in Bavaria, they have a New York office and a special address in New Jersey to which you send $4.00 for their huge catalog. Three dollars of that is refundable if you place an order. The merchandise will come from Germany, however (their overseas address is D-8510 Fürth/Bay., West Germany). The catalog is in German but with it you'll get a booklet giving an English translation of their "Fashion Section." Once upon a time you could get a bargain at Quelle, but now the clothes cost about the same as those in the American mail-order houses (exceptions being the kind of items our mail-order houses import from Germany—and not always then); and, with shipping costs and customs duties, not to speak of soaring prices, they could go higher. The clothes, except for some of the prints, look about the same as ours, too, now (the outer clothes, anyway). Gone are the fetching dirndls and peasant costumes of yesteryear. (But don't despair; you'll find an abundance of them in Chapter 3, C.)

Another big German mail-order house is **NECKER-MANN**, WW, P.O. Box 1, Frankfurt 6000, Germany. Their catalog is almost as large as Quelle's, and they say it's free except for packing and postage. I wrote to ask how much that would be; since I haven't heard from them, I'd say a dollar seems fair. Their clothes are in the same moderate price range as Quelle's and, again, styles are on the whole similar to ours, although you'll see one or two models that might seem a little different. The catch here is that Neckermann's catalog is in German, so you'll need either some knowledge of the language or a German-English dictionary.

Although the mail-order house of Wenz is located in Pforzheim, and you send your orders to Germany, it has, like Quelle, a U.S. office from which it sends out catalogs. They're $2.00, of which 5 marks (whatever the mark's worth by the time this comes out) is refundable on your first order, and the address to which you send it is **WENZ**, c/o Bergamo, 181 Nelson Ave., Jersey City, N.J. 07302. (The home address is Schulberg 17, Postfach 30, D. 7350, Pforzheim, West Germany.) Women's clothes are similar to Quelle's and Neckermann's, although I think some of the prints may look rather dowdy to American eyes. There's an extensive line of handsome knits for men, plus some attractive casual wear. Like Quelle, Wenz supplies you with an appendix in English that translates only the women's clothing part of the catalog.

For French-speakers, there's **JELMOLI**, WW, Mail Order Dept., 8021 Zurich, Switzerland, which belongs to SwissAir. If you fly on one of their planes, you get the catalog free; otherwise it'll cost you $3.00; and, with the prudence for which the Swiss are noted, no mention is made of your getting any of it back. Their clothes seem to be in the same price and style range as the German houses, except that they seem to have a lot more sweat suits for joggers and gymnasts in more colors than any place else. It's also the only mail-order catalog I've seen that offers a chef's hat among the regular work clothes.

If you prefer to communicate in English, you might write to Britain's celebrated **ARMY AND NAVY STORE, LTD.**, WW, Victoria St., London SW1E 6QX, England, which offers a small selection of clothes in its free catalog. Also free is the catalog from **OXENDALE INTERNATIONAL, OXENDALE AND COMPANY, LTD.**, WW, Galleon House, P.O. Box 150, Manchester X, England, which is devoted almost entirely to clothes. Styles and prices are very similar to those you'll find in the American mail-order houses, but, of course, you might find something of special appeal to you.

B. AMERICAN CASUALS

The **CARROLL REED SKI SHOPS**, WW, North Conway, N.H. 03860, actually show few, if any, ski clothes in their catalog; what they offer mainly is an attractive group of country casuals, for men, women, and children (the children's things seem rather expensive but fetching). **DUNHAM'S OF MAINE**, WW, Waterville, Me. 04901, offers classic suburban clothes, mostly in well-known brands. **FBS**, WW, 650 Main St., New Rochelle, N.Y. 10801, offers a group of somewhat less conservative casuals. Other Eastern shops that sell spectator sportswear and casual clothes are **PETER GLENN OF VERMONT**, WW, Box 837, Montpelier, Vt. 05602; **TALBOT'S**, WW, Hingham, Mass. 02043; **JOHNNY APPLESEED'S**, WW, Box 720, Beverly, Mass. 01915. Catalogs are free. **SAY YES**, WW, 1628 Second Ave., New York, N.Y. 10028 has a huge selection of jeans, including all the famous brand names, in denim, corduroy, and brushed cotton. They sometimes put out a catalog and when they do it's free.

Western casuals can be found at **OLD PUEBLO TRADERS**, WW, 622 S. Country Club Rd., Tucson, Ariz. 85716. Catalog is 50¢ (ref.).

For the elegant Florida touch, **LILLY PULITZER**, Mail Order Dept., WW 2901 N.W. 34 St., Miami, Fla. 33142, will send you a catalog of resort clothes fashioned out of her own popular prints. Prices for a polyester and cotton dress (sizes 4 to 18) start at $45.00, and you don't get to pick your own colors. You just tell the firm what color and print type (large, small, mild, wild) you prefer. Also bikinis, golf skirts, slacks, and such, plus shirts, slacks, and shorts for men are available in the same prints. Whatever garment you choose, you can get a stuffed alligator or a panda to match. Catalog is free.

WATUMULL BROS., LTD., WW, P.O. Box 3283, Honolulu, Hawaii, offers the giddy print men's Aloha shirts which used to typify the American tourist back in the 1950s, and seem to be making something of a comeback. They start at around $8.00, and there are women's pantsuits and muumuus in the same prints. The cloth is also available, from about $2.00 per yard. For those to whom Hawaii means hula skirts, you can get them here for around $3.50 up (complete with accessories). Brochure is free.

You'll find a lot of imported casual clothes in the following sections of this chapter, as well as in Chapter 4 (see Leather Goods Section B, especially). Since active sportswear seems to be becoming the American everyday costume, you'll find much more American casual wear in Chapter 20 (Outdoors and Sports).

C. KNITS

For the most part I'm emphasizing foreign sources in this section. Whatever native American knitwear is offered by mail will be in the general and sportswear catalogs, although most of the knitwear listed in the American catalogs seems to be imported, anyway.

Scotland and Ireland seem to have a plethora of knitwear houses. You'd think, since their brochures are in English, that you wouldn't have any language problems; however, when you get them you'll find references made to a mysterious knitted garment called a *jumper,* which bears no relationship to the sleeveless dress to be worn with a blouse that we know as a jumper. (The British call what we call a jumper a *pinafore dress,* which, although it sounds all milkmaid and ruffled, can actually be tailored.) What the British mean by jumper is simply a *pullover* (it can also, apparently, mean a blouse, too). By *lumberjacket* they seem to mean a collarless sweater that buttons up to a high neckline.

1. Scotland

Scotland is the origin of most of the cashmeres that have suddenly sprung back into fashion (although a sturdy segment of Middle America has never given up its twin sets). Their Fair Isle patterns (with border designs in the same tradition as the Scandinavian) have also always been much admired here. You'll be able to buy both of these at prices much lower than they would be here; in general, after duty and shipping costs have been taken care of, at least a third less. You can get even bigger bargains in the non-name brands and unspecific types.

St. Andrews in Scotland is celebrated for its golf course. It is also celebrated for the St. Andrews Woollen Mill, which seems to be right by the golf links. The address is **ST. ANDREWS WOOLLEN MILL,** WW, The Links, St. Andrews, Scotland—you get a little map showing the mill right opposite the eighteenth hole. They sell all kinds of sweaters—Shetland, Aran, lambswool, and cashmere (cashmeres start at around $21.00). They also have stoles and tartan and tweed ties (from less than $2.00).

HILLS LONDON SHOPS, LTD, WW, at Prestwick Airport, Scotland, doesn't put out a catalog as such, but they will send you some brochures of Pringle cashmeres, and probably can get you other brands should you so desire. As they're the airport shop, they're a good source for anything Scottish you can't find elsewhere. The **EDINBURGH TARTAN GIFT SHOP,** WW, 96 Princes St., Edinburgh, 2, Scotland, also shows sweaters by Pringle as well as Hogg of Hawick. The Pringle brochures they include with their main catalog show some jazzier items than does most of the

other Pringle material I've received, although they, too, have the classics. Pringle cashmere pullovers start at around $23.00; Hogg cashmeres start at around $17.00. The catalog is free by regular mail; $2.00 by air.

WILSON OF HAWICK, WW, 30 Drumlanrig Sq., Hawick, Scotland, in the thick of the Caledonian sweater industry, features Lyle and Scot knitwear. Cashmere sweaters start at around $10.00. They also offer lambswool sweaters and skirts, starting at around $8.00. Their catalogs and swatches are $1.00 by seamail; $2.00 by air. **W. S. ROBERTSON,** WW, 13-15 High St., Hawick, Scotland, offers a similar range of knitwear. Catalog is $2.00.

GLEN LOCKHART KNITWEAR, WW, Aberdour, Fife, Scotland KY3 ORF, features women's and men's pullovers and cardigans in lambswool, cashmere, and Shetland, including Fair Isle sweaters and sweater dresses, from around $16.00. For women there are skirts to match or mix, from $16.00; jackets, capes, and coats, from around $55.00, to match. Stock sizes are offered, but for very little more you can have them made to measure. Prices are given in American dollars and the catalog is $1.00.

D. MacGILLIVRAY AND CO., WW, Muir of Aird, Benbecula, Outer Hebrides, Scotland, has handknitted Shetland shawls for around $13.00, in pastels and natural wool colors; pullovers and cardigans in solid colors or with traditional Fair Isle patterns ($16.00); and cashmere and Shetland sweaters. Handknitted Harris wool sweaters are less than $7.00. There are also Harris wool socks and golf stockings. They'd appreciate 25¢ to help pay the postage for their brochures. Knitwear that the people of Shetland make in their homes is sold by the **SEAL ISLAND CO.,** WW, Harbour Rd., Androssan, Ayrshire, Scotland. Body colors are natural—yokes are predominantly blue, brown or green. Pullovers and cardigans start at around $17.00. There are also hats and gloves to match. The mimeographed price list is free.

2. Ireland

The traditional fisherknits, also known as Aran knitwear, are what Ireland is best known for. You'll also find other attractive knitted and crocheted garments here. Most of these are the products of cottage industries; that is, they're made in the homes of workers, who sell them to shops, which, in turn, sell them to you. Some of the workers have organized cooperatives, so that you can buy the goods directly from them. Usually they'll be cheaper that way, and, in many instances, you can have them made to order (some of the shops can arrange for this, too).

You could hardly call the place I'm going to begin with a mere shop. **WESTPORT HOUSE**, Mail Order Division, WW, Westport, Co. Mayo, Ireland, describes itself as the "stately home of the Marquess of Sligo," (though I can't for the life of me see how it can remain stately with all those "boutiques, shops and centres" on the premises), and the business is run by the Earl of Altamont, the present Marquess' son. The catalog, which costs $1.00, features a pleasing collection of Aran sweaters in the traditional *bainin* (natural off-white) starting at around $33.00. Handknitted dresses (black or white) are $27.00 up. There are also some attractive casual tweed clothes. Prices (in American dollars) include shipping.

C. KENNEDY AND SONS, LTD., WW, Ardara, Co. Donegal, Ireland, a well-known Irish specialty store, sells handknit fishermen's sweaters, in bainin only, each one labelled with the name of the knitter. Prices range from around $30.00 to $35.00, for men's and women's sizes, less for children's. **IRISH COTTAGE INDUSTRIES**, WW, 18 Dawson St., Dublin 2, Ireland, offers its fisherknits mainly in the traditional off-white, but they are also available in yellow, emerald green, rose pink, turquoise, violet, and purple. Pullovers for women (in sizes 36 to 40) cost around $27.00 or $28.00. Button-ups (which go up to size 42) are a dollar or two more. Men's sweaters (42 to 46) cost from $28.00 to $30.00. Also on hand are knitted belts, gloves, socks, and hats, all modestly priced. **EILEEN'S HANDKNITS**, WW, Ardara, Co. Donegal, Ireland, also offers colors on request, although the off-white is featured. Prices run from around $20.00 to $27.00, sizes are 32 to 46. All three brochures are free.

A group of craft-minded Irish housewives got together to form their own business, **BALLYMACHUGH HANDICRAFTS**, to handle the various crafts that they work in during their spare time. Although they have a stock of their most popular items on hand, you can arrange to have things made to order. Traditional off-white Aran knitwear in stock sizes includes cardigans from $17.00 to $20.00. Aran coats and dresses are available made to order; also available are many items crocheted of wool in any color you like. Sleeveless tops are $11.00; there are also dresses, coats, and so on. You can get price lists (in dollars) from **MRS. MAUREEN McENERNEY**, WW, Moynagh Lower, Pinea P.O., Mullingar, Co. Westmeath, Ireland. They're handwritten now, but she expects to have them printed in the near future.

A slightly feckless lady named **MARY CARMODY**— she forgot to put her name and address on either her advertising material or the envelope (it's Devon Rd., Templeglantine, Co. Limerick, Ireland)—offers custom-made knits and crochets for men, women, and children. Sweaters start at around $7.00, crocheted dresses and pantsuits (either knitted or crocheted— she's rather ambiguous) from $27.00. She says she's working on a printed brochure. **CRANA HAND-KNITS**, WW, Crana Rd., Buncrana, Co. Donegal, Ireland, is another cooperative knitwear venture. I'm unable to give you the prices of the sweaters, since Mrs. Rosalee Hagerty, who heads the venture, refers me to lists that she forgot to include with the illustrations. However, she did put in the list of special items, like crocheted hostess gowns, buttoned down the front, which cost from $35.00 to $55.00 and are quite lovely. There are also good-looking capes from around $38.00, shawls from $12.00 to $25.00. Both brochures (if they ever get printed) are free.

You'll be glad to know that they're still busily knitting away in Northern Ireland, too. The **ULSTER BOUTIQUE**, WW, 64 Wellington Pl., Belfast, Northern Ireland, offers a free brochure of Aran handknits, mainly in bainin, though other colors can be arranged. In addition to sweaters (starting from $20.00), they have women's coats (beginning at around $45.00), as well as knit trousers, skirts, and dresses. For men, they offer only sweaters.

If you're in a hurry for your fisherknits, you can buy them in this country from the **IRISH SHOP**, WW, 8 Melody Lane, Chelmsford, Mass. 01824. Prices are a great deal higher—$40.00 to $45.00—but there will, of course, be no duty to pay and shipping is included, which would bring them close to the prices of the more expensive Irish shops. You'll also find both Irish and Scottish handknits at the **SHANNON AIRPORT STORE** (See Section D.2).

3. The Continent

HUSFLIDEN, WW, Grunnlagt 1895, 500 Bergen, Norway, was established in 1895 as a nonprofit organization to serve as a center for the cottage crafts of Norway. Among the many free brochures it offers is one devoted to the very attractive Norwegian handknits, with the prettiest being those in traditional allover patterns. Pullovers are from $25.00 to $30.00, sweater jackets are a little higher. There are also mittens and hats (including several clearly meant for trolls) in gay profusion. The brochure has an English insert, but prices are in kroner.

ICEMART, WW, Mail Order Dept., P.O. Box 23, Keflavik International Airport, Iceland (catalog 30¢) offers some very handsome sweaters, knitted according to traditional patterns, in the natural colors of the Icelandic sheep—mostly off-white, with some black, gray, and brown. Prices are about half what they would be here; a man's or woman's pullover costs around $22.00. Also on hand among the knitwear are scarves, slipper socks, caps, berets, mittens, and collars to wear under your coat to keep your neck toasty warm. In addition, there are knitted and woven capes, ponchos, stoles, and vests—some ornamented with traditional Icelandic patterns—plus some bold, modern-looking coats.

WILLIAM SCHMIDT AND CO., WW, Karl Johansgate 41, Oslo, Norway, offers a brochure of attractive, traditional Norwegian sweaters in bright colors for both sexes and all ages. It is, curiously, almost the same brochure that's offered by the export division of **A. S. SUNDT AND CO.,** WW, Postboks 1063, 5001 Bergen, Norway. However, Sundt gives the prices in American dollars (starting at about $35.00), and with Schmidt's you have to struggle with kroner. Prices work out to about the same. Both brochures are free.

TIROLER HEIMATWERK, WW, Meraner Strasse 2, Innsbruck, Austria, sells patterned sweaters similar to the Norwegian from around $22.00. Plain button-up sweaters cost somewhat less. Also available are some mittens and lively knee-length socks. The charming little catalog is free. Prices are given in American dollars.

Usually the more southerly European countries are not noted for their sweaters; however, **MADEIRA SUPERBIA, LTDA.,** WW, av. Dubuque de Loule 75-A, Lisbon, Portugal, shows a group of handknit and handembroidered fishermen's sweaters. I can't imagine any working fisherman wearing them, but they are very pretty and the prices are incredibly low —$5.00 to $15.00. Their handsome catalog is free and prices are in dollars.

4. The Orient

Most of the Hong Kong houses also offer sweaters. Beading is the big item here, although plain cashmere and lambswool sweaters are also offered. A good source for knitwear is **HARILELA'S MAIL ORDER,** WW, P.O. Box 5106, Kowloon, Hong Kong, which has a huge collection of beaded and embroidered cardigans, $8.00 to $17.00, plus bulky knits and sweater coats. They also offer plain Pringle sweaters for men ($19.00 to $26.00) and women ($27.00 up); also Jaeger sweaters for men ($15.00 to $19.00). **CANDLELIGHT ASSOCIATES MAIL ORDER SERVICE,** WW, P.O. Box 1243, Hong Kong, also shows both beaded and embroidered sweaters in lambswool (around $9.00 to $11.00) and cashmere ($15.00 to $17.00) in its attractive trilingual (French, Spanish, English) catalog. Seamail shipping is included in the prices, given in American dollars. Both catalogs are free, if you order them by seamail, $2.00 each by airmail.

Beaded and embroidered Oriental sweaters may be obtained stateside from **THAI SILKS,** WW, 393 Main St., Los Altos, Cal. 94022, for $15.00 to $20.00, and there's no duty to pay. Unornamented sweaters are much cheaper. There are also many other kinds of Oriental garments and merchandise, in some cases priced almost as low as they would be in the Orient. SAE for brochures.

5. The Americas

Solid color sweaters from Ecuador are offered in classic styles and American sizes. Prices start at $18.00, and, for an additional $1.50, you can have an indigenous design woven into your sweater. There are also floral-design sweaters from the cooperative "Chompas de los Andes," plus cardigans trimmed with embroidered woollen fabrics ($25.00), and skirts to match ($15.00). All from **ANDEAN PRODUCTS,** WW, Apartado 472, Cuenca, Ecuador, whose charming little catalog in English is free. Prices are given in American dollars and shipping is included. You'll find other handknits of the Americas in Chapter 3, B.

D. OUTERWEAR—COATS, SUITS, WRAPS

1. The British Isles

BURBERRY'S, LTD, WW, Burberry's in the Haymarket, London SW1Y 4DQ, England, will send you a free catalog of the British coats and raincoats that have made their name a household word. Their men's coats start from around $50.00, the women's from about $65.00.

I didn't know that the poncho was a traditional Scottish garment, but, under the traditional name of *mhor*, it apparently is a Highland classic. So says **EGERTON'S,** WW, 5 Fore St., Seaton, Devon EX 12 2LB, England, which shows several types of mhors in its general gift catalog (50¢), from around $11.00 to $17.00, in basketweaves and mohair. On the other hand, **WILSON OF HAWICK** calls a poncho *tonag mhor* (which they translate "big shawl") and sells it for $17.00 to $18.00. (Their plain *tonag*, "wee shawl," is $12.00 to $13.00.) **BROOMBERY COTTAGE INDUSTRIES,** WW, by Ayr, Scotland, in Burns country, also sells ponchos, but they maintain that the traditional Gaelic name is *tunag*. Anyhow, their tunags, in blue, green, or red plaids, are around $12.00 to $13.00, shipping included. They also have brushed mohair tartan and plain wool scarves, from $3.00, as well as sweaters. Their little leaflet is free.

To return to Egerton's, they show some suits and coats made to your measure in Wales, from the region's distinctive tapestry cloth. A vest and skirt combination costs from around $30.00 to $40.00. Prices are given in American dollars. You can also order tapestry coats, capes, and skirts, in styles different from those offered by Egerton's, directly from the **LLYSWEN WELSH CRAFT CENTRE**, WW, Templar House, Temple Way, Bristol BS1 6HD, England, at much the same prices. At Llyswen you can get handbags to match your outfit, from around $6.00 to $9.00. Llyswen's handsome swatch-filled brochure is free. (Egerton's will also send swatches if you ask for them.)

MacGillivray has a tailoring service that will provide women's and men's suits from around $50.00 to $70.00, coats, $55.00 to $70.00, plus the cost of the fabric. Glen Lockhart will make tweed coats and suits for women at lower prices (they include the fabric). **WILLIAM ANDERSON AND SONS, LTD.**, WW, 14 to 16 George St., Edinburgh, Scotland, also offers made-to-measure tweed and tartan skirts and "pinafore" dresses for women, plus coordinated knitwear. Catalog is free.

You can buy reasonably priced Harris tweed jackets imported from Scotland on this side of the Atlantic, from the **FREED CO.**, WW, Box 394, Albuquerque, N.M., for less than $35.00 each. Freed also has women's Yorkshire tweed English riding jackets for $30.00 to $35.00. (They also import from the rest of the Americas; ponchos handmade of alpaca-llama are under $20.00, and Mexican serapes from around $2.50 to $15.00. Brochures are free.)

2. Ireland

SHANNON, WW, Mail Order Stores, Shannon International Airport, Shannon, Ireland, has pure wool Connemara rug coats (very loud) at prices ranging from $30.00 to $35.00, also Connemara rugs not made into coats at around $11.00. There are lots of cashmere and lambswool sweaters, at very reasonable prices; Viyella robes for both sexes and Viyella shirts and Aquascutum jackets for men alone. There are also Irish fisherknits for all and woollen dresses for women. Their marvelous catalog, which shows a little of everything (mainly at prices that I have rarely seen beaten elsewhere), is 60¢.

One of Ireland's poshest shops, **BROWN THOMAS AND CO., LTD.**, WW, Grafton St., Dublin, Ireland (catalog 50¢) offers a group of good-looking local tweeds. A skirt is $10.00; women's suits start at less than $60.00. Prices in American dollars.

S. & M. JACOBS, LTD., WW, 20 Dawson St., Dublin 2, Ireland, established as custom tailors for over 60 years, offers both women's and men's custom-tailored garments in their Donegal handwoven tweeds (the men's are said to be thornproof). Women's suits start at less than $50.00, men's (English or American styling) around $80.00. The price for the catalog and

swatches is $1.00; and, the proprietor says hopefully, "A dollar note, or coin, is the simplest way to send it."

E. MAINLY FOR WOMEN

1. Britain and Ireland

W. BILL, LTD., WW, 40 South Motton Rd., London W1Y 1AT, England, sells pantsuits for women, from around $40.00, and skirts from $30.00, plus lots of knitwear. Brochures are free.

CLEO, WW, 3 Molesworth St., Dublin, Ireland, shows some really gorgeous capes. A heavyweight wool cloth cloak is around $55.00, a short-length tweed cape with sleeves is less than $30.00. And the hooded velvet Munster cloak for evening wear leaves no doubt as to why Red Riding Hood had trouble with wolves (although she's generally depicted as wearing the day-length version, which is also offered); it's less than $75.00. There are all kinds of stoles and shawls—a "fine tinker's shawl for cocktail or evening wear" (a tinker is a sort of indigenous gypsy) is $15.00. Shown with it is a red flannel "peasant" skirt at $17.00. Also offered are very good-looking crocheted and woven hostess skirts, plus knitwear, and a most engaging donkey who is not for sale.

COLETTE MODES, WW, 66 South St. George's St., Dublin 2, Ireland, sells colorful Donegal handwoven tweed skirt and pantsuits, in the $45.00 to $55.00 price range, as well as some dresses, $25.00 to $30.00. Only stock sizes (10 to 18) are offered. And from **BALLYMACHUGH** (C.2) you can get Carrickmacross lace blouses (around $40.00), mantillas (average $12.00), and stoles ($20.00), plus collar and cuff sets ($3.00 to $12.00). They'll also make you a wedding veil, which will be a real heirloom, from $38.00.

2. The Continent

The well-known Belgian house of **MARIA LOIX**, WW, 52-53 rue d'Arenberg, 1000 Brussels, Belgium, has lace blouses from around $25.00 to $35.00, mantillas and lace scarves from $10.00, and wedding veils from $35.00. If you're interested in anything in particular, you can get a picture of it for a small charge. Similar offerings are made by "Brussels' largest lace store" which is how the **LACE PALACE**, WW, 1-3 rue de la Violette, 1000 Brussels, Belgium, describes itself. They also sell a lot of items you don't see at the other lace houses, such as lace fans, $11.00 to $16.00; pure lace hostess aprons, $3.00 to $5.00; and lace gloves and lace jewelry. Both lists are free; both give prices in dollars.

Lovely linen and silk blouses from Portugal, embroidered in the distinctive Madeira mode may be obtained from Madeira Superbia (C.3) at most reasonable prices (from around $11.00 to $25.00). Both American and European sizes are given. Blouses in the same genre are available from **SWATOW** (G).

All kinds of Florentine articles are what **EMILIO PAOLI**, WW, Via della Viona Nuova 24-26-28R., 50123 Florence, Italy, makes, but the catalog shows only crocheted straw clothes, starting at around $30.00 for a sleeveless dress, and with a top of around $65.00 to $70.00 for an evening gown. There are also straw suits and straw coats. They're all very pretty, but they don't look practical to me; and, when I wrote to the firm to ask whether they were dry-cleanable, they evaded the question. I assume the catalog is free, since they were evasive about that too.

3. The Orient

The **MAY FASHION HOUSE**, WW, Box 6162, Hong Kong, shows a selection of attractive dresses in stock sizes (8 to 18); however, for 10 percent extra, you can have them made to order. Dresses in a variety of luscious-colored silks start at less than $25.00; there are also lots of nice pantsuits, starting at less than $30.00. Particularly worthwhile are the coat and dress ensembles in silk-and-wool combinations at less than $70.00. May can also make up anything you want from a sketch or clipping. The catalog costs $1.00, and prices are given in dollars.

CANDLELIGHT ASSOCIATES (C.4.) has good-looking silk and satin dresses and robes, in sizes 8 to 22 (American; they also give French and German sizes). A beaded Thai silk cheongsam is around $25.00, a full-length beaded Thai silk evening dress is $37.00. There are also silk blouses, $4.00 to $5.00, and many other pleasing things.

The **PACIFIC MAIL-ORDER SYSTEMS, LTD.**, WW, P.O. Box K-9282, Kowloon City Post Office, Hong Kong, B.C.C., puts out a handsome "Dynasty" catalog (free) of their holiday and resort fashions. Prices seem somewhat higher than at the other Hong Kong houses, and they don't offer special tailoring or dress-making services; moreover, there seems to be little that's Oriental about the clothes—except for the loungewear. However, they're not expensive (mostly $60.00 to $100.00) for styles that aspire to high fashion. You may very well see something you like.

TESORO'S, WW, 1352 A. Mabini, Ermita, Manila D-406, Philippines, has some very attractive dresses and blouses in dacron, ramie-tetoron ("wash and wear linen") and voile, in a variety of styles, all custom-made, so you can pick the collar, sleeve length, etc., you want. Most are embroidered; some are decorated in cutwork; some combine the two. Prices are remarkably low, starting at $12.00 for a dress, and you get

fabric swatches along with your catalog (which is $2.00, and includes the whole roster of Philippine handicrafts).

F. MAINLY FOR MEN

1. Custom-Made

O'BEIRNE AND FITZGIBBON, LTD., Export Dept., WW, 14/15 Upper O'Connell St., Dublin, Ireland, puts out a sample card of the Donegal tweeds and tweed mixtures they use to make their men's jackets (at prices in the $45.00 neighborhood). Their brochures are $1.00 (ref.), but one of them includes a poem that ends, "Och, on looms of enchantment/Donegal fairies weave it/Donegal tweed, O Donegal tweed!"—which is worth at least part of the price.

MAIWO YANG AND CO., WW, G.P.O. Box 2798, 14 Queen's Rd. Central, Hong Kong, B.C.C., will send you free a thick bundle of fabric swatches for men's suits. There are somber traditional swatches and colorful modern swatches. A polyester and wool suit starts at around $58.00, 100 percent wool around $61.00, the doubleknits at $75.00.

SANGWOO INTERNATIONAL, LTD., WW, Far East Mansion, Middle Rd., Kowloon, Hong Kong, says it's been approved by the U.S. Army Uniform Quality Control Office in Washington for making military uniforms, so you ought to be able to trust them with your civvies. They have a big book of swatches in knitted crimplene worsted, polyester knits, worsted sharkskin, all-wool worsted, dacron, sharkskin, and so on. Suits start at around $60.00, jackets around $42.00. Seamail shipping is included.

The **YANGTZEKIANG GARMENT MANUFACTURING CO., LTD.**, WW, 30 Queen's Rd. Central, Hong Kong, will also send you swatches of various materials, plus their brochures and price lists. Although they offer ready-made suits—cut, they say, "to American, British, and Continental specifications," and priced under $40.00, sports jackets around $27.00, slacks around $12.00—for $10.00 extra you may have a garment custom-tailored.

You'll also find some custom houses in Section D of this chapter.

2. Ready-to-Wear

CABLE CAR CLOTHIERS, WW, 211 Sutter St., San Francisco, Cal. 94108, calls itself "San Francisco's great natural shoulder stores since 1946." Much of its stock is imported, but I have a feeling that their "Lederhosen style slacks by Rough Rider" are indigenous. These come in corduroy and poplin and are $13.00 (less for the shorts). There's a comprehensive collection of jump and jog suits ($16.00 to $35.00), plus classic suits ($85.00 to $175.00), sport coats, and such. Because this is a Western firm, the hats naturally include Stetsons. The catalog is free.

That well-known bastion of the conservative, **BROOKS BROTHERS**, WW, 346 Madison Ave., New York, N.Y. 10017, puts out catalogs from time to time, which they may or may not send upon request. They asked that I not list them in my *Family Circle* articles, and I didn't; but I feel they do belong in the book, as a kind of monument, if nothing else.

Somewhat different from Brooks' wares are the men's clothes offered by **LIMBO**, WW, P.O. Box 961, Madison Square Station, New York, N.Y. 10011. Because styles change so fast here, the items I list are only to give you an idea of the general tenor of the place. A used Texas Department of Correction cotton T-shirt is $1.50, work jeans by A. Smile in several shades of cotton twill and pinwale corduroy are $9.00 to $11.00, a Western shirt made of imported velvet is $20.00, a green Canadian battle jacket $5.00, a "funky Italian knit snugge" is $12.00. The catalog is free. Prices, considering that a lot of the stuff is second-hand, are not exactly low. (See Chapter 20 for a lot more government and other institutional surplus clothing.)

Very cool characters will be attracted by the clothes that **ELEGANZA**, WW, Pearl St., Brockton, Mass. 02403, vends. You don't see items like, for example, a polyester doubleknit maxicoat with cotton suede inserts and matching flared slacks everywhere. Available only in bright blue, it's $70.00 for the set (and there are even matching shoes with 2½" heels). Other equally dramatic suits are even less. Another eye-catcher is the extra-full cut hooded kaftan of purple nylon, at $25.00. There are also distinctively colored shirt suits, all kinds of slacks—bell-bottoms, kick pleats (in contrasting colors), two-tone, studded—everything you could think of, with complementary shirts and loads of other accessories. In much the same genre is **FLAGG BROTHERS**, WW, 492 Craighead St., Nashville, Tenn. 37204, well-known for its innovative work in men's shoes. (See Chapter 4, E.) They've now added a group of maxi and toga suits. A really spectacular toga suit, with tunic and slacks of acetate and nylon, in burgundy, black, and beige, the tunic trimmed with imitation Persian lamb, is $43.00. Also all kinds of distinctive slacks and shirts. Both catalogs are free.

JOEL McKAY, INC., WW, 707 South Raymond, Pasadena, Cal. 91105, specializes in jump suits in practically any fabric you can think of. Prices range from about $17.00 to $45.00, and there are rubber-soled casual shoes to match, from $15.00, as well as other

items of casual clothing. Shipping is included. Catalog is free.

In its free folder, **TRIMINGHAM'S**, WW, Hamilton, Bermuda, shows Indian madras items for men; shirts and shorts run from $7.00 to $9.00, trousers $14.00, jackets $30.00. There are also other types of shorts from $7.00 to $30.00, and shirts from $9.00 up.

3. Shirts

If you send a dollar to **A. GARSTANG AND CO., LTD.**, WW, 213 Preston New Rd., Blackburn, Lancs. BB2 6BP, England, they'll send you all sorts of swatches from which you can order custom-made shirts. Fabrics include cottons, nylons, drip-dries, silks, Botany wool, Viyella fancies, and the like, with prices from around $10.00 to $20.00. They also make pajamas. To the East, the **WAYSTON SHIRT CO.**, WW, P.O. Box 15114, Hong Kong, will make you a shirt in any style you like, from around $8.00 to $12.00, in cotton, drip-dry, Swiss voile, etc. Brochure and swatches are free. And so much further East it's West again . . . **J. PACKARD, LTD.**, WW, Custom Shirtmakers, Terre Haute, Ind. 47808, makes shirts in a variety of fabrics, mainly knit and permanent press, to your specifications. They are priced from around $8.00 to $11.00, with discounts on quantities. Shipping is extra.

Ready-made shirts are offered at many of the firms described elsewhere in this chapter. Particularly interesting are **TESORO'S** *jusi barong* Tagalong formal dress shirts, handembroidered on banana fiber, as well as everyday shirts, either hand- or machine-embroidered, from $4.00 to $15.00. You can also get handembroidered wash and wear shirts made to your specifications, from $12.00 up.

The Portuguese firm of **JABARA AND SON**, although located in Funchal, Madeira, has a New York office at WW, 281 Fifth Ave., New York, N.Y. 10016, to which you can write for their free catalog. They have handembroidered men's dress shirts, available in white and blue but with fabric unspecified (I suspect it's linen), at $15.00. Special sizes are a few dollars extra.

You wouldn't expect to find men's shirts offered at an art gallery, but the bright-colored fast-dyed batik shirts created by the **SERENDIB GALLERY**, WW, 100 Galle Rd., Colombo 4, Sri Lanka (Ceylon), were created by artists, and are priced very reasonably, from around $8.00. Price lists are free and include many other fascinating things. After all, wasn't it the Three Princes of Serendib who kept making those unexpected discoveries? Address your request to the manager, Mr. Watson Fernando.

G. MAINLY FOR CHILDREN

MOTHERCARE-BY-POST, WW, Cherry Tree Rd., Watford, Herts. WD2 5SH, England, will send you, free of charge, a fat little catalog containing everything to outfit the infant from birth through toddlerhood, at very moderate prices. For instance, little girls' trouser suits in damson (purple) acrylic jersey, with braid trim, are around $5.00; and a brown and white three-piece orlon ski suit—presumably for either sex—is under $7.00. As you can see, no color choice. There are also some reasonably attractive clothes for the expectant mother at very low prices indeed.

C.H.I.C., WW, CCPO, Box 1189, Makati, Risal, Philippines, offers a group of very inexpensive handmade and handembroidered Tetoron (I assume that's a synthetic) infants' wear at extremely low prices. You have to buy them in sets. For instance, six sunsuits for toddlers, or four baby gowns are $9.25 per set; eight diaper shirts or six pairs of panties are $8.75. Postage is $1.00 extra for each set. Brochure is free. **TESORO's** not only offers handembroidered dresses for babies and infants for from $6.00 to $9.00; they also have them for pre-teens at $7.00 to $11.00. Fabrics are dacron and banana fiber.

Both The **LACE PALACE** and **MARIA LOIX** have lace christening robes from around $22.00 to $60.00 and lace-trimmed bibs, bonnets, and booties, $2.00 up. The Lace Palace also offers baby dresses from $27.00 to $30.00. **BALLYMACHUGH** will make you a Carrick-macross lace christening robe for around $27.00. Madeira Superbia offers an enchanting selection of children's clothes, handembroidered in traditional Madeira fashion. Bibs start from less than $1.00, a sunsuit is under $2.50, and dresses are around $2.00 to $8.00. Colors are mainly pastel, but there are also items in cherry and royal blue.

The **SWATOW DRAWN WORK CO., LTD.,** WW, P.O. Box 455, Hong Kong, has some exquisite embroidered drip-dry cotton things for babies and toddlers. Smocked dresses run from around $2.00 to $5.00, rompers are $2.00 or so. They also show some beautiful embroidered blouses for women. Catalog is free. Another Hong Kong firm, the **WELFARE HANDICRAFTS SHOPS,** WW, Deck 1, Samun Gallery, Ocean Terminal, Salisbury Rd., Kowloon, Hong Kong, operates under the auspices of a number of Hong Kong welfare organizations that supervise its production standards. Its small, rather general brochure offers some especially good buys in clothing for smaller children. Drip-dry smocked cotton dresses and rompers cost from around $3.00 to $5.00, denim and corduroy playsuits from $3.00 to $7.00. Also on hand, pajamas and robes for older children as well as adults.

UNDER THE NAME OF SAUNDERS, WW, 140 West 92 St., Apt. 2B, New York, N.Y. 10025, makes, it says, "hand-sewn clothes from original designs, in durable, machine-washable natural fabrics. They are real clothes for real children." They also are a lot more expensive than the other sources described here; fabric dresses for little girls can run as high as $20.00 or more. However, if you go in for hardhat chic, you might be interested in workmen's overalls for babies, from $6.00 to $8.00. There are also classic sailor suits (sizes 1 to 6) as seen in Kate Greenaway illustrations, $12.00 to $15.00. Brochure is free.

H. UNDER AND LOUNGEWEAR

I was going to head this section *lingerie,* but, since President Pompidou of France has made such a point of taking the English out of the French language, I feel I have to retain the honor of the English-speaking peoples. Anyhow, as I am covering both men's and women's clothes here, perhaps *underwear* is a more tactful term (although I don't see why, actually, since *lingerie* merely means linen). Most of the European mail-order houses seem to have larger and more colorful selections of textured and opaque tights (or *panty hose* as Americans call them; I prefer the British term, or the German *strumpfhosen*), especially the warmer ribbed and knitted types, than are generally available here. You'll also find more sizes and colors of tights and leotards at the dance supply houses (Chapter 2, J) you'll find them in larger sizes, too, because a lot of larger ladies use the dance to attempt to get rid of their avoirdupois.

The lingerie is where you'll find a great difference between the European and American mail-order houses, mainly because central heating is not as ubiquitous as it is here; I understand that even today modern apartments on the Continent are built without it. Quelle has some sexy warm woolies for ladies, plus some more or less standard underwear in bright blue, lilac, rust, tearose, and splashy prints (they also have the conventional black and white, of course). Gentlemen's undies make a bright splash, too (as it does here too, of course, nowadays). Neckermann also has cheerful underwear for women though they don't go as heavy on the warm woolies.

LA ESTRELLA, WW, Heerenstraat 30 Punda, Curaçao, calls itself Curaçao's most complete department store, but the only item for which they put out a specific brochure is men's Norwegian *Brynje* string underwear in both white and colors, priced from $1.75 to $2.50. They also put out a list describing their wares in general terms. Included on it are Arrow shirts, Italian bathing suits, ski sweaters from Norway, Austria, and Israel . . . and practically everything else listed in this book. Since prices in Curaçao are usually much lower than here, you might think the matter worth further investigation. Both the general list and the *Brynje* brochures are free.

Most of the English catalogs that I've seen show underwear like ours, to go with those swinging minis, but **HELIOS HOME SUPPLIES**, WW, Macclesfield, Cheshire, England, offers "Gigi" stretch nylon underwear. The knee-length "pantaloon" comes in white or pink, is trimmed with rows of lace, and costs around $2.00. A bra-top vest (undershirt) to match is slightly higher. There are also knickers (panties) and cami-knickers (combinations, I guess you'd call them). I thought the Gigi pantaloon was a winter garment, but they have an equally frilly pantaloon in wool-nylon, for about a dollar more, with other items to match. Catalog is free.

In an entirely different genre, **FREDERICK'S** of Hollywood, WW, 6608 Hollywood Blvd., Hollywood, Cal. 90028, has acquired a worldwide reputation for its unabashed underwear. There are panties and panty hose without crotches, as well as other items that cover up the less usual parts of the body and expose those usually covered. There are bras in all sizes (A to DD) and shapes, including some that paste on, others that blow up, and Tender Tips "for the gal who can't make it on her own" (flat-chested ladies wear these under sheers). They all have names like "Secret Shaper," "Bare Necessity," and "Little Sneaky." For those who feel inadequate in the rear, there are girdles that "fix your flats," or you can come right out and buy Fanny Falsies. Underlying all these coquetries is a kind of strangely old-fashioned innocence, for to justify the purchase, it has to be assumed that these illusions can be sustained for a measurable length of time. Since I last wrote them up, they've added a line of seductive loungewear for both sexes, including see-throughs for men. Prices seem moderate, considering the passions involved. Catalogs are 50¢ each, $1.50 for a two-year subscription.

ORIGINALS, WW, Treasure Island, Fla. 33706, also offers seductive lingerie under the heading "The Turn-Ons." There's some loungewear, too, and a line of "obedient bras," to fit all figure sizes from 32B to 48DD (apparently they've never even heard about A cups here). The catalog is apparently free.

One-time ecdysiast **LILI ST. CYR**, WW, 8104 Santa Monica Blvd., Hollywood, Cal. 90046, is now engaged in selling "way out lingerie from the undie-world of Lili St. Cyr." Her brochure is merely a folded broadsheet, but the merchandise is similar to Frederick's raunchiest, with some imitation leather items for kinky types on a budget. (Well-heeled kinks should investigate the wares of **WALTER WRIGHT**, Chapter

4,B. Prices are moderate, and the brochure, so far as I can tell, is free.

More conventionally, **CHATHAM HOUSE, INC.**, WW, P.O. Box 646, Siler City, N.C. 27344, offers a large line of slightly-irregular panty hose at what they claim are half store prices or less (from around $12.00 to $24.00 per dozen; you have to buy at least three pairs at a time). These include sheer support and maternity styles. There's underwear for both men and women, tights and leotards ($3.00), also virgin wool cardigan sweaters for men and women (around $12.00 each). Everything, they declare almost belligerently, is American made, and the catalog is free.

Specialist in terrycloth leisurewear for both sexes is the **TOG SHOP**, WW, Lester Sq., Americus, Ga. 31709. For women, in addition to classic wrap-arounds and dusters (starting at around $18.00 for a cornflower-blue smock style), there is an intriguing collection of hostess robes—a multicolor striped hooded kaftan at $24.00, a two-toned green striped aba for $33.00, even a terrycloth jumpsuit at $12.00. Pastels are offered as well as deep colors. For men, there's the classic robe at $20.00—printed in a tiger pattern it costs a dollar more—and a group of very practical jog and jump suits, from $20.00. Women's sizes run from 6 to 20, men's from 34 to 48.

The **SWATOW DRAWN WORK CO.** (G) shows some good-looking pajamas for both men and women. The drip-dry dacron (with embroidery, for women) is priced from around $5.00 to $7.00, the pure silk from $10.00 to $14.00. There are also women's silk night-gowns, slips, and half slips, in white and pastels very modestly priced (a silk nightgown is less than $10.00). In another part of the world, the **BAZAAR GANDHI**, WW, Front St., Colon, Republic of Panama, offers, among a variety of diversified wares, brocade robes for both men and women, smoking jackets for men ($10.00 to $13.00), and silk pajamas for men, women, and children (from $3.50 to $5.00). They also sell men's *panabrisa* shirts, Ecuadorian ponchos, and linens of all kinds. Prices are in American dollars and catalog is free.

One of the most prestigious sports shops in the world, **LILLYWHITE'S, LTD.**, WW, Piccadilly Circus, London SW1Y 4QF, England, puts out a colorful little brochure called "Lillywhite's Leisure," which shows some very smart-looking terrycloth dresses and coats from around $20.00, also some glamorous patio dresses in a variety of fabrics, costing around $40.00 to $50.00. Some have swimsuits to match; there are also other swimsuits, from the exceedingly skimpy to very covered-looking ones with skirts (and these have cover-ups to cover them up) starting at around $17.00. The brochure is free, and you can send for it when you send for the main catalog, described in Chapter 20,A.

I. IN-SIZES AND OUT-SIZES

People with what are euphemistically called "figure problems" will find the custom houses a boon. Many of the foreign firms described in the preceding sections will make garments to order at prices no higher than ready-mades here. If your problem is more one of general proportion rather than odd bumps here and there, you'll find that most of the big American mail-order houses, especially **MONTGOMERY WARD**, offer a wide range of sizes beyond the range of what is usually considered average, from the smaller than standard to the larger, from the shorter to the taller. If you are a female of ample proportions, you will discover that the German houses include sizes that Americans regard as overgenerous within their normal range. However, there are several shops that cater specifically to people in the larger-than-average ranges. For women there are **ROAMAN'S**, Saddle Brook, N.J. 07662; and **LANE BRYANT** and **HAYES**, both at 2300 Southeastern Ave., Indianapolis, Ind. 46201, for they're actually divisions of the same company. Lane Bryant deals primarily with full sizes (although they have some half sizes) and Hayes with half sizes (although they have some full sizes). Roaman's has both half and full sizes. At the same address as Lane Bryant and Hayes, is the **TALL GIRL'S SHOP**, for tall women. All four are in the moderate price range, although prices tend to be a bit higher than similar items in the regular mail-order houses, when they carry them.

Lane Bryant has a brother firm, **LEWIS BRYANT**, for bigger men (same address as Lane Bryant). Other firms that serve the heroic-type male are **JOSEPH M. KLEIN**, WW, 118 Stanton St., New York, N.Y. 10001; and the **KING-SIZE CO.**, WW, 2333 King-Size Building, Brockton, Mass. 02403

J. DANCE AND ATHLETIC WEAR
ALGY DANCE COSTUMES, WW, 410 N.E. First

Ave., Hallandale, Fla. 33000, offers a group of very attractive leotards from around $8.00 to $13.00. Although they're intended for dance costumes, a lot of people will want them for general sportswear. Brochure is free, but, if you want the full catalog of costumes for majorettes, cheerleaders, and band members, it'll cost you $1.00.

KLING'S, WW, 218 South Wabash Ave., Chicago, Ill. 60604, also has lots of leotards and tank suits, from less than $5.00 up; plus jazz pants, tights, and, of course, shoes. Tights are in sizes 8 to 22; there are even women's leotards that go up to size 20 ($7.50). A particularly pretty "Victorian body suit," with ruffles at neck and wrists is $12.00. Catalog is free.

SELVA AND SONS, INC., WW, 1607 Broadway, New York, N.Y. 10019, also offers dance costumes and accessories. There are lots of nice tights and leotards that could be used for regular wear, and some charming things that can't (unless you happen to be a sylphid). There are not only ballet slippers, but gym, jazz, and acrobatic shoes, all very inexpensive. Catalog free.

The Sportswear International Division of **BALLET SCHOOL SUPPLIES' LTD.**, WW, 25 Queen St., Newcastle upon Tyne NE1 3UG, England, also has a selection of particularly nice-looking leotards, moderately priced, including some which may be used for tennis and other sports, others with skirts to go over them to make complete costumes suitable for street or patio. Prices range from about $3.00 up. Tights, tutus, and ballet slippers are also available.

A. CHATILA AND CO., WW, 5719 18 Ave., Brooklyn, N.Y. 11204, has dance costumes for children and adults. And, of course, Capezio ("dancing since 1887") has a complete catalog of footwear strictly for dancing, as well as leotards and tights and such. Address is **CAPEZIO**, WW, 1855 Broadway, New York, N.Y. 10023. **STUDIO IMPORTS**, WW, P.O. Box 143, South Pasadena, Cal. 91030, offers a free brochure of dance footwear.

> **Remember:** *Write for the catalog first.* All prices given were valid only at the time of writing and probably have been changed.

Chapter 3

ETHNIC AND REGIONAL COSTUMES

A. AMERICAN INDIAN

Most of the American Indian handicraft and supply houses sell Indian ceremonial costumes, including war-bonnets, bustles, roaches, belts, headbands, leggings, fans, powwow bags, shawls, sashes, rattles, etc. Since most of these firms are also described in other chapters (Jewelry, Art, Collectors, Crafts), I'll just list the bulk of them—so you'll be able to know where to look for the garb of a particular region—giving details only on those that seem to specialize in items aimed at the general public, and those which deal primarily in costumes. So far as I have been able to determine, all of the clothes are authentically Indian-made, but not all of the firms are Indian-owned and/or operated. Where there is a charge for a catalog, I've listed it; if no charge is given I got the catalog free and assume it's free to everyone.

CHEYENNE LODGE, WW, Box 717, El Reno, Okla. 73036; WA'KE-DA TRADING POST, WW, P.O. Box 19146, Sacramento, Cal. 95819 (15¢; OZARK TRADING POST, WW, Box 25644, Oklahoma City, Okla. 73125 (50¢); LONE BEAR INDIAN CRAFT CO., WW, 5 Beekman St., New York, N.Y. 10028 (Eastern Woodland craft work); OKLAHOMA INDIAN MARKETING AGENCY, INC., WW, P.O. Box 4202, Tulsa, Okla. 74104; DAKOTAH ARTS AND CRAFTS, WW, 116 Oak St., P.O. Box 103, Sisseton, S.D. 57262 (Sisseton-Wahpetah Sioux); OJIBWA WIGWAM, WW, Rt. 2, Luck, Wis. 54853; PEYE'SHA TRADERS, WW, P.O. Box 765, Painesville, Ohio 44077 (25¢); SUPERNAW'S OKLAHOMA INDIAN SUPPLY, WW, 301 East W. C. Rogers Blvd., Skiatook, Okla. 74074 (25¢); ROBERTS INDIAN CRAFTS AND SUPPLIES, WW, 211 West Broadway St., P.O. Box 98, Andarko, Okla. 73005 (25¢); DEL TRADING POST, WW, Mission, S.D. 57555 (25¢); TREATY OAK TRADING POST, WW, 5241 Lexington Ave., Jacksonville, Fla. 32210 (25¢); OKLAHOMA INDIAN ARTS AND CRAFTS COOPERATIVE, WW, P.O. Box 966, Anadarko, Okla. 73005 (25¢).

TOUCHING LEAVES INDIAN CRAFTS, WW, 929 Portland, Dewey, Okla. 74529, seems to deal in nothing but costumes of the Delaware Indians, made to order and featuring the characteristic ribbonwork. The mimeographed catalog is in English, but the names of all the items are given in Indian.

The SEMINOLE OKALEE INDIAN VILLAGE ARTS AND CRAFTS CENTER, WW, 6073 Sterling Rd., Hollywood, Fla. 33024, is owned and operated by the Seminole Indians, who have always been known for their colorful patchwork garments—more popular than ever now that patchwork is so much in vogue. You can buy women's skirts from $17.00 to around $50.00, men's shirts from $23.00 to $39.00. Aprons and children's clothes are also available.

The CHEROKEE CRAFT CENTER, WW, P.O. Box 807, Tahlequah, Okla. 74464, has stoles, capes, and ponchos, handwoven by Cherokee weavers and selling at $12.00 to $23.00. So far as I can see, there's nothing particularly Indian about them but they are very good-looking.

KI-KIT-TA-MUET ARTS AND CRAFTS CO-OP, WW, Shishmaref, Alaska 99772, includes in its price list sealskin caps from $25.00 to $35.00, slippers from about $20.00, and mukluks from $35.00. They'll make jackets and parkas to order.

At IROQRAFTS, LTD., WW, R.F.D. 2, Ohsweken, Ont. Canada, you can get, in addition to a vast array of ceremonial attire (much of it of museum quality) Indian-made Cowichan raw-wool sweaters with patterns in natural color wool, priced from around $50.00 to $70.00. There are moose-hide jackets, starting at around $70.00, mukluks, moccasins, and so on. (Catalog is 25¢).

NIZHONIE, INC., WW, 810½ Broadway, Box 729, Cortez, Colo. 81321, sells sweatshirts with kachinas on them ($6.00 to $8.50), and sport and western shirts ($12.00 to $20.00).

INDIAN ORIGINALS, WW, 521 7 St., Rapid City, S.D. 57701, is the brainchild of LaVerne Heiter, an Oglala Sioux designer, who has blended the basic elements of traditional Indian costume with modern haute couture to produce a very wearable collection of clothes. The catalog that I saw includes some handsome Powwow Pantsuits, with tops patterned after the traditional Sioux ghost shirt, for $55.99, and a really stunning handbeaded pantsuit in white homespun for $135.00. A wide-legged pants costume, available in a variety of designs and fabrics, called the Tipi Creeper, is $55.00. Also skirts, shorts, and jumpsuits.

B. THE OTHER AMERICAS

It's hard to find mail-order houses in Mexico, outside of **SANBORN'S** (Chapter 4,B), which is in Mexico City and very tourist-oriented. However, I've discovered two firms that seem very promising. **REY-COSIJOEZA**, WW, Av. Morelos 17, Mitla, Oaxaca, Mexico, which specializes in typical Zapotec arts and crafts, sells different types of woolen rebozos at very low prices. The least expensive is a plain one in natural-colored wool for about $3.00, the most expensive, a Keshquemett type with crochet work trimming for about $9.00. The rest of the list (which is typed, so don't write for it unless you're seriously interested) breaks into Spanish—of which I can just make out that they also offer short-sleeved blouses for around $6.00, as well as quilts, scatter rugs, and handbags. They also carry all kinds of regional clothes and there is a member of the firm who is able to correspond in English. The other Mexican firm, **TEXTILES HER-NANZ, S.A.**, WW, Real de Guadeloupe, Num. 28, San Cristobal de las Casas, Chiapas, Mexico, offers cotton and woollen rebozos, ruanas (like ponchos only open down the front), and other garments whose identities I can't quite figure out since the printed list is in Spanish and my dictionary seems unequal to the occasion. Anyhow, the prices seem to be on the same modest levels as Rey-Cosijoeza's. The firm appears to correspond only in Spanish, although it is a mail-order house. Both price lists are free.

MANUEL ANTONIO PILON, WW, P.O. Box 268, Guatemala City, Guatemala, offers a whole array of attractive, very reasonably priced local crafts, including handmade woollen capes for women in numerous colors, from around $10.00 to $18.00. There are also colorful Guatemalan *chalecos* (men's fringed vests, but women can wear them, too), at $7.00; and women's ponchos, $8.00 to $9.00. Prices are given in U.S. dollars, shipping is included, and the minimum order is $10.00.

The **WIESENFELDS**, WW, Apartado Aereo 22456, Bogotá, Colombia, offers handwoven, handbrushed ruanas, available in 12 different colors, and reversible —one side solid color, the reverse a complementary multistripe pattern. They cost around $28.00, and they're made out of industrially spun wool. You can also get them in handspun wool, in the natural off-

white only, for around $35.00, Prices, in American dollars, include shipping; lists are free.

Ecuador seems the most mail-order oriented of the South American countries, because I've unearthed three sources there. **ANDEAN PRODUCTS** (Chapter 2,C.5) offers men's and women's fiesta shirts, as worn by Ecuador's northern Indians, made of handwoven off-white wool, elaborately decorated with native embroidery, $10.00 to $16.00. Also, dresses and aprons, plus *Gualaceo* shawls, as worn by campesino women in the Cuenca Valley, $12.00. **FOLKLORE**, WW, Av. Colon 260, P.O. Box 64, Quito, Ecuador, sells handwoven ruanas and ponchos from several different regions, from $6.00 to $8.00 for orlon, $11.00 to $18.00 for wool. Also belts, handbags, and slippers. Their unillustrated brochure is free. **AKIOS**, WW, P.O. Box 219, Quito, Ecuador, is back in business after suffering a disastrous fire. There are ponchos in all shapes and styles, in cotton or wool, with woven or embroidered designs, in prices ranging from around $3.00 to $25.00. A group of woollen ones, handwoven by the Saraska Indians, is $10.00. There are embroidered cotton and woollen skirts, jackets, blouses, etc., plus handknit sweaters in handspun wool and orlon. They also have some items of Jibaro native costume. Their very full catalog, listing hundreds and hundreds of items, is $1.00.

C. EUROPE

You'll find Scottish kilts and the appropriate accouterments, as well as tartan garments of all kinds, at virtually all of the Scottish firms already described in Chapter 2,C and D. In addition, you'll find a large supply of tartan and Scottish wear at **HUGH MAC-PHERSON, LTD.**, WW, 17 West Maitland St., Edinburgh EH 12 SEA Scotland; and **WILLIAM ANDERSON AND SONS, LTD.**, WW, 14-16 George St., Edinburgh 2, Scotland. Both catalogs are free.

You can also get a full range of Scottish products in the United States from **SCOTTISH PRODUCTS, INC.**, WW, 24 East 60 St., New York, N.Y. 10022. In addition to traditional items of costume, they offer 109 Clan Crest badges, Clan blazer badges, and so on. In general they're more expensive than the firms in Scotland, but in certain areas, like jewelry, they seem to be about the same or so little more that it might not be worth the trouble of ordering from abroad, particularly in the case of small orders. The catalog is free.

The 100-year-old firm of **LODEN-PLANKL**, WW, Michaelerplatz 6, A-1010, Vienna, Austria, specializes in dirndls, national costumes, and loden and hunting clothes. The dirndls, of which there are a great variety, festive and plain, cost from around $15.00 to $70.00. There are blouses, aprons, and stockings to accompany them (with minature versions for little girls), as well as capes and ladies' lederhosen ($18.00 to $25.00). For men, there are also lederhosen (slightly higher-priced), classic hunting suits at $80.00 to $90.00 (women's are slightly less), capes, hunting coats, and jackets, plus some elegant regional dress suits and duffle coats, all extremely becoming. Catalogs are in German, but descriptive brochure and price lists are in English.

JAHN-MARKL, WW, Residenzplatz, A-5020, Salzburg, Austria, is even older than Loden Plankl—it was founded in 1844—and has belonged to the same family ever since. They used to be purveyors of leather clothing to the Austrian court, when there was an Austrian court. Their handsome free catalog, in both English and German, tells you all about the origins of leather and leather breeches (lederhosen), and about the history of the firm. There are leather swatches and careful instructions on how to measure yourself. There are pictures of various types of lederhosen (both shorts and knee-length), traditional hunting jackets and capes, and leather accessories, as well as some modern leather garments. The only thing you won't find there are prices.

If you'd like to buy lederhosen locally, you can get some Bavarian imports in gray suede trimmed with green leather from **MUNICH HOUSE**, WW, P.O. Box 326, Niantic, Conn. 06357. Men's are $25.00 to $38.00, women's, $21.00 to $29.00. Brochure is free.

You can get Portuguese aprons, embroidered woollen shawls, and head scarves from **MADEIRA SUPERBIA**. **JABARA** also has hostess aprons (also hot-roll covers and pot holders) gaily decorated with regional hand embroidery. Aprons are about $2.00.

Although I do have a number of sources in Greece, I haven't as yet been able to locate an overseas firm that will sell Greek clothing by mail. However, there is a firm in New York, the **GREEK ISLAND, LTD.**, WW, 215 East 49 St., New York, N.Y. 10001, that offers an attractive, if rather high-priced, selection of Greek clothes and accessories. Catalog is free.

Again, I don't have a direct Russian source, but **SURMA**, WW, 11 East 7 St., New York, N.Y. 10003, an authentic Ukrainian shop, will make Cossack tunics to order for men and women (who can wear them as mini dresses). Prices range from $20.00 to $35.00 in dacron-cotton, hopsacking, velour, or wool, and I doubt you could do as well in Moscow or Kiev. They're planning to expand their ethnic line to include embroidered clothing from the Carpathians and Transyl-vania and 25¢ is obviously a small sum to pay for brochures depicting all of these.

D. THE ORIENT

Clothes from India and other Near Eastern countries are very popular, offered both in their original form and adapted to Western styles. You'll find both at **PAKISTAN ARTS AND CRAFTS, INC.**, WW, 35 West 30 St., New York, N.Y. 10001; and **TANTRA IMPORTS**, WW, P.O. Box 489, 355 Westminster St., Providence, R.I. 02901. They have dresses and accessories. Shirts for both men and women are in the $6.00 to $12.00 range. You can buy these shirts (*mulmul kurtas*) much less expensively from **DEEPAK'S ROKJEMPERL PRODUCTS**, WW, 61 10th Khetwadi, Bombay, India, from $8.00 to $25.00 per dozen (prices depend on length and color), but you have to take potluck, since this is a wholesale house. The price list (containing many other things) is free, and there are several firms, mostly gemstone suppliers, on it, so don't write more than once to the same address, as you'll just be getting several copies of the same catalog.

HARILELA'S has a catalog devoted entirely to saris. A pure silk one with a blouse and long slip to go with it costs $40.00. There are also items made of sari cloth. Other excellent sources of Indian saris and other garments are described in the Fabrics Section of Chapter 18, B.2. Note particularly **BENGAL HOME INDUSTRIES, KAVERI MYSORE STATE HANDICRAFTS**, and the **LEPAKSHI HANDICRAFTS EMPORIUM**. For similar items from Ceylon (now Sri Lanka) see **LAKLOOMS, DEPT. OF SMALL INDUSTRIES**, and the **SERENDIB GALLERY**.

K. HAYASHI AND CO., LTD., WW, International Arcade, 2-4 Yurakucho, Chiyodaku, Tokyo, Japan, claims to have the most comprehensive stock of kimonos under any one roof in Japan. Their lovely free catalog and brochures show men's, women's, and children's kimonos in all varieties from the inexpensive cotton to the glamorous silk, in practically any color and price range you might want. My catalog shows the silk ones starting as low as $20.00 but the yen was floating freely when I last heard, and who knows what the prices will be by the time this comes out? There are also happi coats, lounging pajamas, and obis (with directions for tying same).

E. AFRICA

From **INKENTAN CRAFTS, LTD.**, WW, P.O. Box 1356, Nairobi, Kenya, you can get colorful cotton *kitenge* dresses for women and bush shirts (it's not clear whether they're for men or women, or both) at very modest prices—dresses are around $8.00 to $12.00; shirts $5.00 to $8.00. Price lists and catalog are free.

The **CRAFTSMAN GALLERY OF STUDIO 68**, WW, P.O. Box 7904, Nairobi, Kenya, aims, it says, "to present the skill and originality of the African people as shown through their products," and they sell their wares on behalf of the local Kenyan craftsmen and women, who benefit directly from sales. Most of the apparel offered is more for costume or ceremonial use—like the women's beaded skin aprons, or the decorative waistbands fashioned either from the "toe bones of the deer-like duiker or the vertebrae of a gnu." There are lip plugs and other jewelry. For men there are nose plates, purses, and two-legged stools, to be carried around the neck (I suppose they are to be considered as ornaments). Prices are fairly high, though not when you consider that for the most part these are museum pieces. Price lists are free.

F. HERE AND THERE

You'll find other regional clothing under Handicrafts (Chapter 11,C). For example, you can get Tibetan Sherpa jackets from the **NATIONAL TRADING CO.**; more African clothing from **LA ROSE d'IVOIRE**; Lebanese costumes from **ELIE G. NSEIR**; and aboriginal Australian garb from **QUEENSLAND ABORIGINAL CREATIONS**.

Remember: *Write for the catalog first*. All prices given were valid only at the time of writing and probably have been changed.

Chapter 4
ACCESSORIES

Most of the mail-order houses described in the preceding chapters offer plenty of accessories. All the knitwear firms (Chapter 2,C) sell knitted gloves, hats, and scarves; some have socks, belts, even handbags as well. **HIGHLAND HOME INDUSTRIES**, WW, 94 George St., Edinburgh, Scotland, is another good source of Scottish accessories, knitted and otherwise. The houses that specialize in lace and embroidery (Chapter 2,E.2)—**LACE PALACE, MARIA LOIX, MADEIRA SUPERBIA, TESORO'S, SWATOW, BALLYMACHUGH**—offer collar and cuff sets, dickeys, jabots, handkerchiefs, etc. Most of the firms specializing in ready-made men's apparel (Chapter 2,F.2) sell scarves, ties, shoes, belts, hats and other accoutrements.

All of the shops described in Ethnic and Regional Costumes (Chapter 3) are very heavy on items which are intended as accessories or can be worn as accessories. Some specialize in this area. An example is the **OKLAHOMA INDIAN ARTS AND CRAFTS CO-OPERATIVE**, which is an Indian-owned and operated arts and crafts enterprise, representing more than twelve Indian tribes of Oklahoma. They put out a brochure, for 25¢, of handsome suede fashion accessories—handbags from around $40.00, eyeglass cases, $3.00 up, and so on, plus lots of beadwork and German silver jewelry. You'll find more American Indian (as well as East Indian) houses in Chapter 5 (Jewelry).

A. GENERAL

There are some mail-order houses that specialize in accessories, generally. For instance, the famous **HERMÈS**, WW, 24 Faubourg Saint-Honoré, Paris, France, will send you a catalog of its well-known accessories—handbags, gloves, belts, and the like—as well as sports clothes, at prices just as high as they are in American shops (and, believe me, that's high). However, if you don't have a Hermès outlet in your town (and there aren't too many of them), you might like to write for a catalog. It's free and it's in French. Also from France is **OBÉRON**, WW, 73 Champs Elysées, Paris, France, which puts out a beautiful catalog for $1.50 (ref.), which they tell you to keep, as most of these items will run for many years. There are bags, gloves, scarves, umbrellas, Lacoste shirts—in short, the widest range of French items that I've seen in any catalog (including other things you'll find described in later chapters). Prices are unquestionably on luxury levels, but they're much lower than the same items would be here. Similar, but less extensive lines are offered by **FREDDY**, WW, 20 rue Auber; **MICHEL-SWISS**, WW, 16 rue de la Paix; **LYNDA**, WW, 3 rue Caumartin; and **BENLUX**, WW, 277 rue Saint-Honoré, . . . all Paris, France. Their catalogs and brochures are free.

In Germany, **STEGMANN**, WW, Jungfernstieg 45/46, 2 Hamburg, West Germany, issues pretty little color catalogs called simply *Accessoires*. They show costume jewelry, belts, scarves, dickeys, hats, and other frou frous from all over the world. In the current issue there are some nice big globby necklaces, from around $2.00 to $15.00, and some charming little Swiss scarves from $3.00. Send 3 IRCs to cover postage.

In addition to the many Caledonian houses described in the previous chapters, you'll find that the **SCOTTISH CRAFT CENTRE**, WW, Acheson House, 140 Canongate, Edinburgh EH8 8DD, Scotland, is a worthy source of scarves (around $3.00), lambskin slippers (around $3.50 to $6.00), and silk and wool ties ($2.00 to $10.00), all designed by Scottish craftspeople. Catalog is free.

Many of the firms written up under Handicrafts in Chapter 11,C and under Fabrics in Chapter 18,B.2, sell accessories as part of their often vast stocks. For example, the **BENGAL HOME INDUSTRIES ASSOCIATION**, WW, 57 Chowringhee Rd., Calcutta 16, India, has handwoven cotton shoulder bags from around $3.00 up, men's silk ties starting at a little over $1.00, and small leather goods (wallets, spectacle cases, etc.) priced with equal modesty. The beautiful illustrated catalog is free so far. And **NARAYANA PHAND**, Thai Handicrafts Center, WW, 275/2 Lun Lunag Rd., Bangkok, Thailand, has a brochure of Thai cotton hats, scarves, handbags, stuffed animals, and such. However, the only price list I got was for carved teak. Teak prices seem reasonable, however, so why not cotton? Then there's **SILK OF SIAM**, WW, 297 Suriwongse Rd., G.P.O. Box 1802, Bangkok, Thailand, which is American-owned and operated, so you'll have no communications difficulty. Their big full-color brochure is one of the loveliest I have seen, and so far as I can tell it's free. An attractive line of accessories includes scarves and men's ties from around $3.00 up, plus an intriguing line of jewelry. Prices are in American dollars.

Meanwhile, back at the ranch, **BEREA COLLEGE**, WW, Berea, Ky. 40403, sells gay dirndls—designed, woven, and made up by students—from $30.00. Also shopping bags ($12.00), shoulder bags ($15.00), and woollen scarves ($3.00 to $12.00). There are ponchos, available either in "a patchwork of bright colors or subdued natural undyed yarn," at $36.00, plus shawls, belts, and throws. Catalog is 25¢.

Accessories of a very special sort are offered by **LIBERATION ENTERPRISES**, WW, General Delivery, G.P.O. Brooklyn, N.Y. 11202, which calls itself a "unique mail-order boutique owned and run by women for women." The items offered in its free catalog certainly are not designed for shrinking violets. For instance, you have to be pretty sure of yourself to carry their roomy canvas shoulder bag emblazoned with the slogan "Liberation is my bag" in red, at the very liberated price of $8.00. There are also aprons with appropriate inscriptions, some of them mildly obscene, and jewelry.

B. LEATHER GOODS

A number of houses devote themselves to accessories, and sometimes clothes, made out of leather. There are some overseas houses in this category. **LOEWE**, WW, Barquillo 13, Madrid-4, Spain, is celebrated throughout the world for its fine leather goods. The brochure they sent me showing a sampling of their goods shows gloves from around $7.00, handbags in suede or box calf from $70.00 to $80.00, wallets at around $12.00 to $14.00, and a really stunning attaché case at a stunning price, about $78.00. They also have men's jackets and women's coats, starting at well over $100.00. I assume the brochure is free, although they refused to commit themselves.

In a wholly different genre is **ARTIKRAFTS**, WW, P.O. Box 1944, Bombay-1 BR, India, which puts out an unillustrated price list that offers small leather goods—handbags and tote bags from around $4.00 to $10.00, as well as sandals, wallets, and cushion covers all priced comparably. The firm also sells handprinted silk scarves and jewelry. The trouble is, because there are no illustrations, and this is a wholesale house, you might have to take a chance on samples. Price list is free.

Going West, you'll find Scottish deerskin products featured at **PERTHSHIRE CRAFTS, LTD.**, WW, Dunkeld, Perthshire, Scotland. Their brochure is free.

You'll need to send an IRC to **WALTER WRIGHT**, WW, 28 Dorothy St., Liverpool L71 QP, England, to get the brochure of his rather unusual leather garments.

HARILELA'S (see Chapter 2,C.4) offers a separate catalog of suede and leather garments for women in the 6 to 16 size range, along with its regular catalog. The mail-order houses like **EGERTON'S**, **ICEMART**, **QUELLE**, **NECKERMANN**, **WENZ**, **JELMOLI**, etc., all offer leather assortments, and the Austrian houses, **JAHN-MARKL** and **LODEN-PLANKL** (see Chapter 3,A.3) offer other things made of leather besides their breeches.

South of the border, **SANBORN'S**, WW, Avenida Madero 4, Mexico, 1, D.F., offers some attractive leather items at moderate prices. A woman's fringed leather vest is around $15.00, a fringed leather mini-skirt around $13.00. Handbags run from $6.00 to $23.00. There are also eyeglass cases (or lens purses, as the free catalog says), wallets, coin purses, and so on.

However, leather goods emporia seem to be most characteristic of North America; at any rate that's where I've unearthed a number of them. There's **AL-VORD'S DEERSKIN PRODUCTS**, WW, Adirondack Trail Route #30, North Mayfield, N.Y. 12117. They used to specialize in deerskin gloves, and they still have plenty of them, from about $6.00 to $15.00 (for a pair lined with fur). Now they've added an equally wide range of moccasins, starting at $4.00 and going up to $25.00. They also sell handbags, hats, jackets, belts, and so on. They'll make gloves out of your skins (deerskins, that is), or buy them. Their catalog is 25¢. A similar catalog is offered free of charge by **BERMAN BUCKSKIN**, WW, 26 Hennepin Ave., Minneapolis, Minn. 55401. (In fact, in the last issue I saw, some of the pages in their catalog seemed exactly the same as Alvord's, with slightly lower prices in some instances.) Berman has moccasins, gloves, coats, jackets, hats, and doodads, in all kinds of leather, not only buckskin. Prices for moccasins run from $8.00 to around $30.00; gloves start at $6.00.

The **DEERSKIN TRADING POST**, WW, 119 Foster St., Peabody, Mass. 01960, claims to offer the largest selection of leather goods in the world, and their free full-color catalog does, indeed, show a large collection of inexpensive moccasins, boots, and slippers, for all sizes and sexes, at prices ranging from $6.00 to $12.00. There are also casual shoes, from $14.00 to $20.00, hiking boots at somewhat higher prices, gloves beginning at around $6.00, and a number of nifty-looking handbags (plus several rather peculiar-looking ones). The **VERMONT COUNTRY STORE**, WW, Weston, Vt. 05161, also offers some leather accessories— gloves (from $5.00), bags, moccasins. Catalog is 25¢.

NAUSET LEATHER, WW, Box 1011, Rte. 6A, Orleans, Mass. 01553, purveys handbags from around $6.00 to $40.00, both shoulder and non-shoulder types; brass-buckled belts, $8.00 to $9.00; also numerous small items, like keycases, wallets, and something you don't see around too much—leather visors, $7.00. They also make sandals to order. Shipping is included and the catalog is free.

C. GLOVES

Although all of the preceding houses naturally carry gloves, there are some firms that are glove specialists. Overseas, Italy is where you're likely to get the best buys in leather gloves. Three good sources are ANTICOLI, WW, via del Tritone 143, Rome 00187; CATELLO D'AURIA, WW, Via due Macelli 55, Rome 00187; and AMEDEO PERRONE, WW, 92 Piazza di Spagna, Rome. Prices generally start at around $3.50 and go up to a top of around $15.00, with most of the gloves averaging around $4.00 to $5.00 for women, $5.00 to $6.00 for men. Anticoli also carries men's silk ties, from a little over $3.00 to $5.00, and some small leather goods—wallets, belts, and so on—very attractively priced. Perrone also has ties, $5.00 up, and scarves, $3.00 to $6.00. They show Borsalino hats for women (from about $10.00), but merely list hats for men on their price list. (I imagine if you wanted a specific type of Borsalino hat, you could query them.) All three lists are in American dollars. Anticoli's and d'Auria's are free; Perrone's requires one IRC.

As for American gloves, the SARANAC GLOVE CO., WW, 6-8 Main St., P.O. Box 680, Littletown, N.H. 03561, sells deerskin (and other leather) gloves and mittens from $4.00 up to $18.00 (for goosedown mittens). They also sell cold-weather face masks made out of sueded deerskin rather than the more usual knitted type. They're $3.00, and should be of special appeal to bandits. Catalog is free.

D. BAGS

The French accessory houses are particularly good for *petit point* and beaded bags, at prices that are lower than here, but by no means low. From Portugal, JABARA'S (Chapter 1,F.3) has *petit point* and *gros point* tapestry evening bags from $45.00 to $80.00. (They also have them in kit form for do-it-yourselfers.)

Most of the Oriental houses described in Chapter 2 sell beaded bags, and the MAY FASHION HOUSE, WW, P.O. Box 6162, Kowloon, Hong Kong, offers (for 50¢) a leaflet showing a selection of handbeaded trimmings and handbags.

The Middle East is known for its leatherwork, and you can get some very handsome handbags at remarkably low prices from ANTRANIG S.CHILINGURIAN, WW, P.O. Box 1129, Beirut, Lebanon. Most of them seem to be shoulder bags, averaging from $5.00 to $7.00; the leaflet shows them mainly in tan and red, but I should think other colors would be available. There are also belts and Oriental slippers (around $3.00), plus travel bags modestly priced in the $5.00 to $6.00 range. The catalog is $1.00. As Chilingurian is a wholesaler, you may be asked to pay a small surcharge per item if you order samples. Another good Lebanese source is ELIE G. NSEIR, WW, Bliss St., Beirut, Lebanon. He has leather drawstring bags for about $2.50 (apparently for a set of three; although the catalog is in English, it's not too clear), and travel bags (actually large handbags) costing from $4.00 to $6.00. Catalog is free.

Most of the Caribbean and South American firms are strong on handbags. For instance, The DOMINICA HANDCRAFTS CO., WW, P.O. Box 22, Roseau, Dominica, West Indies, offers an attractive selection of straw, raffia, and sisal tote bags and handbags, both in the unadorned natural fibers ($2.00 to $5.00) and ornamented with either woven strips or embroidery (these go up to around $8.00). Also on hand is a huge variety of hats for all ages and both sexes, from less than $1.00 up to around $2.00. Particularly appealing are the girls' roseau straw bonnets, at less than $1.50. Brochures are free.

The TIPCO Division of SHEICA (Société Haitienne d'Enterprises Industrielles, Commerciales, et Agricoles) WW, P.O. Box 396, Port-au-Prince, Haiti, has some straw and sisal handbags and tote bags from around $2.00 to $5.00. There are also hats and mats. The catalog, which shows many other interesting items, is free. And, in Guatemala, PILON (Chapter 3,B) sells leather handbags at less than $7.00, and some extremely handsome shopping bags made of cloth woven in native designs and trimmed with natural leather at $6.00 each—also sisal shopping bags for around $1.00 each. The Ecuadorian houses (Chapter 3,B) all have excellent buys in leather, straw, and fabric handbags.

I've found some very nice native buys here, too. At GURIAN'S, WW, 276 Fifth Ave., New York, N.Y. 10016, you can get some extremely pretty handembroidered crewel-work tote and shopping bags for $6.00 each. (These aren't kits; they're all finished.) The colorful brochure is 50¢. MARCIA S. MACK, WW, 21 Westward Rd., Woodbridge, Conn. 06525, makes white tote bags with delightful animals on them. There's a raccoon, a fox, a frog on a fern, and an owl, at prices ranging from $9.00 to $11.00 postpaid. Brochure is free.

SUDBERRY HOUSE, WW, Wesley Ave., Westbrook, Conn. 06498, will make linen and wool bags to order, in any color you like, from $12.00 to $17.00 postpaid. **CAPE COD FISHNET INDUSTRIES**, WW, North Truro, Mass. 02652 has fishnet bags that can double as hats, at $1.25, fishnet shopping bags at $3.00 to $4.00, and all kinds of fishnet accessories. Prices include shipping. Both brochures are free.

The **PORT CANVAS CO.**, WW, Deck Sq., Kennebunkport, Me. 04046, puts out all kinds of carrying things made of canvas, at prices often lower than similar items I've seen in New York. A big shoulder bag is $10.00, strong shopping or tote bags $6.00 to $8.00, and an artist's portfolio at $18.00. Even your skis and your skates and ski boots and tennis racquets can find totes for themselves here. Also some wearing apparel (for people). Everything is offered in navy blue, Breton red, and/or natural, and the catalog is free.

E. SHOES

1. General

If you've never had shoes made to order, a new experience awaits you at **LEE KEE BOOT AND SHOE MAKER, LTD.**, WW, 65 Peking Rd., Kowloon, Hong Kong. The firm will make shoes (and, of course, boots) to your specifications at prices ranging from around $16.00 . . . in calfskin and kid suede. They also make handbags and other leather items. The free brochure, which includes a booklet of leather swatches, gives explicit instructions about how to measure your feet. Lots of interesting ready-made shoes are offered for men alone at **ALAN McAFEE, LTD.**, WW, 38 Dover St., Piccadilly, London W.1, England. They offer a large selection of men's shoes in the medium- to high-priced bracket, about a third cheaper than they would be here. The catalog is $1.00.

And, a firm that is as American as McAfee is English, the **AUSTIN BOOT CO.**, WW, P.O. Box 12368, El Paso, Tex. 79912, sells authentic Western boots in traditional and contemporary styles, made in American standard sizes 4 to 13D in widths A to EEEE. They're sized to fit your particular measurements (the company is very anxious to make sure your boots are comfortable), and the instructions given for telling them all about your feet and calves are as detailed as Lee Kee's. Prices range from $33.00 for the classic old-timer up to $60.00 for the elaborate Grand Champion. Any style can be altered to suit your personal taste. The brochure is free.

Another very American firm is **FLAGG BROTHERS**, WW, 492 Craighead St., Nashville, Tenn. 37204, who have attained celebrity through their popularization

of high-heeled shoes for men; others may now be following the same trail, but the Flaggs were the ones who blazed it. Their free catalog shows lots and lots of them, priced from around $18.00. There are solid colors, two-tones, and multi-tones, as, for instance, Rainbow Rider, described as "navy with ice blue, red, and yellow appliqués on toe and side, cushion crepe rainbow sandwich heel and platform sole. Cool navy and white laces." Color catalog is free.

In a different vein is **BLOOM'S SHOE SHOP**, WW, 311 Sixth Ave., New York, N.Y. 10014, situated for 75 years in Greenwich Village. They sell the "Village" kinds of shoes, which have by now permeated our entire culture. All kinds of sandals for both sexes start at around $12.00. Wooden shoes or clogs from Sweden cost around $10.00. Their International Men's Shoe Gallery includes such conventional items as Wallabees ($28.00 up) and the inexplicably named Manachevitz (high-heeled, brown suede, $45.00). Brochure is 25¢.

You can buy wooden shoes even more inexpensively from **A.W.G. OTTEN**, WW, 102-104-106 Albert Cuypstraat, Amsterdam-2, Holland, which makes nothing else but *kloempen,* as they so onomatopoetically call them in their native land. (To the French they're *sabots,* to the Germans, *holzschuhe.*) Although some of these are extremely decorative, they are all meant for wearing. Prices, given in American dollars, are from around $2.00 to $7.00. Brochures, in both English and Dutch, are free.

2. Moccasins

Virtually all of the Indian houses listed in Chapter 3, A sell moccasins, and some of them sell both the authentic and the "commercial" types. There is no way that I can distinguish them except by the prices (the higher the prices, the more likely the moccasins are to be authentic, since the elaborate beadwork takes a lot of time). Incidentally, many of the commercial moccasins are actually produced by Indians. The **WINNEBAGO PUBLIC INDIAN MUSEUM**, WW, P.O. Box 411, Wisconsin Dells, Wis. 53965, offers moccasins made by Indians (who also operate the museum) from around $7.00. Here's a group of moccasin vendors who, I can assure you, are strictly commercial.

The **CASCO BAY TRADING POST**, WW, Freeport, Me. 04032, calls itself the world's largest supplier of Indian-style moccasins, and they certainly do seem to offer a good many, in prices ranging from $12.00 to about $22.00 for Cherokee boots. They also have gloves, hats, and tote bags. Their catalog is free, as is the colorful "Minnetonka Moccasin" catalog available from **HECKLER'S NOVELTY CO.**, WW, 401 West Sheridan Ave., Oklahoma City, Okla. 73102. They sell moccasins and casual footwear at reasonable prices. Women's fringed softsole "squaw boots" are around $8.00 to $9.00, hardsoles from $9.00 to $10.00. Men's boots are a dollar or two higher. **QUODDY MOCCASINS,** WW, 222 Anderson St., Portland, Me. 04101, offers both indoor and outdoor leather moccasins for men, women, and children. Indoor moccasins start at less than $5.00. Their best rugged outdoor handsewn moccasins of "heavy oil-tanned leather" start at $12.00. There are also ankle-high styles, from $10.00. Brochure is free.

FRANK DREW, WW, 2899 South 6 St., Klamath Falls, Ore. 97601, offers casual footwear for the whole family, from around $7.00 up. Particularly attractive are the fake, plush-lined sealskin boots, from $10.00 up. The shoes are mainly of the moccasin variety; all of them have names such as Ojibwa and Navajo and Comanche—which, I suspect, have little to do with their origin (or how would you explain Minnehaha?). Catalog is free.

Particularly unauthentic but very snug-sounding are the sheepskin moccasins offered by **CAMBRIDGE WOOLS, LTD.,** WW, 16-22 Anzac Ave., Auckland 1, New Zealand, in a variety of colors, from around $4.00 to $5.00. There are also moccasin kits and handbags, for about $4.00 to $13.00; plus sheepskin rugs, car seat covers, and medicated bed mats. If you're wondering about these, why not send for the free brochure?

You'll also find an abundance of moccasins at the houses described in Chapter 20 (Outdoors and Sports).

3. Specialties

You'll be able to find shoes that are wider or longer than average at the houses listed in Chapter 2,I; or you can, of course, have them made to order. Or, if you're a wide-footed woman, you can send for the free catalog put out by **SYD KUSHNER,** WW, 1204 Arch St., Philadelphia, Pa. 19107, who specializes in wide-width shoes for women, in sizes 4 to 12, C to EEE. There's a large number of attractive styles, at prices averaging around $15.00; boots around $20.00. There are handbags to match some of the shoes. On hand also are outsize panty hose and hosiery. **SHOECRAFT,** WW, 603 Fifth Ave., New York, N.Y. 10017, sells shoes for tall women, in sizes from 9 to 14. Prices range from $12.00 to $45.00. Both catalogs are free, as is the catalog for large-footed men put out by **HITCHCOCK SHOES,** WW, 165 Beal St., Hingham, Mass 02043.

POKORNY'S, WW, 123 St. Charles St., New Orleans, La. 70130, is a retail men's shoe store that doesn't put out catalogs. However, they issue free mailers at Christmas, and it's about the only place I know of where you can get red velvet shoes with the Shriners' emblem embroidered in gold (to make you "the talk of the temple"). They're $22.00 postpaid.

F. SCARVES, TIES, WHIPS, AND UMBRELLAS

RAMA JEWELRY, WW, 987 Silom Rd., Bangkok, Thailand, offers handwoven Thai silk stoles (around $9.00 to $20.00), neckties, and scarves ($2.00 to $3.00); they also have some small leather goods in their free catalog. The other Thai houses offer similar items.

ROWLAND WARD, LTD., WW, P.O. Box 40991, Nairobi, Kenya, offers some unusually attractive 30" pure silk scarves with animal designs—prides of lions, sitting leopards, small zebras, and a semi-abstract zebra head. They cost around $9.00. Catalog is free.

REGIMENTALS, WW, Box 2348, Williamsburg, Va. 23185, sells pure-dye, pure repp silk, woven in the United States "in the traditional stripes and colourings of the regiments, clubs, and schools of Britain." They're $6.50 postpaid. The pretty, color brochure (free) also shows authentic regimental blazer badges handembroidered in Britain of gold bullion and silver wire; they're $4.00. (I particularly like the Royal Army Pay Corps—the lion has a mean comptroller's expression.) There are also specially made civilian-size copies of British officers' tunic buttons, and authentic obsolete British officers' regimental buttons made into cufflinks ($12.50). Prices include postage.

SWAINE ADENEY BRIGG AND SONS, LTD., WW, 185 Piccadilly, London W.1, England, is an amalgamation of two nineteenth-century firms of whipmakers. The original founder of the firm was royal whipmaker to King George III, but he turned to umbrella making in the reign of Queen Victoria, and the company has furnished the Royal Family with their bumbershoots ever since. They're very expensive, but mostly they're made of silk with silver-mounted handles, so you'd expect high prices. The firm hasn't forgotten its origins, however, and still purveys hunting, beagling, bull, dog, ladies', children's, pole, dressage, and riding whips. The catalog is free.

If you're interested in a less sober type of umbrella, check the French houses listed in Section A. Their *parapluies* are very gay, indeed, and a lot less expensive, though by no means cheap.

Chapter 5
JEWELRY AND WATCHES

A. JEWELRY

You will find jewelry here in all price ranges, from less than a dollar up to thousands of dollars, with emphasis on the less expensive, because it makes me nervous to think of anybody ordering something that costs several thousands of dollars sight unseen from a mail-order catalog. I've tried to hunt down as many bargains as I could, and to provide something for everyone, including people who don't wear jewelry.

1. Europe

GARRARD AND CO., LTD., WW, 112 Regent St., London, W1A 2J5, England, "the crown jewellers," offers a handsome brochure of jewelry and silverware. Prices and merchandise are approximately on the Tiffany level, but TIFFANY's (727 Fifth Ave., New York, N.Y. 10021) charges a dollar for its catalog, and Garrard's is free.

Many of the Scottish houses described in Chapters 2 and 3 sell traditional Scottish jewelry—Luckenbooth brooches, silver set with cairngorms (smoky quartz), and Scottish pebbles (agates), and the like—most of it relatively inexpensive (under $50.00), and some of it downright cheap (under $10.00). **WILLIAM ANDERSON AND SONS** and **EDINBURGH TARTAN** probably show the most in their catalogs. On more of a Tiffany level, **HAMILTON AND INCHES, LTD.**, WW, 87 George St., Edinburgh EH2 3EY, Scotland, puts out a free catalog of beautiful and rather expensive jewelry.

On the continent, **QUELLE** still has some good buys in semiprecious stone necklaces, although they're not the steals they used to be. Baroque rhodochrosite, coral rose quartz, and garnet are a little over $10.00 each, turquoise around $20.00, amber around $30.00. **WENZ** has some rather pleasing real silver jewelry in both modern and traditional design, some set with semiprecious stones. A charming snake ring, with more loops than your usual snake ring, is a little under $5.00, an ornate silver and rhodochrosite pendant, $10.00. Also offered is a silver ring with six interchangeable stones to suit your costume or your mood. I've seen these before, but never with a real amethyst, sodalite, rhodochrosite, tiger-eye, rose quartz, and green agate, all for just about $10.00. There are necklaces, too—baroque turquoise, with a silver clasp, for about $24.00, symmetric amethyst with a 14-karat gold clasp for around $40.00. (See Chapter 2,A for details on both catalogs.)

A. E. KÖCHERT, WW, Neuer Markt 15, 1010 Wien I, Austria, puts out beautiful brochures of the jewelry the firm makes and markets. Inexpensive it isn't, but the naturalistic flower and fruit sprays for which Köchert is noted stay in the low hundreds—a very charming lily of the valley spray, made of rock crystal, nephrite jade, and diamonds, set in 14-karat gold, is less than $300.00. There are even a few small pins under $100.00, but the prettiest range from around $150.00 up.

In Finland, **KALEVALA KORU**, WW, Keskusatu 4, Helsinki, creates some unusually lovely jewelry either faithfully reproduced from, or adapted from, mediaeval Finnish jewelry. There are brooches, neckchains, bracelets, necklaces, and earrings, in the authentic bronze or in silver, and sometimes in gold plate. Brooches start at around $4.00; an elaborate bracelet that is a copy of one based on an ancient ornament of the Merja people is around $15.00. (I was so taken by this when I saw the catalog, that I sent away for it, and it's just as nice as the picture, although I had some difficulty working the ancient Merja fastener, which was reproduced perhaps too faithfully from the original.) Brochures are free, but they're sometimes reluctant about parting with them. You can, however, always get a Kalevala Koru brochure from **STOCKMANN AB**, Export Service, WW, Aleksanterinkatu 52, P.O. Box 10220, Helsinki 10, Finland, when you send them a dollar for all their other brochures (also described in Chapters 8, 9, and 18). **ICEMART** (Chapter 2,C.3) has a particularly nice line of silver jewelry, which I've described in some detail in Chapter 14,B.3.

More from Scandinavia's celebrated silversmiths . . . **DAVID-ANDERSON**, WW, Karl Johansgate 20, Oslo, Norway, offers stunning jewelry created by contemporary Danish artists at remarkably low prices. A winsome fish brooch, in multicolored enamel on sterling silver is less than $9.00; silver rings set with amethyst, labradorite, tiger-eye, among other stones, begin at $10.00; bracelets also start in that neighborhood, with the majority of the *bijoutrie* offered under $20.00.

They also offer their own beautiful Saga silver flatware. Prices are given in American dollars; brochures are free.

H. WALTER—RASMUSSEN, WW, Østergade 57, DR-1100 Copenhagen K, Denmark, has no catalog as such, but, upon request, the firm will send you a catalog of charming jewelry by Gaveider. Particularly nice are the delicate silver pieces; exquisite, icy-looking pendants and rings begin at less than $5.00.

GIOVANNI APA, WW, Torre del Greco, Naples, Italy, has been manufacturing cameos and coral jewelry for over 125 years. The cameos, which are very handsome indeed, are offered both mounted and unmounted. Set in sterling silver, they start as low as $6.00 for a pair of earrings, and go up to around $40.00. In gold, they are, of course, much higher. The coral jewelry is also quite reasonably priced—a pretty little floral spray pin set in silver gilt is less than $10.00. The attractive color catalog is free.

From **TREASURES OF ITALY,** WW, P.O. Box 1513, Florence 50100, Italy, you can get the charming inexpensive Venetian glass jewelry that seems to represent Italy. Necklaces cost from around $4.00 to $8.00, earrings from $2.00. There's also Venetian glass mosaic jewelry, and some very nice filigree jewelry finished in gilt and enamel, which starts at around $4.00 —a charming bracelet with a series of little blue flowers that look like forget-me-nots is $9.00. They also sell silk scarves, small leather goods, and lots of other attractive souvenirs.

TUZEX, Foreign Trade Corp., WW, Export Department, Opletalova 15, Prague 1, Czechoslovakia, will send you a free brochure of their famous Bohemian garnet jewelry. There are pendants, earrings, bracelets, necklaces, brooches, etc., in the familiar traditional styles. Earrings start at around $12.00, bracelets at around $40.00. Prices are in American dollars and include shipping.

ACHILLES SCORDILIS, WW, 44 Perikleous St., Athens 125, Greece, puts out a free catalog of the distinctive jewelry made in his workshops, which blends traditional Hellenic art with contemporary fashion. There are handsome, modern-looking pendants, necklaces, bracelets, earrings, and belts, offered either in the natural bronze or finished in silver and gold. Prices start at less than $1.00, and go up to $15.00 or $16.00. They're given in American dollars.

2. The Middle East

RODED, LTD., WW, P.O. Box 29090, Tel Aviv, Israel, is a wholesale jewelry firm that is willing to sell to retail customers. They have some interesting Oriental-looking silver jewelry pendants, some with precious stones (notably the blue eilatstone, or azurite, which is particularly characteristic of Israeli jewelry), cost from about $4.00 to $15.00; brooches start at $15.00. Also on hand are rings, earrings, and dogcollars. In addition, Roded offers a line of even more inexpensive olivewood jewelry, starting at less than $1.00. The illustrated catalog is free.

THE GOOD SHEPHERD'S STORE, WW, P.O. Box 96, Bethlehem, via Israel, makes and sells some very pretty mother-of-pearl pendants with geometric designs, priced from less than $1.00 to $2.00. Similar brooches fall into the same price range, and mother-of-pearl crosses cost from less than $1.00 to slightly over $5.00. There are also some attractive mother-of-pearl jewelry boxes, priced from around $5.00 to $20.00. Prices are in American dollars; catalog is free.

ELIE G. NSEIR offers some beautiful silver filigree jewelry, starting at around $2.00 for earrings; including some extremely handsome Crusaders' crosses, at $5.00 and up. Also available is some stunning 18-karat gold jewelry—a pair of gold and alexandrite earrings costs about $20.00; an intricate gold necklace set with turquoise is under $100.00; a gold bracelet with four topazes is about $60.00. Prices are in American dollars. **CHILINGURIAN** offers some handmade silver jewelry, mostly rings, at very low prices—from $2.00 to $3.00. (See Chapter 4,D for both.)

3. The Far East

K. MIKIMOTO, INC., WW, 5-5, 4-Chome, Ginza, Chuo-ku, Tokyo, Japan, are said to be the originators of cultured pearls, and the name of the firm is still almost synonymous with them. They will send you a free, full-color brochure offering their pearls and other jewelry at prices well below the prices the Mikimoto line sells for here. Necklaces, for example, start at around $35.00. You may be able to get Mikimoto pearls more cheaply from some of the Hong Kong houses; and, of course, there are anonymous cultured pearls that cost a good deal less. For instance, the **QUEEN PEARL COMPANY,** WW, C.P.O. Box 1446, Tokyo, Japan, sells cultured pearls for as low as $12.00 a string and going up to several hundred dollars. Shipping is included, and the necklaces are supplied temporarily strung—unknotted and without clasp—to save duty. Price list is free, and prices, as in Mikimoto's catalog, are given in American dollars.

However, you might not need to write to Japan to get a good buy in cultured pearls. The **CROWN CULTURED PEARL CORP.,** WW, 580 Eighth Ave., New York, N.Y. 10018, which is actually the American branch of a Japanese firm, often has closeouts of cultured pearl necklaces starting at about $8.00. They also offer a full line of regular cultured pearl necklaces, at prices that don't seem too much (if at all) higher than Queen's, let alone Mikimoto's. Furthermore, you can buy them already strung without having to worry about duty. They also have pearl earrings, many as low as $2.00 and $3.00, plus semiprecious stone carvings to be used as pendants—a jade fish is around $4.00, a coral heart, around $2.00. Also on hand are some charming semiprecious stone figurines. The catch is that this is a wholesale house, so you may have to buy certain inexpensive items in small lots rather than individually. For instance, one of their current lists shows a dozen cultured pearl tietacks set in silver at $8.00. The minimum order for merchandise is $15.00.

The **AMITA JEWELRY CORP.**, WW, Kyoto Handicraft Center, Kumano Jinja Higashi, Sakyo-ku, Kyoto 606, Japan, is celebrated for its lovely damascene jewelry in silver and gold-plated settings. Prices for earrings range from around $7.00 to $12.00, bracelets are $15.00 to $35.00; also on hand are brooches, rings, pendants, cufflinks, and little gewgaws like pillboxes, combs, and atomizers. Amita also sells some attractive silver and semiprecious stone jewelry and sterling silver pocket knives. The catalog is free.

You can get cultured pearl necklaces from India, too. **DEEPAK'S ROKJEMPERL PRODUCTS**, WW, 61, 10th Khetwadi, Bombay 4, India, offers them at prices ranging from $8.00 to $20.00. They also carry some inexpensive ivory jewelry. Price lists are free.

KAVERI MYSORE STATE HANDICRAFTS DEVELOPMENT CORPORATION, LTD., WW, 26/45 Mahatma Gandhi Rd., Bangalore-1, India; **LEPAKSHI HANDICRAFTS EMPORIUM**, WW, Gunfoundry, Hyderabad, India; and **BENGAL HOME INDUSTRIES ASSOCIATION**, WW, 57 Chowringhee Rd., Calcutta 16, India, all offer lovely silver filigree (and other types of silver) jewelry from around $1.00 to $2.00 for a ring, and $3.00 to $4.00 for a bracelet or a necklace (with tops rarely more than $10.00). There are also silver boxes and trinkets at very low prices. Gold is, of course, much higher, but reasonably priced—rings are around $8.00 to $30.00; necklaces from $20.00 to several hundred dollars. All three catalogs are free, and in English.

ORIENTAL HANDICRAFTS, WW, Captain Sham Lal Rd., Civil Lines, Ludhiana, India, will send you a free list of handcarved camel bone jewelry. Don't shudder —you don't know whose bones the other bone jewelry described in these pages is derived from. As a matter of fact, ivory is elephant bone, and a lot of work that's offered commercially as ivory is really made out of the bones of an animal other than an elephant. (Not by reputable firms, however, and I have endeav-

ored to list no other sort here. I would also like to limit the ivory and the bone carvings to those made out of animals who have died of natural causes, but I haven't quite figured out how to set about acquiring the requisite information.) Bone should be much cheaper than ivory, as you can see by the prices at Oriental. Necklaces of "down-trunk" elephant beads run from 75¢ for 12 to $2.25 for 40; "up-trunk" (which, being luckier, are naturally more expensive), from $1.40 to $4.50. There are also necklaces of rose, peacock, lion, camel, and fretwork beads; plus bracelets (25¢ to 40¢), earrings, brooches for women (elephants), and coat badges for men (birds). Also sold are bookmarks, salt spoons, and tooth or ear cleaners, all at less than a dollar a dozen; paper knives, cigarette holders, scent buds (your guess is as good as mine); $2.75 to $9.00 per dozen. Since this is a wholesale source, there's a minimum of $25.00, but this includes postage and packing.

RAMA JEWELRY, WW, 10/6 Surasak Rd., Bangkok, Thailand, has very inexpensive (from less than $2.00) silver cufflinks, either engraved or in nielloware, as well as all sorts of small silver items like pillboxes, mostly under $5.00. They also have more expensive jewelry set in 14-karat gold, not only the princess rings ($17.00 up) that you see all over, but more expensive models—for example, a black star sapphire with a diamond on either side is a little over $80.00. They also carry brooches, bangles, and bracelets. Prices (in American dollars) go up to over a thousand dollars for some of the really lavish models, but they're lower than the same things would be here. Catalog is free. **SILK OF SIAM**, 297 Suriwongse Rd., GPO Box 1802, Bangkok, Thailand, also shows some jewelry in its free catalog.

The **DEPARTMENT OF SMALL INDUSTRIES**, WW, Hemas Bldg., Bristol St., Colombo 1, Sri Lanka, puts out a free unillustrated price list describing all kinds of jewelry at what seem like fantastically low prices. For instance, a 3.5 cm. circular silver brooch with a carved lion in the center, surrounded by other animals, is less than $2.00. A silver bracelet set with 9 moonstones is around $3.00, a necklace of garnets and tourmalines on a gold chain is $25.00. They also have tortoise shell jewelry—a tortoise-shell and silver brooch is less than $2.00—and other tortoise shell items. Unfortunately, there are no illustrations. **SERENDIB** (Chapter 2,F.3) also lists sterling silver jewelry at very low prices—rings and brooches are $2.00 to $3.00, moonstone cufflinks are around $5.00.

FRANK AND CO., WW, Box 30072, Taipei, Taiwan, will send you free a lovely, colorful brochure showing green jade and coral jewelry set in 14-karat gold. Jade and gold rings start at around $11.00 and go up to around $35.00. Jade earrings start at around $13.00 and coral is slightly higher. There are also some lovely elaborate pieces, resembling the types so popular in Austria and Italy, but much lower in price—a gold brooch of pink coral roses with jade leaves is slightly over $50.00, as is a necklace of green jade and white coral.

The **TAIWAN GIFT SHOP**, WW, P.O. Box 12120, Taipei, Taiwan, has a brochure of unusual and very pretty T-stone lacquer jewelry. According to the brochure, the art of T-stone lacquercraft is over eight centuries old and has been popular ever since the heyday of the Sung Dynasty. It's made by lacquering one layer on another over and over in many different colors—it takes more than 100 separate layers to make the thickness of one third of an inch. Prices for this unusual craft are minimal—necklaces and pendants, less than $2.00, some less than $1.00; earrings all under $1.00. There are also bracelets, brooches, hair ornaments, cufflinks, and so on. Catalog is free. I would imagine, however, that you'd have to order enough goods to make it worth the firm's while to send the items to you. (No minimum was specified, but most overseas wholesalers who will deal with retail customers set a guideline of $20.00 to $25.00 as a minimum.)

TAIWAN VARIETY AND NOVELTY SUPPLIES, WW, 2 Alley 11, Lane 174, Section 2, Patch Rd., Taipei, Taiwan, puts out a catalog and group of brochures showing lots of nice things. The jewelry is so inexpensive that you have to order it by the dozen. Jade earrings are around $30.00 per dozen; mother-of-pearl brooches and earrings less than $8.00 per dozen; jade tie clasps less than $9.00. Jade, agate, and tiger-eye rings are $25.00 to $35.00 per dozen; nut necklaces (that is, made out of nuts) $3.00 to $4.00. There are many sample special offers, however, so you can order a selection of various types. Minimum order is $20.00. Catalog is $1.20.

ALIPIO'S PIONEER CURIO SHOP, WW, P.O. Box 96, 153 Kennon Rd., Camp 7, Baguio City, Philippines, offers Philippine jewelry made out of ipilipil seeds and shells. All of them cost well under a dollar. The catalog is free. More expensive Philippine jewelry may be obtained from **TESORO'S** (Chapter 2,E.3), which has some attractive silver filigree jewelry. The ones set with osmeña pearls are especially lovely, and the complete set of earrings, necklace, and bracelet costs around $15.00.

4. Africa and Down Under

INKENTAN CRAFTS (Chapter 3,E) offers African bead necklaces and belts at very modest prices.

M & B GIFTS OF AUSTRALIA, WW, P.O. Box 17, The Basin 3154, Australia, sells attractive opal jewelry in plain sterling silver or gold-plated sterling silver settings. Pendants cost from $16.00 to $23.00, bracelets (with 3 opals) are $40.00. Most unusual are the womens' watch bands, set with opals, and priced from around $35.00 to $55.00, depending on the number of stones. M & B also offers Australian charms and souvenir spoons. Airmail shipping is included, and circulars are free.

HETTIE'S ROCKSHOP, WW, 110 Birdwood Ave., Christchurch 2, New Zealand, offers gemstone jewelry made of New Zealand jade and paua shell, as well as jade figurines and other New Zealand novelties. Catalog is free.

5. South of the Border

In Mexico, **SANBORN'S**, WW, Avenida Madero 4, Mexico 1, D.F., sells handsome Mexican jewelry at prices that are about the same as they would be here, but you might find some styles that have particular appeal for you. The catalog is free, as is the one put out by the **CASA DE LAS ARTESANIAS DE JALISCO,** WW, Parque del Agua Azul, Guadalajara, Jalisco, Mexico. They sell some beautiful jewelry at incredibly low prices. For instance, a handengraved bracelet inlaid with turquoise is less than $8.00, filigree rings set with turquoise, onyx, or abalone are less than $1.00. Aztec calendar fanciers will find lots of Aztec calendar jewelry. Catch is, you have to buy at least a hundred dollars' worth, because they seem to sell jewelry only wholesale. (However, they might let you buy less if you pay a surcharge.) The catalog's in English and prices are in American dollars.

Most of the Central and South American houses described in Chapter 3,B have jewelry assortments to offer. **PILON** has an unillustrated price list of silver and gold-plated necklaces and pins made by Guatemalan Indians, from $3.00 to $7.00. **ANDEAN PRODUCTS** has beautiful silver and gold filigree jewelry fashioned by the artisans of Chordeleg after colonial originals. Earrings cost from $4.00 to $15.00 in silver, $19.00 to $45.00 in gold. **AKIOS** also has a jewelry line worth looking into.

TIMI'S, WW, P.O. Box 1144, San Juan, Puerto Rico, is an American house, but it is definitely south of the border. Its wares consist of pleasing tortoise-shell jewelry created by a California artist transplanted to the Caribbean. Necklaces cost from around $7.50 to $17.50; earrings are $3.00 to $5.00 a pair. There are also bracelets—the wide, plain ones at $7.50 are particularly satisfying—hair ornaments, and combs. Brochure is free.

The **TIPCO** Division of **SHEICA**, WW, P.O. Box 396, Port-au-Prince, Haiti, also offers tortoise-shell jewelry. The selection is much more limited than Timi's, but prices are lower. Earrings are mostly under $1.00 per pair, bracelets and "armrings" start at $2.00, belts at $3.00. Catalog is free.

6. North of the Border

Virtually all of the American Indian firms described in Chapter 3,A sell jewelry, with the emphasis on beadwork and German silver pieces. However, there are some firms whose primary output is jewelry, so I'm listing them separately here. You'll notice that prices range from inexpensive-souvenir-type to costly museum quality. They are all, to the best of my knowledge, completely authentic; but you must not expect to buy a rare potential heirloom piece for 50¢.

Really gorgeous jewelry handmade by Navajo silversmiths is available directly from **NAVAJO ARTS AND CRAFTS GUILD**, WW, Drawer A, Window Rock, Ariz. 86515. Plain sterling silver (the Navajos use only sterling) pins cost from around $3.00 to $18.00; with turquoise, they go from $6.00 to $24.00. Necklaces start at $24.00 and go up to $500.00. Available, too, are table silverware, and ornamental pieces, like boxes and candlesticks, as well as larger items. Every piece is a work of art and is likely to increase in value with time. The sumptuous, but not too informative, catalog is free.

The **APACHE ARTS AND CRAFTS BEAD ASSOCI-ATION**, WW, P.O. Box 1026, Whiteriver, Ariz. 85941, was organized by the women of the Fort Apache Indian Reservation to enable them to market the traditional beadwork, which they do by hand. A variety of necklaces is offered, from $2.00 up. The beautiful elaborate "T" necklaces start at $20.00. There are also medicine-ball necklaces, dolls, pins, belts, and so on, all exquisitely made by hand. In fact, they'll bead your name to order on your belt, if you like, although I personally prefer the traditional designs. Belt prices range from $15.00 to $25.00. The little color catalog is 50¢.

DAKOTAH CRAFTS, WW, 116 Oak St., P.O. Box 103, Sisseton, S.D. 57262, offers the fine beadwork for which the Sisseton—Wahpeton Sioux tribe is renowned. Prices range from as low as $1.50 for tiny, beaded turtle pins to $27.50 for a triple-medallion choker. The full-color folder is free.

The **INDIAN HILLS TRADING POST**, WW, Indian Hills Reservation, P.O. Box 229, Petoskey, Mich. 49770, has some attractive Ottawa and Chippewa jewelry. In addition to beadwork, there are necklaces made of quills, seeds, corn, acorns, leather, and vari-

ous other natural materials, most of them costing around $3.00. Catalog is free.

The **PIPESTONE INDIAN SHRINE ASSOCIATION**, WW, Pipestone National Monument, Pipestone, Minn. 56164, "is a non-profit organization dedicated to preserving the vanishing Indian handicrafts and providing a sounder economic base for the individual craftsmen," according to the free brochure. Pipestone offers a large selection of beadwork made by the local Sioux Indians—pendants, necklaces, and headbands. Necklaces cost from $4.00 to $11.00. There's also some jewelry made of pipestone, or catlinite—a red mineral prized by the Indians. Earrings and pendants are from $2.00. There are also turtles, owls, bears, and other figurines in animal shape; tomahawk and arrowhead paperweights; and ashtrays of all kinds, at prices starting at less than $1.00.

The **SIOUX PIPESTONE WORKS**, WW, P.O. Box 74, Box Elder, S.D. 57719, is the one-man enterprise of Joe Dudley, a Yankton Sioux, who makes and sells all the items featured in his little free brochure. There are brooches, necklaces, earrings, and so on, beginning at less than $1.00 and going up to a top of $3.00 or so. Ask for the retail catalog (unless you'd like to buy a a dozen or so at a clip).

QUALLA ARTS AND CRAFTS MUTUAL, INC., WW, P.O. Box 277, Cherokee, N.C. 28719, is a cooperative enterprise owned and operated by Cherokee Indian craftspeople of the Qualla Indian Reservation in North Carolina. Their folder includes an entire brochure devoted to their charming and extremely inexpensive beadwork (starting at 30¢ for a ring) Some very pretty beaded necklace and earring sets cost from $3.00 to $6.00 (other necklaces start as low as 75¢). Beaded belts run from $14.00 to $18.00, and there are many other interesting items.

For something quite different in jewelry, write to **NBWC**, WW, P.O. Box 476, Rialto, Cal. 92376, for their brochure, which shows pendants, tie clips, cufflinks, bracelets, and so on, featuring black widow spiders bred in their own laboratories and embedded in clear plastic. I don't know that I'd wear them myself, but they'd make wonderful gifts for certain very special people. Brochure is free.

MANDARIN HOUSE, WW, 12 East Church St., Blackwood, N.J. 08012, offers those gay Terra Sancta ecology pendants you've been seeing all over. This brochure, however, is devoted completely to them, so you'll find more than usual. There are half a dozen different kinds of dove, as well as spaceship earth; and pendants saying things like "Peace," "Shalom," "Love," "Save our Farm," and so on. There are fish (those are fertility symbols, folks), and attractive neck ornaments named "Genesis Rainbow," "Celebrate Earth," and "Peace with Nature," which can be enjoyed as designs alone. All of them are from $2.50 to around $4.00, on chains or thongs. If the designs really grab you, you can get them as coat hooks, belt buckles (You've got to take the belts along with them), door knockers, bookends, candleholders, letter openers, key rings, and trivets. There are also some religious items. The brochure is free.

7. Reproductions, Antiques, and Odds and Ends

Some of the jewelry purveyed by the above firms includes reproductions of ancient originals. In addition, many of the museum shops described in Chapter 11 offer handsome pieces of jewelry reproduced from items in their collections. Real antique jewelry may be obtained from some of the shops in Collections (Chapter 15). I'd also like to call your attention to the gemstone and jewelry houses in Chapter 17. You can buy gemstone beads from the East Indian houses far more cheaply than you can buy them here. Many of the American gemstone houses offer finished jewelry pieces, which you might be interested in. Incidentally, if you like costume jewelry, you can save a lot (usually, at least half) by buying the parts and putting them together yourself. It's not terribly creative, but it's fun. (Don't get kits; you save less money that way, and it's more interesting to pick out your own colors and combinations.)

B. WATCHES

Name brand watches are one thing you should never buy at list price, if you can help it, and there are a number of firms abroad that offer hefty discounts. It's impossible for me to estimate how much you might be able to save, because I can't check out each watch, model by model; moreover, a lot of firms here also offer discounts on certain brands. What you have to figure out, once you've decided on your watch, is whether you'll still come out ahead if you order from

abroad after shipping costs and duty have been added to the cost. In most cases, I think you will.

If you've set your heart on a Swiss watch, you could write to **BUCHERER**, WW, Bahnhofstrasse 50, Zurich, Switzerland, which puts out a catalog of Bücherer, Rolex and Piaget watches. Bücherer's prices are given in American dollars. If you want a Gübelin, Patek Philippe, Omega, or Audemars Piguet, write to **GÜBELIN**, WW, Schweizerhofquai 1, 6000 Lucerne, Switzerland, which puts out a catalog in francs. Both catalogs are free. If Bücherer and Gübelin get rotten and refer you to their U.S. branches, write to the **ARTLAND WATCH CO., LTD.**, WW, P.O. Box 857, Hong Kong, which says it can give you discount prices on practically every brand of watch there is. So, when you write, tell them the specific brand or brands you're interested in, and they'll send you free brochures.

STECHERS, WW, 62 Independence Sq., Port of Spain, Trinidad, W.I., offers a similar service. Tell them what brand you're interested in and they'll send you brochures and let you know what kind of discount you'll get. They say their prices average about 40 per cent less than in the United States, but they sell a lot of other things, so there's no way of telling whether that applies to watches.

T. M. CHAN AND CO., WW, P.O. Box 3881, Hong Kong, will give you discounts on Seiko watches. The catalog, in American dollars, is free. And **UNIVERSAL SUPPLIERS**, WW, P.O. Box 14803, Hong Kong, puts out three catalogs, one of Rolex and Girard Perregaux watches, another of Titoni and Tugari watches, and a third of Breitling chronographs. The catalogs are free by seamail; by airmail, $1.65 if you want just the watch catalogs; $3.30, if you want their full repertory (described in other chapters).

Many of the Caribbean houses described in Chapters 8 and 9 also can get you discounts on Swiss watches.

Remember: *Write for the catalog first.* All prices given were valid only at the time of writing and probably have been changed.

Chapter 6

BEAUTY AND HEALTH

A. TOILETRIES AND AROMAS

1. Perfume

As I mentioned in the Introduction, French perfume is one thing it really pays to order from abroad. Even when you add on postage and duty (and nowadays duty always has to be paid on perfume, even when it is sent as a gift), it costs approximately half of what it costs here. The larger the bottle you buy, the greater the saving. There *are* restrictions on the amount of each kind you may buy, and some manufacturers require you to obliterate the trademark before you can bring their perfume into this country. The booklet *U.S. Customs Trademark Information,* described in Chapter 1, will give you specific information about this.

Good places to buy all the big-name French perfumes, as well as some less celebrated ones, are **OBÉRON**, WW, 73 Champs Elysées, Paris, France; **FREDDY**, WW, 10 rue Auber, Paris, France; **LYNDA**, WW, 3 rue Caumartin, Paris, France; **MICHEL SWISS**, WW, 16 rue de la Paix, Paris, France; **BENLUX**, WW, 277 rue Saint-Honoré, Paris, France; and **SHANNON**, WW, Mail Order Store, Shannon Airport, Ireland. Oberon's and Shannon's good-looking color catalogs are $1.00 and 60¢ respectively (but both offer a wide range of different products . . . described elsewhere in this book). Freddy's bright little catalog is free, as are the brochures put out by Lynda, Michel Swiss, and Benlux. (Most of these French shops also offer Limoges and Lalique dressing-table fripperies, like atomizers, mirrors, lipstick holders, and such.)

But French perfumes aren't the only ones in the world. There are English ones, too, such as the floral and bouquet perfumes manufactured by England's famous **FLORIS OF LONDON**, WW, 89 Jermyn St., London SW IV 6JH, England, which has been perfumer to the court of St. James since 1730. There are Scottish perfumes, too. **D. MacGILLIVRAY AND CO.** (Chapter 2,C.1) offer Hebridean perfumes, hand-blended by crofters in the highlands. From Israel come two very new perfumes—*Chutzpah* (impertinence), created by Aviva Dayan; and *Mazal Tav* (good luck). Both are attractive, light, crisp scents, which can be worn by either men or women. They're avail-

able as toilet water, perfume and after shave lotion, as well as in sets. A 52-cc bottle of perfume in either fragrance is less than $10.00, postpaid and allegedly duty-free (I don't know how they'd work that unless they mailed them from the States, so don't count on the duty-free part); cologne is about half the price. Free brochures describing them are available from **T.S.Q., LTD.**, WW, 9 Moshe Hess St., Tel-Aviv, Israel.

America has some very lovely perfumes of her own. **MAY COVE**, WW, P.O. Box 227, Colonial Heights, Va. 23824, hand blends traditional flower fragrances to make perfumes based on the ones beloved by our great grandmothers, and equally popular with their nature-loving descendants—perfumes considered so authentically Early American that they're sold at Colonial Williamsburg and other museum shops. *Eau de May Cove,* stronger than cologne, lighter than perfume, is offered in 40 fresh flower fragrances—including stephanotis, nicotiana, mimosa, tea olive, and arbutus, in addition to the more familiar rose (5 different types), lilac, lavender, lily of the valley, etc. A 2-oz. bottle costs $3.75. Small, purse-size flacons are also available. These scents are also offered in perfume and bath oils (the latter available with atomizer for unreconstructed showerers, at $3.00 for a 1-oz. bottle). Postage and packing are included.

Also distinctively American are the Hawaiian perfumes available from **HAWAIIANA PACIFICA**, WW, Waikiki Box 15266; and **HAWAIIAN THINGS**, WW, Waikiki Box 15276—both Honolulu, Hawaii 96815. Pacifica offers several scents—*white ginger, plumeria* (frangipani), and *pikake* (jasmine). Hawaiian Things offers one scent—*Hawaii Calling.* Prices for colognes are around $6.00 for 2 oz. One of the two firms sent me a tiny plastic tube containing a sample, and it was heavenly, whichever of the scents it was.

2. Cosmetics and Soaps

All of the French firms mentioned in the preceding section offer cosmetics and soaps in the same lines as the perfumes. Most of them also offer extensive lines of Orlane and Lancome cosmetics. Obéron's list is the most comprehensive. It includes not only makeup, but such specialties as "anti-wrinkle cream" and "body milk." Michel-Swiss also offers several kinds of "embryo" treatments (very expensive), and a line of

Stendhal cosmetics. **BREMEN HOUSE**, WW, 200 East 86 St., New York, N.Y. 10028, has a selection of beauty and health aids from Germany. Because at this point the catalog (free), up until now in English, breaks into German, I can't tell you any more about them—especially as I am not sure whether some of the names are simply the brands or refer to some awful skin condition. But, if you are interested and speak German, have a look.

There's no point in listing standard lines of American cosmetics because these are readily available all over the country (and seldom, if ever, discounted). However, you might not always be able to get the "natural" cosmetics that are so big these days. Of course, some of the name brands are beginning to jump on the bandwagon, although it has not yet been established to everyone's satisfaction that their cucumber and strawberry and (yet to come) tossed green salad lines are actually made with those substances rather than merely *scented* with them.

A drugstore that's almost as old as the Republic itself is the **CASWELL-MASSEY CO., LTD.**, WW, Catalog Order Dept., 320 West 13 St., New York, N.Y. 10014 (catalog $1.00 for several issues). The company takes pride, the catalog says, "in the fact that we pioneered the making of pure, 100% natural beauty creams in America," and names among satisfied customers Adelina Patti, Lillian Russell, and Sarah Bernhardt. It guarantees that Caswell-Massey cosmetics "sold under the registered name of *Certi-Natural* contain the products of natural origin mentioned on the label, absolutely," and offers three *Certi-Natural* moisturizing creams—peach for dry skin, banana for normal, strawberry for oily. A 4-oz. jar is $5.00. The firm also purveys an incredible selection of soap from all over the world. All are rather unusual and, like most of Caswell-Massey's wares, rather expensive, ranging from $1.00 up per cake. Postage and shipping are extra, but $1.00 is tops.

The health food and herb stores have always offered "organic" and "natural" cosmetics, and many of those listed in this chapter and the one following carry lines of varying fullness, as well as the materials for those free spirits who want to make their own cosmetics. **STUR-DEE** and **BARTH'S** (both described more fully in Section B of this chapter) have rather extensive offerings. Stur-dee has fruit and vegetable face creams—the cucumber, they aver, is "not a mere scent from cucumbers, but made with fresh cucumbers"—as well as all kinds of other things for the body. Barth puts out a special catalog of "natural products to protect your beauty and personal hygiene." They're heavy on the cucumbers, too; also strong on strawberries and avocado. Many of the health food stores

carry the Orjene line of natural cosmetics. However, if you prefer, you may order directly from **HEATHER GARDEN**, P.O. Box 526, Woodside, N.Y. 11377. They will send you free brochures describing their broad range of products which, they say, are not only natural but nonallergenic. In addition to the usual creams and lotions, they have complete lines of lipstick, powder, eyeshadow, and so on, at quite moderate prices.

Long before natural products came into vogue here—at least commercially—they were much in demand in other countries. **MEADOWBROOK HERB GARDEN**, WW, Wyoming, R.I. 02898 (catalog 25¢), has on hand the well-known Weleda herb toiletries from Switzerland, including rosemary and chestnut shampoos ($1.25 to $1.50), rosemary and iris toilet soap, and so on. (**HEALTH 4 ALL PRODUCTS**—see B—also carries them.) Meadowbrook also has Bio-Kosma cosmetics, produced from "pure vegetable oils, dried blossoms and extracts of medicinal herbs," plus "organically cultivated cucumbers." Actually they seem to be mostly cucumber—cucumber day cream ($2.25 per tube); cucumber night cream ($2.50 per tube); and cucumber tonic, for closing the pores ($2.75 for 3½ oz.). **APHRODISIA**, WW, 28 Carmine St., New York, N.Y. 10014, includes in its piquant little catalog, which disclaims (perforce) any aphrodisiac properties to its wares (and costs 35¢) Aditi cosmetics from India. These are not only organic, it is claimed, but hypoallergenic. Among items seldom seen amidst the relentless roll of cucumbers are grapefruit oil skin freshener, lotus leaf moisturizing cream, and sesame oil moisturizer (all $3.50 to $4.00 for 2 oz.).

If you'd like to order natural cosmetics directly from abroad, Britain's famous herbalists **CULPEPER LIMITED**, WW, 59 Ebury St., London SW 1 WDN2, England, will send you a free brochure describing a long line of herbal cosmetics. These include elder flower and red elm creams at around $1.50 for 24 gr.; green lettuce and Black Forest pine soaps, around 60¢ for a toilet-sized cake; and rosemary and jaborandi hair lotion, around $1.25 for 113 cc. Shipping is extra.

Other sources of soaps that may or may not be natural but are certainly appealing in scent, color, and shape (as well as less expensive than most of those offered as natural) are the **CAROLINA SOAP AND CANDLEMAKERS**, WW, Southern Pines, N.C. 28387; and the **PINEHURST HANDMADE SOAP AND CANDLE CO.**, WW, Pinehurst, N.C. 28374. Carolina's catalog is 25¢, Pinehurst's 35¢.

If you're looking for theatrical makeup, write to **STUDIO IMPORTS**, WW, P.O. Box 143, South Pasadena, Cal. 91030. They'll send you a free brochure of the cosmetics made by the famous firm of Leichner, which has served the London theater for nearly a century.

3. Potpourris and Pomanders

The **POTPOURRI SHOP**, WW, P.O. Box 108, Redding Ridge, Conn. 06876, informs us in its catalog (25¢) that *potpourri* is a French word meaning "rotten pot." They offer five different kinds of potpourris at $1.00 per cup. You can also get a white ginger jar or a moon-and-star pattern glass apothecary jar each filled with two cups of potpourri at $4.00 and $5.00 respectively. They have a very original and engaging idea here; they've made tea cosies (or muffin cosies or casserole cosies) out of quilted calico, trimmed them with eyelet embroidery, and filled them with a spice mixture. As the heat of the pot inside warms the cosy the air fills with fragrance. The cosies are $4.00, and large potholders (or small table protectors) to match are $2.00. On hand also are sachets, pomanders, potpourri makings, and do-it-yourself kits. The potpourri kits each make six cups and cost $5.00, while the pomander kits each make six pomanders and cost $3.50. Prices seem low, but it's hard to tell since herbs are priced by cup rather than weight (most botanicals are, of course, extremely light). Prices are also very reasonable at **CAPRILANDS HERB FARM**, WW, Silver St., North Coventry, Conn. 06238, which offers hop pillows (for insomnia), peace pillows, and herbal moth preventatives, all for around $1.50 each; there are also potpourri and pomander makings and many other sweet things in its small brown brochure (10¢).

The **HERB FARM**, WW, Granville, Mass. 01034, offers potpourris and supplies, plus a small selection of culinary herbs, and all sorts of herb items, including tussie mussies (dried herb bouquets, $4.00 to $6.00). Particularly interesting here are the herbal Christmas cards with little packets of herbs and spices attached. One comes with rosemary, one with assorted spices, and one with poultry stuffing—50¢ to 65¢ each. Catalog is 25¢.

Aphrodisia has potpourris and pomanders "handmade by local craftsmen," presumably the merry peasants of New York City. Kits for the do-it-yourselfer are $9.00 for the potpourri, $4.25 for the pomander. They're postpaid but shipping is extra on the loose herbs and spices and the fragrant oils. Although Floris of London was first mentioned under Perfumes, it's probably best known in this country for its exquisite potpourris and china pomanders. The pomander balls come in several styles and sizes (not only the traditional ball, but a key fob and a pendant), from around $1.50 to $7.00. Other items in their repertory include a variety of potpourri jars, perfumed-candle lanterns, and potpourris reviver essence plus a pomander reviver essence to ginger up your fading fragrances.

Caswell-Massey has a section in its self-consciously fascinating catalog entitled "The Compleat Pot Pourri and Perfume Oil Providers." The prices for potpourri ingredients are quite a bit higher than at most other places, but the catalog tells you what color each herb, petal, and wood is—which, to my knowledge, no other catalog does. It has the usual fragrant and/or essential oils; particularly interesting is the firm's very own potpourri oil, which you use in case you've goofed and concocted something that smells awful. It's $5.00 per ½ oz. bottle. Also on hand are musk, ambergris, and civet oils for fixing the perfume odors (or your own odors).

Potpourri ingredients are also offered by virtually all of the other herb stores described in this chapter and in Chapter 7,D. Some offer incense as do virtually all of the occult supply shops. A firm devoted entirely to incense—they have 30 different kinds of India Temple Incense and 15 different kinds of Mission (ritual) incense—is **INDIACRAFTS**, WW, P.O. Box 853, San Francisco, Cal. 94101. Also offered is a large group of fragrant oils (all the herb shops sell these). Everything here is $1.00, but sizes aren't specified. (The pictured oil bottle looks as if it says ¼ oz.) Brochure is free.

B. FOOD SUPPLEMENTS

There are many firms that offer vitamins and minerals, plus other food supplements; most of those listed in the Health Foods section (E) of Chapter 7 sell them. You'll also find food supplements of one kind or another at some of the firms listed in Section C (Medicines and Remedies) of this chapter. In addition, there are some firms that specialize in food supplements, and they sell them at prices that compare very favorably with those prevailing at most neighborhood health food stores—and many drug stores, too.

STUR-DEE HEALTH PRODUCTS, INC., WW, Island Park, N.Y. 11558, puts out a free catalog—in fact, a series of free catalogs, because they seem to come out every month or two—listing all kinds of food supplements. Postage is free and there are free gifts (at Christmas they offer a delicious organic fruit cake). If your first catalog happens not to be a sale catalog, wait. All the others will be, and prices will be very reasonable. All the catalogs put out by the **NATURAL SALES COMPANY**, WW, P.O. Box 25, Pittsburgh, Pa. 15230, are sale catalogs. It offers similar merchandise and free gifts as well. In addition, there are cut-rate one-to-a-family offers on a selected group of supplements, which are outstanding bargains. For instance, the current catalog shows 100 kelp or bone-meal tablets at 25¢. **BARTH'S**, WW, 270 West Merrick Rd., Valley Stream, N.Y. 11582, puts out a line of vitamin and mineral supplements, which are sold both by direct mail order and through health food stores. Gifts are offered with mail orders here, too.

NATUREX, INC., WW, 1125 Mont-Royal Est, Montreal 176, P.Q., Canada, puts out a thick catalog that's mainly in French. They don't send food to the United States (not even their organic *petits pains à "hotdog"*) but they will ship vitamins and minerals and probably cosmetics and bath products. I suspect they will also ship their books (my favorite title is Dr. Passebecq's *Adieu Constipation*). **NATURE FOOD CENTRES**, WW, 292 Main St. Cambridge, Mass. 02138; **HERRSCHNER PHARMACEUTICALS**, WW, Benton Harbor, Mich. 49022; and **HEALTH 4 ALL PRODUCTS**, 326 College St., Toronto, Canada, all sell food supplements (and natural cosmetics). Health 4 All's is in both French and English. All the catalogs offered under *Food Supplements* are free.

C. MEDICINES AND REMEDIES

1. Conventional Medicine

There may be some people so lost to the retrograde sweep of progress that they still prefer the chemical nostrums being pushed by the medical establishment. These people may be interested in the **CELO DIRECT DRUG SERVICE**, WW, 6905 4 St. N.W., Washington, D.C. 20012; and the **GETZ PRESCRIPTION CO.**, WW, 916 Walnut St., Kansas City. Mo. 64199. Both of them offer to fill your prescriptions by mail at discounts of up to 40 percent (it's not clear on what, because there are usually no list prices available for prescription drugs). Their free catalogs give partial listings of the most commonly prescribed drugs and their comparative prices, so you can judge for yourself whether the prices would represent substantial savings for you. Remember, though, you still will need a prescription from your doctor in order to buy them.

2. Medicinal Herbs

The new generation—and some leftover members of old generations—seems to be into herbs and herbal remedies in a big way. Since herb lore tends to overlap food to cosmetics to medicine to the occult, you will find herbal sources listed in all of the chapters that deal with these matters; and, sometimes, repeated where a firm's line is strong in more than one area. Aphrodisia, for instance, has a particularly good line of botanicals (herbs, barks, and spices), though not as extensive as the one at **WIDE WORLD OF HERBS, LTD.**, WW, 11 St. Catherine St. East, Montreal 129, Québec, Canada. That firm calls itself "Canada's largest dealer in botanicals," and it offers the longest

list of botanicals I've seen, totaling at a rough estimate some 1500 varieties. (And they say they stock over 2000, so that, in the unlikely event that you don't see what you want, you can ask for it.) Prices are very reasonable, but shipping and handling costs will jack them up quite a bit. Other sources, such as the **HERB PRODUCTS CO.**, and **NATURE'S HERB CO.**, are described in Chapter 7,D.

Once upon a time, American ginseng was shipped to the Orient, because it wasn't used here except by a select few. Now that living styles have changed, the traffic is going the other way; we are getting our ginseng (as well as *fo-ti-tung* and *gota kola*) from the Orient. Most of the herb stores included here (except for the New England ones, which tend to be more the tussie mussie type) now sell it. However, because most of the ginseng sold here comes from Korea, where it is a government monopoly, you might like to write directly to the **KOREA GINSENG CENTER**, WW, P.O. Box 2288, San Francisco, Cal. 94126, which is the American address of the Republic of Korea's Office of Monopoly. They may try to tout you on to a local health food store, but they do have a form for ordering from them by mail directly, and they will send it to you if you persist.

Or you might like to order your ginseng from China, where most of the ginseng lore comes from. I can't give you a mainland China address yet (I'm working on it), but the **CHINESE MERCHANDISE EMPORIUM**, WW, 92-104 Queens Road C., Hong Kong, which deals only in goods from China, offers both ginseng root and ginseng extract, as well as such Old World remedies as deer's antler, tiger-bone pills, Peking royal jelly, and other items unfamiliar to me or partly familiar, like essence of chicken with cordyceps. (The Emporium's free catalog is described more fully in Chapter 7,A.1). If you prefer American ginseng, as many do (the American variety is reputed to have somewhat different properties from the Oriental), write to the **SMOKY MOUNTAIN GINSENG CO.**, WW, P.O. Box 861, Asheville, N.C. 28802, for their free folder. Don't expect the American variety to be inexpensive, because it isn't. (They also sell ginseng roots and seeds in case you want to grow your own.)

3. Herbal and Homeopathic Remedies

Some firms offer ready-made herbal remedies, many based on secret recipes of their own. **CATHAY OF BOURNEMOUTH, LTD.**, WW, 53 Curzon Rd., Bournemouth, England, is a firm operated by herbalist Violet Mitton, who learned her art in Hong Kong and South Africa, together with her husband. It offers what it modestly describes as "world-famous herbal preparations of outstanding quality and efficacy" in its engaging catalog written in an elegant Edwardian style.

There's The Empress of China's Own Recuperative Elixir, the function of which is "to improve digestion, sluggish elimination, and tone up the system." There are Tiger Headache Pills, which are supposed to relieve headaches; Temple Garden Tablets, which "offer quick, speedy relief for biliousness and sickness arising from upset stomach." Restoral Chest Elixir is not only "a most excellent herbal fluid restorative that relieves influenza, heavy chest colds, and comforts the cold and despondent . . . induces sleep and aids the circulation and digestion." In addition, "it is quite delightful to drink, as it cheers and lifts the spirits wonderfully." There are also Lightning Lung Balm, Excel Embrocation, and Mrs. Mitton's Vivacity Drops, plus plain herbs, cosmetics (the Quick Recuperative Cream sounds especially good), and Nefertiti Cream Perfume (derived from a secret perfume of ancient Egypt). The colorful catalog is free, and orders from America are welcomed. Culpeper also has a long line of remedies.

Bournemouth appears to be an herbalists' haven, for **GERARD HOUSE, LTD.,** WW, 736B Christchurch Rd., Bournemouth, England, also is a purveyor of herbal preparations (and vitamins). *"Priory*, cleansing herbs for inner freshness," costs $4.00 for 4 packets; *Gerard Natural Herb Nervine* containing valerian, asafoetida, lupulus, skullcap, and gentian is $4.50 for 360 tablets; and a combination of extracts from raspberry leaves, marshmallow, and partridgeberry, sold as *Gerard Raspberry Compound,* is $4.00 for 400 tablets. This is for such female disorders as menstrual troubles, vaginal discharge, and pregnancy. Prices are given in dollars; shipping is included and with their price list you get a copy of their fascinating little book-catalog, *Health Digest,* which gives you information about all kinds of relevant topics, like Vitamin E, slippery elm, and the prostate gland, along with some very appetizing recipes. The one for quick wheatmeal bread, baked in a flower pot, is a must. They also put out a very interesting natural health magazine called *Grace.*

Let it not be thought that the New World cannot rival the Old in this sphere. The 70-plus-year-old **INDIANA BOTANIC GARDENS,** WW, P.O. Box 5, Hammond, Ind. 46325, also seems to make time stand still in its Almanac (15¢), which offers BIM, "for better nutrition," Peptocel, "for gas and bloat," and Myra, "medicine and perfume of kings and queens. . . . When diluted with warm water, Myra is a soothing gargle. . . . Myra is a palliative to cankers, fever blisters, and mouth sores of superficial nature. . . . It [is] useful for a variety of minor conditions such as skin irritations, burns, cuts, bruises, poison ivy, innocuous insect bite, etc." A satisfied customer, Mrs. W. A. P. writes, in her "unsolicited" letter, "Myra sure is a wonderful medicine

to have around." The Almanac has lots of useful information,too—a planting guide and weather forecast for every month of the year; recipes for candying leaves and flowers and for warming the stomach (which you do by mixing 4 oz. of ginger with 1 qt. of gin); directions for making your own soap, getting rid of fleas (pennyroyal), getting rid of blackbirds (baking them in a pie, honestly! They even give the recipe). Incidentally, this is the only mail-order house I've noted where you can get empty capsules that you can fill with your powdered botanicals—or whatever. (In addition to the Almanac, Indiana has a catalog of botanicals, which you must ask for specifically.)

ROLLY'S HEALTH STORE, WW, 634 Yonge St., Toronto, Ontario, Canada, offers therapeutic products, including some herbal preparations with names that are unfamiliar to me but doubtless well-known to those who seek them—such as Luri (with or without oil) and Beverol, which I take it you drink; or Anthyllis and Imperator, which you apparently rub on yourself. They also have food supplements. **LUYTIE'S PHARMACAL CO.,** WW, 4200 Laclede Ave., St. Louis, Mo. 63108, "manufacturing pharmacists since 1853," issues a list of its homeopathic remedies, including the rather sinisterly named *Aconite Napellus* and *Arsenicum Alb,* as well as *Echninacea Angustifolia, Spongia Tosta, Thuja Occ,* and other doubtlessly well-known old-time remedies with botanical bases. The firm also carries "the twelve Schuessler remedies," which seem to include one for almost every ailment, especially unpleasant ones with slimy discharges. Both brochures are free.

D. COMFORT

Virtually all of the firms mentioned in this chapter offer items to make life easier for you—heating pads and special toothbrushes, massagers of divers kinds, foot baths, water filters, bunion regulators, exercise equipment, and all kinds of other gadgets. Caswell-Massey has items like *Germann* ear plugs from Italy (a tin of 12 is $3.00), smelling salts, menthol sticks for the relief of headaches, loofahs and sponges in profusion. *Heros Chiropody Sponge* ($1.50) is said to wash away corns. They have French friction mitts and straps for use after the bath ($6.50 to $27.00). (Barth's has an Austrian back-scrubber for only $5.00).

Then there are firms with specialties. **CHARLES NESSLER PRODUCTS CO.,** WW, Box 27, Avon, Conn. 06001, puts out an unusual English-made hairbrush with single-set flexible brushes in a rubber air-cushion pad. I've been using one for years and never found anything to match. It comes in maple, ebony, lime, and hot pink and costs about $4.50 postpaid. A brochure, with tips on how to care for your hair, as well as for the brush, is free.

1. Garments and Exercise Machinery

DAMART, INC., WW, Posen, Ill. 60469, sells special thermal undergarments for arthritis- and rheumatism-sufferers, as well as for elderly people generally. **MAGIC MOLD, INC.,** WW, 10 Taylor St., Freeport, L.I., N.Y. 11520, offers slimming, controlling, and supporting devices, including surgical supports and, oddly, a small selection of sexy underwear, which sorts ill with the front buckle side-opening belt for dropped stomach. Both catalogs are free. For 25¢ **FRANK BETZ & CO.,** WW, 44 Park Dr., Glenview, Ill. 60025, will send you a catalog full of all kinds of exercise machines and gadgets, plus a variety of miscellaneous health aids. They have many different types of heating pads for many parts of the body; as well as a lot of invalid aids.

2. Sleep

There are two firms dedicated to the poor sleeper, as well as the good sleeper who wants to become a great sleeper. Both, by coincidence, are situated in New Jersey. **BETTER SLEEP, INC.,** is at WW, New Providence, N.J. 07974, and **WUENSCH'S NORMAN DINE SLEEP SHOP** is at WW, 33 Halsted St., East Orange, N.J. 07018. Both have slant boards, bed boards, blanket supports, all kinds of pillows (antiwrinkle, neck supporting, travel, bath, backrest, etc.), and antisnore devices. Better Sleep also has a *Compat-a-Pillow,* which, they say, "has been designed, tested and modified with the advice and aid of marriage counselors, both religious and medical, to assure greater satisfaction and marital joy." It's $7.00 and comes with a pink acetate satin zipper cover and an "authoritative text."

Wuensch (whose prices seem slightly higher) goes in for more expensive installations, like a kingsize round bed at $330.00 (the price also includes a blanket, four sheets, and a mattress pad). It has bedding to fit all sorts of outsize and odd-sized beds. They also carry some exercise machines. Both catalogs are free.

One time-honored way of relieving insomnia is by taking advantage of the well-known soporific properties of hops. A country hop pillow is known to have enabled George III to enjoy a refreshing slumber after all others had failed—and perhaps it will prove equally beneficial for you. The **MALTINGS,** WW, Horsecraft Rd., Bury St. Edmunds, Suffolk, England, offers 18" by 27" pillows that contain selected dried English hops enclosed in "quality feathers" and covered with strong, white ticking. They should, the firm says, last for years. There are three grades, costing from a little over $8.00 to around $13.00. Descriptive sheet is free.

3. Breathing

If you have trouble breathing—who doesn't these days?—you might send for the brochure (free) put out by **SURVIVAL ASSOCIATES', INC.,** WW, P.O. Box 8, Old Chelsea Station, New York, N.Y. 10011. It describes their filter masks (which cost around $18.00 to $23.00 postpaid), and can be fitted with replacement cartridges. The masks are meant to be used outdoors, but, if you're self-conscious about going out in the street looking as if you expected an enemy attack momentarily, you still might like one to wear on special occasions, not only Halloween, but when there's a smog alert or when you're dusting or using sprays. The firm says it's safe to wear them even when you're using insecticides. Although they're meant for everybody, they're a special boon for people who suffer from respiratory ailments and allergies.

4. Seeing

If you wear eyeglasses, you may be interested in **PRISM OPTICAL, INC.,** WW, 135 West 41 St., New York, N.Y. 10036, which will undertake to make you spectacles from your eye doctor's prescription. Prices are not high, though they are far from being the "rock bottom" that the firm claims, and the catalog is free.

5. Strictly for Southpaws

Here's a happy note. People who have been suffering all their lives from the trauma of being born left-handed into a doggedly right-handed world can take comfort from the knowledge that somebody cares. **ANYTHING LEFT-HANDED LIMITED,** WW, 65 Beak St., London W.1, England; **THE ARISTERA ORGANIZATION,** WW, 9 Race's Lane, Westport, Conn. 06880; and The **LEFT HAND,** WW, 145 East 27 St., New York, N.Y. 10016, have left-handed scissors, pinking shears, potato peelers, playing cards, eggbeaters, spatulas, mustache cups, ladles, corkscrews, ice cream scoops, address books (which might also appeal to Near Easterners), golf clubs, T-squares, wrist watches, gardening tools, palettes, potholders, and so on and so forth, including many items you would never think of as having any specific orientation.

Anything Left-Handed has a crochet hook for left-handers and Aristera has a knitting book and a needle-point book, plus a button that says, "Kiss Me, I'm Left-Handed," while the Left Hand sells left-handed boomerangs and posters of legendary lefties, including Napoleon, Michelangelo's David, and Robert Redford. Anything Left-Handed's catalog is 25¢, Aristera's is 50¢, and the Left Hand's is free. The British firm's prices seem to be generally lower but shipping costs (additional for all three) will probably be higher, and there might be duty on some of the items. In any case, if you're left-handed, or know someone who is, you'll want to have all three catalogs, because each has many items the others don't show.

Chapter 7

FOOD

You can get lots of interesting food by mail that you may not be able to obtain locally, but don't expect to save any money that way. Even though many of the firms listed in this chapter list store prices no higher than those in the supermarkets, the tremendous cost of packing and shipping will push prices way, way up.

You'll note that I've tried to exclude highly perishable foods, like fresh meat, from this chapter, since I don't think it's practical to ship them by mail unless you live very close to the store. However, some of the catalogs that have been included do carry perishables in addition to their other lines. If you order them, you have only yourself to blame if they're not in good condition when you get them. Also, if a firm advises against shipping some of their products during certain months, take their advice.

A. FOREIGN FOOD

1. From Abroad

There are many restrictions on ordering food from abroad, and it's so costly and difficult to import in small quantities that—except for things like candy and tea—you'll really find it simpler to order foreign food from stateside mail-order houses. In addition, they often can supply you with United States-made equivalents of certain foreign foods that cannot be imported legally. However, in case it gives you a sense of daring and adventure to get your food directly from abroad, there are certain overseas firms that regularly send parcels to the United States and thus are familiar with all necessary rules and regulations.

One of these is the famous French food house of **FAUCHON,** WW, 24 Place de la Madeleine, Paris 8e, France, which offers such delicacies as goose liver (or, as we call it, *pâté de foie gras*), at prices ranging from about $24.00 up for an 8-oz. crock. There are *marrons glacés,* at about $6.00 for a 14-oz. can, chestnuts in syrup, Bar-le-Duc jelly, French tuna fish, sardines of various kinds (including spiced sardines with truffles— around $1.00 for a 4-oz. can), French herbs, mustards, snails, canned cheese, and various kinds of pâtés —including hare, thrush, baby wild boar, blackbird, lark, etc., at about $1.75 for a 4½-oz. can. As you can see, it's all very expensive, but terribly chic.

The equally famous British house of **FORTNUM AND MASON, LTD.,** WW, Piccadilly, London W1A 1ER, England, puts out a handsome Christmas catalog (plus brochures during the year), featuring a group of smashing food hampers at even more smashing prices. They begin modestly at about $12.00 and soar up to $200.00 and more. Included are such delicacies as a whole roast pheasant in aspic, selected ox tongue, Old English mincemeat, real turtle soup, selected brawn, etc. They also have beluga caviar; all kinds of English cheeses; tea in wonderful Staffordshire ironstone and Wedgwood jars; their famous Christmas puddings (a three-pounder is a relatively modest $5.00); plus all kinds of food appurtenances, like a bonbon box in the shape of a giant gilt walnut, and a Wedgwood vacuum ice bucket.

Both catalogs are free, and both firms are food stores, so they will probably be able to get you any exportable local food you desire. **EGERTON'S,** WW, 5 Fore St., Seaton, Devon EX12 2LB, England, however, is a mail-order service and all it offers in the way of food are the gift packages described in their catalog (60¢, and it includes many other things—described elsewhere in this book). These range from about $6.00 to $17.00. A variety of English chocolates and other sweets, cookies, cakes, and tea is available. Prices are in American dollars.

You might want to get your tea directly from a tea merchant. **MARK AUSTIN,** WW, 169 Kingston Rd., Wimbledon, London S. W. 19, England, specializes in sending tea, done up in charming packages, to Americans. His catalog, with prices in American dollars, is free. For Indian tea, get in touch with **R. N. AGARWALA,** WW, Nehru Rd., Darjeeling, India, who offers 4½ lbs. of "Golden Flowery Orange Pekoe Tea" for $10.00, packing and postage included, which looks like a very good buy. He has no catalog, but puts out a standard form, which is free. You can get both tea and coffee from **P.G.C. HAJENUIS,** WW, Rokin 92-96, Amsterdam-C, Netherlands. His free brochure is in Dutch, but it is readily comprehensible so far as the tea and coffee are concerned.

For delicious Dutch candy, write to **CHOCOLATERIE "DAUPHINE" PETER REYNHOUD,** WW, 24 Prof. Oranjestraat, Amsterdam, Netherlands, for a colorful free catalog. The candy is not inexpensive—although no higher in price than comparable American confections—but you must remember that postage and packing are included in the price. There isn't any point to sending for the more common varieties, like *hopjes,* which you probably can get more cheaply in your own neighborhood. However, when it comes to the types of chocolates obtainable only in fancy fooderies, you'll do better at Dauphine. For example, a 3-lb. "Royal" box of assorted chocolates costs around $12.50 delivered. (Although the catalog doesn't warn you, the liqueur chocolates are illegal in this country.) All the boxes and packages are very beautiful and would make splendid gifts. Prices are in American dollars.

It may never have occurred to you to order goodies from Morocco, but once you see the attractive folder put out by **LIJAC,** WW, 80 Av. Lalla Yacout, Casablanca, Morocco, you'll have a wild craving for the various dates, nuts, and bonbons depicted therein. Prices seem most reasonable, starting at around $4.00 for a kilo, and the packages look fantastically lovely. Lijac also offers a few other Moroccan food specialties, like sardines, anchovies, octopi, mussels, and tuna fish. Since the brochures are aimed primarily at customers in France, they're in French, and prices are in francs.

For a really exotic food source, how about mainland China? Direct communications have not yet been established, but **THE CHINESE MERCHANDISE EMPORIUM,** WW, 92-104 Queens Rd. C., Hong Kong, deals only in goods from the People's Republic of China. It puts out a free 44-page catalog in both English and Chinese, merely summarizing the range of its wares, which from the descriptions, seem to outdo Macy's in scope and variety. Because no prices are given, I have no idea of how much the different Chinese teas, preserved fruits, confectionery, and dried and canned foods would cost. You have to write and make specific inquiries, which, they say, are welcome. And they say they are equipped to pack and despatch both large and small orders all over the world.

Although Canada is, of course, a foreign country, it doesn't seem cricket to classify the **INDIA TRADING CO., LTD.,** WW, 113 Dupont St., Toronto 180, Ontario, as a foreign firm, because the food it offers is not typically Canadian. However, it does offer an extensive selection of Indian products at moderate prices. Price lists are free.

Some of the firms already mentioned in Chapter 2 also sell food. **SHANNON** (D.2) has Irish cakes, chocolate, and tea. **ICEMART** (C.3) has a package of all kinds of fish products, with the emphasis on herring. And where else could you get cod liver pâté?

2. Local

You can, of course, buy more kinds of foreign foods locally than you probably could, as an individual, get from abroad. Some firms here specialize in foreign food. For instance, **THE GOURMET CLUB,** WW, Box 366, Dayton, Ohio 45401, sends out an odd little list (free) that includes such diverse comestibles as an 8-oz. can of red pepper purée from Africa at 60¢, an 8-oz. package of water chestnut powder at 80¢, and a 1-lb. can of Oriental plum sauce at $1.25. Because the prices apparently include postage and packing they seem very reasonable. The firm also professes to offer "culinary paraphernalia," but the list I saw includes only a wok. There are also some cookbooks at slight discounts.

H. ROTH AND SON, WW, 1577 First Ave., New York, N.Y. 10028, has an attractive selection of food from all over the world. A 14-oz. can of Hungarian fish ragout *a la Bakony* is $1.70, sheep cheese Bryndza is $2.00 per can, 14 oz. of *hummos tahini* (chickpeas with sesame), also $2.00. They have a delectable assortment of confections, plus many other things to eat and to facilitate eating. **PAPRIKAS WEISS,** WW, 1546 Second Ave., New York, N.Y. 10028, puts out a similar catalog with a somewhat different selection of foods. There are Hungarian salads, tinned goulash ($1.60 per lb.), Czechoslovakian pickled gherkins ($1.25 per lb.), Israeli gefilte fish (10½ oz. for $1.10), and lots of other comestibles. Roth's catalog is free, Weiss' is $1.00 for a year's subscription.

LE JARDIN DU GOURMET, WW, Ramsey, N.J. 07446, has a catalog that lists French foods at prices not only far more reasonable than Fauchon's, but (even with postage and packing), cheaper than you'll find them at many other gourmet shops. They also have German, Greek, English, Italian, Mexican, and Indonesian foods. Be careful to ask for their food catalog (25¢), as the owner seems to be more interested in his garden leaflet (which you'll find described in Chapter 10,C.2). In fact, he wrote me that he was thinking of selling his food division, but, since he hasn't advised me to the contrary, I assume it's still continuing under his aegis.

MANGANARO FOODS, WW, 488 Ninth Ave., New York, N.Y. 10018, will send you, for 10¢, a complete little catalog of Italian food. There are both imported and local Italian cheeses—imported provolone is a little over $3.00 per lb., imported bel paese and gorgonzola, $2.50. Also on hand are sausages of all kinds, prosciutto, mortadella (both $1.90 domestic and $2.20 imported), pepperoni, antipastos, herbs, condiments, imported pastas, coffee and tea, fish, and confections. There are also a few utensils and gadgets.

BREMEN HOUSE, WW, 200 East 86 St., New York, N.Y. 10028, long a Yorkville landmark, sells all kinds of German as well as other European specialties. There are wursts (shipped at the buyer's risk) in profusion. In addition to more familiar types, they include plockwurst, touristenwurst, and schinken speck, at prices averaging from $2.00 to $3.00 per lb. Also on hand are tinned boar and venison products, cheeses, confectionery, preserves, and about everything else you can think of that's edible. Their catalog is free.

DELI-DELITES, WW, P.O. Box 32, Maspeth, L.I., N.Y. 11378, puts out a free brochure that gives a mouth-watering selection of Hebrew National kosher food.

OLD DENMARK, WW, 135 East 57 St., New York, N.Y. 10022, has Danish cheeses—Hillerod, Tilsit, Royal Danish Blue, etc.— all in the $2.20 to $2.50 per lb. price range; smoked meats and fish (smoked eel is $4.20 per lb.); and confections—a 3½ lb. Kobenhavner stollen is $3.00. Prices include postage and packing. **TRE KRONOR**, WW, 244 Main St., Farmington, Conn. 06032, also lists some Scandinavian food in their otherwise mostly gift catalog. Both catalogs are free

MONEO AND SON, INC., WW, 210 West 41 St., New York, N.Y. 10011, puts out a very comprehensive listing of Mexican foods, including cheeses, sausages, chilo' and chiles, and beer, plus more exotic specialties. A 22-oz. can of diced *nopalitos* (cactus) is $1.00; 12 oz. of *jalapeño* relish is 85¢; 3 oz. of *mole* powder, 60¢. Catalog, in both English and Spanish, is free.

KATAGIRI AND CO., INC., WW, 224 East 59 St., New York, N.Y. 10022, puts out a free price list containing a fascinating variety of Japanese foods. There are no less than 19 different kinds of dried seaweed, 13 kinds of soya sauce, and 11 kinds of *tsukudani* (I don't know what that is, but if it comes in 11 different varieties, it must be popular). They have Japanese noodles, pickles, cereals, dried fish, tea, candy, canned goods, and so forth, at what seem to be reasonable prices. You can find Japanese cooking and eating utensils here, too. Japanese foods are also available at many of the health food stores in Section E (Health Foods). Greenberg's has an especially extensive selection.

KALUSTYAN'S, WW, 123 Lexington Ave., New York, N.Y. 10016, is a store devoted entirely to Oriental foods. You can get betel nuts; all kinds of pickles, chutney, and spices; dry curry leaves; soap-nut powder (*cheekai*); *moth* beans; *urad* flour; *ghee;* tamarinds; and the like. Prices seem moderate, as far as I can determine. **APHRODISIA**, WW, 28 Carmine St., New York, N.Y. 10014 offers an attractive line of Indonesian and Malaysian specialties. In addition there are Indian condiments and liquid spices, and a group of Chinese specialties that includes chrysanthemum flowers ($1.50 per oz.), tree fungus (cloud's ear, 75¢ per oz.); and lotus root ($1.15 for ¼ oz.). Aphrodosia's catalog is 35¢, Kalustyan's 25¢.

B. REGIONAL AMERICAN FOODS

1. New England

When you think of New England, you think of seafood, and **EMBASSY SEAFOODS**, WW, P.O. Box 165, Gloucester, Mass. 01930, offers a variety of tinned products of the deep, including lobster meat (5 oz. are around $4.00); codfish cakes ($1.00 for 10½ oz.); lobster Newburg ($3.20); plus spreads, dips, chowders, and so on. Shipping is included, and price lists are free.

The **VERMONT COUNTRY STORE, INC.**, WW, Weston, Vt. 05161, includes New England foods among the many and varied offerings in its catalog (25¢). There are 3 different kinds of beans with pork, dandelion greens, creamed clams with mushrooms—all in cans—and Vermont's famous cheese. A house specialty is the New England common crackers (1½ lbs. packed in a useful split-ash tote basket is $3.00).

As a matter of fact, Vermont seems to offer more mail-order food than any other state. The **BENN-BURRY SHOP**, WW, Rte. 7, Shaftesbury, Vt. 05262, is noted for its cheddar cheese, sold at $1.40 per lb. in the store, mailed at from $1.80 to $2.00 per lb., depending on where you live—a wheel comes cheaper. There are also other cheeses, canned New England foods (3 kinds of chowder, baked beans, and Indian pudding at slightly less than $5.00 postpaid for the lot), country pickles, smoked country hams and bacon, honey, and, of course, all kinds of maple products. In addition to maple syrup and maple sugar, there are walnut crunch and peanut brittle made with maple syrup—2 10-oz. boxes are $4.75 postpaid. **HICKINS' MOUNTAIN MOWINGS FARM**, WW, Rte. 1, Black Mountain Rd., Brattleboro, Vt. 05301, purveys cheese, smoked meats, and whole hams (which average $1.60 to $1.70 per lb.; Canadian bacon and boned ham run higher). Also sold are maple syrup products (including pickles sweetened with maple syrup), preserves, and the like. **THE GREEN MOUNTAIN SUGAR HOUSE**, WW, R.F.D. 1, Ludlow, Vt. 05149, offers its own maple syrup and maple sugar products (a 1-lb. 14-oz. tin of old-fashioned soft maple sugar is slightly under $4.00 at the Sugar House, a dollar or two more if shipped). **HARWOOD HILL ORCHARD,** WW, Bennington, Vt. 05291, offers cheese, apples, maple syrup, jams and jellies, at comparable prices. I must admit to a certain degree of resentment at the statement in their brochure, which says, "Shipments to postal zones 1, 2 and 3 *except New York* receive an extra apple bonus." (The italics are mine—I live in New York.) All these brochures are free.

2. New York

The **FORSTS,** WW. P.O. Box P, Kingston, N.Y. 12401, offer a group of "Catskill Mountain Delicacies," including several types of smoked bacon, smoked pheasant, smoked turkey, and smoked ham. Turkey is around $1.80 per lb., ham about $1.70, bacon, $2.50. They also sell New York State giant McIntosh and Delicious apples at $5.00 to $5.50 per carton of one dozen. Prices are prepaid east of the Mississippi.

3. Pennsylvania

THE GREAT VALLEY MILLS, WW, Quakertown, Bucks County, Pa. 18951, includes some Pennsylvania Dutch specialties in its catalog of flours and cereals. Beer bolognas and Lebanon bolognas cost $1.50 for the midget size (weight unspecified). There are also other smoked meats; canned scrapple; pretzels; fruit butters (apple, maple, peach, and quince); and Pennsylvania Dutch cheese, at $1.75 per lb. The **NATURAL DEVELOPMENT CO.,** WW, Box 215, Bainbridge, Pa. 17502, offers a line of preserves, candies, and canned fruits, packed under its own Pennsylvania Dutch label. Both catalogs are free.

The **ROMBINS' NEST FARM,** WW, Fairfield, Pa. 17320, charges 25¢ for its catalog. It sells many other things besides its Pennsylvania Dutch specialties— scrapple, pretzels shipped directly from the bakery, jars of peanut and prune butter, potato salad, various dressings, and blueberry syrup—all made in small batches by local people. Both Natural Development and Rombins' Nest sell Pennsylvania Dutch hex signs; Natural Development has Irish ones, too.

4. Midwest

For food characteristic of the Hudson Bay area, write to **HERTER'S, INC.,** WW, Waseca, Minn. 56093, for its big, fascinating catalog, which seems to have a little bit of everything under the sun. It costs a dollar, but it's worth it. You can get a 1-lb. package of "Genuine Hudson Bay World Famous French Canadian and French Crêpe Suzette Wild Rice Pancake Mix" for less than $1.00. There is dry and canned wild rice, Benedictine fruit cake ($2.70 for a 1-lb. cake packed in a box that gives its complete history), beef jerky, Minnesota Fort Saint Charles whiskey cherry bon bons, and all sorts of unusual foodstuffs.

Herter's also puts out its own "Three-Alarm Sauce," proudly proclaiming that "there's nothing at all like it on hamburgers, hot dogs, meat, duck, venison; in soups, beer and whiskey." A 14-oz bottle is around $1.20, and is said to have been a favorite of Wild Bill Hickok, Buffalo Bill, Teddy Roosevelt, and Black Jack Pershing. For a few cents more you can get the "Five-Alarm Sauce," which was favored by Doc Holliday, Wyatt Earp, Bat Masterson, and Chief Sitting Bull. (Incidentally, you may notice that Herter's occasionally advertises a free catalog, but that's a skinny little thing, with only a feeble sampling of the many delights of the complete version.)

You'll find a lot of Wisconsin foods in C.3 (Cheese).

5. South

The famous cuisine of Louisiana is brought to you by the **CREOLE DELICACIES CO.,** Inc., WW, P.O. Box 51042, New Orleans, La. 70151. There are soups— turtle, crayfish bisque, shrimp creole, gumbo—all at around $1.15 for a 10-oz. can; pralines ($3.45 for 1 lb.); rémoulade sauce, la cuite syrup, Creole seasoning, and so on. Postage is included, catalog is free.

The **LYNCHBURG HARDWARE AND GENERAL STORE,** WW, P.O. Box 239, Lynchburg, Tenn. 37352, sells what it calls "real Tennessee ham" at around $1.90 per lb.; hickory-smoked sausage and bacon (an 8- to 9-lb. slab is $13.00 east of the Mississippi); and a 2-oz. package of sassafras, either ground or in chip form, at 75¢. The catalog (which also includes a lot of Jack Daniels items, but no whiskey), is 25¢. **MOUNTAIN DEW SASSAFRAS PRODUCTS,** WW, Cotter, Ark. 72626, offers sassafras candy (60¢ per bag) and other old-fashioned candies, sassafras "tea bark," country sorghum, molasses, and various syrups and spices. Price list is free.

6. West

From the Pacific Northwest come marine delicacies. **HEGG AND HEGG,** WW, 801 Marine Dr., Port Angeles, Wash. 98362, has a free folder listing Dungeness crab meat at around $1.70 per 7½-oz. can; smoked sturgeon, $1.35 per 6½-oz. can; shrimp meat, around $1.00 for a 4½-oz. can, postpaid west of the Rockies. Smoked salmon and all kinds of sea food appetizers are also available.

The **NICHOLS GARDEN NURSERY,** WW, 1190 North Pacific Hwy., Albany, Ore. 97321, offers a whole section of gourmet foods in its garden catalog (35¢). It includes Oregon's Tillamook cheese (a type of cheddar), sold at $5.00 for 3 lbs., postpaid west of the Rockies, slightly higher east. There's also other southern Oregon cheese—goat cheddar, raw milk cheddar, Oregon blue cheese, and Greek *kasseri*-type cheese. Also on hand are smoked Pacific Ocean salmon, and salt-free canned salmon and what seems to be genuine Oregon halvah. (It was claimed by the ancient Egyptians that halvah gave strength and virility; today, all that can be promised is additional inches on the waistline.) The mimeographed catalog also contains many things of interest to those who eat and/or grow organic and macrobiotic foods.

You'll find other western food, especially fruit, under Specialties (C), and under Health Foods (E), where California is particularly well represented.

7. Hawaii

Under the heading "Hawaiian Candy and Foods" in the brochure put out by **HAWAIIAN THINGS**, WW, Waikiki Box 15276, Honolulu, Hawaii 96815, are offered macadamia nuts, chocolate-covered macadamia nuts, macadamia nut fritters, coconut chips and twists, and tropical twists. A 5-oz. can of macadamia nuts is $1.75 delivered. All very toothsome, to be sure, but don't the Hawaiians eat anything but goodies? **KEMOO FARM**, WW, P.O. Box 3973, Honolulu, Hawaii 96813, isn't very helpful, because fruit preserves, coconut syrup, and fruit thins aren't exactly what you'd call farm foods. The fruit thins, which are candies, come in guava, toasted coconut, pineapple, mandarin mint, and passion fruit flavors, which at least sound Hawaiian; $3.50 per lb., postpaid. **HAWAIIAN HOLIDAY, INC.**, WW, P.O. Box 707, Honukaa, Hawaii 96727, sells macadamia nuts in many forms. All three lists are free.

8. Alaska

From the **SOURDOUGH TRADING POST**, WW, Box 40175, Anchorage, Alaska, you can get real sourdough starter mix in an earthenware crock for $6.00 postpaid, and chocolate-coated wild berry candy at $4.50 per lb. They used to sell canned blubber and seal liver and the like, but you can't get them any more because of the game laws. However, as a matter of academic interest, Sourdough sells an Eskimo cookbook, which gives you recipes for these delicacies. Catalog is 25¢.

C. SPECIALTY FOODS

1. Fruit and Nuts

HARRY AND DAVID, WW, Bear Creek Orchards, Medford, Ore. 97501, specializes in fruit. A 25-lb. ranch pack of their big Royal Riviera pears is $16.00 delivered. These are family pears, they say, not as pretty as the gift pack pears, which cost quite a bit more. They also offer "renegade apples," which were "just a bit too rambunctious for our ultra-fancy gift baskets and boxes," at $15.00 for 18 lbs. delivered. Also available are preserves made from Oregon fruit

and all sorts of other goodies. **PITTMAN AND DAVIS, INC.**, WW, Harlingen, Tex. 78550, specializes in "tree-ripened fruit from pampered orchards," mainly red grapefruits and navel oranges. A 65-lb. sack is around $15.00 delivered. There are also gift parcels, and 2 lbs. of orange blossom honey in a ceramic jug that's said to be an exact copy of an ancient Egyptian honey pitcher. It's $5.50 (but you can get 4 lbs. of 3 different honeys in simple cans for the same price). **THE FORTY ACRES RANCH**, WW, P.O. Box Y, Lakeland, Fla. 33602, sells Florida citrus fruits. A huge 1 1/3-bushel box of oranges and/or grapefruit is around $18.00 delivered. There are smaller packages and attractive gift baskets. All brochures are free.

PETE'S CALIFORNIA DATES, WW, Box 863, Camarillo, Cal. 93010, puts out a free brochure describing every kind of date and date product imaginable. There are "redi-dates" (pitted), at $2.70 for 40 oz., as well as fancy Deglet Noor and Madjhool dates. There are date-nut rolls, date butter, chocolate-covered dates ($2.35 for 24 oz.), date-nut loaf, and mysterious dates stuffed with assorted ingredients. There is even a do-it-yourself date-stuffing kit for $4.40. Shipping is included, and, if you buy in large quantities, the dates come down to supermarket prices.

KAKAWATEEZ, LTD., WW, 130 Olive St., Findlay, Ohio 45840, sells yummy dry-roasted "Totem Nuts," with a distinctive flavor, in 6½-oz. glass jars, ranging from 75¢ for peanuts to $1.60 for macadamias; there are also cashews, almonds, filberts, pistachios, and brazil nuts. They're sold in gift packs of three of any kind. **SUNNYLAND FARMS, INC.**, WW, Albany, Ga. 31701, offer pecans in the shell or out, plus pecan brittle, pecan pralines, and other goodies. A 5-lb. box of pecans in the shell is $6.30, including shipping. Both brochures are free.

THE STERNBERG PECAN CO., WW, P.O. Box 193, Jackson, Miss. 39205, offers nothing but packages of their wonderful fancy mammoth pecan halves. Prices start at $6.75 for 2 lbs. and go up to $27.00 for 10 lbs., all postpaid. The brochure is 15¢.

You'll also find a lot of nuts and fruit (mostly dried) under Health Foods (E).

2. Tea and Coffee

There are a number of tea and coffee firms that offer an impressive number of different varieties of coffee and tea; plus blends, instant coffees, tea bags, and some tea- and coffee-making appurtenances. Coffee in the bean generally averages about $1.00 to $1.50 per lb., and tea averages around $2.50. There are, of course, price variations among the houses, but they seem to average out to approximately the same.

Two of the oldest and best-known firms are the **EM-PIRE COFFEE AND TEA CO.**, WW, 486 Ninth Ave., New York, N.Y. 10018, and **McNULTY'S**, WW, 109 Christopher St., New York, N.Y. 10014. **SIMPSON AND VAIL, INC.**, WW, 53 Park Pl., New York, N.Y. 10007, comes recommended by Raymond Sokolov of *The New York Times* (from whose column I learned of it). Other good sources are **THE NORTHEASTERN COFFEE MILLS STORE**, WW, 217 North Broadway, Milwaukee, Wis. 53202, a company owned and operated by a group of teachers and students; **THE RED WAGON STORE**, WW, 136 S.W. Jefferson St., Portland, Ore. 97201; and **MURCHIE'S TEA AND COFFEE**, WW, 1008 Robinson St., Vancouver, B.C., Canada. You can get Hawaiian coffee from the **MAUNA KEA COFFEE CO.**, WW, P.O. Box 828, Captain Cook, Kona, Hawaii 96704. All catalogs and brochures are free.

3. Cheese

You'll have found lots of cheeses in the Foreign and Regional Food sections (A and B). Bremen House and Manganaro also have types of cheese other than the German and the Italian. **PLYMOUTH PRODUCTS**, WW, Plymouth, Vt. 05056, specializes in cheese; its lists are free.

Next to New England and New York, Wisconsin is most famous for its cheese. There is a group of firms in Wisconsin that started out originally as purveyors of local cheeses, as well as sausages and smoked meats, and now specialize in gift packages, many made up of cheese or including cheese, but many wandering far afield. There are plain (but fancy) boxes of assorted cheeses, or cheese combined with sausage, or with such other delicacies as pâtés, anchovies, sardines, and meat and fish spreads. There are also combinations of cakes, jams, jellies, nuts, and candies—with cheese and without cheese. And then there are all kinds of comestibles packed into containers that are themselves gifts—baskets, casseroles, serving dishes, electrical appliances, and so on. Prices seem reasonable enough, considering that the gifts are packed, wrapped, and delivered directly to the recipients' doors without your having to do more than write out a check and mail it. Many of the gifts are similar—for instance, for some curious reason almost all of the firms feature electric hot doggers filled with cheese), but each house has some individual concepts of its own.

For example, **THE WISCONSIN CHEESEMAN**, WW, P.O. Box 1, Madison, Wis. 53701, offers a package that combines cheese with golf balls ($10.00); while the **WISCONSIN CHEESE MAKERS GUILD**, WW, 6048 West Beloit Rd., Madison, Wis. 53219 combines a small Parsons table with anchovy paste, chicken liver, sardines, cheese, and a few other snacks

for $15.00 delivered. The **SWISS COLONY**, WW, Monroe, Wis. 53566, offers a 30-ft. sausage (4½ lbs.) for $15.00 delivered. At Christmas they offer a gingerbread chest filled with 28 oz. of cookies for $12.00 delivered. Since the chest is edible, this is an ecological plus. Also available are gingerbread Christmas cards, for those who trust the postman. At **FIGI'S, INC.**, WW, Marshfield, Wis. 54449, you can get 4 14-oz. antiqued aluminum tankards, filled with cheese and sausage, for $10.00 delivered. You'll find that all the houses also offer bulk cheese if you hunt through the catalogs (free) hard enough.

In Canada, the **BLACK DIAMOND CHEESE CO.**, WW, Black Diamond Rd., P.O. Box 1, Belleville, Ont., is noted for its excellent aged cheddar. You can buy a 10-lb. black waxed circle delivered to the United States for around $17.00 (a 2½-lb. cheese would be around $6.50). Black Diamond also goes in heavily for gift packages, although the foodstuffs accompanying them are almost invariably cheeses. Among the attractive looking packages are 6 imported lead chrystal wine glasses, at $19.00; a Canadian hand-crafted miniature wooden spinning wheel at $11.00; 4 Canadian-made pottery onion soup bowls at $14.00; delivered in the United States (slightly less in Canada). Each comes packaged with, so far as I can determine from the pictures, about 2 lbs. of assorted Canadian cheeses. Brochure is free, and it lists the various people on your gift list who would doubtless be happy to receive a cheese gift, including, rather surprisingly, your milkman.

4. Sweets

Of course you'll find cakes, candies, and such at many of the houses already described, especially those in Section C, but there are one or two worth special mention. **BISSINGER'S**, WW, 205 West 4 St., Cincinnati, Ohio 45202, offers a tempting catalog (free) of what they modestly describe as "the world's most elegant chocolates," at prices starting from around $4.00 per lb. They also offer other goodies and gift boxes.

5. Other

PERMA-PAK, WW, 40 East 2430, South Salt Lake City, Utah 84115, sells dehydrated low-moisture lightweight foods, not only for camping and for emergencies (the firm is very insistent on emergencies, and even provides candles with the kits), but recommends them for daily use as well—they keep longer and are much easier to store than either canned or frozen foods. One lb. of the dried food, Perma-Pak says, is usually equivalent to about 7 or 8 lbs. of fresh fruit or vegetables. There are red and green peppers, at around $4.00 to $5.00 for 1½ lbs.; sliced onions, around $2.00 for 1½ lbs.; plus other vegetables, as well as fruits, eggs, powdered peanut butter, and so on.

You'll find many other freeze-dried foods in the camping catalogs listed in Chapter 20,C, some even giving their caloric content. These foods are rather handy to have around the house; I've tried them.

D. HERBS AND SPICES

Contrary to the advice I gave you for food in general, it *does* pay to buy botanicals (herbs and spices) by mail. Very few supermarkets carry more than a limited range, and very often some of the more slow-moving items aren't as fresh as they should be. Moreover, the herbs and spices that you buy in the supermarket are packaged in such small quantities that most of what you pay goes for the container. If you use enough herbs and spices so that you can order them by the half pound or pound (most of the mail-order firms will sell you smaller quantities but then it might not pay to order from them), you can save quite a bit of money. If you can't use that much all by yourself, you might be able to get together with a friend or two to combine an order—or you could save the pretty jars your supermarket herbs come in to fill with your herb excess for very welcome gifts. Don't ever stockpile herbs, however; no matter how tightly you seal the containers, herbs and spices lose their savor after a while. (Although, in Indiana Botanic Garden's Almanac, you will find a 1730 recipe for restoring ancient cloves.)

Prices vary a lot among the different firms listed. This does not necessarily bear any relationship to quality, so do compare the catalogs before you order.

THE WIDE WORLD OF HERBS, LTD., WW, 11 St. Catherine St. East, Montreal 19, Canada; and **INDIANA BOTANIC GARDENS,** WW, P.O. Box 5, Hammond, Ind. 46325, both described in the previous chapter, are two firms with the widest selections of herbs of all kinds, culinary as well as medicinal, that I've come across. Both catalogs are, as you will recall, free. **APHRODISIA,** already described earlier in this chapter, as well as in the one preceding, also has a large selection of culinary herbs, including some exotic types not readily available elsewhere.

Other firms that offer large herb selections are **NATURE'S HERB CO.,** WW, 281 Ellis St., San Francisco, Cal. 94102; the **HERB PRODUCTS CO., INC.,** WW, 11012 Magnolia Blvd., North Hollywood, Cal. 91601; **HARVEST HEALTH,** WW, 1944 Eastern Ave. S. E., Grand Rapids, Mich. 49507; **THE MAGIC GARDEN HERB CO.,** P.O. Box 332, Fairfax, Cal. 94930; and **THE HERB LADY,** WW, P.O. Box 26515, Edendale Station, Los Angeles, Cal. 90026.

Most of the herb stores described in the preceding chapter also offer tea herbs, herb seasonings, and spices. Spices and herbs seem to be natural concomitants of coffee and tea, so you'll find that most of the coffee and tea stores listed in the preceding section also offer them. Some of the other firms mentioned earlier in this chapter also carry large supplies of them, particularly **H. ROTH** and **PAPRIKAS WEISS.** In addition, you will find herbs and herb teas sold at many of the health food stores listed in the following section.

E. HEALTH FOODS

The terms *natural, organic,* and *health foods* seem to be used in general to apply to foods that are raised without the use of chemicals—including both insecticides and chemical fertilizers—and prepared without the use of any additives. I'll use the term *health foods* simply as a matter of convenience, not because I am either supporting or disavowing the various claims and controversies. You'll find further definitions, most of them conflicting, in the catalogs themselves.

More and more supermarkets are beginning to offer health foods, but their stocks are usually quite limited. Although health food stores are beginning to spread throughout the country, they're still not really abundant outside of California, New York, and a few other localities. Moreover, a lot of them tend to be overpriced, so here's another area where it might pay you to order food by mail. In fact, although health food is usually more expensive than ordinary food (nonprocessing costs a lot more than processing), if you buy it in bulk, you can sometimes bring the price down to the price of regular groceries. You'll save money if you choose the supplier that's closest to you. (Canadians might want to buy their health foods from **NATUREX, INC.,** WW, 1125 Mont-Royal Est, Montreal 176, Québec, Canada, described for American customers in the preceding chapter. Catalog is free.)

Most of the firms listed in this section go into detail about bulk buying and the various methods of shipping. Some of them even indicate which of their products they know are definitely organic, which are semiorganic, and so on. As far as I know, all the firms listed are reliable, but, as I said generally in the Introduction, I cannot vouch for any of them.

All of them carry, broadly, the same type of food. This will include, first of all, various kinds of stoneground (hopefully organic) flours, meals, and cereals; and products made from them—mixes, pastas, breads, cakes, cookies, etc. The breads are multifarious—whole wheat, sprouted wheat, gluten, soy, potato, rye, raisin, onion, and so forth. (Most of them taste very good, but that's a by-product, not a requirement.) There are seeds, not merely for cooking or sprouting, but also to be eaten as snacks—raw, roasted, and sometimes honey- or carob-coated. There are nuts, especially raw nuts; candies made out of such natural products as carob, honey, sesame seeds, rose hips, etc.; raw honey; preserves; unsulphured dried fruit; cold-pressed, nonhydrogenated vegetable oils; and canned fruits, fruit juices, and vegetables. A few offer canned meats; others have canned meat substitutes for vegetarians.

Some firms are based at farms and so produce a good deal of their own merchandise; some are millers; others are packagers (I'd better not say processors in this connection) that put out food under their own label, but may also have stores as well. In all of these cases, the larger companies generally carry each other's products, as well as their own, to increase their range. Some firms are merely retail shops that sell by mail; however, they may offer as wide or wider a range than the others. Usually all of them, even the farms, sell food supplements (vitamins, minerals, brewer's yeast, and so forth). All the lists are free unless otherwise specified.

1. Farms

DEER VALLEY FARM, WW, R.D. 1, Guilford, N.Y. 13780, has been, it says, "devoted to organic farming since 1947." They have their own bakery, which specializes in "baking 100% organically grown whole-grain bread, cookies, and rolls." All the flour and raw milk and eggs used come from their farm. In addition to the standard products, they sell New York State cheddar cheese made from raw milk, at around $1.10 per lb.

VITA-GREEN FARMS, WW, P.O. Box 878, Vista, Cal. 92083, specializes in organic produce that you'd probably have to have shipped airfreight if you live any distance away. There are plenty of other items, though, that can be shipped via parcel post. You'd better hurry if you want to order anything; alarmed by creeping chemicals, the owners are contemplating leaving "this U.S.A.-polluted holocaust," and moving to Australia within the next few years.

The owners of **WALNUT ACRES,** WW, Penns Creek, Pa. 17862, one of the best-known organic farms, say, "we've been growing, preparing, and shipping whole unchemicalized nature foods by mail for over 26 years." In addition to a vast line of the standard foods, they also put out their own baked goods, and proudly state that all eggs used come from free-run chickens. They also have canned meats from free-run steers (not inexpensive—a 1-lb. can of beef chunks or

of ground beef is around $2.00), and put up a large variety of their own soups.

The **NATURAL DEVELOPMENT CO.,** WW, Box 215, Bainbridge, Pa. 17502, has, in addition to the usual offerings, "Trappistine" candies (caramels made from pure ingredients without additives by the monks at St. Joseph's Abbey in Massachusetts), at $1.75 per lb. box, and organic green soy beans developed on their own experimental farms. Five lbs. are $2.25, and postage east of the Mississippi is prepaid.

2. Millers and Mills

The **SIOUX MILLERS,** WW, RR 1, Whiting, Iowa 51063, "believe that all grains should be ground FRESH just before our customers get them, thus retaining the full natural flavor and vitamin content. As soon as they are ground, whether flour or cereals, we put them in air tight bags or containers. This prevents contact with the oxygen of the air. Keep them that way at your home." They have a long list of regular health foods in addition to their whole-grain products.

EL MOLINO MILLS, WW, 3060 West Valley Blvd., Alhambra, Cal. 91803, offer, as part of their line of whole-grain foods, four different types of bread mixes at a little over $1.00 for a 3-lb. package (makes 3 loaves). For those anxious to get back into the kitchen, **STERLING H. NELSON & SONS, INC.,** WW, 525 South 4th West, Salt Lake City, Utah 84110, offer handgrinders at $12.00 "that will reduce hard winter wheat into flour in one single grinding operation," and will also grind beans, nuts, etc., and crack grain for cereal. If you're ambitious, there's an electric flour mill for home use (no price given); also a bread mixer that can make enough dough for one to four loaves at a time, for $19.00.

The **BIRKETT MILLS,** WW, Box 440, Penn Yan, N.Y. 14257, best known for its stone-ground brown buckwheat groats (kasha), offered in any one of 4 grinds, also manufactures a whole line of stone-ground flours, including white buckwheat groats, German grits, graham flour, rye flour, whole wheat flour, and wheat germ milled to order. Prices range from 25¢ to 50¢ per lb. As long as supplies last, you get a nice little kasha cookbook along with your free price list, if you ask.

3. Packagers

The **BETTER FOODS FOUNDATION, INC.,** WW, 300 North Washington St., Greencastle, Pa. 17225, sells what they call "'Bio-factured' foods from Mennonite Country," but, aside from cheese made from whole raw milk, their list contains what seems to be basically standard health foods (although varieties, of course, are always different). **STUR-DEE, NATURAL**

SALES, and **BARTH**, all described in Chapter 6, offer some natural foods—Barth more than the others—plus some kitchen equipment and appliances.

4. Stores

PANACEA HEALTH FOODS AND HERBS, WW, 323 Third Ave., New York, N.Y. 10010, and **GREENBERG'S NATURAL FOODS**, WW, 125 First Ave., New York, N.Y. 10002, put out thick complete catalogs that seem to list every health food imaginable, including numerous items I haven't seen listed elsewhere. Panacea's is free; Greenberg's is 50¢.

Other health food stores that offer interesting (and free) lists of somewhat more limited scope are **NORTHERN HEALTH FOODS**, WW, Box 66, 13 South 4 St., Moorhead, Minn. 56560; **HARVEST HEALTH, INC.**, WW, 1944 Eastern Ave. S. E., Grand Rapids, Mich. 49507; The **NATURAL HEALTH FOODS AND BARBELL CENTER**, WW, 6981 Market St., Youngstown, Ohio 94512; and **CLIFFROSE**, WW, 129 Coffman, Longmont, Colo. 80501.

5. Specialists

SUNRAY ORCHARDS, WW, Myrtle Creek, Ore. 95957, specialize, in prunes prepared without the use of any preservatives or additives. Four types are available—Italian, Date, Perfection, and Brooks—ranging from $2.40 to $3.60 for 6 lbs., depending on size. Organically grown dried Bartlett pears are $4.80 for a 6-lb. box and walnuts are $3.50 per 10-lb. box. **SIERRA NATURAL FOODS**, WW, 2408 26 St., Sacramento, Cal. 95818, specializes in organic dried fruits and nuts "as Mother Nature intended." They also have mixed fruit packs, like "a rococo of apricots, peaches, pears and dates," at $4.00 for a 36-oz. package. **LEE ANDERSON'S COVALDA DATE CO.**, WW, P.O. Box 908, Coachella, Cal. 92236, says that "over 30 years of natural soil building goes into making Covalda Ranch products the most tasty and wholesome dates, pecans and citrus produced today. We have over 100 acres all under natural organic soil culture." Offered in 15-lb. flats are such delicacies as Desert Brownie Dates, at about $7.00; figs, $19.00 to $22.00, seedless raisins, $11.00; and other fruit from $15.00 to $30.00. They also have stuffed dates, honey, date cookies, grapefruit and tangerines. Free price lists from all.

Bob and Sue, proprietors of **WILD JAMS AND JOLLY JELLYS**, WW, Box 255, South Otselic, N.Y. 13155, say "all our fruit jams and herb jellies are absolutely pure and undiluted. They are sweetened with natural turbinado sugar only, no colorings or preservatives are used, ingredients are either gathered wild or grown organically." There are some relatively usual ones—wild elderberry, rose hip, wild raspberry—and

some decidedly unusual ones—coriander, horehound, lavender, fennel. Packed in 4-oz. jars at around 75¢ each.

DANDELIONS UNLIMITED, WW, 450 N.E. 28 St., Pompano Beach, Fla. 33064, offers ground roasted, organically grown dandelion root as a coffee substitute for $2.50 for 8 oz. It's also available in instant form. They also sell slippery elm food and a honey carob drink mix.

The **ESTEE CANDY CO.**, WW, 135 West Central Blvd., Palisades Park, N.J. 07650 (catalog 10¢) puts out a line of natural sweets that contain no chocolate.

SUNSHINE VALLEY, WW, 8725 Remmet Ave., Canoga Park, Cal. 91304, manufacturers of the "original natural enzyme line," offer a group of nut products, including such unusual items as powdered malted almonds and cashews ($1.45 for 8 oz.), acidophilus and bulgaricus cultures ($2.60 per pint), and a fruitcake made without heating (24 oz., $2.50). They are, they say, "pioneers in special sub-zero freeze dehydrated foods (lyophilized)."

6. Addenda

Some of the firms already listed in this chapter under Regional Foods carry natural foods (and some will write indignantly after this book is out to tell me that their products are natural, too). They include **THE GREAT VALLEY MILLS**, the **VERMONT COUNTRY STORE**, and **HERTER'S**—which offers herbicide and insecticide-free fruit syrups, made from wild blueberries and wild chokeberries, at around $4.50 per qt.

F. DIET FOODS

Diet food, as used here, is for people who are on restricted diets because of specific ailments other than obesity. The foods mentioned here are not necessarily nonfattening, although those dieting to lose weight will probably be interested in the water-packed foods offered by most of the larger houses in the preceding section. Virtually all of them also have salt-free products (including soups and soup mixes), as well as salt substitutes. You'll also find gluten-free and wheat-free cereal products for those with wheat allergies or specific ailments that require the avoidance of wheat and gluten. Also on hand are carob-flavored sweets and carob flavoring for people allergic to chocolate.

Although diet foods are found, for the most part, in health food stores, not all of them are natural foods. Among the firms already described in the preceding section, **PANACEA** has an especially extensive line of dietetic and salt-free products. They even carry salt-free pickles, unsalted mustard, and imitation catsup, as well as saltless instant soup, unsalted natural cheeses, and baked goods.

ESTEE'S puts out a large selection of sugar-free candies and cookies. A 4-oz. chocolate bar (real chocolate; their "natural" bar is carob) is around 60¢. **HERTER'S** also manufactures candies for diabetics and others on sugar-restricted diets. Sorbitol is used for sweetening. Their white Swiss fondue pine-nut flavored candy, Belgian butter violet hard candy, and English candy cost about $1.00 to $1.50 per lb.

NECKERMANN'S (Chapter 2,A) has a large selection of diet, as well as health foods in its catalog, and if you can cope with the German, you might be interested in looking over its repertory. Although the food is not inexpensive, especially when you consider shipping costs, there are some items you rarely see offered here; and, to the jaded diabetic, they might be well worth their cost.

ENER-G FOOD, INC., WW, 1526 Utah Ave., South Seattle, Wash. 98134, puts out under its "Jolly Joan" label wheat-free and gluten-free bread mixes, and egg replacers for those allergic to eggs. They also have rice flour, rice polish, instant soy meal, and pollen products.

Remember: *Write for the catalog first.* All prices given were valid only at the time of writing and probably have been changed.

Chapter 8

KITCHEN AND DINING ROOM

A. FOOD PREPARATION

1. General

You'll find a lot of kitchen equipment available at the places that sell food (Chapter 7). **PAPRIKAS WEISS** and **ROTH** have particularly large selections of gourmet cooking equipment imported from all over the world. Many of the health food stores offer devices to facilitate your consumption of health foods—seed sprouters, yogurt makers, even mills for grinding your own meal. The big mail-order houses, both domestic and foreign, also have lots of things to make life easier for the cook and homemaker (watch out, though, at the foreign ones, for the exotic items imported from the United States).

There are two British firms that offer free brochures of British food accessories. **DAVID MELLOR IRON-MONGER**, WW, 4 Sloane Sq., London S.W.1, England, has some things that are rather unusual. I, at least, have never seen a ham stand before (made of white earthenware, it's around $7.00). There are teak scoops handmade in Devon, from around $1.50 to $8.00 (for the "monumental" scoop); a handcarved thistle shortbread mold from Braemar, around $12.00; blue or pink Sussex pigs (the pig's head becomes a mug and its body is a jug) at around $3.00. Also available are black cast iron candleholders for fat candles, made by Mr. Mellor himself; a set of brown glazed pottery made expressly for Mellor's; a replica of an eighteenth century beechwood lemon squeezer; Norfolk herring baskets, and lots of other indispensables. **CUCINA**, WW, 46 Ladbrooke Grove, London W.11, England, shows things from all over the world; however, there are some English-made items, like a moon egg flower holder for a little over $3.00, and a stoneware salt jar for around $4.00.

Back in the United States, the **VERMONT COUNTRY STORE**, WW, Weston, Vt. 05161, has all kinds of kitchen things—New England custard cups (6 for $4.25); cast iron early American iron cookware (skillets cost from a little over $2.00 to a little over $5.00); an early American food crock ($5.00); a metal breadmaker ($25.00); a Vermont soapstone griddle ($18.00); plus lots of imported utensils. Catalog is 25¢.

The **CHINA CLOSET**, WW, 6807 Wisconsin Ave., Bethesda, Md. 20015, sells nice things from all over the world for cooks and housekeepers. Some attractive plastic items from the United States include a smoke-colored lucite cutting board with a leather thong for $3.00, and a long-handled opaque acrylic dustpan in red, orange, or green, for $4.50. Also on hand are an oyster shucker for $5.50, a Mexican tortilla press for $5.00, and a 6-at-a-time taco fryer for $3.00. Catalog is 25¢.

2. Pots and Pans

Practically every sort of imported (mostly French) cooking utensil and appurtenance you could dream of is available from the **BAZAR FRANÇAIS**, WW, 666 Sixth Ave., New York, N.Y. 10010. There are muffin rings (50¢), china coquille shells ($1.50), old-fashioned custard cups ($1.10), *coeur à la creme* molds ($2.00 to $8.00), steel chestnut pans ($2.50), Pullivuyt oval terrines and bake dishes ($20.00 to $40.00). The **BAZAAR de la CUISINE INTERNATIONAL, INC.**, WW, 1003 Second Ave., New York, N.Y. 10022, offers a similar range of imported (and domestic) kitchenware. Included in its repertoire are . . . a French deci-litre measuring glass ($1.75); a mincing knife by Peugeot (they are versatile, aren't they? $4.00); silver decorating skewers "attelets" ($5.00); iron or aluminum paella pans, ($10.00 to $18.00); oblong pâté casseroles ($16.00 to $40.00); Dutch ovens from France ($15.00 to $17.00); and so on. Bazar and Bazaar both have some of the same things and sometimes Bazar charges more and sometimes Bazaar does, and sometimes prices are the same. Each one also has lots of things the other doesn't, and since both catalogs are fascinating and free, everyone who likes to cook will want them.

BON APPETIT, WW, 113 South 19 St., Philadelphia, Pa. 19103, offers "cooking and serving aids for gourmet dishes." They have some of the same things as Bazar and Bazaar in their neat little catalog, and some things neither would dream of having, such as their Dirty Old Man apron ($6.00). **CROSS IMPORTS**, WW, 201 Hanover St., Boston, Mass. 02113, have, they say, served the Italian, French, and gourmet cook for over 40 years. They put out a thick, well-indexed catalog (25¢), featuring some things I haven't seen in the others, like their own pizzelle makers ($8.00 to $10.00 for the regular, $24.00 to $26.00 for the electric). Unlike the other catalogs, theirs includes lots of recipes . . . for such delicacies as *quiche lorraine* and *madeleines.*

Perhaps you'd like to go directly to the source of many imports. **E. DeHILLERIN**, WW, 18-20 rue Coquillière, 51 rue J. J. Rousseau, Paris 1e, France, puts out a handsome catalog (with a picture of their huge shop on the cover—it's on the corner; hence, I suppose, the two street addresses) of the fine French cookware for which it's famous. The catalog is intended mainly for restaurants, hotels, and institutions, but they'll send it free of charge to anybody. (However, it's in French.) Because of economic fluctuations, they say, they can't quote prices until you tell them exactly what you're interested in. Once I did manage to get a price list out of them, but I imagine, now that the franc is floating, it will be even more difficult. However, if you're a serious cook, you should look into their wares, which I've heard very well spoken of.

On the local level, the **LYNCHBURG HARDWARE AND GENERAL STORE**, WW, P.O. Box 239, Lynchburg, Tenn. 37352 offers, in its 25¢ catalog, cast iron cooking utensils. A 9-quart Dutch oven is $15.00, a fetching 4-quarter is $8.50. There are also griddles, and muffin and corn stick pans. They seem to be postage paid, except, curiously, for the 4-quarter. You'll also find lots of cast iron cookware at **PRESTON'S** (Chapter 9,B.3).

3. Specialties

There are three firms that offer catalogs specializing in items for cake and candy making and decorating. They are **GENERAL SUPPLIES CO.**, WW, P.O. Box 338, Fallbrook, Cal. 92028; **MAID OF SCANDINAVIA CO.**, WW, 3245 Raleigh Ave., Minneapolis, Minn. 55416; and **CAKE DECORATORS**, WW, Blacklick, Ohio 43004. The catalogs are 50¢ each. Their lines include lots of molds for chocolate, sugar, candles, or plaster. (I vote for chocolate.) All of them sell miniatures and feature some other crafts.

Solingen is noted for its steel, and **J. A. HENCKELS**, WW, Zwillingswerk AG, Postfach 100864, 5650 Solingen 1, West Germany, is well known for cutlery. The firm has some brochures, in German, showing the scissors, knives, and strange (to me) implements for which they have achieved distinction. Also available are manicure tools and some exceptionally handsome stainless steel tableware. Unfortunately, they won't quote prices; you have to write and tell them what you want, and they'll write and tell you how much the merchandise will cost and what the shipping charges will be. I assume they're expensive, but the firm has a worldwide reputation for fine-quality steel. Brochures are free.

You have to pay $1.00 (ref.) for the attractive color brochures put out by **J. WILLIAMS**, WW, 533 Koenigswinter 51, Postfach, West Germany, depicting the European merchandise they've assembled for you. There is elaborate staghorn-handled cutlery, with four-color etched Solingen steel blades, starting at $30.00 for a two-piece carving set; also gold-rimmed German beer glasses or goblets, each with the coat-of-arms of a different brewery at $12.00 for 8; plus other glassware. Prices are in American dollars, the brochures are in English, and, if you order more than $20.00 worth (it's difficult to order less), goods are postpaid.

Making wine at home these days seems to have become a very popular hobby, and numerous suppliers have sprung up—they offer complete lines of appurtenances, including concentrates for those too lazy to stomp their own grapes (they sell presses, too); gadgets of all kinds; bottles; kegs; and—for earthier types—brewing equipment. Some of them are: **ARBOLYN**, WW, P.O. Box 663, West Columbia, S.C. 29169; **BACCHANALIA**, WW, 273 Riverside Ave., Westport, Conn. 06880; **CONTINENTAL PRODUCTS**, WW, P.O. Box 18223, Indianapolis, Ind. 46218; **R. S. DANENBERGER**, WW, P.O. Box 276, New Berlin, Ill. 62670; **JIM DANDY**, WW, P.O. Box 30230, Cincinnati, Ohio 45230; **WERTH WINE**, WW, P.O. Box 1902, Cedar Rapids, Iowa 52406; and the **WOLLERSHEIM WINERY**, WW, H'wy. 188, Prairie du Sac, Wis. 53578.

Naturally all the aforementioned firms sell corks, but they're limited to corks to fit wine bottles. If you need any other size or shape cork, you can get it from the **BOTTLE STOPPER**, WW, Highland Lake, N.Y. 12743. Hitch is, they don't sell less than half a gross of any one size (the #1 size is only 85¢ for 72 corks, so you can see why), and you can't order less than $5.00 worth—but sometimes it's worth ordering a lot of corks in order to get the few you really need.

THE WESTON BOWL MILL, WW, Weston, Vt. 05161, makes all sorts of nice things out of wood for your house. Most of them are offered both finished and, slightly cheaper, unfinished, in case you are either a do-it-yourselfer or want a special finish. Salad bowls cost from around $1.70 for an unfinished 6-inch, up to $17.00 for a finished 17-inch whopper. Seconds (about half the price) reappear later on in the catalog modestly described as chopping bowls. Weston also has nice pine sugar buckets to put all kinds of things in besides sugar (from $3.75 to $14.00); an immense selection of cutting, chopping, and serving boards; the whales ($2.00 for mama,

$1.00 for baby) are especially fetching, although I don't for a minute believe that they're made of Vermont blubber the way the catalog says. Then there are all the other things you'd expect to find in wood—salt and pepper sets, cruets, candlesticks, and so on, very much less expensive than their often quite similar European counterparts. Catalog is 25¢.

The **SAWMILL**, WW, P.O. Box 145, Lafayette, N.Y. 13084, puts out a folder showing some very inexpensive hard rock maple products—a sandwich board is $3.00, a chef's grill weight, $2.00, a boot jack is $4.00. Collectors might be interested in the plate and/or spoon rail, offered by the foot, from $1.25 up. Folder is free.

For nostalgia lovers who refuse to give up modern convenience, the **HOUSE OF WEBSTER**, WW, Box 488, U.S. 62, North Rogers, Ark. 72756, sells electric ranges made like old-fashioned stoves (about $475.00). They also have electric cast iron skillets ($35.00) and electric cast iron bean pots ($50.00). On the other hand, if you insist on complete authenticity you can get old-fashioned wood- or coal-burning cookstoves from the **PORTLAND STOVE FOUNDRY, INC.**, WW, Portland, Me. 04104. Both catalogs are free.

B. FOOD SERVING

1. General

The **OLD GUILFORD FORGE**, WW, Guilford, Conn. 06437, specializes in Early American reproductions. There's lovely diamond thumbprint glassware (a tumbler is $2.50, candlesticks $8.75), as well as moon and star pattern, and lovely dolphin candlesticks. Stainless steel flatware is shown in classic sterling patterns. Also sold are ironstone and stoneware dinnerware (mostly made in England), pewter, and lots of lighting devices. The pretty color catalog is 25¢ (coin). You'll find similar assortments offered at **COHASSET COLONIALS**, the **STURBRIDGE YANKEE WORKSHOP**, and **JENIFER HOUSE**, all described in the next chapter.

The **KILKENNY SHOP**, WW, Castle Yard, Kilkenny, Ireland, is the retail sales outlet of the Kilkenny Design Workshops, sponsored by the government of Ireland. Their address is more than merely romantic-sounding, for they're located in a crescent of eighteenth-century stone buildings that used to be the stables, storerooms, and dairy of Ormonee Castle, just across the street. Their free colorful catalog shows a variety of objects for table and cupboard strictly in the modern idiom. There's brown ironstone stoneware lined in white—cup and saucer are around $2.00; a tea or coffee pot, less than $5.00; a covered oven-to-table casserole in a very satisfactory shape is called an

Irish stewpot and comes complete with a recipe for Irish stew (around $7.50). There's attractive pottery, too. On the expensive side is a selection of handsome handwrought sterling hollowware, made to order. The cheapest item I saw was a silver wine coaster for around $16.00. At the other extreme is a smashing wine jug, 190 mm. high (600 grams in weight) for $270.00.

SWITZER AND CO., WW, Grafton St. & Wicklow St., Dublin 2, Ireland, put out a small free brochure with a sampling of the many items they offer. It shows only a very limited selection of their china and crystal. They do have separate catalogs for Wedgwood, Royal Doulton, Waterford, etc., with a schedule of charges too complicated to put down here. Tell them what type of thing you're interested in, and they'll tell you how much that particular catalog costs when they send you your brochure. Their silver department offers reproduction antique and modern sterling by Royal Irish. There is an extremely handsome George II sterling teaset patterned after a Dublin original made in 1728. The teapot is around $380.00. Other pieces are priced accordingly.

FÖCKE AND MELTZER, WW, 152 Kalverstraat, Amsterdam, Holland, want a dollar for the colorful folder they put out at Christmas (although usually it's available for much of the rest of the year). It's full of interesting things, including the delightful Herend multicolor pottery, Battersea enamels, Metawa pewter, Warmink clocks, and so on, at prices lower than they would be here. They also deal in crystal and china (including figurines) from all the popular continental, as well as the British and Irish, manufacturers, and can quote prices on your particular desires.

DEN PERMANENTE, WW, Vesterport DK-1620, Copenhagen V, Denmark, is an organization of several hundred Danish craftsmen who maintain a permanent sales exhibition in Copenhagen. They put out a very handsome and elaborate catalog, which costs $3.00. It includes sterling silver, stoneware, glassware, etc., plus some bric a brac. Some of the items shown don't seem to me appreciably cheaper than I've seen them offered in New York stores, and some are a great deal cheaper. You'll have to take them piece for piece and judge for yourself.

THE CHINESE MERCHANDISE EMPORIUM (Chapter 7, A.1) offers lacquerware tea and coffee sets, as well as cloisonné, porcelain, etc., from mainland China.

2. China, Crystal, Silver

CHINACRAFT, LTD., WW, 499 Oxford St., Marble Arch, London W1R 2BH, England, has a thick, colorful catalog of fine bone china and crystal, which they'll send you free on request. Don't get too excited by the prices (in American dollars); when duty, insurance, and shipping costs are added, you'll find they average only about 25 to 35 percent less than the same pieces would cost here—although there can be greater savings on the really costly items. In general, the more expensive the china, the lower the duty; moreover, the postage is the same for a one-dollar as for a hundred-dollar plate. Here you'll find Worcester, Staffordshire, Coalport, Wedgwood, Royal Doulton, Crown Derby, and so on, and what isn't shown in the catalog Chinacraft can probably get for you. They have lots of crystal, too, including Edinburgh, Tudor, St. Louis, and Waterford.

The **GENERAL TRADING CO.**, WW, 144 Sloane Sq., London S.W.1, England, puts out a free color brochure showing a few of the many things they sell, including the various types of English bone china, plus Waterford, Baccarat, Orrefors, and many other types of crystal. They say that, "after allowing for U.S. duty and for shipping charges, English china bought from us in this way is still up to 50 per cent cheaper than current prices in a U.S. retail store." No doubt it is, if they're referring to one of New York's elegant East Side shops (or its equivalent) but I'd say a third would represent a more realistic estimate—and that's certainly not to be sneezed at.

HAMILTON AND INCHES, LTD., WW, 87 George St., Edinburgh EH2 3EY, Scotland, offer Edinburgh thistle crystal, and their stunning free catalog also shows a selection of the fine Scottish silver, for which they're noted. Prices start as low as approximately $12.00 for a silver pin tray, and then soar. The most expensive item shown is a four-piece coffee set, at around $850.00, but I'm sure they have other, even more expensive, items that they can produce upon demand. I doubt that you'll find any bargains here, but, if you're interested in fine things that you don't see all over the place, you'll find this firm well worth looking into.

"Many folk, living outside our shores, must assume from the press that Ulster is a devastated desert!" begins one of the brochures put out by **ROBERT HOGG AND CO., LTD.**, WW, 10 Donegall Sq. West, Belfast BT 1 6JQ, Northern Ireland. However, the firm says, they have been in business since 1850, and have no intention of giving up now. "Our stocks," they declare, "are better today than ever before." Since Hogg is a Northern Irish firm, they are in a better position than most to provide you with the hard-to-find Belleek. In addition, they offer all the well-known brands of English bone china (and probably the obscure ones too, if such is your fancy), as well as figurines by Royal

Doulton, Worcester, Copenhagen, and Hummel. They have Royal Worcester porcelain oven-to-tableware, and, of course, Waterford glass. Prices are in American dollars and brochures are free, but it will help if you tell them exactly what you're interested in.

SHANNON MAIL ORDER STORES, WW, Shannon International Airport, Ireland, seems to be one of the most reliable sources of Waterford glass. Be sure to ask for their Tramore Suite brochure when you write for their catalog (60¢, with prices in American dollars). It also includes Aynsley bone china, which turns out to be a Waterford subsidiary. The catalog also shows Wedgwood and Coalport. In addition, there's a separate catalog of Galway crystal, which I've heard well spoken of, particularly by those shops that seem unable to get Waterford crystal in sufficient supply to meet the voracious demand. It seems to be more expensive than the Waterford.

If you're interested in Waterford glass, write to **BROWN-THOMAS AND CO., LTD.**, WW, Grafton St., Dublin, Ireland, for their Waterford glass brochure, which costs 50¢ (that's in addition to the cost of its regular catalog). Prices are given in American dollars; glasses cost from around $3.50 to $11.00, decanters average $21.00 to $30.00. They're not as inexpensive as they seem, however, because the firm points out packing and postage will add about 20 percent to the total, on top of which there will be duty. Although Brown-Thomas profess themselves readier than most to get you what you want in the way of Waterford glass, they warn you to write for confirmation that an item is available before you send money. Remember, if you order Waterford glass from any firm, be prepared to wait a long time for it.

Cork crystal was first produced in 1783; then its making was discontinued during the nineteenth century. In 1971 the craft was revived, and today you can buy it directly from the **CORK GLASS CO.**, WW, Ballincolig, Co. Cork, Ireland. It's handsome and rather expensive—a decanter is around $45.00, glasses and goblets average about $10.00 each. The attractive catalog, with prices in American dollars, is free.

You can buy the traditional Oriental-inspired Dutch Delftware from Föcke and Meltzer, but why not go directly to the source **DE PORCELEYNE FLES**, WW, Postbus 11, Delft, Holland, which is the mail-order export division of the Royal Delftware Manufactory itself? They'll send you free a beautiful little color catalog in English (but with Dutch prices), showing the popular blue Delft, Polychrome, and Pijnacker (the last two both multicolored). In the remote event that you don't see exactly what you want, ask for it—if they don't have it, who else will?

OBÉRON (see Chapter 4,A) offers Lalique crystal and Limoges, mostly of an ornamental nature, though they have some practical pieces of china and earthenware, too, and say they can get you practically anything of French manufacture, if you ask for it. If you're interested specifically in porcelain, LES PORCELAINES SALMON ET CIE, WW, Bôite Postal 204, Limoges 87, France, will send you free their big catalog of luscious-looking Limoges porcelain, in both traditional and modern styles. Prices are by no means low, but they're substantially less than you'd pay for Limoges here; and I doubt that you'd be able to find many of the items shown, on this side of the Atlantic; although, of course, I haven't checked every china shop. Collectors will be interested in their "fantasie de grand luxe," which includes, among a lot of other expensive knicknacks, a series of figurines of Empire soldiers, either in *blanc* or painted. The catalog is full of all sorts of useful information about porcelain making; unfortunately, for non-linguists, you have to be able to read French in order to take advantage of it.

SVENSKT GLAS, WW, Birger Jarlsgatan 8 S-11434 Stockholm, Sweden, puts out a charming export catalog showing selected handmade crystal from the best-known Swedish glassmakers—Orrefors, Kosta, Kjellander, Färe Harcolin, Strömberghyttan, Boda, and so on. Prices (in American dollars) are, by and large, 30 to 40 percent less than they would be in most places here.

H. WALTER-RASMUSSEN, WW, Østergade 57, DR-1100, Copenhagen, K, Denmark, doesn't put out a catalog as such, but does send out free brochures of some of the most beautiful silver and stainless steel tableware you've ever seen. There's sterling silver by Hans Hansen, Monica of Denmark, W. and S. Sorenson (including their delightful fairy tale cutlery with designs derived from Hans Christian Andersen's stories), and Georg Jensen; stainless steel by Dansk and Frigast; tin by Just Andersen Mylius; pretty Danish Christmas spoons by Michelson; etc. Brochures are in Danish with some English. Prices, where given, are not low, but a lot lower than here. Tell them what lines you'd be interested in so they can send the appropriate brochures.

The ROSENTHAL CHINA EXPORT STORE, WW, 8 Theatinerstr., 8 Munich 2, West Germany, sent me a big beautiful catalog of their china, crystal and tableware free of charge, so they should, hopefully, do the same for you. Prices are considerably lower than they are here, and, although they will unquestionably have gone up by the time you read this, so will the prices of Rosenthal here. Catalog is in both English and German.

If you're fond of things Scandinavian, you have a treat coming from STOCKMANN'S EXPORT SERVICE, WW, Aleksanterinkatu 52, P.O. Box 10220, Helsinki 10, Finland. The store doesn't put out a catalog as such, but, if you'll send a dollar for postage, you'll get heaps of brochures showing the famous Wärtsilä Arabia pottery, Rosenlew cast iron kitchenware, Hackman stainless steel tableware and glass, glass, glass. The Finnish glass and china are simply fabulous, and prices seem so incredibly low, it could be worth the trouble and expense of having the breakables shipped. Some of the brochures are in English and some are in Finnish; some give American prices and some give Finnish.

You can buy beautiful Bohemian crystal directly from TUZEX, WW, Export Dept., Opletalova ul. 15, Prague, Czechoslovakia, which is an agency of the Czech government. Vases cost from around $15.00 to well over $100.00; ashtrays start at $7.00. A complete punch set consisting of 1 punch bowl, 12 cups, 1 ladle, and 1 tray is about $180.00. Catalog is free, prices are in American dollars, and the minimum order is $50.00.

NORITAKE SALES, LTD., WW, 1 Taranomon, Minatoku, Tokyo, Japan, puts out a catalog of china so that customers who have broken pieces of their Noritake sets may obtain replacements, as long, the firm says, as the patterns requested remain available—they're making no rash promises about keeping them in open stock indefinitely. However, they tell you how much a whole set will weigh, so I assume they're not averse to sending you one if you want to start from scratch. They don't tell you how much the pieces cost. What they want you to do is write to them and tell them what you want, and then they'll tell you exactly how much it will cost. What I suggest you do is write to UNIVERSAL SUPPLIERS (Chapter 5,B) for their catalog of Noritake, which does give prices; then, when you hear from Noritake (their catalog is free), you can decide which will give you the better deal. I suspect that Hong Kong will prove cheaper than Japan, but you never can tell.

The THAI CELADON CO., LTD., WW, G.P.O. Box 869, Bangkok, Thailand, puts out a detailed catalog (in English) of the beautiful jade-green celadon ware for which Thailand is noted. There is a lot of celadon tableware (tea-pots start at around $6.00), as well as casseroles, so it must be ovenproof. Outstanding are the lamps, of all kinds from the classically simple to the intricate, in prices ranging from around $20.00 up well past $100.00. Prices are in dollars, and, the firm says, they apply only to "our average beautiful ware. On pieces that come out of the kiln with an exceptional glaze transfiguration, a rare translucence of color, or a peculiar mark attesting to the ordeal the ware has gone through, we reserve the right to increase the price in an amount commensurate with the beauty of the piece."

ROWLAND WARD (EAST AFRICA), LTD., WW, P.O. Box 40991, Nairobi, Kenya, has produced in its own design a series of Bavarian-made glasses depicting big game animals, at prices ranging from around $4.50 up; a decanter is a little under $20.00. A set of 6 Royal Brierly crystal tumblers etched with African birds is around $18.00. Ward also sells big game mats and cocktail mats. The catalog is free.

You'll find a lot of reproduction American glassware at the general houses described earlier in this chapter and in the one following. If you're interested in Sandwich glass, the **SANDWICH GLASS MUSEUM,** WW, Town Hall Sq. and Rte. 130, Sandwich, Cape Cod, Mass. 02563, puts out a small folder of authentic Sandwich glass replicas in the diamond-thumbprint pattern. A tumbler is $2.50; a celery vase, $8.00.

And **ROMBINS' NEST FARM,** WW, Fairfield, Pa. 17320 (catalog 25¢) offers "South Jersey Clevenger glass completely hand-blown by the old masters, whose art is disappearing." You can't pass up the opportunity to buy from perhaps the only old masters still extant. There's a sunflower jug, a daisy pitcher and creamer, as well as a crown and diamond bottle, at $6.00 each. **HOLLY CITY BOTTLE** (Chapter 15, B.2) also sells Clevenger glass.

CASA DE LAS ARTESIANAS, WW, Parque del Aqua Azul, Guadalajara, Jalisco, Mexico, offers a catalog that shows its beautiful handblown glass in full color. Pitchers start at less than $1.00, and go up to a tops of $6.00. There are also glasses, mostly less than 50¢, cups, candlesticks, and so on. The catalog is free.

AVALOS, WW, Av. Revolucion 324, Guadalajara, Jalisco, Mexico, has a stunning color catalog of its beautiful prize-winning glass, which comes in amber, green, cobalt, marine blue, clear, and amethyst. There's an English introduction; otherwise it's in Spanish. Prices (incredibly low) are in pesos. Although the catalog is free, they cometimes seem reluctant to send it; if it arrives at all, it may take many months.

TREASURE TRADERS, LTD., WW, P.O. Box N 635, Nassau, Bahamas, offers an export plan that will be of enormous interest to you if you're after name brand china, crystal, and silver. They offer bone china from England (Royal Crown Derby, Royal Worcester, Aynsley, and Coalport) at approximately 40 percent below the U.S. price, *including* postage and insurance, which they pay. After you have paid the duty, they figure that you will have saved around 35 percent. The catch is that your minimum order has to be

$50.00, and, if you order Stuart and Royal Brierly crystal from England, it must be $100.00 (here you get 30 percent below the U.S. price). If you buy larger quantities of the English products, you get additional discounts. St. Louis and Baccarat crystal from France (minimum order $100.00) is offered at 40 percent off the U.S. price (after duty has been paid, they say, your savings should be 35 percent). Galway crystal from Ireland is offered at 20 percent below the U.S. price; for some reason, there is no duty on the Galway, or so they say, and you merely have to buy a minimum of 12 glasses. Now, here's something. You get most of the well-known brands of silver (Towle, Gorham, Wallace, Reed and Barton, etc.) here at 25 percent off the suggested retail price ($50.00 minimum). And that's what it will cost you. Postage and insurance are, as usual, included in the price; and there's no duty to pay, because the goods are of American origin. Moreover, when these firms have sales, Treasure Traders has them too, so you'll get the discount on the sale price. Isn't that nice?

STECHER'S, WW, 82 Independence Sq., Port of Spain, Trinidad, W.I., puts out a general brochure without prices. However, from what they say, it appears that you can get good buys here on glassware, especially those types not offered as frequently in the other firms' catalogs—Baccarat, Lalique, and Baum from France; Val St. Lambert from Belgium; Lobmeyr and Riedel from Austria; and Murano from Venice. They also have china and porcelain, including Hummel figurines; and silverware. They say they figure you'll save about 40 percent on U.S. prices, but it's not clear whether that's before or after postage and insurance have been paid. When you write for their free brochure, tell them specifically what you're interested in.

MERCURIO, S. A., WW, P.O. Box 2151, Panama 1, Panama, say they can deliver sterling silver flatware—including Reed and Barton, Wallace, Lunt and Alvin—at 34 percent below U.S. list prices, and there is, apparently, no minimum. But they don't say anything about postage and insurance, either. They also carry Swiss watches and jewelry. Again, they have no catalog as such, but if you write and tell them what lines you'd like to know more about, they'll send you the appropriate brochures.

3. Pewter and Other Metals

Many countries seem to feature pewter. The antiques have a high lead content; today, in the United States and in many other countries it's illegal to use lead in making pewter. If you're buying pewter for use, rather than for decoration, make sure that it has no lead content (where I know the pewter is lead-free, I will so indicate).

In Holland, the **CHOCOLATERIE "DAUPHINE" PETER REYNHOUDT**, WW, 24 Prof. Oranjestraat, Amsterdam, Holland, shows in its colorful free catalog an extensive selection of Royal Dutch and/or Metawa pewter, at prices much lower than they'd be in the States. They also have Delft, both blue and multicolor, wooden windmills, both musical and plain, and a variety of Dutch knicknacks.

SELANGOR PEWTER, WW, 231 Jalan Tuanku Abdul Rahman, P.O. Box 15, Kuala Lumpur, Malaysia, offers lead-free pewter that, they say, does not tarnish ... in many handsome shapes and forms. A very beautiful water pitcher (in what is identified as "Huggin's design") is offered at prices ranging from around $50.00 to $65.00. Ashtrays start at less than $5.00, napkin rings at less than $3.00. A lovely tea set on a 12-in. tray is around $150.00. Prices are given in American dollars. Brochure is free.

THE CHINA REFUGEE DEVELOPMENT ORGANIZATION, WW, P.O. Box 5861, Kowloon, Hong Kong, (See Chapter 11, C.8 for a description of its work) offers some extremely inexpensive pewterware. Jugs that cost dollars more elsewhere, even in other Oriental countries, run from less than $1.00 up to around $7.00. They also have some very inexpensive wooden items—teakwood salad bowls from $2.00 to $8.00, a cheese tray for around $3.00, plus lots of other attractive things. Brochure is free.

Many of the U.S. firms dealing in Americana feature pewter. In addition, there's the **COLONIAL CASTING CO.,** WW, 443 South Colony St., Meriden, Conn. 06450, which specializes in handcrafted lead-free (of course) pewter. Most of the items in their attractive collection are reproductions of Early American originals. Plates cost from around $5.00 to $18.00; a two-handled porringer is around $10.00. The brochure costs 25¢. **THE BEACON PEWTER WORKS,** WW, 19 Elmer St., Cambridge, Mass. 02138, puts out some attractive pewter pieces in classic shapes. Plates begin at around $10.00. Catalog is free.

S. SAMRAN THAILAND CO., LTD., WW, G.P.O. Box 740, Bangkok, Thailand, sells the bronze tableware for which Thailand is noted. Handles are of bronze, horn, and rosewood, and the pieces are available individually, but a full set for 6 (75 pieces) is less than $50.00. There are also bowls and trays (a salad bowl is around $16.00). Prices, in American dollars, include shipping. Brochures are free.

The **JAMES HANNA WORKSHOP,** WW, 11 Greenwell Pl., Newtownards, Co. Down, Northern Ireland, makes and sells handmade copper "tinker" kettles for around $10.00; "tinker" tankards and jars for around $4.00 to $5.00; as well as a good deal of other decorative copper items. Brochure is free; prices are in American dollars.

For antique copper utensils imported from the Near East, see **DICK OAKES** in Chapter 15,A.7.

4. Linens and Basketry

Many of the firms described in Chapter 2 sell table linens. Both the **LACE PALACE** and **MARIA LOIX** offer linen tablecloths and mats trimmed with Belgian lace. **BALLYMACHUGH** has table mats (averaging around $3.00), tablecloths ($45.00), tray cloths, and other items, either made entirely of or trimmed with Carrickmacross lace. Also available are crocheted tea cosies and a whole group of very modestly priced basketwork—table mats, baskets, pincushions, ornaments—priced as low as 25¢ (a bread basket is less than $1.50). (On hand also are natural color lambskins to use as rugs, $10.00 to $15.00.)

MADEIRA SUPERBIA shows the exquisite Madeira embroidery, cutwork designs, and appliques on linen and organdy tablecloths, napkins, doilies, placemats, etc., in both white and colors. Prices for these tablecloths start at less than $30.00 and go up into the hundreds. Much less expensive are the colored handwoven linens with woven decorations, which start at around $8.00 for a bridge-sized cloth with 4 napkins, and go up to around $45.00 for a banquet-sized cloth with 18 napkins. **JABARA** has a large supply of attractive table linens (some drip-dry) of all kinds. The **SWATOW DRAWN WORK CO., LTD.,** WW, G.P.O. Box 445, Hong Kong, makes and sells beautiful table linens with all kinds of ornamentation—cutwork, drawn work, embroideries of several kinds, Venetian lace, applique. . . . The linens themselves are white or colored, the prices extremely reasonable, starting at around $10.00 for a bridge cloth with 6 napkins and going up to around $250.00 for a 72" x 126" fine-point Venice lace banquet set with 12 napkins (there are also banquet cloth sets for less than $30.00). There are luncheon sets and other linens, including some expensive but exquisite sheets and pillow cases (the cottons are, of course, much cheaper than the linens).

Of those firms mentioned earlier in this chapter, Brown-Thomas has Irish linen tablecloths, mats, and napkins in great profusion. There's white double damask, and colored double damask (table cloths here start under $9.00), embroidered cloths, hemstitched linen cloths, linen embroidered with shamrocks. An Irish linen basketweave luncheon set, consisting of 4 mats and 4 napkins, is around $3.00; however, a hand-embroidered banquet set, with 12 napkins, can run you well over $100.00. There are also linen sheets, starting at around $33.00. Shannon's and Switzer's also offer some table linens.

Panama, surprisingly, appears to be a good source for linens. **HELEN'S LINEN CENTER**, WW, P.O. Box 3002, Panama 3, Republic de Panama, puts out a multipaged mimeographed list describing more kinds of table and household linens, as linens, than I'd ever imagined existed. There are literal linens, cottons, and organdies—white and colored, plain, appliqued, embroidered, decorated with Venetian lace (or wholly of Venetian lace) or cutwork. Prices, which are most reasonable, start at around $5.00 for a white linen applique and go up to around $250.00 for a white Venetian point lace banquet cloth. There are also some gay, inexpensive handwoven cloths from Guatemala. (**PILON**—see Chapter 3,B—also sells such cloths.) **BAZAAR GANDHI**, WW, P.O. Box 776, Colon, Republic of Panama, offers embroidered ecru and white "linette" tablecloths, from $4.00 up, as well as a variety of other table and househbld linens in white and colors and in a variety of fabrics. Both brochures are free.

TROPICRAFTS, LTD., WW, P.O. Box 43, Roseau, Dominica, W. I.; and the **DOMINICA HANDCRAFTS CO.,** WW, P.O. Box 22, Roseau Dominica, W. I., offer good-looking straw mats and baskets at extremely low prices. Both brochures are free.

5. Specialties

BLAIR, LTD., WW, 404 Ward Ave., Honolulu, Hawaii, sells a selection of household items—bowls and trays and such—in monkey pod and kea woods, made by native craftsmen. They're similar to the Philippine and Haitian wood carvings (see Chapter 11,C for more wooden tableware), but are more expensive. Brochure is free.

DON ROBERTO, WW, 205 Calle del Cristo, San Juan, Puerto Rico, offers an attractive array of stoneware products, including vases and planters, lamps, ashtrays, candelabra, and very distinctive tableware. Pitchers, for example, cost from $7.00 to $9.50. There are also mahogany plates—$2.50 to $3.75—and salad bowls—$2.00 to $19.00—plus papier mâché fruits and vegetables made in Don Roberto's own studios (starting at $1.00 for a lime and going up to $5.00 for a cauliflower). Price lists are free.

Remember: *Write for the catalog first.* All prices given were valid only at the time of writing and probably have been changed.

Chapter 9

AROUND-THE-HOUSE

A. GENERAL

HAMMACHER SCHLEMMER, WW, 147 East 57 St., New York, N.Y. 10022, puts out catalogs from time to time of wild and wonderful things for all parts of the home. They're expensive, often extravagantly so, but you won't see a lot of the items they carry elsewhere. In fact you may not even know that a lot of the items they carry exist (and that you can't live without them) until you see Hammacher Schlemmer's catalogs, which, they assured me when we last corresponded, are free.

CASA DE LAS ARTESIANAS (see Chapter 8,B.2) offers a variety of attractive Mexican things for the home. They have handsome lanterns, around $5.00 to $15.00; and all kinds of wrought iron candlesticks and strange things (a set of what look like either fireplace or barbecue tools is marked "chimney"). They also have some handcarved wood items and small pieces of furniture at very modest prices. Little 6" x 8" carved wooden chests with lion-faced hardware are less than $4.00 each.

In spite of the current changes in lifestyles Early American still seems to be the most popular style for home decor in America, or, at least, the one most frequently offered by mail order. There is a number of firms that offer everything to turn your life into a reproduction Early American one. The **STURBRIDGE YANKEE WORKSHOP**, WW, Brimfield Tpke., Sturbridge, Mass. 01566, puts out a catalog that lists 1000 basic items for furnishing an Early American home. These include authentic reproduction furniture: they sell the 60 different chairs made by Nichols and Stone in 14 different finishes (a bowback chair in a choice of finishes is $60.00); Hitchcock furniture (chairs start at $40.00, chests at $185.00); pine hutches, corner cupboards, dry sinks; trestle tables (a drop-leaf tavern table is $230.00 to $240.00). In addition they have a huge group of reproduction glassware—Sandwich, cranberry, cameo, Westmoreland milk, pressed glass (made from the original molds), etc. A Westmoreland milk glass candy dish with a pussycat on it is $10.00; salt dips in daisy and button or moon and star patterns are $3.00 to $4.00 per pair. Also on hand are ironstone, pewter, and lots of other things. **WILLIAM SPENCER**, WW, Ronconos Woods, N.J.

08069, also has furniture—the popular hutchback dining table is here adapted into a hutchback coffee table (around $60.00); also dry sinks and rolltop desks and armoires. The catalog has pages and pages of reproduction old-fashioned lamps and lanterns (and parts thereof), candlesticks, chandeliers (many of their own make), and Tiffany lamps (not what I'd call Early American, although they are indubitably American and are earlier than now, anyway). There are clocks, rocking horses, antique hardware, trivets ($1.50 up), white porcelain canisters ($21.00 per set), and so on. **JENIFER HOUSE**, WW, Great Barrington, Mass. 01230, offers a selection of merchandise so aggressively Colonial that its order blank sternly warns you, "if married, use husband's initials." They have Early American pressed glass in stipple star, daisy and button, moon and star, panel grape, strawberry and currant, Jersey swirl, diamond quilt, and hobnail. Prices start at $3.50 for a wine glass. Also on hand are handhooked rugs, dinner and tableware, pine furniture, pewter plates, clocks—all kinds of things for around the house. Spencer's catalog is 50¢, the other two are 25¢ each.

On a more formal level, the **CRAFT HOUSE**, WW, Williamsburg, Va. 23185, shows a line of authentic eighteenth-century furniture meticulously reproduced from originals in the Williamsburg collection, plus an impressive array of accessories—fabrics, glassware, lighting fixtures, etc.—to go with them. All of these fine things are very expensive, and so is the catalog— $2.95—but not if you think of it as a source book for furnishings of the period.

B. FURNITURE

1. Traditional

Again, Early American furniture lovers will find no dearth of merchandise to please them here—both in faithful reproduction and imaginative adaptation. Many of the items shown are available in kit as well as finished form. **COHASSET COLONIALS BY HAGERTY**, WW, Cohasset, Mass. 02025, offers kits of furniture patterned after authentic Early American originals, many of them museum pieces. Ladderback chairs reproduced from prototypes in the Boston Museum of Fine Arts are around $24.00 to $31.00; a sleigh seat is $17.00; a small Salem drop-leaf table, $46.00; a water bench after the original in the Samuel Wilson House in Hingham, Mass., $100.00; a candlestand from an original in the Metropolitan Museum is $12.00. As you can see, they're much cheaper than you could possibly buy them in finished form. Also available are lots of accessories. Catalog is 50¢.

OLD BENNINGTON WOODCRAFTERS, WW, Bennington, Vt. 05201, specialize in Early American furniture which, they say, they custom finish themselves in their carriage barn. There's a handsome reproduction Governor Winthrop desk, around $170.00 ($225.00, with a secretary top); solid cherry tables; and chests in the Queen Anne style (a coffee table is $110.00). In a less formal style there's lots of pine—handsome trestle tables are $190.00 to $200.00; also hutches, other kinds of tables, loads and loads of reproduction chairs, including some Hitchcocks. There are some nice small accent pieces—little tilt top tables of native pine, $16.00 to $17.00, and a rolling pin footstool at $12.00, which any cat would take to be his, exclusively; also lots of things to go with the furniture. Catalog is 25¢.

EPHRAIM MARSH, WW, Box 266, Concord, N.C. 28025, puts out a catalog of handsome reproduction eighteenth- and early nineteenth-century furniture, both the formal and the country styles. They have a particularly good assortment of traditional desks. Huge roll tops with piegonholes galore are $330.00. They also put out a catalog of office furniture, which includes some good-looking contemporary pieces as well. The regular catalog is 50¢ (probably if you ask for the office-furniture catalog at the same time you can get it as well).

NEWCOMB'S REPRODUCTIONS, WW, 3231 Hillsborough Rd., Durham, N.C. 27705, makes handsome eighteenth-century reproduction furniture, handmade, they say, according to "true eighteenth-century cabinetmakers' principles." Price of catalog is $1.00.

SHAKER WORKSHOPS, WW, the 1747 Wright Tavern, 2 Lexington Rd., Concord, Mass. 01742, sells furniture that is faithfully reproduced from the much-admired nineteenth-century Shaker prototypes. It's usually sold in kit form (although you can get it completely finished on special order), with each kit containing all necessary materials, including hardware, glue, stain, sandpaper, and instructions; the only things you don't get are hammer and screwdriver. A large drop-leaf table is $95.00; the largest rocker is $55.00. The smaller pieces, like the hanging cupboard, $25.00, and the clothes hangers (assembled and finished), $5.00, are particularly satisfactory. If you've been looking for those handsome oval Shaker boxes,

which are probably the best known of all the Shaker pieces, you can find them here, from $12.00 to $20.00 (or $70.00 for a nested set of 5). Catalog is $1.00.

CHARLES E. EMERY, CABINETMAKER, WW, North Conway, N.H. 03860, puts out a brochure of hand-made furniture, again most of it faithfully reproduced from Early American originals. A copy of a small Early American half-round pine table with mortice and tenon joints pegged in place, and an interesting looking handpegged ratchet candle stand are less than $40.00 each. A handpainted tote chair is less than $30.00. Brochure is free.

The **GREEN BOUGHS CABINET MAKER'S SHOP, INC.,** WW, 2021 Valentine Dr. N.E., Grand Rapids, Mich. 49505, offers pieces of small handcrafted furniture in traditional eighteenth-century styles in the finish of your choice. For example, several styles of corner table cost from $42.00 to $46.00 postpaid. Also sold are candle stands, book stands, and display stands. Brochure is free.

At **PINE COLONIALS BY HEDDERIG,** WW, Rte. 106, Loudon, N.H. 03301, you can get a number of Colonial adaptations and reproductions in knotty pine. There are stools from around $7.00; a 42" bench at $40.00; a wagon seat blanket chest, $70.00; and a huge pine hutch for $400.00. Free brochure.

YIELD HOUSE, WW, North Conway, N.H. 03860, offers adaptations of Early American furniture, both kits and finished. Some of the adaptations are reasonably faithful, such as the Chesapeake slantfront desk ($85.00 kit, $150.00 finished). Some are primarily utilitarian, like the Colonial file cabinets ($50.00 kit, $65.00 finished). The wood is pine in both instances. Very good buys here are the unfinished chairs in beechwood—captain's is $20.00, mate's is $15.00. The very solid oak riverboat captain's chair is $50.00. Yield also has a cupola kit at $20.00 and all sorts of things for around the house, and their catalog is now 25¢.

HUNT GALLERIES, INC., WW, 2920 North Center St., Hickory, N.C. 28601, sells handsome traditional furniture of unspecified period at moderate prices. There's a wide choice of fabrics (a big swatch book is included in the $1.00 price for the catalog), or you may send your own; also, a choice of six finishes.

MARTHA M. HOUSE, WW, 1022 South Decatur St., Montgomery, Ala. 36104, puts out reproduction Victorian furniture made from solid mahogany with all carving done by hand. Catalog is 50¢.

2. Contemporary

DEN PERMANENTE (see Chapter 8,B.1) shows a lot of furniture, priced more reasonably than you can get it here. As I've said in the Introduction, I do not think it's a good idea to order furniture from outside the country. However, if you insist, Den Permanente will make all the arrangements for you and let you know in advance how much they will cost, *except* for the customs broker, which they don't mention. It's possible that they can advise you about that, too. In any case, there are smaller items in the home furnishings area—lamps, curtains, wall hangings, and so on—that are mailable.

The **WORKBENCH** and the **CHILDREN'S WORK-BENCH,** both at 470 Park Ave. South, New York, N.Y. 10016, offer imported contemporary furniture in the medium to higher price ranges (although you'll find some good buys for adults at the Children's Workbench). Each catalog is $1.00.

BON MARCHÉ, WW, 74 Fifth Ave., New York, N.Y. 10011, sells imported and domestic furniture, very reasonably priced. Those of you who want to order furniture from abroad might take a look at Bon Marché's leaflets (they don't have a catalog, but they'll send you a sheaf of reproductions of their advertisements). The ones I got show a teak Wahl Iversen design writing table from Denmark at $150.00; Gunnar Bjoerklund swivel chairs, two for $90.00; chrome-finished steel chairs from Italy, $32.00; and 75' rosewood storage walls from Denmark for $400.00.

There are also several dealers who sell their furniture in unfinished kit or modular form. **FURN-A-KIT,** WW, 140 East Union Ave., East Rutherford, N.J. 07073, puts out a catalog of oak and walnut furniture, either in the natural finish or with their finishing kits in a variety of colors. They say that "everything—from a simple chair to an entire wall system of shelves and cabinets—goes together with just a few turns of a screwdriver and some knocks to join things solidly." And, if you have to move, or you change your mind about the arrangement, you just take it apart and put it together again. Their catalog is $1.00; but you pay only 25¢ for the one put out by **FURNITURE-IN-THE-RAW,** WW, 47-11 35 St., Long Island City, N.Y. 11101, which also shows knockdown furniture . . . in ready-to-finish, lacquer, or mica. **COUNTRY WORK-SHOP,** WW, 95 Rome St., Newark, N.J. 07105, sells modern, ready-to-finish furniture in modular units. Hardwood only—poplar and black walnut—are used, and prices are reasonable. Catalog is free.

3. Casual and Occasional

Wicker furniture is as popular today as it was in the days of our grandmothers and great-grandmothers,

and the three sources listed below seem to carry just about everything there is in wicker. One source is **FRAN'S BASKET HOUSE,** WW, 29 Calumet Ave., Rockaway, N.J. 07866, which sells wicker furniture, mainly in willow and rattan, from all over the world. You'll find all the curlicued old favorites plus some uncluttered new models. Prices start under $10.00 and go up to over $300.00. Catalog is 25¢. **JOAN'S WICKERWARE,** WW, 8010 Old York Rd., Elkins Park, Pa. 19117, puts out a big catalog, which has more baskets and rattan furniture than I've ever seen gathered together in one place. You can have them in the natural wicker or any of 24 colors. All the usual types of wicker furniture are offered, plus some unusual, and occasionally improbable, items—like the wicker lamp in the shape of a nude female torso ($40.00), and the sacred cow end table ($35.00). A rattan chaise lounge is $210.00 and a turntable bookshelf, $125.00. The catalog will cost you $1.00. Last, the **WICKER GARDEN,** WW, 400 Jacksonville Rd., Hatboro, Pa. 19040, offers decorative rattan furniture painted to your order. Prices start at around $9.00 and go up to a little over $100.00 (for a "love settee"). If you want anything in natural, it's 10 percent less. Brochure is 25¢.

The **J. F. DAY CO.,** WW, 2820 Sixth Ave. South, Birmingham, Ala. 35275, issues a catalog of beautiful aluminum reproductions of antique cast-iron garden furniture, which are supposed to be just as durable as cast iron and a lot easier to move around. A rose and lyre chair is around $62.00; a settee in the same pattern is $140.00; a harmonizing table is under $75.00. In addition to furniture, there are lots of decorative garden pieces—a most engaging juvenile lar with a basket on his head for offerings is $210.00. For indoors, there's a gorgeous oak pattern hat tree and umbrella stand at around $300.00 (less expensive umbrella stands start at $40.00). Catalog is $1.00. **THE PATIO,** WW, P.O. Box 2843, San Francisco, Cal. 94126, sells lots of casual summer furniture, and pads and replacement parts for furniture you already have. They also offer very attractive garden statuary from Mexico. Catalog subscription is $1.00.

The **LEATHERCRAFTER,** WW, 303 East 51 St., New York, N.Y. 10022, offers handmade leather furniture crafted according to the techniques used by Early American saddle makers. However, styles are, by and large, more in the contemporary vein. Directors' chairs start at around $35.00, British officers' chairs at around $50.00; prices go up to $650.00 for the firm's fabulous Ultima chair. Also available are handbags, tote bags, and sandals. Catalog with leather samples is 50¢. **JENSEN-LEWIS,** WW, 156 Seventh Ave., New York, N.Y. 10011, sells a large variety of directors chairs at very sensible prices, as well as some other casual furniture. Brochure is free, as is the one put out by the **HOUSE OF HAMMOCKS**, WW, Box 263, Cotuit, Mass. 02635, which offers old-time hammocks (imported from Brazil), priced from about $10.00 to $40.00. **HERTER'S** (see Chapter 7) has some small solid walnut tables, carved in French Canada, from $18.00 to $28.00, plus other pieces of occasional furniture.

For $1.00 The **BUTCHER BLOCK**, WW, 298 Bowery, New York, N.Y. 10012, will send you a catalog of their butcher block furniture, meant now for other rooms in the house besides the kitchen. Tables start at around $75.00 for an 18" x 18" square small kitchen table up to around $300.00 for a dining table.

The **GEORGES NADER GALLERY**, WW, P.O. Box 962, 104 rue Bonne Foi, Port-au-Prince, Haiti, offers a few small pieces of decorative furniture, made by an artist-craftsman—a Renaissance type of armchair made of acajou is around $55.00, a carved oak coffee table, around $80.00. The reason I mention them, in spite of my reservations about ordering foreign furniture, is that airfreight is prepaid, so there should be no problem with brokers. The catalog is free. It's in English, but the native tongue is French, so there may be some communication difficulty.

Did you think Franklin stoves were a thing of the past? Not a bit of it. The **PORTLAND STOVE FOUNDRY, INC.**, WW, Portland, Me. 04104, is still busily turning them out. They have cast iron folding-door Franklins, starting at $145.00 for ordinary stove black, and soaring to $340.00 for the "1742 Eagle" in colored porcelain enamel. (All models are available in both stove black and porcelain enamel.) Also on hand are the traditional beloved potbellied coal stoves, wood parlor stoves, and wood cook stoves—everything you could think of in that line, with all the necessary fittings and replacement parts. And the **PRESTON DISTRIBUTING CO.**, WW, Foot of Whidden St., Lowell, Mass. 01852, also offers Franklin stoves, from around $145.00—coal and wood heating, and cooking stoves, and lots and lots of accessories. In addition, there's an impressive array of cast iron cookware, some made from antique patterns, including cauldrons from $27.00 to $67.00 (that last holds 30 gallons and could hold almost anyone). Both brochures are free.

C. FABRICS

Household fabrics by the yard will be found at many of the fabric firms described in Chapter 18 (Needle and Loom). Some also sell bedspreads and hangings.

The Scandinavian firms offer many fabric items. **HUSFLIDEN** (see Chapter 2) has Rya rugs, embroidered hangings, pillows, and aprons, at prices that seem well below U.S. prices for similar items. **STOCKMANN** (see preceding chapter) has curtain and drapery fabrics, and might be able to get you the *Marimekko* fabrics if you ask (Marimekko itself refuses to deal directly). In both cases, don't forget to ask for brochures of the special items in which you're interested. The **KILKENNY SHOP**, described in the preceding chapter (B.1), has a group of woollen bedspreads, all of them fringed, except for Dripsey, a single-weave lightweight number ($20.00 to $25.00), and Kilcarr ($30.00). Others are Kilkenny, a folk-weave, and Foxford, Cashel, and Patchwork, all jacquards (prices run from around $36.00 to $70.00). Colors are luscious. Also on hand is a collection of printed cotton curtaining, 48" wide, at around $2.50 per yard, plus mohair travel rugs and blankets from Kerry. Many of the Irish houses sell glass cloths (I'd call them dish towels), but the ones here are a particularly good buy, not because of the price, which is $1.25, and more or less standard, but because of the designs on them. I'd use them for decorative hangings. Who would want to dry dishes on Orpheus playing to the animals, for heaven's sake? There's another one with just plain animals, and the rest have Irish proverbs (*sean thocail* to you) in Gaelic, but translations are offered. My favorite is the one on tea—"Dead with the tea and dead without it." Then there's "Many a time a man's mouth broke his nose," and, "There's no feast till a roast, there's no torment till marriage" . . . all so exquisitely lettered the non-Gaelic reader would have no idea that they are not just designs.

1. Curtains and Draperies

COUNTRY CURTAINS, WW, Stockbridge, Mass. 01262, offers café and full-length curtains in bleached and unbleached muslin, as well as floral prints, ticking, osnaburg, and other traditional provincial fabrics. Ruffled unbleached café curtains start at $3.50 per pair. **RONNIE DRAPERIES**, WW, 145 Broad Ave., Fairview, N.J. 07022, says it offers the world's largest selection of ready-made fiberglass curtains, draperies, and bedspreads, and they certainly do seem to offer an enormous variety in practically every length and width you could want—in solids, textures, and prints, lined and unlined, opaque and sheer. Both catalogs are free.

Extra-wide curtains and draperies, as well as yard goods, may be obtained from **HOMESPUN HOUSE**, WW, 9024 Lindblade St., Culver City, Cal. 90230. Catalog is 50¢.

2. Linens and Bedding

You'll find the big U.S. mail-order houses (Chapter 2,A) excellent for stocks of bed linens in more sizes and colors than you're likely to find in any one store. If you're allergic to (or don't care for the clammy feeling of) the ubiquitous drip-dry finish, which seems to have taken over the market, the mail-order houses may be the last place you can still get the untreated kind. However, the way things are going, by the time this comes out, it's possible that even they won't be carrying them any more, in which case, try the big European mail-order houses—**NECKERMANN, QUELLE, WENZ, JELMOLI,** etc.—which have equally large stocks. Remember, though, that their standard bed and pillow sizes are different from ours, so don't get fitted sheets unless you've checked your measurements carefully. You'll also find bed linens there that are much different from the ones you see here. In addition to muslin and percale, they have regular sheets made out of flannel, damask, satin, and, sometimes, plissé; the colors and prints, too, are quite different from the ones we're accustomed to. You'll also find some specialized bed linens (mostly to fit odd-sized beds) on sale at the sleep shops—**BETTER SLEEP** and **WUENSCH**—described in Chapter 6,D.2.

HELIOS HOME SUPPLIES, WW, Macclesfield, Cheshire, England, offers luxurious sheets and pillowcases at prices that they say are below normal retail in the United Kingdom, and that may well be below normal retail for linens of the same quality here. Be that as it may, they look pretty expensive to me. Helios also sells pure wool blankets at reasonable enough prices ($10.00 to around $60.00, but mostly under $20.00); also quilts, bedspreads, and curtains. Catalog is free. **FANNY'S SHOP,** WW, Curaçao, N.W.I., sells embroidered cotton and linen sheets and pillowcases, as well as Irish linen in "all required colors" (from "snow white to black"), by the yard, in widths from 36" to 108"; and all kinds of table linens. The little catalog is free, but there are no prices. It says, "ask for price-lists," and I did, and did not receive. It also says "catalog on dinnerware, crystalware, flatware on request," and there, again, I requested and did not get. Still, their brochure says they have Waterford, Bohemia crystal, Royal Dutch crystal, Jensen and Dragsted stainless steel, Dresden, Bavarian, Haviland, Meissen, and Limoges china and porcelain, all insured against breakage, so I thought you might feel the matter was worth pursuing. Most of the linen shops mentioned in the preceding chapter also sell bed linens. Note **BROWN-THOMAS** for real luxury.

3. Bedspreads and Quilts

Lots of bedspreads have already been mentioned incidentally in the course of this chapter and the preceding ones, and all of the big all-round mail-order houses, carry extensive stocks. Firms described in Chapter 2 that seem to offer particularly good buys in this area are **MacGILLIVRAY,** which sells Highland and Shetland all-wool bedspreads, from $10.00 to $15.00, plus cheviot wool blankets at $16.00; and **TEXTILES HERNANZ,** which offers what I think are bedspreads, but which might be quilts, in cotton and cotton and wool, very inexpensively indeed. **REY-COSIJOEZA** has some nice buys in quilts, too.

VIRGINIA GOODWIN, WW, P.O. Box 3603, Dilworth Station, Charlotte, N.C. 28203, and her family have been weavers since 1813, and remain, she says, "as far as our information has revealed to date—the only weavers to reproduce authentic antique hand-loomed patterns in coverlets woven without a seam." They include the traditional Morning Star, Lovers' Knot, Whig Rose, and Honeycomb, at prices from around $55.00 to $90.00. Very new here is a lovely colorful Crazy Quilt pattern of mostly wool pieces, each with a crewel flower. It's $200.00. Fabric by the yard is also available. Brochures are 25¢ in coin.

LAURA COPENHAUER INDUSTRIES, INC., WW, "Rosemont," Marion, Va. 24354, is the result of a plan formed during the Depression to help the impoverished country families of Virginia by utilizing their native handicrafts. The organization puts out a small booklet (50¢) describing the traditional mountain crafts they offer. These include wool and cotton coverlets, from $37.00 to about $70.00; quilts, $110.00 to $250.00; curtains, canopies, and so on—all they say, authentic reproductions of items of the past.

GURIAN'S, WW, 276 Fifth Ave., New York, N.Y. 10001, sells imported hand-embroidered crewel bedspreads ($50.00 to $80.00) and pillow covers ($5.00), as well as tablecloths ($35.00 to $45.00). They also sell crewel by the yard in 36, 45, 48, and 50-inch widths. Prices start at around $10.00 per yard. Catalog is 50¢.

Quilts are very popular right now, and, in addition to the ones described in the following section you'll find down quilts offered by many of the houses in Chapter 20 (Outdoors and Sports). Note especially **ANTARCTIC PRODUCTS** and **YETI ENTERPRISES.** The **J. SCHACHTER CORP.,** WW, 115 Allen St., New York, N.Y. 10022, specializes in fine quilts. Dacron-filled patchwork quilts start at $85.00, and white European goosedown quilts covered in satin and "stitched in the old-fashioned Continental style" begin at $130.00. Also available are other types of quilts in various fabrics, running up to $300.00 for a huge featherbed. At the same source you'll find blankets, pillows, and bedspreads, plus all sorts of bedroom accessories. The full-color brochure is 50¢.

Much more modestly priced are the "patch quilts" made by **RUSSELL'S QUILT CO.**, WW, 4032 Tweedy Blvd., South Gate, Cal. 90281, at prices ranging from $25.00 for a dacron-filled one 63 by 84 inches up to $100.00 for a 90 by 108-inch one filled with down (wool-filled ones are available as well). They'll also re-cover your old quilts. Brochures are free. **APPALA-CHIAN TRAILS**, WW, P.O. Box 247, Arlington, Va. 22210, offers handmade patchwork from Appalachia. Quilted bedspreads start at $85.00, tufted pillows at $11.50, shipping included. Send 10¢ for brochure and swatches.

The **PIKE COUNTY CITIZENS' ASSOCIATION**, c/o Sue Ramsay, WW, 1917 North Oakland, Milwaukee, Wis. 53202, puts out an odd little offset sheet that tells you about their group, an association of women in eastern Kentucky and Tennessee (and mentions, by way of explaining the address, that their corre-sponding member has moved to Wisconsin). Anyhow, they have drawn pictures of a variety of quilt pat-terns—stars, cat, simple patchwork, crazy, grand-mother's flower garden, etc.; and then state that "our basic quilt is double-bed size, hand-tacked, hand-hemmed, and comes in any pattern and color." And costs $25.00. (They must mean just the quilt *top*, don't you think? Even so, it seems like a bargain.) They also sell patchwork skirts at $4.00 and aprons, $15.00, and poke bonnets, $3.00. If you write, I think they might appreciate a stamp.

If you're looking for blankets, you'll find them sprink-led casually through the chapter, and, when you get catalogs from some of the houses that I've featured for other things, you'll find that they have blankets, too. However, if you want something special, such as a cashmere blanket, you'll need to be directed to **EGERTON'S** (Chapter 2,D.1), which has them from around $85.00 to $120.00. There are also pure wool merino blankets, much more modestly priced (from $18.00), and down quilts. **ICEMART** (Chapter 2,C.3) has "cuddly-warm" Icelandic blankets in 13 different designs, with such interesting—and not especially ap-propriate—names as Surtsey (you'd think something named after a newly created volcanic island wouldn't be just a striped brown and white blanket), Lala Fire (a plaid), and Saga (that, at least, has a traditional de-sign on it). They're priced from around $15.00 to $20.00. They also have eiderdown quilts ($109.00) and pillows ($12.00); plus soft, soft sheepskin rugs.

4. Rugs

You can get sheepskin and other types of rugs from many of the firms already mentioned. The **NAVAJO**

ARTS AND CRAFTS GUILD (Chapter 5,A.6) offers, as might be expected, handwoven Navajo rugs (from $5.00 to $10.00 per square ft.). **NSEIR** (Chapter 4,D), shows some lovely Middle Eastern rugs, but their price list ends suddenly just before Textiles, so I have no idea what they might cost.

SOL'S, WW, 3 Maragou St., Glyfada Sq., Athens, Greece, which describes itself as "the store which loves Americans," will send you a small full-color brochure of their handwoven wool *flokati* rugs, shown in solid colors, although they say combinations of 2 and 3 colors are available. Prices of the plain rugs range from around $20.00 for one 2' by 6' to around $200.00 for one 9' by 12'. They offer to match any color sample you send them. There are also rather charming circular rugs, with a pentafoil in the middle and a Greek key border. The two-foot one is $17.00; one 7' in diameter is $165.00. Shipping is included. **ATTIKA GIFTSHOPS**, WW, 6 Karageorgi Servias St., Constitution Sq., Athens, Greece, also offer *flokati* rugs. Both catalogs are free.

D. ACCESSORIES

1. Lamps and Lighting

THE KING'S CHANDELIER CO., WW, P.O. Box 667, Eden (Leaksville), N.C. 27288, sells chandeliers made of Czechoslovakian crystals combined with U.S. metal parts. When you buy one of their chandeliers, they say, you're investing in an heirloom of the future. Prices range from less than $100.00 to $4000.00. The catalog is 50¢. For other sources of crystal chan-deliers, see the firms in the preceding chapters that sell Waterford glass and Bohemian crystal, especially **TUZEX**.

SHEMITZ LIGHTING, WW, 1501 Boston Post Rd., Milford, Conn. 06460, puts out a portfolio of tradi-tional, Colonial, and contemporary lighting devices. The **HOUSE OF LIGHTS**, WW, Box 1901, Fairview Heights, Ill. 62208, has a selection of pretty chain lights and lamps from $20.00 to around $50.00. Note-worthy are the hanging colored glass lights in tradi-tional styles. Both catalogs are free. **GEORGE KO-VACS**, WW, 821 Madison Ave., New York, N.Y. 10021, sells contemporary lighting fixtures that start at relatively modest prices. Catalog is 50¢.

The **BRASS LANTERN**, WW, 353 Franklin St., Dux-bury, Mass. 02332, handcrafts reproductions of Early American lanterns, as well as original models in solid brass, and very handsome they are, too. All those shown in the folder are for outdoor use, but some may be used indoors as well. Their most popular, and the one I like best, is the "Night Watch"—a simple square in polished brass and antique rippled amber (or clear glass), which costs from $23.00 to $32.00. Other lamps cost from $38.00 to around $100.00. The Brass Lantern also makes custom lamps to your specifications. **HERITAGE LANTERNS,** WW, Sea Meadows Lane, Yarmouth, Me. 04096, has reproductions of early Colonial lights, made by hand out of copper in the traditional way. Although they're meant mainly for outdoor use, again, they may be used indoors as well. Prices range from $35.00 for a small onion glove to $240.00 for a Boston post light, with the average in the $65.00 to $75.00 range. Both brochures are free.

SANBORN'S (Chapter 5,A.5) has metal and hand-blown glass lamps, from around $3.00 to $7.00. Most of the furniture houses sell complementary lighting fixtures.

2. Clocks

MASTERS ASSOCIATES, WW, 82 rue Doudeauville, Paris 18, France, puts out a color brochure (free by seamail, $1.00 by airmail), of clocks that reproduce the most important inventions in horological history. These include the first wheel clock, with its foliot escapement; the short-beat pendulum wall clock (with Leonardo da Vinci's improvements); Galileo's long pendulum clock; the flying pendulum clock, patented in 1883; etc. Prices range from around $50.00 to $125.00, including surface shipping. In addition to the unusual appearance and authentic historical background, which will make these clocks of interest to collectors, they are also guaranteed to keep good modern time—which should make them of interest to everybody. There are even assembly kits for do-it-yourselfers, from around $35.00.

PRECISA INTERNATIONAL, WW, Postfach 1465, 899 Lindau (Bodensee), West Germany, shows an attractive selection of good-looking clocks. Many are battery operated, and there are also 8- and 400-day clocks. Prices run from around $15.00 to over $100.00. Also available are the traditional Black Forest cuckoo clocks, and clocks with similar happenings (roving-eye animals, etc.), priced from less than $10.00 to $17.00 or so. Prices all include shipping, and the catalog, actually a bunch of colorful brochures, is $1.00.

For other interesting German clocks see **SELVA** in Chapter 15,E.

3. Other

If you have a yearning for a traditional Coromandel screen, the **FORTUNE HAND WORK FAMILY CO., LTD.,** WW, P.O. Box 6066, Kowloon, Hong Kong, shows striking examples of that craft in its free but uninformative color folder. No prices are given; the Fortune Family refuses to so much as give a hint un-

less you tell them *exactly* what you want (and I'm always afraid to do that lest, through a gap in communications, a costly Coromandel screen, or whatever, should suddenly arrive collect on my doorstep), but I don't doubt that they're expensive, because Coromandel screens are expensive. However, since Hong Kong prices are almost invariably much lower than elsewhere, you ought to be able to save a considerable sum of money, unless you get hung up on freight and brokerage (but even that might be worthwhile on something like this).

KLODS HANS, WW, 34 Hans Jensenstraede, DK.5000, Odense, Denmark, has a small color catalog (35¢) that shows surprisingly inexpensive Danish wares. There are gaily colored ceramic and wooden candlesticks, $2.00 to $3.00; bright wooden eggcups, under $2.00; some really smashing ceramic eggcups shaped like fat birds, under $1.50; and handmade copper ladles with oak handles, $3.00 to $5.00. Brass candlesticks are around $5.00, and there are some delightful extinguishers to go with them. Tin-lined copper mugs are $5.00 to $6.00.

H. S. LOLLING, WOODCRAFT, WW, Hartsburg, Ill. 62643, sells carved rustic redwood signs with any words you want on them for $2.00. They also offer some very inexpensive Early American accessories—a quaint screw-top candle stand with a drawer in the base is $5.00 to $7.00, depending on the wood. A hanging salt box is $2.00, a wall pocket is $3.00; and there are spice and knicknack shelves, spoon trays, redwood hanging baskets, wooden plates, and so on. No charge for the brochure.

The **TENNESSEE CHROMIUM PLATING CO.,** WW, 206 Louise Ave., Nashville, Tenn., sells black iron andirons in owl or pussycat shapes for $19.00 per pair postpaid; fire sets with cats or owls on them; owl and cat bookends; owl and cat knockers; plus other metal items. Brochure is 10¢. **LEMEE'S FIREPLACE EQUIPMENT,** WW, Rte. 28, Bridgewater, Mass. 02324, has a nice selection of andirons in black and brass, from $19.00 to $50.00. The traditional Hessian soldiers are around $37.00; owls with glowing eyes are $14.00 to $20.00; glowy-eyed cats, $25.00. There are dachshund andirons, hitching post andirons, anchor andirons, and plain andirons, plus fire-sets, grates, and a variety of iron and brass household accessories and ornaments. Brochure is 25¢.

JUBI, WW, P.O. Box 662, Holyoke, Mass. 01040, prints a little catalog of modestly priced wrought iron home accessories, in the curly Mediterranean manner. Candlesticks are around $5.00 a pair, a little plush-topped footstool is $16.00. There are sconces, lamps, lanterns, and knicknacks. In addition, they can make anything in wrought iron to your specifications. Catalog is 10¢.

The **YANKEE WORKSHOP,** WW, 48 Hoyle St., Norwood, Mass. 02062, specializes in aluminum weather vanes either painted black or covered with 23-karat gold, at $35.00 to $50.00. They'll also design weathervanes to order for an additional charge. Brochure costs 10¢. **ROMBINS'** (Chapter 7,B.3) has all kinds of weathervanes, from the 9½-inch midget with the traditional rooster (a bantam, of course), at $2.00, to their $20.00 number, which comes with a large rooster, dog of any breed, ship, owl, etc. (If you want a cupola, they'll sell you one for $70.00.)

P. E. GUERIN, INC., WW, 23 Jane St., New York, N.Y. 10014, has been selling "artistic hardware" to the well heeled inhabitants of New York since 1857. Their merchandise is frankly in the luxury bracket. Bathroom fittings and accessories include basin sets (tap and handles) in the shape of snarling jaguars' heads, birds, pineapples, etc., at prices from $200.00 to $400.00 (there are some less expensive, less interesting ones, but not many). There's also builders' and furniture hardware. You can get a small cabinet knob for as low as $1.00, but an espagnolette bolt, such as I have seen only in the grandest old-fashioned Hollywood movies, can cost you close to $450.00. Catalog is $1.00.

Remember: *Write for the catalog first.* All prices given were valid only at the time of writing and probably have been changed.

Chapter 10

GARDEN

Although I've broken this chapter down into Seeds, Bulbs, and Plants for convenience, most firms don't specialize that narrowly. With few exceptions, the seed houses carry some plants, and the plant houses usually carry seeds. Unless a price is specified, the catalogs are free so far as I can determine.

A. SEEDS

1. General

The firms in the following group consist for the most part of well-known seedsmen who put out large glossy catalogs of fruit and vegetable seeds. They offer substantially the same kinds of merchandise, although some items will be very different. A few offer more modest catalogs, and this is often reflected in lower prices.

BURGESS SEED AND PLANT CO., WW, P.O. Box 218, Galesburg, Mich. 19132; **W. ATLEE BURPEE CO.,** WW, P.O. Box 6929, Philadelphia, Pa. 19132; **WILLIAM DAM SEEDS,** WW, Hwy. 8, West Flamboro, Ont., Canada (many special Canadian varieties; seeds are untreated); **HENRY FIELD SEED AND NURSERY CO.,** WW, 141 Oak St., Shenandoah, Iowa 51601; **JOSEPH HARRIS CO., INC.,** WW, 51 Moreton Farm, Rochester, N.Y. 14624; **J. W. JUNG SEED CO.,** WW, Randolph, Wis. 53956; **MEYER SEED CO.,** WW, 600 So. Caroline St., Baltimore, Md. 21231; **ROBERT NICHOLSON SEED CO.,** WW, Dallas, Tex. 75215; **OLDS SEED CO.,** WW, Box 1069, Madison, Wis. 53701; **GEORGE W. PARK SEED CO., INC.,** WW, Greenwood, S.C. 29646; **ROBSON QUALITY SEEDS, INC.,** WW, Hall, N.Y. 14463; **P. L. ROHRER AND BRO., INC.,** WW, Lancaster Co., Smoketown, Pa. 17576; **SCHELL'S SEED HOUSE,** WW, Tenth and Market Sts., Harrisburg, Pa. 17104; **R. H. SHUMWAY,** WW, Rockford, Ill. 61101; **STOKES SEEDS, INC.,** WW, 737 Main St., Box 548, Buffalo, N.Y. 14240 (this is both a Canadian and a U.S. house, with offices on both sides of the border); **GEORGE TAIT AND SONS, INC.,** WW, 900 Tidewater Dr., Norfolk, Va. 23504; **WETSEL SEED CO., INC.,** WW, P.O. Box 791, Harrisburg, Va. 22801.

Almost all of the preceding firms offer larger quantities for commercial growers; there are also some firms that deal primarily with market gardeners and florists, though usually they do offer small packets as well.

These include: **D. V. BURRELL SEED GROWERS CO.,** WW, Rocky Ford, Colo. 81067; the **DeGIORGI CO., INC.,** WW, Council Bluffs, Iowa 57501 (catalog is 25¢; prices of seeds exceptionally low, starting at 10¢ per packet); **MIDWEST SEED GROWERS,** WW, 505 Walnut St., Kansas City, Mo. 64106.

2. Special

GREENE HERB GARDENS, WW, Greene, R.I. 02827, puts out an unusually long list of herb seeds. In addition to your run-of-the-mill herbs, they have nettles, two kinds of thistles, and two kinds of teasels, as well as books and herbal information. (You'll find more herb seeds and herb plants at many of the other herb stores listed throughout the book, as well as at most of the other firms in this chapter.)

SHIRLEY MORGAN, WW, 2043 Encina Ave., Alameda, Cal. 94501, puts out a very unusual and comprehensive list of herb seeds, which contains hundreds and hundreds of herbs, including many that are difficult to obtain. There are also dye plant seeds, seeds for salads and greens, unusual fruits and melons, and so on, most of them priced at 50¢ per packet. Send an SAE for the list.

The **KITAZAWA SEED CO.,** WW, 356 West Taylor St., San Jose, Cal. 95110, offers a small list of unusual vegetable seeds. There are edible burdock, *mitsuba* (Japanese parsley), edible-podded peas, etc., plus Japanese varieties of familiar vegetables. The **NICHOLS GARDEN NURSERY,** WW, 1190 North Pacific Hwy., Albany, Ore. 97321, also offers, in addition to an unusually extensive line of herbs, some offbeat vegetables, such as Kikuza winter squash, Montezuma red beans, Crowder peas, beets crapaudine, *Wong Bok,* Sicilian purple cauliflower, *Lagenaria Langissima,* and so on. They also carry "native plants that serve mankind" (usually by being edible). Their mimeographed catalog is full of odd bits of information, recipes, and random thoughts and costs 35¢.

THE NATURAL DEVELOPMENT CO., WW, Bainbridge, Pa. 17502, which specializes in organic foods, offers vegetable and flower seeds in their catalog, but they don't specifically say that the seeds have been organically raised. They do offer organic plant food, however, and insecticides they claim are nontoxic (except, of course, to insects). **VITA-GREEN FARMS ORGANIC NATURAL SEEDS**, WW, P.O. Box 878, Vista, Cal. 92083, puts out a line of vegetable and herb seeds which, they say, are "natural, untreated, old-fashioned, unhybridized, and uncrossed." They also carry organic and rock fertilizer.

Ever since 1876, **HERBST BROTHERS**, WW, 1000 North Main St., Brewster, N.Y. 10509, have been supplying tree seeds for nurserymen and foresters, plus flower and vegetable seeds for commercial growers. Their thick unillustrated catalog doubles as a price list. Seeds here are offered by the oz. and lb., so you're not likely to be interested unless you're going to do a lot of planting. However, if, say, you and a lot of your friends are anxious to grow *koelreuteria paniculata* (which, as we all know, is panicled gold raintree), it might pay for you to get together and blow around $1.50 on ¼ lb. (plus $23.50 on something else, as the minimum order is $25.00). They have a lot of trees and shrubs I haven't seen elsewhere. (Though you ought to check with **MELLINGER'S**—Section C.2—before you order a lot of seeds you don't need in order to get the few you want; they're good on tree seeds, too, and they sell them by the packet rather than by the forest.) The **F. W. SCHUMACHER CO.**, WW, Sandwich, Mass. 02563, also sells seeds for nurserymen and foresters. The **WOODLAND SEED CO.**, WW, Norway, Mich. 49870, has seeds of evergreen and decidious trees and shrubs. Both brochures are free.

CLYDE ROBIN, P.O. Box 2091, Castro Valley, Cal. 94546, specializes in native flower and wild tree seeds, plus some plants. In addition, they offer seed mixtures for special purposes—to plant in the desert, along the roadside, on a mountain slope. There are fire-control mixtures and erosion-control mixtures—also vacuum-sealed, naturally grown, unfumigated, untreated vegetable seeds for organic gardeners. They also sell earthworms, which they describe as "loveable little creatures . . . especially bred by us." Although the emphasis is on California culture, you'll find plants hailing from and suitable for other areas as well. The price of the colorful, unusual catalog is $1.00.

JOHN BRUDY'S RARE PLANT HOUSE, WW, Box 84, Cocoa Beach, Fla. 32935, offers the seeds of some unusual plants. Here you will find the *Boobyala*, the *Porra Tree*, the *Muchukundu*, the *Giant Wooly Morning Glory*, the *Pongam* (or *Poonga-Oil*) tree, and the *Roxburgh Fig* (a rubber plant with leaves the size of dinner plates—but can you imagine seeds at $45.00 for ¼ oz.?). (Before you get scared, the others are mainly 75¢ per packet.) You're warned that you must save your catalog—and why not, since

you've already paid 50¢ for it—because it gives the only cultivation instructions you're going to get.

3. Foreign

There are many restrictions about ordering plants from abroad; however, there's usually no problem with seeds. As a rule, the English firms know what seeds may be sent to the United States (Thompson and Morgan has a very handy system of asterisking no-nos), but the Australian and New Zealand houses are not always aware; so, if you're planning to order something exotic, it might be a good idea to check with the local office of the Department of Agriculture.

THOMPSON AND MORGAN, LTD., WW, Ipswich, England, says it puts out the world's largest and most famous seed catalog; and they certainly offer as extensive a collection of flower and vegetable seeds in their handsome publication as I've ever seen. On the other hand, **SUTTONS SEEDS, LTD.**, WW, Reading RG6 1AB, England, are seedsmen by appointment to both the Queen and the Queen Mother. They say, in their pretty color catalog that they have great experience in shipping their flower and vegetable seeds to all parts of the world. **ALLWOOD BROTHERS, LTD.**, WW, Hassocks, Sussex, England, are carnation specialists. You can buy seeds of their own particular carnation, pink, and dianthus seeds from them, but don't let yourself be tempted by the plants. You can get organically grown English herb seeds from **E. and A. EVETTS**, WW, Ashfields Herb Nursery, Hinstock, Market Drayton, Shropshire, England, who put out a special export list.

L. S. A. GOODWIN AND SONS, WW, "Milford," Mangalore, Tasmania, Australia 7406, "an international seed service," will send you a group of mimeographed catalogs in return for 4 IRCs. Most interesting probably will be the tree and shrub list, which contains many native Australian plants. **KANDELKA NATIVE SEEDS**, WW, 70 Sun Valley Rd., Valley Heights, N.S.W. 27777, Australia, specializes in the seeds of native Australian species only. Guidance notes are included with all orders and you can get their mimeographed list for 1 IRC (2 if you want it by airmail). **WATKINS SEEDS, LTD.**, WW, P.O. Box 468, New Plymouth, New Zealand, puts out a fat little unillustrated catalog of vegetable and flower seeds from down under, and they'd like you to send 36¢ (add 48¢ if you want it sent via airmail). Prices at all three firms are given either in Australian or in New Zealand dollars, which are worth much more than ours, so don't make any mistakes.

HAZERA SEEDS, LTD., WW, P.O. Box 1565, Haifa, Israel, issues an attractive, informative catalog of vegetable, field, and forage seeds in varieties especially adapted to subtropical conditions. It's in English; it's free; and prices are given in American dollars.

B. BULBS

The Dutch have an arrangement whereby bulbs destined for the United States are inspected before shipping, so you won't have to worry about any export formalities. I've found two firms from which you can order direct. **DUTCH GARDENS, INC.**, WW, P.O. Box 30, Lisse, Holland, puts out one of the most beautiful full-color catalogs I've ever seen. I couldn't believe it was free, but they assured me it is. Bulbs are shipped directly to you from the Dutch lowlands at what they claim are wholesale prices. You don't even have to pay shipping costs if you order at least $30.00 worth. (They suggest that gardeners get together and combine their orders for maximum savings.) **J. B. WIJS AND ZOON,** WW, Koninklijke zaadhandel n.v., Singel 508-510, Amsterdam, Holland, has a colorful bulb brochure, with a price list in English (though the prices themselves are in guilders).

A good local source for bulbs is **P. de JAGER AND SONS, INC.**, WW, 188 Asbury St., South Hamilton, Mass. 09182.

C. PLANTS

1. General

All these firms offer large and varied selections of shrubs, trees, plants, etc. You'll save shipping costs (and wear and tear on your plants), if you try to order from those located closer to you. **ARMSTRONG NURSERIES,** WW, 1265 South Palmetto, Ontario, Cal. 91764; **VERNON BARNES AND SON NURSERY,** WW, P.O. Box 250-PL, McMinnville, Tenn. 37110; **EMLONG NURSERIES, INC.,** WW, Stevensville, Mich. 49127; **EARL FERRIS NURSERY,** WW, 375 Bridge St., Hampton, Iowa 50441; **GIRARD NURSERIES,** WW, P.O. Box 428, Geneva, Ohio 44041; **KELLY BROTHERS NURSERIES, INC.,** WW, Dansville, N.Y. 14437; **LINWOOD GARDENS,** WW, Linwood, N.J. 08221; **J. E. MILLER NURSERIES, INC.,** WW, Canandaigua, N.Y., 14424; **NEOSHO NURSERIES,** WW, Neosho, Mo. 64850; **PUTNEY NURSERY, INC.,** WW, Putney, Vt. 05346; **SAVAGE FARMS NURSERY,** WW, P.O. Box 125, McMinnville, Tenn. 37110; **STARK BROTHERS' NURSERIES,** WW, Louisiana, Mo. 63353; **STERN'S NURSERIES,** WW, Geneva, N.Y. 14456; **WAYSIDE GARDENS,** WW, 501 Mentor Ave., Mentor, Ohio 44060 (catalog is $2.00, ref.); **WHITE FLOWER FARM,** WW, Litchfield, Conn. 06759 (catalog is $2.50–$2.00 ref.); **ZILKE BROS. NURSERY,** WW, Baroda, Mich. 49101.

2. Specialties

Water Gardens. There are several firms devoted entirely to selling plants and equipment for water gardens. They offer water lilies and other shallow water and bog plants, as well as equipment for maintaining—and, in some cases, making—your fish pond or lily pool. Van Ness also sells supplies for fountains. Most of them offer tropical fish and snails, and some sell frogs as well. Bee-Fork claims their frogs are intelligent looking. Free catalogs are put out by **BEE-FORK WATER GARDENS,** WW, Bunker, Mo. 63619; **WILLIAM TRICKER, INC.**, WW, 174 Allendale Ave., Saddle River, N.J. 07458; **VAN NESS WATER GARDENS,** WW, 2460 North Euclid Ave., Upland, Cal. 91786; and **SLOCUM WATER GARDENS,** WW, Winter Haven, Fla. 33880. **THREE SPRINGS FISHERIES,** WW, Lilypons, Md. 21717, charges 50¢.

Trees. The **DUTCH MOUNTAIN NURSERY,** WW, Augusta, Mich. 49012, specializes in trees and shrubs that supply shelter and sustenance to birds. They'll tell you what to plant so there will be a constant succession of fruits available for your feathered friends, even in winter. They'll tell you which plants certain birds like best (bluebirds are fond of Japanese honeysuckle and Virginia creeper; the cedar waxwing likes to munch on holly and black gum; while the evening grosbeak seldom passes up a chance to snack on Russian olive.) They'll also tell you which trees will do best under such adverse conditions as city life. Seeds are offered according to the kind of bird that will eat them when they've grown into plants. The catalog is 25¢.

MELLINGER'S, INC., WW, 2310 West South Range Rd., North Lima, Ohio, 44452, puts out a simple, sparsely illustrated offset catalog, which includes an incredible number of trees and shrubs at very reasonable prices. They are even in a position to furnish you with a whole arboretum, at prices ranging from $11.00 to $100.00. Their supplies are also modestly priced.

Other good sources for trees are **KRIDER NURSERIES, INC.,** WW, Box 123, Middlebury, Ind. 46540; **MAYO NURSERIES,** WW, Rte. 14, Lyons, N.Y. 14489; and **MUSSER FORESTS, INC.,** WW, Indiana, Pa. 15701.

Alpines and Wildflowers. **GARDENS OF THE BLUE RIDGE,** WW, Ashford, McDowell Co., N.C. 28603, specializes in native mountain wildings. These include herbaceous perennials; plants for rock gardens and naturalizing; native orchids; native ferns; aquatic and bog plants; and so on. **LAMB NURSERIES,** WW, East 101 Sharp Ave., Spokane, Wash. 99202, sells hardy perennials and alpines. **WOODLAND ACRES**

NURSERY, WW, Crivitz, Wis. 54114, puts out a folder of wildflowers, ferns, and perennials for problem areas.

Herbs. **CAPRILANDS HERB FARM,** WW, Silver St., North Coventry, Conn. 06238, has over 200 varieties of herb plants, as well as herb seeds, plus weathered wood and terra cotta garden figurines and shrines. Leaflet is 10¢. **LE JARDIN DU GOURMET,** WW, Ramsey, N.J. 07446, puts out a price list for their herb plants and herb seeds, both domestic and imported from France—the latter including *pourpier* (purslane), *oseille* (sorrel), *scorsoneres* (black salsify), and *arroche* (unidentified). They also sell shallots, for both eating and planting, and leeks.

Roses. **JACKSON AND PERKINS CO.,** WW, Medford, Ore. 97501, have long been celebrated for their roses (though now they're offering other nursery stock as well). Other sources for regular roses are **STAR ROSES,** WW, Box 203, West Grove, Pa. 19130; and **TILLOTSON'S ROSES,** WW, Brown's Valley Rd., Watsonville, Cal. 95076. (Tillotson's catalog, "Roses of Yesterday and Today," is $1.00.) For miniature roses, write to **MINI-ROSES,** WW, P.O. Box 4255, Station A, Dallas, Tex. 75208; and **PIXIE TREASURES,** WW, 12851, Old Foothill, Santa Ana, Cal. 92705.

Berries. **BRITTINGHAM PLANT FARMS,** WW, Ocean City Rd., Salisbury, Md. 21801; **THE CONNOR CO., INC.,** WW, P.O. Box 534, Augusta, Ark. 72006; and **RAYNER BROTHERS, INC.,** WW, Salisbury, Md. 21801, are all sources for berries.

Flower Species. **BRAND PEONY FARMS,** WW, Box 36, Faribault, Minn. 55021, specialize in peonies, as well as irises. **LYN-MAR GARDENS,** WW, P.O. Box 236, Dell City, Tex. 79837, specialize in irises, as do **JONES IRIS GARDENS,** WW, Box 62, Lucerne Valley, Cal. 92356; and **CARMEN'S IRIS GARDENS,** WW, Payson, Ill. 62760. For chrysanthemums, try **DOOLEY GARDENS,** WW, R.R. 1, Hutchinson, Minn. 55350; **NORVELL GREENHOUSES,** WW, 318 South Greenacres Rd., Box 73, Greenacres, Wash. 99016; or **SUNNYSLOPE GARDENS,** WW, 8638 Huntington Dr., San Gabriel, Cal. 91775. Gladioli may be found at **EDEN GLAD GARDENS,** WW, Box 7, Mount Eden, Cal. 94557; geraniums at **WILSON BROTHERS,** WW, Roachdale, Ind. 46172.

For orchid lovers, the **SHANTI KUNZ NURSERY,** WW, "Shanti Kunz," Bong Rd. Halimpong, India, offers a free descriptive price list (in U.S. dollars) of Indian and Burmese orchids, offered at what seem to be very reasonable prices—less than $30.00 per 100. Although you can't buy any single specific variety in

quantities of less than 100, there are also some assortments, 25 different plants for about $30.00; 50 for around $55.00, and these are sent to you airmail postpaid. I believe that because orchids come with their roots in moss rather than in soil, they may be imported into the United States; however, if you want to try, again, it might be wise to check with your local branch of the Department of Agriculture first. (Different states have different regulations.)

Bromeliads. These plants can be found at **CALIFORNIA JUNGLE GARDENS,** WW, 11977 San Vicente Blvd., Los Angeles, Cal. 90049.

Cacti. The **CACTUS GEM NURSERY,** WW, P.O. Box 327, Aromas, Cal. 95004, offers hundreds of cactus varieties priced from 50¢ up; also numerous succulents. Cacti are also available from the **DESERT PLANT CO.,** WW, P.O. Box 880, Marfa, Tex. 79843, which offers a small printed list of West Texas big bend cactus, starting at 35¢.

Carnivores. **ARMSTRONG ASSOCIATES, INC.,** WW, Basking Ridge, N.J. 07920, has a folder describing their "hungry carnivorous plants" which capture their own meals. Cultural instructions are supplied with all orders. However, **PETER PAULS NURSERIES,** WW, Canandaigua, N.Y. 14424, will include instructions along with the brochure of carnivorous plants and supplies they'll send you for 25¢.

House Plants. Many of the plants in this section are house plants, and you'll find other house plants listed at virtually every other firm in the chapter. For 25¢ you can get a long mimeographed list of inexpensive house plants from the **GREENLAND FLOWER SHOP,** WW, Rte. #1, Port Matilda, Pa. 16870.

D. ACCESSORIES

You'll find equipment for indoor and outdoor gardeners plus books at all the firms already listed. In addition, here are some specialists.

GARDEN WAY PUBLISHING, WW, Charlotte, Vt. 05445, puts out a catalog of paperback and hardcover books about gardening and allied arts, such as beekeeping, animal husbandry, etc. Most of the herb stores offer books on how to heal *yourself* with herbs; Garden Way offers an *Herbal Handbook for Farm and Stable* by Juliette de Bairadi Levy, which is "a compendium of simple herbal remedies for ailments of sheep, goats, cattle, poultry, horses, and sheep dogs." **CARRY BACK BOOKS,** WW, Franconia, N.H. 03580; and **ZIMMER'S, INC.,** WW, 1344 Santa Fe Dr., Denver, Colo. 80304, also specialize in gardening books.

NORTH CENTRAL PLASTICS, INC., WW, Ellendale, Minn. 56026, sells lightweight, heavy duty plastic lawn and garden tools, which, the company says, are "immune to garden chemicals and weather," in pleasing shades of red, blue, green, and yellow. A set of four very pretty hand tools in a plastic bag is $1.00 or so; rakes are less than $2.00 each, delivery included. Brochure is free.

The HYDROPONIC CHEMICAL CO., WW, Copley, Ohio 44321, offers not only the firm's famous plant foods, but all kinds of useful and interesting things for both indoor and outdoor gardens. There are planter poles, downspout extensions, trellises, fences, and nice white sand for people who have trouble finding small quantities for horticultural (or decorative) purposes. The NATIONAL FARM EQUIPMENT CO., WW, 645 Broadway, New York, N.Y. 10012, sells all kinds of things gardeners would probably be interested in, at what seem like reasonable prices (sometimes lower than those in the garden catalogs).

The HOUSE PLANT CORNER, WW, P.O. Box 810, Oxford, Md. 21654, puts out a catalog that lists all the equipment the most pampered houseplant could ask for. There are lights, pots, humidifiers, plant food, planters, misters, soil testers, and so on, in addition to a small selection of house plants. Catalog is 25¢. TUBE CRAFT, INC., WW, 1311 West 80 St., Cleveland, Ohio 44102, sells fluorescent lights and "Floracarts" for indoor gardeners. Brochure is free.

If you want a fountain from overseas, get in touch with GARVENS BROTHERS OHG, WW, Box 29 and 48, Grehberg 32 and 35-37, 3251 Aerzen, near Hameln, West Germany. (Hameln, of course, being the same as Hamelin, where the Pied Piper used to flourish.) They sell illuminated fountains for both indoors and outdoors. Brochures are in English and there are price lists in American dollars. For American fountains, you can get brochures from the RAIN JET CORP., WW, 301 South Flower St., Burbank, Cal. 91503; and REAL FOUNTAINS, INC., WW, 264 West 40 St., New York, N.Y. 10018, which both manufactures and sells indoor and outdoor fountains.

For greenhouses of all kinds, from small window models to elaborate numbers that look like glass palaces, write to LORD AND BURNHAM, WW, Irvington, N.Y. 10533; and the STURDI-BILT MANUFACTURING CO., WW, 11304 S. W. Beenes Ferry Rd., Portland, Ore. 97219, for their handsome color catalogs.

Remember: *Write for the catalog first.* All prices given were valid only at the time of writing and probably have been changed.

Chapter 11

ART

A. PRINTS, POSTERS, AND REPRODUCTIONS

Here are three catalogs, lovely as only the Japanese can make them. The 60-year-old **RED LANTERN SHOP**, WW, 236 Shimmonzen St., Higashiyama-ku, Kyoto 65, Japan, features modern Japanese prints, all in signed and numbered limited editions. Prices are most reasonable, starting at less than $5.00 and going up to around $175.00, with most under $35.00. The catalog is free. The **YOSEIDO GALLERY**, WW, 5-15, Ginza 5-Chome, Chuo-ku, Tokyo, Japan, specializes in contemporary Japanese woodblock prints, to fit all budgets, because they also range from less than $5.00 and to up to a little over $100.00, with plenty in the lower price brackets. Catalog costs $1.00 by seamail, $3.00 by airmail. The **UCHIDA ART CO., LTD.**, WW, Kyoto Handicraft Center, Kumano Jinja Higashi, Sakyo-ky, Kyoto 606, Japan, offers attractive and very inexpensive woodblock prints, mostly in the $6.00 to $12.00 range; also lovely woodblock Christmas and gift cards, at around $15.00 for 50 cards; stationery; miniature screens, $5.00 to $10.00; and full-size screens, too. Catalog is free. All three prices are in American dollars.

ASSOCIATED AMERICAN ARTISTS, WW, 663 Fifth Ave., New York, N.Y. 10022, sells signed limited editions of original etchings, lithographs, serigraphs, and woodcuts, at prices starting at $15.00. All are matted, but frames are extra. Send 25¢ for catalog.

The **HUNTERS' CLUB, LTD.**, WW, P.O. Box 1, Great Missenden, Bucks., England, publishes 24 sets of handsome British military prints, at around $6.00 surface mail, $7.00 airmail, per set of 4. There is no charge for the price lists. And in Ireland, **HOBSON MORRIS, LTD.**, WW, Walinstown Ave., Dublin 12, Ireland, offers prints of ancient Irish scenes at a little over 50¢ for the black and white, $2.50 for the colored. They also have Irish scenic ceramic tiles at a little over $1.00. Illustrated price list is free.

The **GOLDEN AGE PRESS**, WW, Box 3196, Boulder, Colo. 80303, publishes limited editions of nineteenth-century prints "that have artistic merit, are of his-toric interest or . . . simply nostalgic reminders of the everyday life of the past century." Each is lithographed on heavy stock and is 11½" by 14½" overall, and costs $3.00. Included are such names as Whistler, Winslow Homer, Frederick Remington, Maxfield Parrish, as well as lesser lights like Rufus F. Zogbaum. Catalog is 25¢.

CAULDRON PROMOTIONS, WW, 98 Mill Lane, West Hampstead, London NW6 1PA, England, have a large variety of posters which they will despatch to any country in the world, even Yugoslavia (although they say they can't accept dinars at a very good rate). Included are such subjects as the tarot, an Aztec mandala (so they say), a werewolf, Mick Jagger, signs of the zodiac, some lovely illustrations by Aubrey Beardsley and other familiar artists, views of old London, etc. Available here, too, are antiqued reproductions of authentic old maps and documents, which include such items of interest as the original deed to Manhattan and Long Island for around 75¢. Catalog is 8 IRC's.

If you find it a thrill to order your posters from England, you can write to **POSTERS BY POST, LTD.**, WW, 43 Camden Passage, London N1 8EB, England, for their free brochure. There are engaging Veale animals for around $1.65 per poster, art nouveau posters for a little under $2.00, plus fairy tale posters, charts, photographs, all very reasonably priced. However, if you'd like to get your posters somewhat more rapidly, without having to worry about paying conversion charges on your checks, you can write to **POSTERS BY POST, LTD.**, WW, P.O. Box 798, Oak Park, Ill. 60302, for their free brochure. They have engaging Veale animals for around $1.75 per poster, art nouveau posters for a little over $2.00, charts, photographs, etc., all priced very little higher than their British cousins' merchandise.

POSTER ORIGINALS, LTD., WW, 16 East 78 St., New York, N.Y. 10021, sells limited editions of art posters, describing exhibits of such notables as Magritte, Dufy, Kandinsky, and so on. All are in full color, many are lithographs, some are silk-screened. Prices range from about $5.00 to $30.00. Brochure is free.

You'll find antique prints and posters offered by several of the houses in Chapter 15 (Collections), A.4; and modern ones at several of the houses in Chapter 22(A.2). Note Paperchase and Happy Things especially.

ALINARI BROTHERS, WW, 24 R. Lungarno Corsini, Florence, Italy, offer large (mostly 11" by 15") color reproductions of famous art works. In addition to the usual Giottos, Botticellis, and other name artists (not only Italians), there are some particularly nice Etruscan and Pompeiian frescoes. These are priced at around $2.00, and are available mounted on wood with gold-leaf borders for a little over $7.00. Also available are wooden triptychs and diptychs, with appropriate reproductions, from around $15.00 to $19.00; and alcohol-proof wooden trays ($9.00 to $12.00), with reproductions on them—for some reason the round trays, which are less expensive, are more effective than the rectangular. The catalog shows wooden boxes, bookends, and lamps (the reproductions are on the shades, and, since the bases are quite simple, the end result is a lot more attractive than you might expect—from $30.00 to $40.00); and some Christmas cards. The beautiful color catalog is free; it's in English; and the prices are given in dollars.

The **GREEN TIGER PRESS**, WW, 7458, La Jolla Blvd., La Jolla, Cal. 92037, sells full-color postcard-size reproductions of fairy tale and fantasy book illustrations by Arthur Rackham, Beatrix Potter, Howard Pyle, John A. Neill, and many others, at 20¢ to 30¢. The free brochure is unillustrated, but the names alone were enough to evoke the pictures for me, and perhaps for you. Most of the museum shops in the following section also sell reproductions.

B. MUSEUM SHOPS

Probably the most handsome and elaborate of all the catalogs put out by museums is the set published by the **METROPOLITAN MUSEUM OF ART**, WW, Box 255, Gracie Station, New York, N.Y. 10028, at 25¢ (coin) for each. One is their Christmas catalog. Last year it included a reproduction of a mid-eighteenth-century Meissen plate, at $18.00; reproductions of Early American blown and pressed glass—a pair of Sandwich glass dolphins are offered at $30.00; calendars, ancient jewelry (starting at around $7.00); and so on. There is also a catalog of "Museum reproductions"; their famous 8-inch blue faience ancient Egyptian hippopotamus, William, is $10.00; a nameless blue faience hippopotamus, half William's size, and very angry, is $5.00. Also $5.00 is a shawabti (Egyptian burial figure) almost 9" high. Then there's a charming 2-headed ancient Cypriote horse, under $5.50; an enchanting duck vase of similar provenance

is $10.00; a bronze Greek lion almost 3" high is under $13.00. A Greek silver-plate on pewter kylix (wine cup) is $23.00. In the higher price range is a gilded medieval bronze falcon mounted on a block of marble, $150.00. Another catalog features "Early American Silver," in sterling, from $7.50 for a teaspoon to $285.00 for a teapot. Still another catalog, called "Presents with a Past," has some reproduction sculpture, glass, and silver, plus notepaper, needlework kits, and two Shaker candle stands ($160.00 and $190.00). Finally, there is a catalog of slides.

As you can see, the Metropolitan has plunged whole-heartedly into the mail-order business, offering practically everything you need to furnish an Early American home or a tomb. The merchandise is rather expensive, however, and you may be able to do better (so far as price goes) elsewhere. (In some cases, originals cost very little more than the reproductions.) On the other hand, there are many items you may not be able to get elsewhere, and the catalogs are pretty.

The **BROOKLYN MUSEUM GALLERY SHOP**, WW, 188 Eastern Pkwy., Brooklyn, N.Y. 11238, puts out the most mouth-watering catalog of handicrafts from all around the world, offered at very reasonable prices. They practically never have the same thing twice, so please understand that I'm telling you about a few of the items they had last year only to give you an idea of the sort of thing they stock—miniature silver boxes from Cambodia, in the shapes of birds and animals, $7.00; a big wooden owl with a hook for hanging clothes, $6.00; a set of tiny wooden soldiers from Germany, $3.00; a straw egg with a parrot inside, from Ecuador, $2.00; a tapestry panel from Israel, $17.00; and so on. The catalog is 25¢, and if you see something you like, write fast; they sell out quickly.

The **MUSEUM OF FINE ARTS**, WW, Sales Desk, 474 Huntington Ave., Boston, Mass. 02115, offers a handsome selection of greeting cards; some very nice jewelry, mostly inexpensive ($3.00 to $10.00, although there are some costlier items); art match books, 25¢ to 35¢ for 6; needlepoint kits ($8.00 to $75.00); and sculpture reproductions. Also on hand are sterling silver reproductions of important pieces in the Museum's collection (a letter opener adapted from a Paul Revere skewer is around $12.00). The catalog is 25¢, which seems to be standard for most museum Christmas catalogs.

However, the Christmas card catalog put out by the **NATIONAL GALLERY OF ART**, WW, Washington, D.C. 20565, is free, and contains items just as nice as do the 25¢ catalogs. The Gallery also puts out a fat unillustrated catalog of their color reproductions (very inexpensive), postcards; slides; and a small selection of modestly priced jewelry (starting from $3.00), based mainly on sixteenth-century Italian originals from their own collection.

The **MUSEUM SHOP, PHILADELPHIA MUSEUM OF ART,** WW, P.O. Box 7646, Philadelphia, Pa. 19101; the **WALTERS ART GALLERY,** WW, 600 North Charles St., Baltimore, Md. 21201; and the **DETROIT INSTITUTE OF ARTS,** WW, 5200 Woodward Ave., Detroit, Mich. 48202; all put out attractive catalogs of Christmas cards and gifts for 25¢ each. Philadelphia also has needlepoint kits and gold- and silver-plated jewelry from $3.00 up. Walters offers art wrapping paper.

The **ATHENEUM SHOP,** WW, Wadsworth Atheneum, Hartford, Conn. 06003, puts out what is one of the nicest collections of Christmas cards I have ever seen, and I only wish they would show some of the other items they sell in their gift shop—if they're as well chosen as the cards, they should be a thoroughly delightful collection. The **NEW-YORK HISTORICAL SOCIETY,** WW, 170 Central Park West, New York, N.Y. 10024, offers an attractive group of Christmas cards, based on items in their collection. They also put out a catalog of prints, postcards, and publications. Both the Atheneum Shop's and the Historical Society's catalogs appear to be free. The Department of Publications, **HISPANIC SOCIETY OF AMERICA,** WW, 613 West 155 St., New York, N.Y. 10032, sells what I have just learned from their catalog is *realia*—notecards, postcards, color prints, and color slides—as well as various publications (many in Spanish). Catalog is free.

The **UNIVERSITY MUSEUM,** WW, 33rd and Spruce St., Philadelphia, Pa. 19104, puts out a handsome catalog of reproductions of art objects from the University Museum's archeological and ethnographic collections. There are masks, and primitive animals and figurines; as well as highly sophisticated artifacts from Africa, the Pacific, and the Americas; plus statuettes, figures, and bowls from India, ancient Egypt, Mesopotamia, the classical world, and ancient China. Unfortunately, prices have been inching up ever since I first wrote about them, but they're still good buys—most of the figurines cost from $10.00 to $20.00, although some start at less. Catalog is 50¢.

The **UNIVERSITY OF ALASKA MUSEUM,** WW, College, Alaska 99701, puts out a free price list describing its postcards, notecards, and slides, as well as the publications it issues.

If you are persistent, the **BRITISH MUSEUM PUBLICATIONS DEPT.,** WW, London, WC1, England, may send you their catalog of Christmas cards, postcards,

and slides (free, if you can get it); although if they're in a surly mood, they may try to fob you off with an American commercial source. There's a huge selection and they're merely listed, so you have to know what they're talking about. But after all, who can go wrong with "King Arthur Asleep on Board of a Ship," or "Expedition of the Duc de Bourbon to Barbary"? They also have little folders by which you can make any of their postcards into a Christmas card. (And then you can take it out and use it as a postcard—another ecological breakthrough!) The **VICTORIA AND ALBERT MUSEUM,** WW, South Kensington, London S.W.7, England, has some particularly nice buys. Reproductions of brass rubbings in the Museum are about 15¢ each; lithographic reproductions of picture sheets of (among others) women's costumes of the nineteenth century, a railway travelling chart, and a view of London, sell from 15¢ to 30¢ each. Price lists are free, and with them you'll get a list of publications that describes their color reproductions, picture books, postcards, books, and pamphlets (mainly on the decorative arts).

The **NATIONAL MUSEUM OF DENMARK,** WW, Oplysningsafdelingen NY Vestergade 10, 1471 Copenhagen K, Denmark, puts out a nice little free catalog showing some unusually interesting Bronze and Iron Age reproductions; as well as—as you might expect—some Viking period items, including some interesting jewelry, and a model of King Harold Bluetooth's runestone, which no desk should be without (there's one on my desk at this very minute).

SERVICES COMMERCIAUX DES MUSÉES NATIONAUX, WW, 10 rue de l'Abbaye, Paris 6e, France, will send you a list of color reproductions from the Louvre and other French museums. There are various sizes and qualities, and prices seem pretty reasonable. Sometimes you'll get illustrations, but sometimes there's just a list. You'll know the pictures, though. You can write to them in English, but if your letter requires an answer, it will be in French.

The preceding three catalogs are all free. In addition, you can get unillustrated free price lists of reproductions, postcards, slides, and publications from: The **NATIONAL MUSEUM OF WALES** (Amgueddfa Genedlaethol Cymru), WW, Cardiff CF1 3NP, United Kingdom; the **ROYAL SCOTTISH MUSEUM,** WW, Edinburgh 1, Scotland; **RIJKSMUSEUM** (Reproductieverkoop), WW, Amsterdam, Holland; **MUSEO DEL PRADO,** WW, Madrid, Spain; and **SZÉPMUVESZETI MÚZEUM,** WW, Dózsa György üt 41, Budapest 62.PF.463, Hungary. Almost all museums put out lists of their publications, so, if there's one you're particularly interested in, write to them!

C. HANDICRAFTS

There are numerous firms that specialize in the arts and crafts of a particular region, ranging from the practical to the decorative, the primitive to the sophisticated. Included will be paintings, carvings, masks, holiday decorations, tapestries, hangings, objets d'art or bric a brac (depending on how you look at them), and such functional items as jewelry, household items, and so on. Many of these will already have been described in previous chapters and, therefore, will be mentioned only briefly here, while others will be written up in some detail. Some of the items offered will be the equivalents of museum pieces; others will be of the strictly souvenir variety. To make it more convenient for you to track down specific types of work in specific areas I've grouped them according to the country of origin.

1. United States

MADE IN VERMONT, INC., WW, Box 67, Waitsfield, Vt. 05673, offers a group of items handmade by Vermont craftsmen. There's a lovely ice blue hand-blown glass globe for $75.00; charming wooden bottles, vases, and weed pots, $6.00 to $8.00; stone trivets in turquoise, tawny, white, and black, $4.00; a most appealing velvet unicorn, $20.00; a sculptured steel lantern that is more a work of art than mere indigenous American handicrafts—quilts from around and sometimes also useful things. Catalog is free.

HOME CO-OP, WW, Rte. 1, Orland, Me. 04472, was formed by the craftspeople of rural Maine working at the craft village they're developing called the Rural Life Center. They make patchwork, braided rugs, and Victorian print dresses, plus the distinctively American two-way dolls—Cinderella before and after; Red Riding Hood and her grandmother and, for a three-way surprise, the wolf. They're $10.00 each.

APPALACHIAN SPRING, WW, 1655 Wisconsin Ave. N.W., Washington, D.C. 20007, offers items created by craftsmen from the 16 Appalachian states. There are patchwork and handwoven items; stoneware pots; plaques; vases (a "lady lamp" is $18.00); cast aluminum mirrors that are also sculptures ($25.00 to $35.00); and some fascinating wind chimes. Catalog is $1.00.

OZARK OPPORTUNITIES, INC., WW, 707 North Vine, Box 400, Harrison, Ark. 72001, specializes in indigenous American handicrafts—quilts from around $16.00 for machine work, up to around $55.00 for all handmade; white oak baskets, from miniatures at less than $1.00 up to big picnic baskets for a little under $6.00. There are wooden items—a working miniature spinning wheel is under $8.00; a Georgia walking plow (not clear whether it is miniature or full size),

around $3.00; butter paddles, stirrers, and crochet hooks, all for less than $1.00 each, at least they were at the time of this writing. Prices have probably gone up considerably since this was an experimental project of the Office of Economic Opportunity.

Most of the Indian houses described elsewhere in this book (mainly in Chapters 3 and 17) offer Indian arts and crafts. Many are one-of-a-kind pieces of museum quality. Although the **TREASURE-HOUSE OF WORDLY WARES,** WW, Calistoga, Calif. 94514, does have folk art from all over the world, proprietor Stevie S. Whitefeather specializes in Indian art, both old and new, aimed primarily at the collector (but there are some inexpensive items always on hand). Various tribes are represented though not all are shown on the list. The list I saw included Navajo sandpaintings, from about $11.00 to $100.00; pottery from various pueblos (some signed by the maker); baskets from different tribes, many of museum quality (an Apache pitch-covered water storage jug was $200.00; a very old Paiute covered bowl basket was $85.00; others start at $15.00). There's also beadwork (some dating from the nineteenth century), and rugs and wall hangings ($35.00 to over $500.00). The lists are free, but there's a charge of 50¢ for each color photograph you request.

The **INDIAN HILLS TRADING POST,** WW, Indian Hills Reservation, P.O. Box 229, Petoskey, Mich. 49770, sells Indian work of the Ottawa and Chippewa or Ojibwa Indians. Much of it is of a souvenir nature, but charming nonetheless—like the barkwork canoes from 35¢ for a 3-inch model to $3.00 for a fancy 18-inch. There are also tiny tepees and totem poles, from 50¢ to $3.00. For the collector, there are porcupine quill on birch bark boxes, starting at $4.00; and, for everyone, a nice assortment of market and sewing baskets.

The **OKLAHOMA INDIAN MARKETING AGENCY, INC.,** WW, P.O. Box 4202, Tulsa, Okla. 74104, offers only items handcrafted by American Indians living in Oklahoma. There are ceramic bowls at $6.50 each, wood sculpture, and paintings. You have to send an additional $1.00 for color slides of these—the catalog itself is 25¢. The Marketing Agency is not to be confused with the **OKLAHOMA INDIAN ARTS AND CRAFTS COOP,** WW, P.O. Box 966, Anadarko, Okla. 73005, which, in addition to Indian crafts, sells prints and original paintings by Indian artists. The **CHEYENNE LODGE,** WW, Box 717, El Reno, Okla. 73036, is owned by the Indian artist, Jerome G. Bushyhead, and, in addition to costume items and craft supplies, offers paintings by Oklahoma Indian artists.

The two families comprising the lower St. Croix band of the Ojibwa Indians put out a small free brochure listing the items they offer for sale. They work in beads and buckskins, and they offer mostly items for ceremonial costumes plus some jewelry. Their address is **OJIBWA WIGWAM**, WW, Route 2, Luck, Wis. 54853.

Handsome handprinted textiles based on authentic Indian motifs are made by **NIZHONIE, INC.**, WW, 810½ N. Broadway, Box 729, Cortez, Colo. 81321, an Indian owned and operated firm. They also offer other Indian handcrafts. **QUALLA ARTS AND CRAFTS MUTUAL, INC.**, WW, P.O. Box 277, Cherokee, N.C. 28719, has some charming carved animals made from various woods, priced from $2.00 to several hundred dollars (most are less than $50.00); also some pleasing masks, priced mostly from $25.00 to $35.00. The best-known craft of the Cherokees, according to the brochure, is basket weaving, and a very handsome selection of baskets is offered, from $5.00 up. (There are also some miniatures under $1.00.) **SEMINOLE OKALEE INDIAN VILLAGE AND CRAFTS CENTER**, WW, 6073 Sterling Rd., Hollywood, Fla. 33024, offers some crafts, many of the souvenir type—miniature canoes and baskets—as well as full-sized baskets.

IROQRAFTS, WW, RR. 2 Ohsweken, Ontario, Canada, offers Iroquois water colors and paintings, Mohawk paintings and jewelry (more for ceremonial than casual use), carvings, and Eskimo art. Although they're aimed mostly at the serious collector (See Chapter 15), they also have lots of inexpensive but authentic souvenir items. Catalog is 25¢.

Other Indian firms that offer large craft selections are **DAKOTAH CRAFTS**, WW, 116 Oak St., P.O. Box 103, Sisseton, S.D. 57262; **SUPERNAW'S OKLAHOMA INDIAN SUPPLY**, WW, 301 East W. C. Rogers Blvd., Skiatook, Okla. 74070 (25¢); and **PEYE'SHA TRADERS**, WW, P.O. Box 765, Painesville, Ohio 44077 (25¢).

SUNARIT ASSOCIATES, INC., WW, P.O. Box 515, Nome, Alaska 99762, is a cooperative, formed in 1968 by the Eskimo families who formerly came from King Island (Alaska), as an outlet for the carvings they had been doing for most of their lives. The catalog shows some very handsome examples of native art in ivory, wood, and soapstone (with prices ranging from $9.00 to $270.00). In addition, there are some attractive block prints from $10.00 to $60.00. Also from Alaska, **KI-KIT-TA-MUET ARTS AND CRAFTS CO-OP**, WW, Shishmaref, Alaska 99772, issues a price list of ivory carvings and walrus

and sealskin products made by the people of Shismaref. Both brochures are free.

2. Mexico

YALALAG, WW, 104 Alcala St., P.O. Box 26, Oaxaca, Oax. Mexico, makes and sells pretty repoussé tinwork items painted in bright colors, at prices much lower than they'd sell for in the United States. Boxes go from a little over $1.00 to $2.00. There is a wonderful band of tin soldier musicians, each over 1' high, at $5.50 each; and some animals on rockers—including a deer and a lion as well as a horse—at a little over $1.00 each. Some large tin owls are $2.50 each. Also on hand are all kinds of other gay and festive things, a lot of them Christmas oriented. Prices are given in U.S. dollars and include postage, packing, and insurance (they say duty, if charges amount to around 8 percent). Brochures are free. The **CASA DE LAS ARTESIANAS** (see Chapter 5,A.5) also has lots of Mexican crafts.

Although the **HOUSE OF ONYX**, WW, Greenville, Ky. 42345, is an American firm, it sells Mexican natural onyx figurines and carvings at prices that are lower than some of the Mexican sources. Miniature animals start at less than 25¢. Other items found here include onyx fruits, idols, ashtrays, bookends, etc. There are also some Tonala Mexican ceramics. Lists are free.

3. Ecuador

AKIOS, WW, P.O. Box 219, Quito, Ecuador, offers an enormous selection of Ecuadorian handicrafts, including tree bark and wood tapestries (from $2.00); figurines carved out of orangewood, cedar, or walnut; wall masks, from $1.00; rugs from $50.00 . . . almost everything you can think of, at incredibly low prices. Catalog is $1.00. Other indigenous Ecuadorian work is available from **FOLKLORE**, WW, P.O. Box 69, Av. Colón 260, Quito, Ecuador; and **ANDEAN PRODUCTS**, WW, Apartado 472, Cuenca, Ecuador. Both catalogs are free.

4. Haiti

The **GEORGES NADER GALLERY**, WW, P.O. Box 962, 104 rue Bonne Foi, Port-au-Prince, Haiti, deals in the work, including painting and sculpture, of contemporary Haitian artists. There are also some indigenous crafts—masks, less than $25.00 postpaid; handsome decorative drums under $70.00, also postpaid. The catalog, in English, is free.

5. Europe

The **SCOTTISH CRAFT CENTRE**, WW, Acheson House, 140 Canongate, Edinburgh EH8 8DD, Scotland, specializes in the arts and crafts of that country. Baskets cost from less than $5.00 to around $10.00, Portjoy marble knicknacks start at $3.00. There are also some lovely ceramics and wooden items, silver, and so on. The catalog is free.

FERGUS O'FARRELL, WW, 24 Duke St., Dublin 2, Ireland, puts out a catalog of Irish craftwork designed and made in his workshops. There are handwrought copper plaques and figures, from around $9.00 to $150.00; bronze figures and carved wood panels starting at around $9.00; a few wooden household items in the modern manner; some attractive jewelry; candleholders, and so on. Free catalog.

The workshops of **OWEN IRISH CRAFTS**, WW, Ballyshannon, Ireland, sell their handmade reproductions of early Irish art forms in turf. I know it sounds peculiar, but the photographs in the handsome free brochure really are quite lovely. Some of them can be worn, as, for example, the Adam and Eve pendant (after the panel on the eighth-century cross of Muiredach, Monasterboice). It costs $4.25. There's a paperweight in the well-known Celtic zoomorphic design, at the same price; and a number of plaques, mainly in the $10.00 area. Most beautiful of all is the big wall plaque after the eighth-century Banacher slab in the National Museum, Dublin, for $37.00. Prices include shipping.

GUNNARSSONS TRÄFIGURER, WW, Drottninggatan 77 S-11160, Stockholm, Sweden, will send you a free list of the wooden figures they make—including country people, sailors, and fishermen, occupational figurines and famous people. Prices run from less than $5.00 to around $40.00 (mostly they're in the $10.00 range). Unfortunately, you'll have to use your imagination, because the list is unillustrated.

TIROLER HEIMATWERK, WW, Meraner Strasse 2, Innsbruck, Austria, shows an attractive selection of Austrian crafts in its delightful free catalog. There are some stunning religious and semi-religious figurines and, in addition to the usual *kitsch,* all kinds of copper and tin and brass and, most surprising (to me, anyway), grotesque (their word) folklore masks (very like the ones you'll see in the Asian and African catalogs), for under $40.00.

You can get a variety of Portuguese handicrafts from **MADEIRA SUPERBIA** (see Chapter 2,C.3). Tiles are less than $2.00; there are also Portuguese pottery, boxes, etc.

ATTIKA GIFTSHOPS, WW, 6 Karageorgi Servias St., Constitution Sq., Athens, Greece, offer what they say is the largest collection of Greek handicrafts in Athens. These include large (10″ to 12″ tall) lovely Archaic style Greek vases and pitchers, mostly from $15.00 to $20.00 (looking very like those you'll find in Chapter 15, and in better condition). Smaller ones

start at around $6.00. Handsome decorated copper amphorae and other urns around 1½′ tall are in the $30.00 to $35.00 price range. There is also all kinds of brass, including door knockers, ashtrays, coffee servers, candlesticks, etc., starting at around $3.00. Greek dolls are $3.00 to $12.00; 18-karat gold Hellenic jewelry starts at around $35.00 for a Byzantine cross. There's also costume jewelry, mainly gold-plated silver. The beautiful free color catalog is in English, and prices (in dollars) include postage and packing, a not inconsiderable expense in the case of the ceramics.

EPIROTAN ARTS, ANDREW HATZIS, WW, 8, Mayor G. Ioannios St., Ioannina, Greece, specializes in the traditional handicrafts of Epirus. Everything they put out seems to be beautiful. Most of the firm's work is in brass. Some stunning candlesticks are priced from around $2.00 to $6.00, and equally stunning candelabra are available in the $10.00 to $25.00 range. Particularly handsome are the ones based on Byzantine motifs. Traditional Kalamari inkstands cost less than $5.00; oil lamps cost from $2.00 to $15.00. Also on hand are some equally beautiful things in beaten copper—lamps, coffee and water pots, mugs, and so on—$2.00 to $7.00. The handsome catalog is free.

Although **SMALOTECHNIKI**, WW, 54 Korai St., Moschaton, Athens, Greece, is a wholesale house, the handmade ceramic coasters and wall plaques are so beautiful that I thought you'd like to know about them—and perhaps you'd be willing to meet their minimum of $45.00 for a mini sample collection. (That's a lot of coasters and wall plaques, considering how inexpensive they are—35¢ to around $1.25.) Classical Greek designs and folk art motifs are both shown in the tiny brilliant-hued free brochure.

6. The Middle East

The **GOOD SHEPHERD'S STORE**, WW, P.O. Box 96, Bethlehem/via Israel, manufactures and exports charming olivewood items, both secular and religious, from the Holy Land. There are appealing olivewood camels, from 7 to 25 cm. tall, plain and painted, priced from less than $1.00 to about $6.00. Complete olivewood nativity sets cost from less than $3.00 to around $9.00, depending on size and intricacy of workmanship. You'll also find olivewood crosses, figures, vases, candlesticks, and boxes at very low prices. Price list is free.

CHILINGURIAN and **NSEIR** (already described in Chapter 4,D) are both excellent sources of Lebanese handicrafts. Chilingurian specializes in leathergoods—hassocks and camel saddles cost from $6.00 to $15.00. Also on hand are some decorative mosaic boxes inlaid with mother-of-pearl, which are from around $6.00 to $14.00. **NSEIR** also has inlaid mosaic boxes. His (which come in smaller sizes) cost from about $2.00 to $6.00. He also offers small mosaic tables ($25.00 to $60.00), brasswork (lanterns are from $16.00 to $30.00), and very Arabic-looking coffee pots ($7.00 up). Available too, are vases, dishes, deeply engraved brass and copper trays ($35.00 to $40.00), and hookahs ($6.00 up).

7. The Far East

NATIONAL TRADING, LTD., WW, Teku, Kathmandu, Nepal, is a Nepalese government agency. They sent me a batch of free, unillustrated price lists. The items within are listed individually (rather than by the dozen) and priced in dollars, so I assume they will sell them on a retail basis, although I haven't been able to get them to commit themselves. They sell bronze figures of the gods, from around $4.00 to $100.00 (that's a 35-inch Badmapani Avalokiteswore). They also offer filigree jewelry, and khukries (Gurkha knives), from $2.00 to around $6.00. Ask for their handicrafts list; otherwise you're apt to get a list of something uninteresting like jute or plastic products (the strangest countries are into plastic these days).

The **NEPAL ART EMPORIUM PVT., LTD.,** WW, G.P.O. Box 101, Kathmandu, Nepal, also is ambiguous about its retail status; however, I believe that an *emporium* usually deals with individual retail customers, so I feel entitled to recommend their free lists to your attention. They have lots of items in what they call gold gilt, including an utterly endearing dragon mask at around $6.00, boxes, ashtrays, figurines, and utensils—a teapot is less than $5.00, holy water jars start at around $8.00. There's a lot of lovely, inexpensive jewelry, in silver metal with real turquoise and coral; in real silver it's a lot more expensive. In copper, there are prayer wheels from around $1.00 up, plus some stunning Tibetan ceremonial pipes. For around $28.00 you can buy an absolutely gorgeous Tibetan tea kettle. There are also loads and loads of bronze figures of deities, prepared by the lost wax method, from around $4.00 up. Both Nepalese catalogs are in English, as are the Indian ones that follow.

BENGAL HOME INDUSTRIES, WW, 57 Chowringhee Rd., Calcutta 16, India, offers some particularly impressive statues of deities in Dokra brass artware, about $9.00 to $11.00 for a 10"-11" size. There are painted wooden and clay toys that are really works of art, most of them less than $1.00. Equally appealing are the painted pith toys, and the collection of papier mâché masks and gods is most engaging. The beautiful color catalog is free, but is in very limited supply.

The **KAVERI MYSORE STATE HANDICRAFTS DEVELOPMENT CORP., LTD.,** WW, 26/45 Mahatma Gandhi Rd., Bangalore-1, India, offers a large variety of "Choicest Handicrafts for Elegance and Grace, Rhythm and Tranquility." They include sandalwood, rosewood, and teakwood carvings; ivory; lacquerware; papier mâché; horn; and metalware—bronze and brass masks cost from $4.00 up, religious figures from $8.00 up. At the **LEPAKSHI HANDICRAFTS EMPORIUM,** WW, Gunfoundry, Hyderabad, India, you will find Bidriware (inlaid metal); Nirmal artware (painted wood); silver filigree from Karimnagar; Perambarti brassware; Eluru and Warangal carpets; and Kalamkari printed cloth. Religious figures (Buddha, Parvathi, etc.) in the exquisite Bidriware are from $5.00 to $15.00. An ivory Lakshmi is about $20.00. Both offer handsome illustrated catalogs without cost.

ARTS AND CRAFTS, WW, 6 Leyden Baston Rd., Colombo 1, Sri Lanka (Ceylon), has some handsome, inexpensive Ceylonese crafts. Lots of nice wooden animals, including stunning cats with moonstone eyes, start at less than $1.00, and cost only a few dollars for the biggest. Other wooden animals go up to $20.00, but most are under $5.00. Horn birds are between $1.00 and $2.00. You'll see lots of nice things in copper, silver, and tortoise shell at equally attractive prices; and some splendid leering devil masks beginning as low as $1.00. The **SERENDIB GALLERY,** WW, 100 Galle Rd., Colombo 4, Sri Lanka, also offers demon masks, from around $2.50 up. (The cheapest is the one for Ginijal Raksa, the demon of fear and shivering.) Palm leaf pictures (from around $8.00), copperware plaques, batik wall hangings, wood carvings, and all manner of lovely things are also sold. Both catalogs are illustrated and free.

The **DEPARTMENT OF SMALL INDUSTRIES,** WW, Hemas Building, Bristol St., Colombo 1, Sri Lanka, is another government agency that isn't clear about its retail status. They have an unillustrated (free) price list of masks described in a most alluring manner. For instance, the Maru Raksha mask, as worn in the "Kolam" folk plays, consists of a "grotesque demon's face with a peacock carried on each ear," and a "human form . . . between the large teeth." It's around $23.00. Other masks start at around $5.00.

There are a number of good sources in Thailand. All brochures are in English and give prices in dollars. **HARPENG LIANG,** WW, P.O. Box 1765, Bangkok, Thailand, offers a variety of Thai handicrafts—buffalo horn and wood carvings, as well as some niello jewelry and bronzeware. Send 3 IRCs for the brochure (and don't forget to seal the envelope well; otherwise they have been known to be removed). Catalogs from the following firms are free. **NARAYANA PHAND,** WW, Thai Handicrafts Center, 275/2 Larn Luang Rd., Bangkok, has all kinds of items in carved teak, as well as temple rubbings and hangings. **SILK OF SIAM,** WW, 297 Suriwongse Rd., G.P.O. Box 1802, Bangkok, presents a beautiful line of Thai handicrafts in its handsome catalog; however, prices seem a little higher than at the other Thai houses. The **THAI CELADON CO., LTD.,** WW, G.P.O. Box 869, Bangkok (its catalog is described in more detail in Chapter 8), offers all kinds of beautiful celadon objects, including small animal figures, starting at around $2.00. A delightful bullfrog is $5.00; larger figures go up to $50.00 or $60.00. There are nice garden lanterns, too. **RAMA JEWELRY,** WW, 987 Silom Rd., Bangkok, offers Thai handicrafts as well as jewelry.

8. The Orient

The **HAKUSUI IVORY CO., LTD.,** WW, Yokohama Port, P.O. Box 40, Yokohama, Japan, will send you a free catalog showing a handsome collection of ivory carvings. Some of the ivory is in its natural color, but more of it is painted. Charming netsukes start at around $8.00 or so, and go up to $60.00; over that, you can get them custom-made to your own desires. I particularly like "monster, assorted designs, our choice" ($9.00). There are animals of all kinds, masks, people, and so on, also over 50 different kinds of birds, ranging from about $5.00 for a one-incher up to $100.00 for a 5-inch hawk. There are statues of gods, men, and geishas that start under $20.00 and go on up to many hundreds. Also on hand are carved flowers and fruit . . . jewelry, too.

KOREAN HANDICRAFTS, INC., WW, I.P.O., Box 3967, Seoul, Korea, makes and sells handsome stone carvings that look like antiques. There are attractive animals—lions, temple dogs, and the most appealing curly dragons, from less than $3.00 up to over $100.00. A plain, very good-looking teapot costs around $5.00, and a dragon pot is about $28.00 (dragons do seem to come higher). There are inkstands, from less than $1.00 to $45.00 for one with double dragons; incense burners (the four-dragon one is the nicest); vases; and lots of chess sets, from around $4.00 up. Catalog is free, prices are in dollars, and remember, these will be very heavy to ship.

The **CHINA REFUGEE DEVELOPMENT ORGANIZATION,** WW, P.O. Box 5861, Kowloon, Hong Kong, was originally organized in 1954 by the refugee and migration section of the U.S. State Department. Now, the managing director says, they are standing "on our own two feet." He says: "At the present time we are supporting 196 families here in Hong Kong by giving them work to do in handicrafts." The work they do is very lovely. Chinese paintings on silk scrolls and pa-

per scrolls, as well as mounted flat on wood panels, cost from less than $2.00 up to around $7.00. There are also very inexpensive handblocked greeting cards; and bronzeware, including a reproduction of an ancient "Wine kettle" ($9.00) and a knocker in the shape of a grinning face ($5.00). Prices are in dollars.

The **TSANG KING KEE IVORY FACTORY,** WW, 23 Wyndham St., Hong Kong, displays its lovely ivory wares in a handsome free catalog. Figurines represent the bulk of the items shown; there are also jewelry, chess sets, and knicknacks. As an example of the modest prices—the god of magic is about $4.00 in the 4-inch size, going up to around $130.00 for one 15 inches tall (9 other sizes in between).

Sources in Taiwan include the **TAIWAN HANDICRAFT PROMOTION CENTER,** WW, P.O. Box 1337, Taipei, Taiwan, which has been more fully described in Chapter 13,B.1. They offer some stunning jade carvings—an 11-inch antique style beast is about $65.00; a 10-inch unicorn is $120.00. There are lions, tigers, sheep, horses, elephants, buffalos, and some plain interesting shapes. (They also have some very inexpensive handicrafts, which I haven't gone into because of the high minimums.)

9. Oceania and Australia

ALIPIO'S PIONEER CURIO SHOP, WW, P.O. Box 96, 153 Kennon Rd., Camp 7, Bagnio City, Philippines, specializes in decorative woodcarvings. Most of the statuettes seem designed to appeal to Europeanized tastes, but there are a few that have a strong indigenous feeling. I like best their wooden salad bowls, plates, trays, and nut dishes. Salad bowl sets consist of 1 big bowl, 6 small bowls, and a salad fork and spoon; and are priced from $6.00 up. Most plates cost less than $1.00 each. There are nice, solid wooden fruits and vegetables at very low prices, and lots of lovely cats from 6" to 18" tall, mostly under $2.00. The catalog is free. **TESORO'S** (see Chapter 2,E.3) also offers an extensive line of lovely Philippine handicrafts.

The **ARGYLE ARTS CENTER,** WW, 18 Argyle St., Sydney 2000, N.S.W., Australia, specializes in Australian and New Guinean primitive art. Bark paintings start at $45.00; wooden *coolamons* (aboriginal carrying bowls), from $35.00; New Guinea masks, from around $150.00. In addition, they have work by leading non-aboriginal Australian artists. **QUEENSLAND ABORIGINAL CREATIONS,** WW, 135-147 George St., Brisbane 4000, Queensland, Australia, also sells bark paintings, but these begin at a modest $5.00. Also on hand are message sticks, *nulla nullas* (clubs), shields, spears, *wannereds* (bullroarers), *woomeras* (throwing sticks), and boomerangs ($1.00 up)—all of these both plain and decorated. They also have *churingas* (totems) and shell necklaces; and, if you buy a boomerang you get a copy of "Boomerang Throwing Made Easy." The **DEPARTMENT FOR COMMUNITY WELFARE,** WW, P.O. Box 39, Rundle St., Adelaide 5000, Australia, also puts out a price list of aboriginal handicrafts. Their boomerangs, carved from the boughs of the *myall* or *mulga* tree, cost from around $3.00 to $10.00. They also have spears and *woomeras, waddies* (clubs), message sticks, and shields, all in the $3.00 to $15.00 price range. Bark paintings, costing from $5.00 to $75.00 are, the list says, "particularly fine examples of Aboriginal art." All three brochures are free, and all three are in Australian dollars, which look like American dollars, but are worth a lot more, so be careful.

10. Africa

INKENTAN CRAFTS, LTD., WW, P.O. Box 1356, Nairobi, Kenya, offers all sorts of wooden items carved in ebony by the "peasant artists" of the Makunde tribe, no two alike (carvings, that is). The abstract carvings are, the firm says, more truly representative of the Makunde sculpture than the naturalistic figurines made to please European taste. There are also Akambe and Wakamba carvings (which may be the same thing, the catalog doesn't make it clear). Prices begin at around $2.00 and go up to $90.00 or more for the really impressive "family logs." Masks here are especially handsome, costing from around $8.00 up. Also available are pleasing banana leaf pictures mounted on plywood, and very inexpensive and attractive banana skin animals ($3.00 up); also batik hangings, jewelry, baskets, and mats. Price lists are free, and you may be lucky enough to get the very handsome catalog free, too, though you'd better not count on it.

STUDIO ARTS 68, WW, P.O. Box 7904, Nairobi, Kenya, which has been described in more detail elsewhere, offers an impressive collection of African art. There are cooking utensils (more to be used as containers than to cook in), weapons, ceramics, and other sculpture, which is merely mentioned in the free lists.

African woodcarvings, most reasonably priced, are available from the oddly named (in view of the wares they offer) **COAST DRAPERS,** WW, P.O. Box 84026, Mombasa, Kenya. Carvings for the most part are the kind you often see here, but are sold at remarkably low prices. Animals start under $1.00, with few over $2.00; masks are $1.00 to $2.00; also on hand are some very inexpensive small drums. Catalog is free.

LA ROSE D'IVOIRE, WW, P.O. Box 8001, Abidjan, Ivory Coast, Africa, issues a lovely catalog in English, French, German, and Spanish (the local European tongue is French), showing 151 pieces of distinguished African art from which you can choose an approximation of what you want; it can't be identical, because every piece is made individually. Since this came in at the last moment, I haven't had a chance to write to ask if they could give me approximate price ranges. Some of the wooden figures are very similar to the museum reproductions offered by the University of Pennsylvania museum (see Section B); however, these are not reproductions—they are the real thing. Also shown are bronze and ivory figurines and jewelry, exciting masks in both bronze and wood, and some musical instruments. The drums are really exciting as art works—the two they show are intricately carved, and one is borne on the head of a small crouching figure; the other has legs made of long-suffering heads. There are also shirts (*dashikis*) and dresses in exquisite patterns; and some equally lovely unidentified textiles (I can't tell whether they're hangings or robes). Sources are not only the Ivory Coast but Dahomey, the Upper Volta, Mali, and Gabon. I assume that the catalog is free.

Remember: *Write for the catalog first.* All prices given were valid only at the time of writing and probably have been changed.

Chapter 12

BOOKS AND MAPS

A. OVERSEAS SOURCES

There was a time when you could save money by buying books from England, and other overseas countries. However, what with inflation, the decline of the American dollar, and the proliferation of discount sources, it no longer pays to order from abroad if all you're interested in doing is saving money. However, the British booksellers are still good sources of supply for books that for one reason or another you are unable to get here, as well as for special editions. I've also found that it often doesn't take any longer for a book to come from an English firm than from a U.S. dealer—and it's not that the British are so outstandingly efficient, either.

Here are two good British sources, both located, you will note, in university towns. **BLACKWELL'S,** WW, 48-51 Broad St., Oxford, England, says it serves 100,000 customers in all parts of the world, offering books on virtually all topics and in virtually all languages. If they don't have a book in stock, they'll order it for you, but they warn that it can take publishers "anything from four days to four weeks to supply us with the books that we order, or even longer if a publisher is in the throes of computerization." (Maybe that's what's wrong with our publishers.) Write for their general catalog of books new and forthcoming, which will include a card listing the various specialized catalogs they issue (over 90 of them). It's free, and so are the specialized ones. **W. HEFFER AND SONS, LTD.,** WW, 20 Trinity St., Cambridge CB2 3NG, England, offer to supply any book, if available anywhere in the world. They, too, put out regular catalogs on various subjects. Send for their free brochure, which also gives a list so you can check off the catalogs (all free) that you want.

Then there's Foyle's. . . . **W. & G. FOYLE, LTD.,** WW, 119-125 Charing Cross Rd., London, W.C.2, England, has always modestly billed itself as "the world's greatest bookshop," and probably it does have more books (cunningly concealed on the premises) than any other store. The trick, of course, is to get at them, for their mail-order service, as I point out feelingly in Chapter 14, leaves much to be desired. However, their catalogs are free.

An interesting source that's both overseas and down under is **DAVID'S,** WW, 214 Kitchener Rd., Milford, Auckland 9, New Zealand. Naturally you'd expect to find books by New Zealand authors and about New Zealand here, and you do; however, there are lots of general things at reasonable prices, which you might just happen to be interested in. The list is free.

A fine South American source is **CASA PARDO,** WW, Casilla 3587, Correo Central, Buenos Aires, Argentina. Founded in 1892, this firm is one of Argentina's oldest and largest bookstores and publishers. A huge assortment of books, both old and new, in Spanish, is on hand here. The catalogs are free.

B. LOCAL SOURCES

In the main, however, you can order foreign-language books locally. You can order German books from **BREMEN HOUSE** (Chapter 7,A.2) or from **ADLER'S FOREIGN BOOKS, INC.,** WW, 162 Fifth Ave., New York, N.Y. 10010. Adler's also carries French, Spanish, and Italian books. Books about mainland China (as well as "The Third World") are available from **CHINA BOOKS,** WW, 95 Fifth Ave., New York, N.Y. 10003. Soviet-oriented Russian books can be obtained from the **FOUR CONTINENT BOOK CORP.,** WW, 156 Fifth Ave., New York, N.Y. 10010, which also carries books from other Iron Curtain countries. For Russian books of all persuasions, from publishers all over the world, send for the catalog put out by **VOLGA RUSSIAN BOOKS,** WW, 77-11 169 St., Flushing, N.Y. 11366. The catalog is in Russian, transliterated into the Roman alphabet, with some English interspersed. Catalogs from all the foregoing are free. However, if you want Polish books, the catalog put out by **KSIEGARNIA LUDOWA,** WW, 5347 Chene St., Detroit, Mich. 48211, will cost you 25¢. (I got a free Polish newspaper with mine, though.) The **MEXICAN BOOK SERVICE,** WW, St. Peters, Pa. 19470, puts out a free list of U.S. publishers' books on Mexico. And, if you send them 15¢, **CYCO,** WW, 25 East 78 St., New York, N.Y. 10021, will send you a list of Yiddish books.

C. DISCOUNTS

A lot of bookdealers offer discounts on regular trade books, but the **DAVID CARIN CO.,** WW, 515 Silver

S.W., Albuquerque, N.M. 87102, offers to give you discounts not only on the books of all publishers in English, Spanish, French, Italian, German, and Russian but on scientific, technical, and reference works as well (10 percent on $5.00 or less, 15 percent on $5.01 to $20.00, 20 percent on $20.01 to $50.00—by arrangement over that). They also handle music of all publishers at similar discounts. Lists are free.

PUBLISHERS CENTRAL BUREAU, WW, 33-20 Hunters Point Ave., Long Island City, N.Y. 11101; and **MARBORO BOOKS,** WW, 205 Moonachie Rd., Moonachie, N.J. 07074, both offer a large selection of remaindered books on many subjects, at discounts that are often fantastic. Prices are the same when the books are the same, but they offer different selections. Publishers Central offers a shade better service.

D. SPECIALIZED BOOKS

Usually you'll find specialized books listed under the area of specialty, which is one reason why this chapter is so skinny. Most of the American Indian firms sell books (and records) pertaining to the American Indian. Then there's **AMERICAN INDIAN BOOKS,** WW, P.O. Box 683, Athens, Ala. 35611, which puts out a free list of Indian books. **MANY SMOKES,** WW, P.O. Box 5895, Reno, Nev. 89503, also offers a list of Indian books. It costs 50¢, but, along with it you get a copy of their fascinating magazine.

BOOKS AND THINGS, WW, 117 Lenox Ave., New York, N.Y. 10026, specializes in black history and Islamic literature.

Specialized books are also listed in the following chapters: Gardening (10), Nutrition (7), Music (13), the Theater (13), the Occult (14), Arts and Crafts (17, 18, 19), and Animals (21). The museum shops listed in 11 all have publications pertaining to their particular areas.

The **MERRIMACK PUBLISHING CORP.,** WW, 85 Fifth Ave., New York, N.Y. 10003, puts out an ir-

resistible catalog featuring children's books reproduced in full color from the antique originals. There are books by Kate Greenaway ($1.25 to $3.00); anonymous books like *The Troubles and Trials of Wandering Bunny* (90¢); anthologies such as *Holly Berries* ($2.70); Beatrix Potter classics ($1.85 each); the Caldecott picture books; and many, many others. Several of the books come with companions—there's a book and mouse (stuffed) set, a *Pinocchio* with a wooden puppet, etc. There are also miniature books, books in cut-out shapes, theater books, and greeting cards and postcards based on antique originals. Catalog is 25¢.

The **COLES PUBLISHING CO., LTD.,** WW, 90 Ronson Dr., Rexdale, Ontario, Canada, offers a free catalog of its Canadiana collection—exact replicas of rare old Canadian books. Most are available paperbound; a few hardcovers are included as well. Among the books . . . *The History of the Indian Nations of Canada* (1747), the *Iroquois Book of Rites* (1883), *The Narratives of Fugitive Slaves in Canada* (1856), *Canadian Savage Folk* (1896), *The Canadian Naturalist* (1840), and so on. Prices start at $2.50.

E. RELATED ITEMS

Old maps will be found in Chapter 15 (Collections). A modern mapseller is the **HAMMOND MAP STORE,** WW, 1 East 43 St., New York, N.Y. 10017, which offers free catalogs of its own publications: "U.S.G.S. Topographical Index," "Cleartype Sales Maps," "H.O. Nautical Charts and Publications," "State Maps," and "Globes." **HUBBARD,** WW, P.O. Box 105, Northbrook, Ill. 60062, puts out a collection of over 300 large raised relief maps, each representing a key area of the U.S. mainland, Alaska, and Hawaii. Each one is about 22" x 33" and costs approximately $10.00.

For bookplates: are available from the **ANTIOCH BOOKPLATE CO.,** WW, Yellow Springs, Ohio 45387; and **BERLINER AND MCGINNISS,** WW, Nevada City, Cal. 95959.

Remember: *Write for the catalog first.* All prices given were valid only at the time of writing and probably have been changed.

Chapter 13
MUSIC AND THE THEATER

A. GENERAL

The **SAM ASH MUSIC CORP.**, WW, 301 Peninsula Blvd., Hempstead, N.Y. 11550, was founded by the bandleader Sam Ash in 1924, and bills itself as "the complete music store." In stock, the brochure (10¢) says, are almost 40,000 different titles of sheet music, including instrumental, vocal, band, and orchestral. They also sell all the instruments they can lay their hands on, from harmonicas to Moog synthesizers, with all name brands included. Discounts are offered, too, though it's not clear whether they are on everything or just selected items. If you're musically inclined, it might be worth your while to investigate.

BLACKWELL'S (See Chapter 12,A) has a separate music shop, which carries not only music and music books but records as well. Write for the specific catalog for the area in which you're interested; general music books; piano and organ music; instrumental music; orchestral music; operas and oratorios; solo, madrigal, and folk music; and gramophone records. All catalogs are free.

B. INSTRUMENTS AND KITS

1. Folk and Popular

KOCH RECORDERS, WW, Haverhill, N.H. 03765, offers a little brochure of its own recorders in cocobolo wood or native black cherry, priced from $10.00 to $100.00. The **RECORDER CENTER**, WW, Amenia, N.Y. 12501, has many brochures describing various kinds of imported records, as well as a big list of music to be played on the recorder (also catalogs of music for antique woodwinds). All this literature is free.

HERE, INC., WW, 410 Cedar Ave., Minneapolis, Minn. 55404, specializes in made-to-order folk instruments, as well as kits for making them yourself. You can get banjos and bancimers (dulcimer-fretted banjos), at $25.00 to $50.00 for kits, $50.00 to $90.00 for instruments; dulcimers, $20.00 to $50.00 for kits, $50.00 to $90.00 for instruments; psalteries, $20.00 to $25.00 per kit, $40.00 to $50.00 per instrument; and thumb pianos (Western versions of the most popular West African instrument, also known as *sansa, mbira, kilimba* and *likembe*), in kit form only, at

around $5.00. Most of the instruments and kits are available in a choice of woods. Complete instructions are included with all kits. Also available are spare parts and music books. Prices include shipping; and catalog is free.

The **HUGHES CO.**, WW, 8665 West Thirteenth Ave., Denver, Colo. 80215, will sell you a balalaika kit for as low as $9.00 (the same instrument in finished form will cost you $37.00). They also have dulcimer kits, beginning at the same price and going up to $65.00 for the double or courting dulcimer—"no chaperon was needed as long as the sound of the dulcimer was heard" (kit is $27.00). There are also, in both kit and complete form, Irish harps, sitars, guitars, even lyres. This may be one of the few places you can buy a primolin—a one-string violin training instrument; they also have *kilimbas*—large thumb pianos, which have, the firm declares, "a rich thumping sound." (These can be electrified at a considerable surcharge.) Brochure is free.

The **STRING SHOP**, WW, 8432 High Ridge Rd., Ellicott City, Md. 21043, sells dulcimers and dulcimer kits. Prices start at $8.00 for a kit to make a dulcimer "suitable for ladies and children with small laps," and go up to $85.00 for their best finished dulcimers. There are also psalteries and psaltery kits ($16.00 to $50.00), banjos and bancimers, and kits thereof ($25.00 to $85.00), thumb pianos (they've got one more name, *lilimba*), and mouth bows. Other dulcimer sources are the **ORANGE COUNTY DULCIMER WORKS**, WW, R.R. #3, Paoli, Ind., which sells two different models in three different kinds of wood, at prices ranging from $40.00 to $70.00; and **CAPRI-TAURUS**, WW, P.O. Box 153, Felton, Cal. 95018, which sells dulcimers at $55.00 to $150.00 (custom models come higher), and accessories, including dulcimer books and records. Both brochures are free.

The **STEWART-MacDONALD MANUFACTURING CO., INC.**, WW, P.O. Box 900, Athens, Ohio 45701, sells banjos ($15.00 to $400.00) and banjo parts. Catalog is 25¢.

HUGH MacPHERSON, LTD., WW, 17 West Maitland St., Edinburgh EH12 5ER, Scotland, is well known throughout the world for his bagpipes, which cost from about $115.00 up to $500.00 (for a set full mounted in chased or engraved silver). For indoor playing there's a miniature set for $60.00; and the practice set at $27.00 is considered good enough for beginners. Also on hand are chanters, accessories, and bagpipe music, as well as drum music.

WALTON'S MUSICAL INSTRUMENT GALLERIES, LTD., WW, Dublin, Ireland, specializes in Irish harps, starting from around $175.00 for the three-quarter size ballad harp, to a top of around $550.00 for the deluxe bardic traditional. They also offer Brian Boru knee harps, for a little under $300.00. Harp strings and other accessories, as well as music books and sheet music (not just for harps, but other instruments), songbooks, and Irish records can also be found here. If you want Irish bagpipes, they sell three-drone models from around $55.00 to $250.00. Prices are given in American dollars.

The **ACCORDION CORPORATION OF AMERICA,** WW, 5585 West Belmont Ave., Chicago, Ill. 60641, sells imported accordions at what they claim are low prices. Brochures are free.

The **TAIWAN HANDICRAFT PROMOTION CENTER,** WW, 11-2 Foo Chow St., Taipei, Taiwan, wants you to buy at least $500.00 of goods from each of their brochures, or else an additional $15.00 is required, in addition to the cost of shipping and insurance. Even so, I imagine they would want you to place a relatively substantial order, which is why I haven't included too many of their other brochures elsewhere in the book. (It's $500.00 for each category, or there might not be any problem.) However, the musical instruments are so interesting, I thought I'd describe them, and perhaps you would like to form an orchestra, a rather large orchestra, because the instruments are so inexpensive. A butterfly lute is around $25.00; moon lutes, $3.00 to $4.00; balloon guitars are around $9.00; temple blocks, $3.00; gongs, about $2.25; ceremonial drums around $4.50; panpipes (really huge—and elaborate), a little over $10.00. Remember, if you get up an order that large, shipping is going to cost a lot. Brochures seem to be free.

Many of the firms mentioned throughout the book offer native instruments. **AKIOS** (Chapter 3,A) has native Jibaro drums, Jibaro flutes, and maracas, all very cheap. (On the same page, they also offer authentic blowguns, with quivers and darts, but you supply your own poison.) Didgeridoos, the only true musical instruments (a wind) known to the Australian aborigines are available from the **DEPARTMENT FOR COMMUNITY WELFARE** and **QUEENSLAND** (see Chapter 11,C.9). And, if you have always wanted a snake charmer's flute, you can get it from the

SERENDIB GALLERY for less than $3.00, but, mind you, there are no guarantees. (You can find antisnakebite kits offered at many of the firms in Chapter 20.)

Many of the American Indian firms (Chapter 3,A.1) offer native instruments, and **SANTA FE DRUMS,** WW, P.O. Box 2522, Santa Fe, N.M. 87501, offers drums made by the Taos Indians. Prices range from around $81.00 for the 23-inch size to $130.00 for the 30-inch drum. Price list is free.

2. Classical

GURIAN, LTD., WW, Canal St., Hinsdale, N.H. 03451, makes and sells classical steel-string guitars, which are warranted to the original owner for life. Prices range from $350.00 to $570.00, and all sorts of accessories are included. The catalog is free, and, for those who like to know the people they're dealing with, there are two photographs, one of Gurian's entire staff, clothed; another of Gurian's male staff in the nude (but copping out by the discreet use of guitars).

If you're looking for an authentic, beautifully handcrafted Renaissance instrument, write to the **RENAISSANCE GILDE,** WW, Cambridge, Wis. 53523, for their free brochure. Three qualities of lutes and theorbos are offered, and none of them is inexpensive. The lowest price is $550.00 (without case), the highest is $1475.00, and special orders may go even higher. However, the instruments are guaranteed without time limit, and your old lute may be accepted in trade. Another source for instruments of an earlier age is **J. WITCHER,** WW, P.O. Box 552, Forestville, Cal. 95436, which sells mediaeval, Renaissance, and baroque instruments, at somewhat more modest prices. These include keyboard instruments—harpsichords, spinets, virginals, and clavichords (priced from $275.00 up); stringed instruments—gigues, citterns, hurdy gurdies, etc. ($75.00 up); and woodwinds—krumhorns, flutes, calumeaux, etc. (from $5.00). If you're a craftsperson as well as a musician, you can save yourself a bundle by buying their instruments in kit form.

SCHERL AND ROTH, INC., WW, 1729 Superior Ave., Cleveland, Ohio 44114, puts out a handsome catalog of their build-your-own Stradivarius (or Guarnerius) violin kits, at prices starting at around $90.00. You also can buy the parts individually, if you want to repair your violin. They also sell books on how to make and repair violins. The **INTERNATIONAL VIOLIN CO.,** WW, 414 E. Baltimore St., Baltimore, Md. 21202, sells not only violins, violas, cellos, and basses, but guitars, accessories, and strings for all, plus instrument kits and a complete line of woods and tools for violin makers. Both catalogs are free. Also coming up with a free price list is **CASCADE MUSICRAFT**, WW, Box 403, Maple Valley, Wash. 98038, which sells floor standards for violincellos, from around $31.00.

The venerable firm of **H. L. WILD**, WW, 510 East 11 St., New York, N.Y. 10009, offers free price lists of material for making Spanish guitars and banjos (also adaptable to *bouzoukis*). They also have a special list of tools for repairing and building not only guitars, but violins, cellos, and double basses, which they will part with for the sum of 25¢.

Well known for their harpsichords are **ROBERT MORLEY AND CO., LTD.**, WW, 4 Belmont Hill, Lewisham, London S. E. 13, England. In addition, they sell clavichords, virginals, and harps, as well as accessories and books, plus some antique instruments. Normally I wouldn't recommend instruments of this size to be shipped from overseas, because they fall into the category of furniture (see Chapter 1). However, Morley has made arrangements with a shipper, who will not only crate and pack your harpsichord, but will act as customs broker for you (even unpack it for you, should you desire). Moreover, the estimated charges for this service are given in a separate brochure, which comes included with your catalog (both free), so that you can tell in advance approximately what the whole deal is going to cost you.

The **GREGOIRE HARPSICHORD SHOP**, WW, Charlemont, Mass. 01339, is a source of the well-known Sassman harpsichords. Their brochure is free but I warn you that, if you send for it, you're likely to get letters from musicians in your area offering to sell you slightly used Sassmans.

3. Mechanical

The **PLAYER PIANO CO., INC.**, WW, 620 East Douglas, Wichita, Kan. 67202, has, it says, the largest stock of player piano rolls in the world at the lowest prices (starting from $1.70). They also have rolls for coin-operated pianos. In addition, there are all kinds of parts and supplies for your player piano, including straight nipples, flanged elbows, and leather nuts. They take a warm interest in the health of your piano, and the catalog (free) includes a number at which the proprietor may be reached day or night. (I wouldn't be surprised if they even made house calls in the area.)

The one thing they don't seem to carry is the player piano itself. For that you'll have to get in touch with **MEKANISK MUSIK MUSEUM**, WW, Vesterbrogade 150, Copenhagen, Denmark, which specializes in cylinder and disc music boxes, organettes, player pianos, coin-operated electric pianos, orchestrions, portable handcranked organs, fair ground and dance organs, and other automatic musical instruments. Prices may be low for this type of merchandise, but this is not an inexpensive type of merchandise. For instance, one of the lower-priced items is $400.00. Prices go all the way up to $7000.00 for a Lösche Titania Orchestrion. Most of the items are old, but a few are modern reproductions. These include handcrafted copies of nineteenth-century automata, set on music boxes, at $300.00 to $500.00. The firm supervises the crating and shipping of all its instruments "to any destination in the world." As a matter of fact, the larger pieces shown in the catalog are located all over the world, many in the United States, so shipping might be the least of your problems. The firm's large, glossy catalog, *Mekanisk Musik Museum Review,* in English, with prices in American dollars, costs $2.00, but you may subscribe to 6 issues for $5.00.

Music boxes and musical movements are obtainable from many of the firms already described in these pages; and some firms feature musical gifts. For example, the **MILL SHOP**, WW, 123 Rokin, Amsterdam, Holland, puts out free price lists in American dollars for their musical windmills, which range from around $14.00 to $36.00, depending on size. They also have larger windmills of some material they do not identify (there are no pictures to give any clues), which not only play music while the sails turn (the others do, too), but light up as well. They cost from about $17.00 to $35.00. Shipping and insurance are included.

E.S.G. BEAVEN, WW, "Swiss Chalet," Hawkcombe, Porlock, nr. Minehead, Somerset, England, makes with his or her own hand some utterly enchanting miniature (mostly 7½" x 3½" x 3½") reproductions of old English chests, fitted with music boxes, and priced from around $12.00 to $35.00. They used to be available without musical movements, as well, and, although the brochure (send 3 **IRC**s to get it) doesn't mention them, perhaps they are still available.

Then there's the **MERRY MUSIC BOX**, WW, 10 McKown St., Boothbay Harbor, Me. 04538, which specializes in music boxes. All have Swiss movements, but many of the housings are made in the firm's own workshop. They offer as large a collection of music boxes as I have ever seen—and they're not all boxes. On hand as well, are musical Toby jugs, musical chalets, musical composers, musical creches, musical plates, musical musicians, and so on. In many cases you can select the tune to go with your music box. According to the firm, the items shown in the catalog represent only the tip of the iceberg; they have tons more on the premises of their music box museum. (Incidentally, they also sell antique music boxes for collectors.) Prices are not low, except when they have a sale, but they're not extravagantly high, and you'll have trouble finding many of the items elsewhere. Catalog is free. **AAA SWISS MUSIC BOXES,** WW, 55 West 42 St., New York, N.Y. 10036, sells Swiss music box movements (around $5.00 each). You may be able to get them for less, but I haven't seen so many different tunes—well over 200—offered in music box movements elsewhere. They also sell discs for the Thorens automatic disc music boxes, and music boxes themselves, and they will make music boxes to order. Price lists are free. The **BOSTON MUSIC CO.,** WW, 116 Boylston St., Boston, Mass. 02116, offers musical gifts for all occasions—musical dolls and animals (including a snake whose head moves in time to the snake charmer's song, at $6.00), musical beer steins, a musical lighter, etc.

A lot of the sources described in Chapter 19 (Workshop) and a few of those in Chapter 17 (Arts and Crafts) also sell music box movements.

C. RECORDS AND TAPES

1. General

The **CHESTERFIELD MUSIC SHOPS, INC.,** WW, 12 Warren St., New York, N.Y. 10007, specialize in selling records, both musical and spoken, by mail. Many of their records are issues that are out of press (or whatever the record equivalent of "out of print" is). Their catalogs and periodic sales bulletins are free.

KING KAROL RECORDS, WW, P.O. Box 629, Times Square Station, New York, N.Y. 10036, who claim to have the world's largest selection of records, offer discount prices on all records and stereo tapes. They'll send you a free Schwann catalog, as well as their own brochure, so you'll have a basis on which to figure out your discounts.

2. Classical

The **MUSICAL HERITAGE SOCIETY,** WW, Box 932, Ansonia Station, New York, N.Y. 10023, offers a free catalog of budget-priced (mainly $3.00) stereo "renaissance, baroque, classical, romantic, and modern music." "Dolbyized stereo cassettes," which can also be played on non-Dolbyized equipment, are available as well (and I hope that means something to some of my readers, because I certainly don't understand it). The catalog, plus periodic mailings of new releases, is free.

The **SOLANA MUSIC SOCIETY, INC.,** WW, 401 South Louise, Atlanta, Tex. 75551, sells inexpensive recordings of classical music from as little as $1.50 per record; and also plan to offer tapes and cassettes.

ROCOCO RECORDS, LTD., WW, P.O. Box 175, Station "K," Toronto 12, Ontario, Canada, sell both their own and Cantilena operatic records. **ED ROSEN,** WW, P.O. Box 97, Freeport, N.Y. 11520, sells tapes of celebrated opera performances, starting at around $13.00 for two operas. All three lists are free (but Rococo also puts out a detailed catalog for $1.00).

3. Ethnic and Foreign

Many of the American Indian firms listed in these pages sell Indian records and tapes. **INDIAN HOUSE,** WW, P.O. Box 472, Taos, N.M. 87571, specializes in them. LPs of traditional North American Indian music are mostly $5.00; tapes, around $6.00. Brochure is free. The **RASHID SALES CO.,** WW, 191 Atlantic Ave., Brooklyn, N.Y. 11201, specializes in Arabic records, tapes, and cassettes. (They also have some Arabic books.) Catalog, in English and Arabic, is free. You can get German records from **BREMEN HOUSE** (Chapter 7,A.2). Irish records and tapes are available from the **IRISH SHOP,** WW, 8 Melody Lane, Chelmsford, Mass. 01824 (catalog free), as well as from **WALTON'S,** described earlier in this chapter. Icelandic records may be obtained from **ICEMART** (Chapter 2,C.3); and Chinese records and musical instruments from our old friend, the **CHINESE MERCHANDISE EMPORIUM** (Chapter 7,A.1).

4. Specialties

Are you a pianist with a mad desire to play concerti but unable to find an orchestra to accompany you? For $6.00, **MUSIC MINUS ONE,** WW, 43 West 61 St., New York, N.Y. 10023, will supply you with a record of your favorite concerto (provided, of course, it's one of the several dozen they list in their free catalog), complete except for the piano part. Similarly, they will provide recorded orchestral accompaniments for a number of different instruments, including the human voice. Both classical and popular works are offered.

UNCLE JIM O'NEAL, WW, Box A, Arcadia, Cal. 91006, puts out a brochure called "Rural Rhythm," listing albums and tapes of country and western music, starting at $2.00 per album (there's no indication that there's more than one record per album). And **ROSE'S COLLECTORS RECORDS,** WW, P.O. Box 7216, 128 Breckinridge Lane, Louisville, Ky. 40207, specializes in unusual records. In addition to country and western, there are old radio programs, jazz and old blues, pop music (old and new), highlights from the popes' speeches, big bands of the thirties, and so on. There are lots of bargain offers, too. Both catalogs are free.

PRO-LOG PRODUCTIONS, WW, Box 6, Dobbs Ferry, N.Y. 10522, sells old radio programs on tape. Their repertoire includes such shows as "Amos and Andy," "Bergen and McCarthy," "The Inner Sanctum," "Pepper Young's Family," "Jack Armstrong," "The Lone Ranger," and so on. Each show is 60 minutes long and costs $4.00 on cassette, $5.00 to $7.00 on tape, $7.00 as a cartridge. The **RADIOLA CO.**, WW, Box H, Croton-on-Hudson, N.Y. 10520, sells old radio programs on records only (usually they're around $6.00 each, less in sets). Their offerings include excerpts from "Allen's Alley," "The Great Gildersleeve," "The Spike Jones Show," "The Aldrich Family," and such one-shots as "The Thing on the Fourble Board." Both brochures are yours without cost.

POLYGLOTTE, WW, Postfach 230147, Fernruf 63191, 4 Düsseldorf 23, West Germany, sells poetry and drama records in over 20 languages (one of which is English). Although the descriptions of the records themselves are in the language of the record, the catalogs are in German. I believe the firm can correspond in English, however, so you might write and tell them in what languages you're interested. I got the catalogs free, but they're rather thick and elaborate, and they may be sorry they wouldn't agree to a token sum when I suggested it.

D. SCORES AND BOOKS

Most of the firms already listed also carry scores and books. Here are some houses specializing in that area. **MARLIN BRINSER**, WW, 643 Stuyvesant Ave., Irvington, N.J. 07111, calls himself "America's most complete source" of books on music. Most of the paperbound books listed in his catalog are from U.S. publishers; hardbacks have been imported from England, and are often, he says, difficult, if not impossible, to get elsewhere in this country. Many of the hardbounds are offered at a discount. (He also imports Italian violins.) The catalog is free.

The **VESTAL PRESS**, WW, Box 97, Vestal, N.Y. 13850, is devoted entirely to the art of mechanical music of the past. They put out a free catalog of historical and technical books and brochures dealing with player pianos, orchestrions, and music boxes; and they also have some recordings of these instruments.

The **DANCE MART**, WW, Box 48, Homecrest Station, Brooklyn, N.Y. 11229, puts out a catalog of books on dance techniques, music for those techniques, and books on physical fitness and acrobatics. Also at the same address is the **OPERA BOX**, devoted to books on the opera, operetta, and musical comedy. Both catalogs are free on request. Be sure to specify which one you want (or, if you want both, specify that).

The famous play publisher, **SAMUEL FRENCH, LTD.**, WW, P.O. Box 64, 26 Southampton St., Strand, London WC2E 7JE, England, offers a fat catalog called *Complete Guide to Selecting Plays* (it's free). Moreover, they say they're also able to obtain any play or book on the performing arts that's still in print, even if it isn't listed in their catalog.

E. THIS AND THAT

FIESTA ARTS' INC., WW, Greenvale, N.Y. 11548, issues a free brochure listing their reproduction first-performance Metropolitan Opera posters, priced at a modest $1.00 each, postpaid.

NORMAN CRIDER, WW, 415 East 53 St., New York, N.Y. 10022, sells ballet books and antiques and puts out periodic free listings.

Do you want a lion's roar, a shake drum, a 3-tone train whistle? There may be other sources that have all three, but the only one I know of is **CARROLL SOUND, INC.**, WW, 351-53 West 41 St., New York, N.Y. 10036. They have all kinds of sound effects, as well as all kinds of unusual instruments. From China and Japan . . . bell trees, $100.00; authentic temple blocks, $75.00; shengs, $60.00; from India . . . manseera, $2.00 to $4.00, daffris, $6.00; dholaks, $35.00; from Africa . . . ngoma-za-mapenzi (tuned leg drums), $110.00 per set of 3. There are also whistles, horns, and calls of divers kinds. All this is just a sampling. "We have combed the world to uncover truly unique musical treasures," the firm says, adding with a certain degree of modesty, "We are not finished but what we offer is miles ahead of anyone else."

> **Remember:** *Write for the catalog first.* All prices given were valid only at the time of writing and probably have been changed.

Chapter 14
THE OCCULT

Under this heading, I have lumped a variety of categories—including metaphysics, mysticism, witchcraft, voodoo, astrology, hermetics, ceremonial magic, divination, and the like—and I trust that no one will take offense at these unavoidable juxtapositions, and that everyone will understand why I have given the serious and the frivolous equal representation without prejudice. I should also like to point out in advance that neither the firms described herein nor I myself ascribe any genuine occult powers to any of the items listed in their catalogs. Everything is offered purely in the spirit of good clean entertainment . . . and you use it at your own risk.

A. BOOKS

With a few exceptions, all of the firms listed under *Supplies* (Section B) also sell books. However, the firms described here are devoted primarily to them; in general, they offer larger and more comprehensive stocks than do the supply houses, which tend to feature popular standards, plus a variety of do-it-yourself pamphlets, and the "long-lost" books of ancient sages, some of rather ambiguous provenance. For the most part, each bookstore catalog will offer some volumes that the others don't list. In some cases, a firm will feature titles that it publishes itself; these are not always the creations of its own scribes, but often reprints of classics that have been out of print for years.

You will sometimes find that, where different firms offer the same books, the prices often are not the same. However, they don't vary consistently, so it's difficult to say that one book dealer is more or less expensive than another. In the main, however, standard books will be offered at list price, though there are some discounted items. If you're looking for bargains, write for the catalogs of the two remainder houses listed in Chapter 12,C, **PUBLISHERS CENTRAL BUREAU** and **MARBORO BOOKS**, both of which almost always have a selection of popular occult books at a fraction of the publisher's original price.

1. General

Probably the best known of the bookstores that specialize in the occult is **SAMUEL WEISER, INC.**, WW, 734 Broadway, New York, N.Y. 10003. This firm was well known for the completeness of its stocks in this area long before the mystic became modish, and those seriously interested in any of the various aspects of occultism will find Weiser one of the most authoritative sources (although popular occult books are also sold). Catalogs are issued several times a year at no charge. **MASON'S BOOKSHOP**, WW, 789 Lexington Ave., New York, N.Y. 10021, is another well-established source of authoritative works on the occult. In addition to the firm's regular book catalog, which deals almost exclusively with occult topics—especially astrology—Mason's sends out special lists on such topics as alchemy, astral projection, hypnotism, occult powers, the Qabbala, etc. All are free upon request.

THE CIRCLE BOOKSHOP, WW, 215 South State St., Ann Arbor, Mich. 48108; and the **AQUARIAN AGE BOOKSTORE**, WW, 813 North Charles St., Baltimore, Md. 21201, both put out free brochures, less elaborate than Mason's or Weiser's, but similar in scope. In addition, Aquarian Age also has special lists on several dozen separate topics. The **VILLAGE BOOK SHOP**, WW, P.O. Box E, Station A, Champaign, Ill. 61820, puts out a fairly large "wholesale" catalog (free), which offers some small discounts. They also profess to be able to get any book you want. In Canada, the **HERMETIC BOOKS AND SUPPLIES CO.**, WW, 998 Coxwell Ave., Toronto, has a free price list of standard works, plus some unfamiliar ones, and a group of Christian mysticism titles—all aimed at serious "esotericists."

All of the British bookstores listed in Chapter 12 have books on the occult, and **FOYLE'S** issues an occult catalog (free), which seems admirable, but is a snare and a delusion. I sent away for a number of books from the list. Some I received, one by one; others I was told were long out of print, while there were two they claimed never to have heard of. From their own catalog, mind you! On the other hand, if you have a particular book in mind, Foyle's is very good at tracking it down for you.

Perhaps a more sympathetic British book source is the **HELIOS BOOK SERVICE, LTD.**, WW, 8, The Square, Teddington, Cheltenham, Glos., G1545 DL, England, which offers a free catalog similar to Mason's and Weiser's, with the prices given in American dollars as well as British pounds. The **METAPHYSICAL RESEARCH GROUP**, WW, Archer's Court, Stonestile Lane, the Ridge, Hastings, Sussex, England, also has a very comprehensive catalog, including classics as well as some unusual items like *Kirk's Secret Commonwealth of Elves.* Their catalog costs $1.00 (bill preferred), but, in addition to the book lists, you get all sorts of booklets offering occult supplies, which will be discussed later in this chapter; so you really get your money's worth in sheer weight. Prices in both catalogs are given in English and American money.

DIETER RUGGEBERG, WW, Postfach 130729, Talstr. 64, D-56 Wuppertal 1, West Germany, puts out a small brochure in English in which he lists only English translations of the Franz Bardon works. However, he says, he sells a broad range of occult books in the German language and, in due course, he plans to offer occult books in English. His lists are free; but specify if you want the German ones as well as the English. (Mr. Ruggeberg is fluent in both languages.) Prices are given in American dollars.

A large part of the little catalog of Spanish books (in Spanish) put out by **LA LIBRERIA "EL CENTRO COMERCIAL,"** WW, P.O. Box 1074, San Antonio, Tex. 78294, is dedicated to "Ocultismo" and related subjects. These are, for the most part, of a popular nature, and include treatises not only on *La Magia Negra* and *Blanca*, but on the less familiar *Verde* and *Roja. La Ultima Palabra de la Magia y del Ocultismo* is $5.00. Other books are mostly in the $1.50 to $2.00 price range, although there are a few more expensive ones . . . as well as some Spanish fortune telling cards. The catalog is free, although you may have given up on it before you get it.

LLEWELLYN PUBLICATIONS, WW, Box 3383, St. Paul, Minn. 55165, which is said to be the largest occult publishing house in the United States, publishes a cross between a magazine and a catalog, for which the firm charges 50¢. It contains a good selection of books, mainly of the popular standard variety; the firm puts out a number of these itself. Its moon sign books and astrological calendars have long been classics of their kind. It also sells some occult supplies. **DR. LEO LOUIS MARTELLO**, WW, The Hero Press, 153 West 80 St., New York, N.Y. 10024, will send upon request a free leaflet describing the books he has for sale. Although he offers a limited selection, and some of them are his own works (he's a well-known witch and author in his own right), he does offer some hard-to-get classics (some of which he has reprinted himself); and he offers unusually speedy

service, something, alas, which is not always true of booksellers, occult or otherwise.

2. Specialized

The **BANYEN BOOKSHOP**, WW, 2739 West Fourth Ave., Vancouver 8, B.C., Canada, offers a rather comprehensive mail-order catalog that features mysticism and the Eastern religions, although other areas of the occult are represented as well. In the United States, the **EMERALD TABLET**, WW, Box 821, Aptos, Cal. 95003, deals with similar subjects in its catalog, which is printed green on green and, in consequence, rather difficult to read. There's also a special section of mystic books for young people. The **CHAPEL OF THE HEALING PRESENCE**, WW, Chapel Bookstore, 6102 Worth St., Dallas, Tex. 75214, puts out a mimeographed catalog that includes "metaphysical, occult, religious, inspirational, and self-help books," including a number that I haven't seen listed anywhere else. And **DeVORSS AND CO.**, WW, 4900 Eagle Rock Blvd., Los Angeles, Cal. 90041, offers a similar line. All four catalogs are free.

The **MARKHAM HOUSE PRESS, LTD.**, WW, 58 West St., Brighton BN1 2RA, England, publishes a series of inexpensive pamphlets and periodicals on various occult subjects, most of them tied in with "the study of the various aspects of Diffusion in the past and of their effects on other cultures." Titles include *Atlantis, Key to the Past; Lemuria Reconsidered;* and *The Garden of Eden,* to give you an idea. Prices are given in dollars. Qabbalists and other interested in Jewish mysticism will want to have the catalog put out by **WORK OF THE CHARIOT**, WW, P.O. Box 2226, Hollywood, Cal. 90028. It's free, and the works included appear to be of a scholarly nature. Most are in English and Hebrew, but there's at least one in Aramaic and Latin. Both catalogs are free.

The **BORDERLAND SCIENCES RESEARCH ASSOCIATION**, WW, P.O. Box 548, Vista, Cal. 92083, puts out a mimeographed list (50¢) of its own publications. It includes such topics as psychic surgery, seance memoranda, animal magnetism, and the ever-popular flying saucers. **PARADICE INTERNATIONAL**, WW, 290 Washington, Vidor, Tex. 77662, devotes itself exclusively to the subject of UFOs. Not only can you buy books on UFOs, maps of UFO sightings, and pictures of UFOs, you can buy your very own professional UFO detector for the very reasonable price of $10.00. Send them an 8¢ stamp (or whatever first class postage is by the time you read this), if you want their catalog.

For books devoted entirely to dowsing, see the **DOWSING SUPPLY CO. OF AMERICA** in the following section.

B. SUPPLIES

1. General

Most of the houses listed here carry lines that include amulets, talismans, incense, oils (both essential and anointing), occult jewelry, gemstones, books, curios, roots, herbs, powders, candles, tarot and I Ching cards, plus a wide variety of ritual and divinatory equipment. Some have large, broad-range stocks; others are more limited in size and scope, but may nevertheless carry items the others don't have. At the same time, although there seems to be a great deal of duplication in the merchandise, the prices are dissimilar. Although in some instances, it is clear that the more expensive item is either of superior quality or handmade on the premises, in others—especially where the very same cut is used in both catalogs to illustrate the item in question—it seems very probable that the same thing is being offered by different houses at widely disparate prices, so do shop very carefully.

INTERNATIONAL IMPORTS, WW, Box 2010, Toluca Lake, Cal. 91602, claims to be one of the largest mail-order supply houses in the world and this seems borne out by the fact that many of the smaller houses use selections from International Imports' catalog (apparently furnished by International Imports) as their own catalogs. It is one of the older occult supply houses in this country, and, for 50¢, it offers a thick, thorough catalog. Included are candles for all occasions (priced from 50¢ to $2.50), magicians' wands, spirit trumpets, rune sticks, ouanga bags ($3.50), seals and talismans (from 35¢), mystic soap, and kits for all kinds of love philtres and spells, at $5.00 each. There are robes of various kinds, voodoo dolls (plus voodoo doll patterns for do-it-yourselfers), and wax images all ready for you to stick pins in (some come complete with pins).

If you'd rather stick pins in anatomical replicas instead, NASCO LIFE FORM, WW, Fort Atkinson, Wis. 53538, puts out the grisliest catalog (gratis). They sent me a finger so lifelike that, when I opened the box, I thought I was being notified that a loved one had been kidnapped. Don't expect that you'll get a free finger, though. I think they were under the impression that I was a practicing scientist when they sent me mine, and you're lucky if you get a free catalog. I imagine the models are intended for science students and such, and they are rather expensive, but, I think, rather less gruesome than some of the things you'll be seeing in the occult catalogs.

To return to International Imports, there are books, mostly of the how-to type, and some small but handsome witchcraft posters at $1.00 each. You'll also find occult music—voodoo music is $6.00 per record, the Satanic mass, $5.25. If you're interested in occult recordings, by the way, OCCULT RECORDINGS, WW, Royal Court, Laindon, Basildon, Essex, England, offers cassette or tape courses in witchcraft and in ceremonial magic, at $21.00 each. Their brochure is free. Several of the other firms described in this chapter also offer courses in such subjects as witchcraft and spiritual development and The Village Book Shop (see preceding section) has some meditation records, plus Israel Regardie's *Twelve Steps to Spiritual Enlightenment* in six cassette tapes.

The TYRAD CO., WW, Box 17996, Minneapolis, Minn. 55417, another old-time house, also offers a vast array of occult and ritual objects, including powdered deer horn (25¢ per capsule), genuine parchment boars teeth ($1.00 each), cobra skins ($6.00), and athamés—witches' ritual knives ($6.00). They also make available genuine skulls—bat skulls are on hand all the time for around $24.00, but human skulls cost $100.00 and must be specially ordered. For those less exacting in their requirements, there is a full-size "castone" skull for only $10.00. The firm will undertake to quote prices on the skeleton of any animal, including the human, if you send them your requirements. Tyrad's selection of hooded robes or tabards is unusually large, and available not only in a range of thirteen colors, but, unlike most other firms' robes, in different sizes. The regular drip-dry dacron-cotton robe is $30.00; the satin, $40.00; the wool blend (for those chilly outdoor ceremonies) and the velvet, both $75.00. For the outsize witch or mage, extra-large sizes are available for an additional $5.00. MISS CAROL, WW, Box 2074, Sepulveda, Cal. 91343, is another well stocked source. Her brochure is 50¢. Tyrad's is 25¢.

The WITCHCRAFT BOOTIQUE (sic), WW, 104 Yorkville Ave., Toronto 5, Ont., Canada, puts out an attractive but very slender catalog for the 50¢ it charges. It, too, offers athamés, at $8.00, and silver chalices for $20.00. There are zodiac seals for $2.00, plus some interesting pendants. Prices seem a little high when compared to similar items elsewhere.

I assume that the catalog put out by the VENTURE BOOKSHOP, WW, Box 249, Highland Park, Ill. 60035, is free, because they sent it to me for nothing in response to a postcard request. The firm does offer books, as well as "psychic appliances," like planchettes ($5.00), and crystal balls made of plexiglass ($8.00 to $40.00). On the other hand most other firms' crystal balls are of molded glass, and Venture does say it's planning a line of authentic rock crystal balls, which, they warn you, are going to cost plenty.

The **METAPHYSICAL RESEARCH GROUP** (already described in Section A) offers a very varied assortment of equipment in the higher price ranges—crystal gazing kits; aura goggles and aura research kits; divining wands, rods, and dowsing supplies; many different kinds of tarot cards; automatic writing equipment; planchettes; Ouija tables—and lots of other good things, some of which I haven't seen included in other catalogs.

The **PANDEMONIUM BOOK SHOP**, WW, P.O. Box 214, Milwaukee, Wis. 53201, puts out a free catalog of modestly priced occult goods, and it is to be hoped that the firm's spells are better than its spelling. Other firms that seem to offer a nice line in the occult are **MR. ASMODEUS**, WW, Drawer 459, Bethany, Okla. 73998; the **HOUSE OF GOOD FORTUNE**, WW, P.O. Box 42, Milford, N.J. 08848; **STANRAY**, WW, P.O. Box 3317, New York, N.Y. 10001; and the **HOUSE OF HERMETIC**, WW, 8906 Melrose Ave., Los Angeles, Cal. 90069. Hermetic's catalog is 25¢; the others are free.

A lot of the firms offer the type of items you see in the windows of botanicas and sometimes in Woolworth's along with more advanced equipment, but the **TEMPLESTAR CO.**, WW, Times Plaza Station, Box 224, Brooklyn, N.Y. 11217, will send you a free brochure containing stock that seems aimed primarily at low-budget and juvenile sorcerors. Most of the items are inexpensive, although where they coincide with the stocks offered in the more sophisticated catalogs, they don't seem to be any cheaper. The **JOHNSON SMITH CO.**, WW, 16335 East Warren Ave., Detroit, Mich. 48224 (whose free catalog will be more lovingly described in a later chapter) offers a similar line of products, but presents them in a frankly frivolous manner along with whoopee cushions and dribble glasses. (Tyrad, I must acknowledge, also has some of these items—well, even a mage must have his or her lighter moments.)

The free catalog offered by the **RELIABLE MAIL ORDER CO.**, WW, Room 403, Borja Bldg., 645 Rizal Ave., Manila, Philippines, contains, in its own words, "different secret teachings, rare mystical books and unique novelties," and presents much of its fascinating contents in comic strip form. There are the talismans, herbs, etc., you'd expect to see, with somewhat different cultural orientations. For instance, I think the locket labeled, "She who wears this necklace will be FREE or PROTECTED from bad HUMAN DESIRES and TEMPTATIONS," is not likely to sell well here. (It's around $6.00.) In addition, there are such unusual items as the "handkerchief of salvation," which will save you from "all kinds of ACCIDENTS from your FELLOW-BEING who is a secret enemy and especially from evil spirits. . . . Just don't take

this with you in the RED HOUSE and night spots, so that it will not lose its power." A steal at $5.00, postpaid.

If you order from another distant source, the **RAHAAJA AGENCY**, WW, P.O. Box 240, Ebute-Metta, Nigeria, you are required to sign the following: "I place the above talismans of my own free will, for I have faith in it." The talismans are different from most of those found in the other catalogs, especially the Nashikrana Mesmerism handkerchief, which "helps the user to vanish anything that is not more than 40 lbs. in weight to do and get the same way." It's quite expensive; less expensive are the talismans to make you pass exams, to gain favor with your boss, to keep yourself from being transferred, and for success in cocoa farming and palm products dealing (both combined in one talisman). The catalog is free.

BICHON'S, WW, 412 Travis St., Houston, Tex. 77002, founded in the nineteenth century by a French family, specializes in handcarved Louisiana occult candles ($1.25). They also sell the usual occult line, including wish bottles, lucky bones, lucky starbags, roots, controlling bath salts, Indian herb oil, jinx-removing offering spray, and so on. In addition, they have a special line of supplies imported from Mexico for the use of *curanderos* (and they imply that they can correspond in Spanish as well as English). Prices for most of these articles are in the 50¢ to $2.00 range. If you want a *mojo,* however, it will cost you $25.00, because it has to be specially handmade for you.

2. Specialties

Everything the novice or advanced dowser could possibly need is available from the **DOWSING SUPPLY CO. OF AMERICA**, WW, Box 66, East Kingston, N.H. 03827, from the Beginner's Pendulum Kit at $1.25, to the Electronic Psychic Detector at $20.00. Also available are a variety of books on dowsing—both pro, and, surprisingly, con—including many scientific treatises. Brochure is free. **MARKHAM HOUSE PRESS**, mentioned earlier in this chapter, also has rods and pendulums for dowsers, including the French Mermet variety, at $3.00 to $6.00.

Despite its name, the **E.S.P. LABORATORY**, WW, 7559 Santa Monica Blvd., Los Angeles, Cal. 90046, puts out a free catalog of "services and supplies" that seems to deal more with the hardcore occult than with parapsychology. And the *Manosophy Metaphysical Catalogue,* obtainable without charge from **TONY PRODUCTS**, WW, Box 783, Costa Mesa, Cal. 92627, has a lot of original offerings. There's a Psychic Food Supplement (rather expensive at $16.00 for a 60-day supply); an Incarnascope, by means of which you may "scan your own past incarnations"; some specialized books and astrological supplies; and, my favorite, the "herbal pot pourri spheres," carefully blended by the firm's psychic herbalist and suggesting "remembrances of sepulchral spicery as if it had been brought from the core of some great pyramid where it had lain on the breast of a mummified pharaoh." It's $4.00, and, the catalog says, "makes an excellent inexpensive psychic gazing ball."

If you want to go directly to the geographical source, you can buy voodoo charms from **TIPCO IMPORT AND EXPORT**, WW, P.O. Box 396, Port-au-Prince, Haiti. "Blessed by the voodoo priest, these charms bring luck to everyone who wears them," the catalog unhampered by any niggling local postal restrictions, tells you. They cost from $2.50 to $3.00, depending on size. There are also voodoo drums priced from less than $2.00 up. Since the largest one is 36" high, and costs only $4.25 (prices are given in American dollars), I'd say they were a bargain irrespective of their occult meanings. There are also all kinds of other Haitian products and curios, all so very inexpensive that I'm sure postage must be additional. The strange little catalog is free.

Mystics with a do-it-yourself bent will be enchanted by the mandalas available from **DORCAS MAN-DALAS, INC.**, WW, 8106 North Lincoln Ave., Skokie, Ill. 60076, at 50¢ each, or $4.50 for a set of twelve. Mandalas, of course, are mystic designs used as an aid to meditation, and they look very like the art works we used to perpetrate in school with our compasses when the geometry teacher wasn't looking. By coloring them yourself, you are supposed to be able to raise your consciousness to incredible spiritual heights. You'll also have some nice wall decorations.

JAMES S. FEINER, WW, P.O. Box 3897, Long Beach, Cal. 90803, puts out a curio catalog that features the 22 gems and minerals in the works of Edgar Cayce. They're offered either as lucky pieces or set in jewelry. Also sold are black mirrors (for psychic elevation) at $4.00; meditation robes in a choice of three colors, and wizards' capes in standard black, both at $10.00; plus all sorts of amulets and talismans. Aside from the gemstones, prices for occult materials seem less expensive than average. **MINERVA'S**, WW, P.O. Box 231, Bayfield, Colo. 81122, also offers a list of "mystical stones" and occult jewelry. Both brochures are free. **RAM IMPORTERS**, WW, 81 Second Ave., New York, N.Y. 10003, puts out a brochure featuring incense, as well as occult books.

Most of the occult houses supply a large variety of herbs. You'll find a lot more herbs (mystic, as well as healing and culinary) listed in Chapters 6 and 7, because folk medicine, food, and witchcraft do tend to overlap. However, the **HERB STORE**, WW, P.O. Box 5756, Sherman Oaks, Cal. 91403, is sponsored by the well-known witch, Paul Huson, so the herbs and herbal combinations offered might be expected to have peculiar potency. In addition, Mr. Huson offers ritual bath sachets and English love sachets, at $1.00 each; astrological sachets at $2.00; plus incense for Beltane, All Hallows, and other important occasions.

Flabby mystics who find some difficulty doing their Yoga exercises will be delighted to hear of the Palm Springs Yoga Institute's Porta Yoga, which will enable you, the brochure says, "to master even the difficult positions easily." For example, "the headstand can be accomplished without your head ever touching the ground." It costs $15.00 plus shipping, and, if you write to the **PALM SPRINGS YOGA INSTITUTE**, WW, P.O. Box 4092, Palm Springs, Cal. 92262, they will send you a free brochure.

3. Other Sources

Many firms that are not primarily occult houses do have items that are either specifically aimed at the esoteric trade, or can be utilized in its service. Some of these items are merely for amusement; others are intended for more serious applications.

On the frivolous side, the **CONTINENTAL TRADING POST**, WW, Box 123, Isabella, Mo. 65676, sells zodiac stationery, astrological decals, and astrological designs for embroidery, plus patterns for various items with signs of the zodiac crocheted into them. **LEMEE'S FIREPLACE EQUIPMENT**, WW, Rte. 28, Bridgewater, Mass. 02314, might be surprised to find themselves in this company, but they do put out a nice line of cauldrons, from $13.00 to $32.00, with cranes to hold them (from $11.00). The catalog is 35¢, but, I warn you, the rest of it *is* fireplace equipment. **PRESTON** (9,B.3) also has some smashing cauldrons.

U.S. GAMES SYSTEMS, INC., WW, 468 Park Ave. South, New York, N.Y. 10016, offers over five different types of tarot decks, most of them in the $4.00 to $5.00 price range, although the Grand Tarot Belline is $24.00. In addition, there are several other types of fortune telling cards, including The Parlour Sibyl, *Le Petit Cartomancier*, Grand Lenormand Astro-mythological Practices, and Gipsy Witch Fortune Telling Cards (all $1.50 to $5.00). There are also books on the tarot, tarot posters (four for $2.00), tarot blocks ($3.00), tarot cocktail napkins ($1.00 per box), and tarot games. The catalog is free and the prices are lower than at most occult houses.

FEDERAL SMALLWARES, WW, 85 Fifth Ave., New York, N.Y. 10003, goes U.S. Games one better by offering a "tiny tarot," ¾" in size, at $1.25; and a regular tarot deck at $2.00. Their catalog is 50¢ and is devoted to toys and games; however, there are other items that could conceivably be of interest to the merry mystic, such as the "New Improved Wobbly Woozer," a wind-up spider modestly priced at around $1.70, and the firm's classic "Go-Away" doormat, at $1.50. Like it or not, for your 50¢, you will also get a catalog of doll-house furniture and miniatures; and perhaps, if the planets are propitious, a catalog of reprints of old-time children's books.

Many items of interest to aficionados of the arcane may be found in other chapters. Gemstones and other minerals, whether for ritual or ornamental purposes, may be purchased much more cheaply from most of the jewelry supply houses described in Chapter 17, F.1. Some, like GRIEGER'S and GEMEX, have "occult" jewelry pieces into which the rankest amateur can set stones (the catalogs tell you how). Others, notably the Indian firms, have beads made of various kinds of gemstones, at ridiculously low prices. There are also crystal stars, gemstone scarabs, bats, Buddhas, and the like at extremely reasonable prices.

Most of the Oriental handicraft houses described in Chapter 11,C.7 offer a variety of gods and lucky symbols. The ICEMART STORE, WW, Keflavik International Airport, Iceland (catalog 30¢), has a fascinating collection of runic jewelry headed "Saga Sorcery in Silver." Included are a love charm, *Fjölnir,* which is "used to ward off ill effects of magical incantations"; the Helmet of Aegir, which is supposed to "assure victory when confronting an enemy"; and the like. (These are all pendants, at around $13.00.) There are also brooches, bracelets, and rings, plus mediaeval crosses for the more conventional.

Many of the museum gift shops (see Chapter 11,B) offer reproductions of ancient jewelry, as well as figurines and bibelots, all of which could be considered to have mystic significance. If you want originals, look under Collections (Chapter 15), where you'll find Egyptian, Minoan, Greek, Roman, and even more ancient artifacts at prices that are sometimes amazingly low (some cost very little more than the reproductions). In the same chapter you'll find fossils, neoliths (elf bolts), and so on. Ceremonial masks from many countries are found in the handicraft sections of Chapter 11, where you'll undoubtedly also find many other items of occult significance. And, of course, virtually all of the American Indian supply houses offer ceremonial objects.

Remember: *Write for the catalog first.* All prices given were valid only at the time of writing and probably have been changed.

Chapter 15
COLLECTIONS

A. ANTIQUES AND COLLECTIBLES

Most of the items in this section will be one of a kind; therefore, the things that I describe are merely to give you an idea of the types of items a firm sells and the kind of prices charged there—chances are that the actual pieces have been sold a long time ago. There is likely to be more delay involved here than in any other type of mail-order buying. A lot of people are likely to want the same items, so the dealers, after sending the desired item to the first person who writes for it, must write to the others, informing them that the particular item is no longer available and, usually, suggesting an alternative or inquiring whether they would want to be notified if a similar item turned up later. As you can see, this entails a lot of correspondence, which explains why many of the dealers prefer that you do not send a check until they can write to confirm your order (and, usually, tell you what the shipping costs will be).

Since most of the firms described here are smallish, there aren't too many people to handle the outpouring of mail; sometimes the dealer takes care of all of it himself. So you should understand in advance that, if you write away for some attractive artifact, you may not get a reply for a long time. Even after your order has been accepted and you have sent your check, months may pass before you get your treasure, because the dealer is probably still working away on the correspondence left over from previous lists. Just because he has you in the hand, he cannot afford to antagonize all those other customers lurking in the bushes. In short, you've got to be patient for all kinds of mail-order buying, but when it comes to antiques, you've got to make up your mind to have the disposition of a saint.

1. General

EDWARD GOLEMBERSKI, WW, 93 Whitemoor Rd., Nottingham NG6 0HJ, England, offers a diversity of items, dating from prehistoric times to pre-World War II (and a few after). At various times he has offered: a bronze Hittite battle axe ($55.00); a set of 6 20-year-old Coalport coffee cups and saucers decorated with Admiralty badges ($12.00); silver-plated sugar tongs from the Isle of Man in the shape of armored legs ($2.00); an eighteenth-century brass Georgian ladle ($11.00); a figure of Henry IV in bisque porcelain ($3.50); Graeco-Roman terra cotta heads ($15.00 each); a Roman bronze pin from the first or second century A.D. ($10.00) . . . and lots of other interesting things (including, from time to time, Egyptian, Palestinian, and Cretan antiquities), at extremely reasonable prices. Subscription to 8 consecutive issues of the catalog is $2.00 by surface mail; $4.00 by air.

BOYNE HOUSE, LTD., WW, Kington, Herefordshire HR5 3DL, England, puts out periodic mimeographed lists of the collectibles they have for sale. The emphasis in their stock seems to be on china and glass. The list I saw had 6-inch Gaudy Welsh plates in a tulip pattern, $3.25 each; a Royal Doulton plate depicting Ophelia (and, appropriately, slightly crazed), $8.00; a 1929 Royal Copenhagen decanter, $37.00; a colored bisque figure of Red Riding Hood, $20.00. Among the nonbreakables, there were a pewter tea and coffee pot, $37.00; a mother-of-pearl card case, $15.00; and some pinchbeck watch fobs, $12.00 to $13.00. Each catalog costs $3.00 (ref.).

BUSAÑAL—IMPORTACÃO E EXPORTACÃO, LDA., WW, P.O. Box 52, Estoril, Portugal, puts out periodic price lists ($2.00 each) of antiquities from all over the world. Included have been seventeenth-century maps of Portugal and Spain, $1.25 each; 100- to 300-year-old tiles, $1.00 each; old Portuguese insulators, $2.00; old ships' lamps, $20.00 to $40.00; 1830 duelling pistols, $250.00; 100-year-old cow bells on leather straps, $3.50; a seventeenth-century suit of Portuguese armor, $1400.00; old French telephones, $40.00; plus old clocks, churns, irons, weapons, portholes, cash registers, etc. They also have new things—Portuguese collectors' plates, ceramics, and lots of reproductions. Prices in American dollars.

GEORGE A. HANSEN, WW, Gammel Kongevej 144, 1850 Copenhagen V, Denmark, offers a price list, in English (American dollars), of Danish antiques and antique reproductions. This includes lots of Bing and Grondahl and Royal Porcelain blue fluted porcelain (coffee and teapots are only around $9.00, so they must be modern), cut crystal vases, painted peasant washstands, old Danish insulators ($2.00 each), German bisque dolls ($20.00 to $50.00), old oakwood carvings ($8.00), old music boxes ($100.00 up), wooden coffee grinders ($7.00), old wooden cheese moulds ($8.00); etc. The catalog costs $2.00, and Mr. Hansen has a broker he can recommend in case you want to buy a carved oak double cabinet with leaded glass doors—at $80.00 to $100.00, it is pretty tempting. He also has collectors' plates.

A. GOTO, WW, 1-23-9 Higashi, Shibuyaku, Tokyo, Japan, is a spendid source of Japanese antiques and collectibles. Netsukes are what you expect first, and netsukes are what they have, in all materials—ivory, wood, jade, mother-of-pearl, coral, metal and other minerals—at prices ranging from $2.00 up (mainly up, with the average in the $15.00 to $20.00 neighborhood). Most of these are 50 to 120 years old. Also available are antique snuff bottles in the same materials plus cloisonné, cinnabar, lacquer, etc., from $35.00 to $100.00 (as well as some modern ones in ceramic and glass, from $5.00). There are antique jade hairpins, buttons, buckles; antique incense boxes, powder horns, scales, wood block prints ($6.00 to $25.00), and so on. New items include soapstone seals, ($1.00 to $20.00), quartz and staghorn opium pipes ($7.00 to $17.00), jade bangles ($17.00), etc. Minimum order is $30.00 and price lists are free.

Here I'm going to break my rule of not including firms that don't put out catalogs, because I know that many of my readers are interested in antiques from the Middle East. Although S. Kaufmann of **KAUFMANN'S ANTIQUES,** WW, 81 Ben-Yehuda St., Tel Aviv, Israel, has no catalog, he (or she) says he/she would be willing to send photographs and quote prices, if you will specify what you're interested in.

2. Antiquities

CHARLES EDE, LTD., WW, 37 Brook St., London W1Y 1AJ, England, specializes in pre-Christian antiquities, mostly of museum quality. Offered in recent catalogs have been Babylonian cylinder seals, $45.00 to $50.00; a Roman statue of Eros in bronze, $275.00; 150,000 B.C. flint handaxes from France, $38.00; Egyptian faïence necklaces, $58.00; an Attic (Greek) lekythos, $90.00; and so on. Illustrated catalogs are free.

G. LAMBOR, WW, 345 Handleton Rd. Hove, Sussex, England, puts out monthly lists of antiquities, which have included a Gandhaa grey schist high-relief head of Buddha, a little under $40.00; a Roman pottery lamp, around $8.00; a fifteenth-century British shoe buckle, $12.00; a Mycenean pottery jar, $45.00. The price of a 6-month subscription is $1.00.

ALADDIN HOUSE, LTD., WW, 648 Ninth Ave., New York, N.Y. 10036, sells ancient oil lamps from Palestine, ancient Egyptian beads and amulets, ancient Roman glass and bronzes, and all sorts of antiquities from the Middle East, many made into jewelry. They also have a large line of reproductions and adaptations including lots of jewelry—ankh lovers will have a field day here. General brochure is free.

3. Military

The **ARMOURER'S SHOP,** WW, 112/114 Buxton Rd., Whaley-Bridge, nr. Manchester, England, specializes in antique arms and armor from all over the world. The periodic lists cost $1.00, and have recently included such items as a pair of Georgian foils, around $38.00; a choice Burmese dha, around $115.00; an eighteenth-century Turkish flintlock pistol, $170.00; an Italian fascist combat knife, $38.00; and so on.

WAFFEN, LTD., WW, 10 Summers Row, London N. 12, England, sells antique American weapons and related items; the last list I saw appeared to have a lot of what seemed to be Civil War surplus. A Union canvas canteen was $25.00; a Confederate bayonet belt and buckle, $14.00; a large Abraham Lincoln funeral buckle, about $16.00. They also have a lot of Wells Fargo items, Tiffany buckles, from around $14.00, and such. Naturally, as the name implies, there will be German items, too.

VIRGILIO NETTO, WW, Avenida Madero 26-R/CE, Lisbon 1, Portugal, specializes in military medals and insignia. They're mostly antique, and mostly Portuguese, but there are some from other countries as well —Iran, Hungary, Imperial Russia, etc. The list is in English, priced in American dollars, and appears to be free.

M. H. KLUEVER AND SON, WW, 1526 North Second Ave., Wausau, Wis. 54401, describe themselves as "purveyors of ancient and medieval armour, swords, battleaxes, and poleaxes, plus associated antiques." They say, "We probably possess the most varied Bronze Age weapons collection in this country." The catalogs I saw included a collection of Bronze-Age weapons and artifacts . . . among them a Luristan dagger, dating back to 1000 B.C., $125.00; a conical Greek pot, $18.00; and a statuette of Osiris, $32.00. More recent items include an English lobster-tail helmet, c. 1650, $155.00; a German sixteenth-century halberd, $50.00; a fighting axe from Fanjore, India, $15.00. The catalog is 50¢, or $1.00 for a subscription (4 issues).

DELTA INTERNATIONAL, WW, Box 361, Lafayette, Cal. 94549, specializes in military antiques (mainly German) from World Wars I and II. The catalog is $1.00. **MOHAWK ARMS,** WW, Interlico, P.O. Box 399, Utica, N.Y. 13503, sells military memorabilia and some other collectors' items, mostly American and German. List is free.

4. Maps and Prints

RICHARD A. NICHOLSON, WW, Wavecrest, Menai Bridge Rd., Bangor, North Wales, will send you 6 issues of his illustrated catalog of antique maps and prints for $4.25 surface, $8.00 airmail. There are maps dating as far back as the sixteenth century, and some as late as the nineteenth, but most of them are seventeenth- and eighteenth-century. Prices start under $10.00.

JACQUELINE BROWN, WW, P.O. Box 177, Baldwin, N.Y. 11510, offers eighteenth- and nineteenth-century prints, both American and European, as well as old maps and miscellaneous Americana—railroad items, old stock certificates, legal papers, etc.—and old illustrated books. Many inexpensive items are available. **ELIZABETH F. DUNLAP,** WW, 6063 Westminster Pl., St. Louis, Mo. 63115, specializes in old maps of the United States. Both lists are free.

5. Americana

HARTWELL KENNARD, WW, 1015 Nyssa, McAllen, Tex. 78501, specializes in authentic pre-Columbian artifacts from Central America, at what he says are 1/3 to 1/2 gallery prices. The last catalog I saw listed Huastec heads, $2.50 to $15.00; terra cotta burial-offering figurines, $10.00 up; burial and ceremonial vessels, $10.00 up. A Colima frog effigy vessel is slightly under $100.00; a Tlatilco vessel in armadillo form, $350.00. The catalog is $1.00.

VAL VERDE CITY FRONTIER VILLAGE, WW, Rte. 1, Box 444, Donna, Tex. 78537, features Southwestern Americana. From time to time they've offered such items as old Spanish spurs starting at around $3.00 each (no pairs), many said to be of museum quality. There are old handforged branding irons, from $4.00, plus other old horse accouterments, and the usual sadirons and trivets. They have old bottles and jars, retablos (from $5.00), soda water and beer tin trays, old Mexican Indian masks (from around $10.00 up), and old santos and crucifixes ($16.00 to $20.00). Lots of pre-Columbian artifacts, beginning as low as $1.25 for clay heads, and going up into the hundreds for museum-quality pieces are also available. To get their illustrated price list, send 2 stamps.

The **WOODEN NICKEL,** WW, 186 Elm St., North Attleboro, Mass. 02760, puts out a list so badly reproduced I had difficulty making it out, but it does seem to offer a lot of inexpensive Americana. For example, the one I saw had an old cribbage travel kit ($4.50), 25 assorted trade cards ($4.50), an old metal sign advertising cigars ($16.00), a John Philip Sousa souvenir spoon ($4.50), and so on. They also have (or had) a number of Civil War and Ku Klux Klan items. Presumably this list is free.

AMERICAN ENTERPRISES, WW, 16260 Ventura Blvd., Suite 630, Encino, Cal. 91316, specializes in western Americana. The list I saw included Wells Fargo buckles ($11.00), 6-pointed marshall and sheriff badges ($4.50), and brass brothel tokens ($1.50 each). I'm not entirely sure whether this firm belongs in this section, because the list (free) doesn't make it clear whether the badges and tokens are antiques or reproductions. The brothel and riverboat posters, at $1.75 for the set of 4 (including "Beware Pickpockets and Loose Women"), are definitely reproductions. Shipping seems to be included.

The **LYON HOBBY MART,** WW, Box 63, Hartford, Conn. 06101, offers monthly lists of Americana—advertising cards, postcards, documents, labels, newspapers, and so on—but don't expect to get more than the first one free unless you buy something. Prices are moderate.

HERTER'S (Chapter 7,B.4), sells antique wooden decoys, and you can tell how old they are from the fact that the now-extinct passenger pigeon is included. There are also widgeons, curlews, snipes, snow geese, and so on, modestly priced from $6.00 to $7.00. (A few big ones, such as the swan, go up to $18.00.) They also have some Early American butter molds ($5.00), old branding irons, copper gold panning pans, Indian arrows, old brass coffee pots, apothecary and provision jars (used by the early French and English traders—$3.00), and all sorts of other interesting old things tucked into their big outdoors catalog. (Remember, you have to look for the antique pages, because there's so much else.)

The **MISCELLANEOUS MAN,** WW, 1728 Thames St., Baltimore, Md. 21231, sells "original nineteenth- and twentieth-century posters and related ephemera." On hand are circus, movie, recruiting, theatrical, and other types of posters, from $5.00 up to over $100.00. Most of them seem to be in the $25.00 to $35.00 range. Also offered are miscellaneous paper items and memorabilia. Catalogs come out every three months or so, and the selection in each, the proprietor says, "is, frankly, more or less random. It does not represent our true inventory, which changes drastically from month to month." He's not being churlish; he's just inviting you to state your wants. A copy of his catalog is $1.00, or $2.50 for the next 3 issues (a year's subscription).

Each year, the **BALTIMORE AND OHIO TRANSPORTATION MUSEUM GIFT SHOP,** WW, Pratt and Poppleton Sts., Baltimore, Md. 21223, puts out a free catalog offering all kinds of things of interest to rail-road buffs. Last year they sold original railroad station clocks, from $125.00; hand lanterns, $8.50 to $10.00; brass locomotive bells, $185.00; brass door-knobs from the B. & O. passenger station in Chicago, $10.00; ticket daters, $21.00; and lots of other fine things . . . real pot belly stoves, authentic bridge lights, original builders' plates, authentic station signs, Pullman car blankets, locomotive oil cans, silver hot plate covers, regulation hat emblems. They probably have some of these things left; if not, I'm sure they've found lots of fresh supplies from the good old days. The catalog usually makes its annual appearance around Christmas.

6. Indiana

The firms that follow deal primarily—or at least extensively—in *old* Indian items. If you collect contemporary Indian work, you'll find many firms that sell pieces of museum quality (as well as less expensive pieces and souvenirs) in Chapter 11,C.1. Many of them also have some antique items.

C. SECRIST, WW, Box 22, Deerfield, Mo., 64741, specializes in Indian relics and artifacts. Arrowheads (some as much as 20,000 years old) start at 35¢ and go up to $35.00 or $40.00. Also present are flint knives, scrapers, effigies, axes, and all kinds of other tools. Then you'll find birdstones ($25.00 to $250.00), antique pipes, discordials (he doesn't explain what these are), old beads, beadwork, war bonnets and other costume items, pottery (starting at $2.50), dolls, etc.—all at prices that seem very reasonable. Also reasonable are the prices charged by **M. NOWOTNY**, WW, 8823 Callaghan Rd., San Antonio, Tex. 78230. His arrowheads also begin at 35¢; scrapers start at 50¢; flint spears, knives, and tangs start at $1.50 to $2.00 per inch. Flint hooks, thunderbirds, ceremonials, old Mexican stone beads, and old pottery idols (mainly priced from $2.00 to $50.00) are listed here, as well as tin retablos ($8.00 to $20.00) and a line of fossils. Both lists are free.

D. A. HUNTER, WW, 4444 McKenzie Hwy., Springfield, Ore. 97477, is a specialist in "Indian relics," so his prices are, naturally, higher. Folsom points are $9.50; a 1930 Northwest coast carved raven frontal piece with abalone eyes, $65.00; on the other hand, an old Navajo silver and turquoise bracelet is only $20.00; a lava grinding bowl from Captain Jack's country, $7.50, and so forth. Price lists are free.

The **INDIAN GIVER**, WW, P.O. Box 2284, Mission Viejo, Cal. 92675, offers modestly priced items for collectors, including arrowheads (50¢ up), small pueblo Indian pottery vessels of the pre-Classic period (around $8.00), terra cotta burial heads with differ-ent meanings—"love, war, fertility, evil spirits, luck, religion"—at around $3.50 (and figurines, $4.50). Also on hand are trade beads, old tribal tokens, old Indian baskets, described as in "average good condition" ($35.00), wooden ceremonial masks of varying ages ($25.00), and stone grinders. Available also are old iron keys, branding irons, and single spurs. Catalog is free.

AMERICAN INDIAN BOOKS, WW, P.O. Box 683, Athens, Ala. 35611, in addition to books, has some Indian artifacts for sale at what seem like low prices. List is free.

IROQRAFTS, WW, RR 2, Ohsweken, Ontario, Canada, offers traditional and ceremonial Iroquois crafts and arts for the collector. Their contemporary masks and false faces are sold with the understanding that they will not be used in pseudo-Indian ceremonies "or other sacrilegious ways." They won't sell old masks at all, declaring haughtily that, "These sacred relics are not for sale; attempts to separate these Old Helpers from The People are to be discouraged." They do, however, sell many old items, described in special lists, which cost 25¢.

7. Assorted Specialties

If you collect old phones, or even have an old phone, you'll undoubtedly want to know about **BILLARD'S**, WW, 21710 Regnart Rd., Cupertino, Cal. 95014, which sells parts for old telephones (and old telephones, as well). They can correspond in French or Spanish as well as English, and their price list is yours free, upon receipt of an SAE. (Both Hansen and Busañal, in A.1, also sell old telephones.)

DENISE POOLE, WW, South Thoresby, Alford, Lincs., England, puts out a catalog of beautiful old, English silver. The cheapest item I found in the catalog I saw was a 1795 Bateman (Peter and Ann) mustard spoon, at a little under $8.00. The dearest, a George II inkstand by Madgalen Feline, was a little under $1200.00. Catalog is free.

The **DICK OAKES AGENCIES**, WW, 2524 19 St. S.W., Calgary 4, Alberta, Canada, sells copper utensils from the Eastern Mediterranean, all of them old, and some of them antique (over 100 years old). An antique and very appealing fat Toparlak water container 12" high is $18.00; antique skimmers and ladles are $9.00. In the less-than-100-year-old category are some very useful-looking teakettles ($11.00 to $13.00), egg poachers ($3.00 to $9.00), and yogurt pails ($10.00 to $18.00). Brochure, with line illustrations, is free.

BALLARD'S ANTIQUE COSTUMES, WW, 517 Wayside Dr., Plainfield, Ind. 46165, offers clothing from the late nineteenth and early twentieth centuries for collectors, designers, students, and people with the urge to garb themselves in period costume. The twentieth-century items seem quite inexpensive—on the list I saw, a multicolored fringed georgette dress from 1929 was $14.50; a 1921 plaid tissue gingham was $9.50. Current lists are 50¢ each.

MANTIQUES, WW, 820 South Hoover St., Los Angeles, Cal. 90005, sells antique vending and penny arcade machines. They're expensive—and the free brochure, the proprietor says, doesn't even list those over $150.00—and irresistible. You'll find antique mechanical musical instruments, including music boxes and devices, in Chapter 13,B.3. Antique dolls are described in Chapter 22,B.

8. Reproductions

Many of the firms in the preceding sections, as I mentioned in passing, offer reproduction antiques as well as originals. Here are two firms that specialize in them. **THE ANCIENT MARINER**, WW, Box 96, Amagansett, N.Y. 11930, issues a beautiful free catalog of nautical decorations. They have stunning reproductions of antique instruments handmade in Europe. There's a particularly attractive 19-inch celestial globe copied from a prototype in the Musée du Mer, Paris. The rings all move, and, when you rotate the earth, the moon circles it automatically. It's $50.00. They also have reproductions of old ships' figureheads, carved out of wood rather than the plastic of the inexpensive reproductions, ranging from $100.00 up. And the **JAMES HANNA WORKSHOP**, WW, 11 Greenwell Pl., Newtownards, County Down, North Ireland, sells battle axes and halberds—primarily, if not exclusively, for decorative use, I suspect—at around $14.00 to $15.00; and reproduction flintlock pistols, which, they claim, only an expert can distinguish from the original, for around $20.00.

You can find reproductions of antique clocks in Chapter 9,D.2 and Chapter 16,E.

B. COLLECTORS' PLATES AND FIGURINES

1. Foreign Sources

Plate collecting has grown to be a very popular hobby; and, because most of the plates being collected are imported from Europe, it seems logical that you should get them more cheaply if you buy them directly from a European source. That is not always true. You can get them as inexpensively in the Caribbean and sometimes in the United States. So, before you place an order, compare prices carefully, remembering that duty and shipping charges are part of your cost.

In England, **JOHN SINCLAIR, LTD.**, WW, 266 Glossop Rd., Sheffield S10 2HS; and **FRANCIS SINCLAIR, LTD.**, WW, Georgian House, 39 Hall Gate, Doncaster, Yorkshire (who are, so far as I know, unrelated), both offer good selections of plates, figurines, mugs, and other items of interest to the collector—from the Continent as well as the British Isles. Both brochures are free and prices are given in American dollars.

OLD WORLD PLATES, WW, P.O. Box 272, DK-1501 Copenhagen V, Denmark, offers Danish collectors' plates of present and past years, as well as some Spode and Wedgwood, and mugs. Prices, which include shipping, seem very reasonable, and, if a plate should break en route, return the pieces and they'll replace it, plus the postage. The mimeographed list (containing what looks like hundreds of offerings) is free. **GILBERT HANSEN**, WW, Vestergade 10, Tune, 4000 Roskilde, Denmark, puts out a price list of old Danish collectors' plates, dating back as far as 1895. Prices are given in American dollars. Still another Danish source is **A/S TORBEN DONATZSKY**, WW, DK-2100 Copenhagen, Freeport, Denmark, which offers both current collectors' plates and collectors' plates of past years, as well as other collectors' items. Prices seem reasonable; however, there's a drawback. The list says, "All items are normally delivered as gift parcels *without insurance at customer's risk,* unless we receive other shipping instructions" (italics mine)—which would undoubtedly push up the price. So, unless they have something you can't find elsewhere, I suggest you buy your plates and such from a firm that automatically insures them. Their lists are free, too.

FÖCKE AND MELTZER, WW, 152 Kalverstraat, Amsterdam, Holland, ask 3 IRCs for their collectors' plate folder, but it does show plates the others don't list, as well as the ones they do have, at similar low prices. It's in color, too.

R. ROESLEN, WW, Taunusstrasse 47, P.O.B. 16628, 6 Frankfurt/Main, West Germany, sells German collectors' plates and related items. He also sells Dresden and other types of figurines (he used to specialize in Hummels) but warns you that there can be a year and a half waiting period for them. If you have your heart set on Hummel, you might try the other houses that sell collectors' plates, as well as the china and crystal firms described in Chapter 8. It may seem odd to approach the Caribbean firms for Hummel figurines, but they seem most confident of their ability to get them. **OBLETTER SPIELWAREN**, WW, Industriestrasse 20, 8034 Germaring, West Germany, puts out a brochure of Hummel as well as other figurines, but it didn't include any price lists. The brochure is free. Roeslen's brochures are free as well.

One Caribbean firm that seems to devote itself to collectors' plates is the somewhat curiously named **AMERICANA, LTD.**, WW, P.O. Box 173, Ocho Rios, Jamaica, W.I. (I say "curiously" because its free mimeographed list offers nothing but imported collectors' plates.) There are Wedgwood, Royal Copenhagen, Bing and Grondahl, Rosenthal, Hummel, Spode, Lladro, Lalique, and so on. Prices seem considerably lower than in the States, higher (in some instances) than in Europe. Another Caribbean firm, **SOLOMON'S MINES, LTD.**, WW, P.O. Box 4801, Nassau, Bahamas, sells Royal Doulton figurines and jugs, Bing and Grondahl figures and plates, Beswick horses, and Lladro figurines, all at discount prices. (Also on sale here are Waterford and Orrefors crystal, and many kinds of china—Coalport, Ridgway and Adderley, and Belleek.) They have no catalogs as such, but probably can supply brochures along your lines of special interest.

Plate collectors will be particularly interested in a source north of the border—**LE GIFT SHOP**, WW, 96 Côté de la Fabrique, Québec 4, P.Q., Canada, which offers a free color brochure devoted almost entirely to collectors' plates. Prices are generally a lot lower than they are here, and mostly on a par with those in Europe. What makes this shop outstanding is that, if you're charged customs duty, all you need do is send them the receipt and the amount you've paid will be credited to your further purchases.

DAHL-JENSENS PORCELAENSFABRIK, WW, Frederikssundsvej 288, 2700 Brønstiøj, Copenhagen, Denmark, will send you free a small brochure of their Copenhagen art porcelains, illustrating a small selection of figures and crackleware from their extensive range of models. A tiny kitten is around $12.00; a pair of most engaging bears, around $45.00; a figurine of a young woman in the Armager costume, $110.00. As for the crackleware, an attractive vase is around $75.00.

2. Local Sources

A Caribbean source that is, at the same time, on native soil is **THE MAISON DANOISE**, WW, St. Thomas, U.S. Virgin Islands, which offers collectors' plates, at, they say, a savings of at least 20 percent over list, when duty and postage have been paid. Brochure is free.

JOYCE McDONALD, WW, P.O. Box 1422, Manhattan Beach, Cal. 90266, sells collectors' plates at discounts that sometimes bring them down to European prices. (She also has plates that go back as far as

1895, if you want to pay over $1000.00.) Send an SAE for her list. **MY GRANDFATHER'S SHOP**, WW, 8055 13 St., Silver Spring, Md. 20910, puts out a thick collector's guide, which is both a catalog of collectors' plates, figurines, bottles, etc., and a collecting guide as well. Subscription fee is $1.00 per year, and, when you buy three or more items, you get a discount (the more you buy, the greater the discount). They tell you that they don't think it's a good idea to order collectors' plates from abroad, but it's possible they're not being wholly objective. Other U.S. sources are the **GRANDE MAISON BLANCHE**, WW, 1621 Boardwalk, Atlantic City, N.J. 08401 (they say they offer discounts); **NORDIC TRADING CO., INC.**, WW, P.O. Box 203, Fort Hamilton Station, Brooklyn, N.Y. 11209; and **JON NIELSEN**, WW, 6166 West Vernor, Detroit, Mich., 48209 (old plates). All lists are free.

HOLLY CITY BOTTLE, WW, P.O. Box 344, Millville, N.J. 08332, offers collectors' plates and antique and modern bottles. From their list, it's a little difficult to determine which is a bottle and which is a plate, but I suppose collectors can tell. Lists are free.

C. FOSSILS

FOSSILS UNLIMITED, WW, 9925 Hwy. 80 West, Fort Worth, Tex. 76116, calls itself "the world's largest fossil dealer," and their lists certainly show a lot of fossils from all parts, starting as low as $1.25 postpaid for a fossil acorn barnacle and going as high as $35.00 for a museum-quality multiple *elrashia kingi* trilobite slab. They have some attractive-sounding collections, too, beginning at $2.00 for a set of 20 examples of fossil life in each major phylum. They also have Indian artifacts. **J. F. RAY'S FOSSILS**, WW, P.O. Box 1364, Ocala, Fla. 32670, have pelecypods, gastropods, cephalopods, and brachiopods, as well as trilobites, bryozoans, protozoans, blastoids, and everything the well-equipped fossil house should have. **XENOPHON**, WW, 6442 Charlesworth Ave., North Hollywood, Cal. 97606, offers California fossils from around 50¢ up to a tops of $2.00 (each one nicely identified). There are specimen sets for students, at about $6.00 each. All price lists are free.

The **BEAVER-HOOD CO.**, WW, P.O. Box 1481, Portland, Ore. 97207, has acquired, it says, "an international reputation" for handling only outstanding specimens of the petrified woods and other plant fossils in which it specializes. The large mimeographed lists include items selling for only a few dollars as well as those in much higher price ranges. Lists are free.

D. MINERALS AND SHELLS

You'll find mineral specimens offered by all the gemstone houses in Chapter 17,F.1. In addition, here are some sources that specialize in specimens. For Swiss minerals (as well as minerals from all around the world) **KÜMINERAL**, WW, 1 ch. Aug. Vilbert, 1218 Grand-Saconnex, Switzerland—send 3 IRC's (ref.) for list. Indian mineral specimens are obtainable from the **PARASMANI TRADING CO.**, WW, 1312 Prasad Chamber, Swadeshi Mill Compound, Opera House, Bombay-4 (BR) India; price list free. **GREG'S SHOWCASE**, WW, 4 Bungula St., Sadleir, N.S.W. 2168, Australia, specializes in Australian specimen crystals. They also sell native gemstone rough. If you're searching for tektites (small meteorites), you can get them dirt cheap from the **DEPARTMENT FOR COMMUNITY WELFARE**, WW, P.O. Box 39, Rundle St., Adelaide 5000, Australia, at prices starting from 15¢ and going up to around $10.00. Both lists are free. **HETTIE'S ROCK SHOP**, WW, 110 Birdwood Ave., Christchurch 2, New Zealand, offers fossils, shells, and mineral specimens from New Zealand. Brochure is free. **W. D. CHRISTIANSON**, WW, 127 Grove St., Barrie, Ontario, Canada; and **CASTAGNE's ROCKS AND MINERALS**, WW, box 594, Station P., Thunder Bay, Ontario, Canada, both offer Canadian mineral specimens. Price lists are free.

Most of the U.S. sources of mineral specimens are in the Gemstone section. However, **THE POWDER MONKEY**, WW, P.O. Box 14283, St. Louis, Mo. 63178, specializes in mineral specimens from Missouri, Oklahoma, and Illinois, and doesn't sell gemstones. List is free.

If you're a sand collector, the **SAND CATS**, WW, P.O. Box 15084, Lakewood, Colo. 80215, have over 250 different kinds of sand from all over the world. Price list is free. The **JAVO DISTRIBUTING CO.**, WW, P.O. Box 13288, Tampa, Fla. 33611, puts out free price lists of shells of all kinds for collectors. "We do not feature or promise quick service—" the firm says firmly, "—only careful service." **DERBY LANE** (see Chapter 17,G) also has collectors' shells.

E. MODELS

The **PIEL CRAFTSMEN**, WW, 307 High St., Newburyport, Mass. 01950, sell completely finished handmade miniatures of famous ships, at prices ranging from $25.00 to $175.00. Ships include *H.M.S. Bounty*, U.S. frigate *Constitution* (Old Ironsides), and the *Cutty Sark*. **PRESTON'S**, WW, Main St., Wharf, Greenport, L.I., N.Y. 11944, offers all sorts of marine items. They have model ships, scrimshaw, and a variety of marine gifts. Preston's catalog is 25¢, Piel's is free. **BLISS** (Chapter 20,D) also offers a catalog of ship models (50¢). Many of the model ships described in Chapter 16,F are available in finished form as well as in kits.

The **NORTH RIVER CO., INC.**, WW, 52 Simon Hill Rd., Norwell, Mass. 02061, sells handcrafted painted pine miniature (8-inch) boats—lobster and shrimp boats, schooners, etc.—for $5.25 to $5.50 postpaid. Larger (over 16-inch) boats are $10.50. Also offered are pewter historical soldiers, 2 3/8 inches high, for $5.50 postpaid. Included are a private in the Forty-second Pennsylvania Volunteer Infantry (1863), a 1781 British grenadier, an officer in the von Bose musketeer regiment (1780), and some historic cannon. **KS HISTORICAL PUBLICATIONS**, WW, P.O. Box 155, Saddle River, N.J. 07458, sells a similar series of 3-inch pewter historical figures, also at $5.50 each (with a few exceptions). These include soldiers who served in the Americas during the sixteenth, seventeenth, eighteenth, and nineteenth centuries. Also offered, are reproductions of American Revolution and Civil War uniform buttons, $1.50 to $2.00 per set of 3; and figurines of American animals, from $7.50 for a raccoon to $10.00 for a great horned owl. Both brochures are free.

The **SOLDIER SHOP, INC.**, WW, 1013 Madison Ave., New York, N.Y. 10021, deals in military miniatures, with a selection of model soldiers hailing from all over the world; it includes Imrie-Risley, Historex, Stadden, Cavalier, Almark, and others, available either in kit form or painted, from $3.00 up and up and *up*. There are also handcolored military prints from around $2.50 up, books, and military antiques and military gifts. They put out a quarterly, half catalog-half magazine for $4.00 per year.

JOSEF KOBER, WW, Graben 14-15, Vienna 1, Austria, is well known as a source of classic tin soldiers. The catalog is free, but in German. You'll find other soldiers in Chapter 22.

APPALACHIAN SPRING, WW, 1655 Wisconsin Ave., N.W., Washington, D.C., creates detailed working miniatures of old-time wagons, for collectors, at prices starting at $40.00. Catalog is $1.00.

Since it was difficult to separate models and miniatures for collectors from models and miniatures for children and frivolers (particularly as many firms offer both types), you'll find many more items in this category in Chapter 22 (Playthings and Diversions). You'll also find figurines and other small collectibles—in ivory and precious stones as well as more mundane materials—in Chapter 11 (Art) and Chapter 17 (Arts and Crafts). Mask collectors will find example after example of the false-face maker's art at nearly all of the handicraft houses (Chapter 11).

Chapter 16

HOBBIES

A. CAMERAS, BINOCULARS

It's said you can get some very good buys in cameras and camera accessories, as well as binoculars, from the Orient, if you know what you're doing. A good place to start, because their catalog is so informative, is **DICKSON AND CO.**, WW, P.O. Box K-3979, Kowloon, Hong Kong. They tell you all the things you'll need to know to order cameras from Hong Kong, including trademark data; and also give you complete instructions on how to return equipment for repair if necessary, without getting unduly involved with customs. Three other good places to write to are: **T. M. CHAN AND CO.**, WW, P.O. Box 3381, Hong Kong; **ALBERT WHITE AND CO., LTD.**, WW, P.O. Box K-202, Hong Kong; and the **FAR EAST CO.**, WW, P.O. Box 7385, Kowloon, Hong Kong. (All three of them also sell hi-fi equipment.) All four catalogs are free and give prices in American dollars.

A Japanese source is the **SUMITOMO TRADING CO.**, WW, P.O. Box 24, Higashinari, Osaka, Japan, which issues a free price list of Japanese cameras and accessories. Again, prices are given in American dollars.

Before you order from abroad, however, see what the home market has to offer. For instance, the **CAMBRIDGE CAMERA EXCHANGE**, WW, 21 West 45 St., New York, N.Y. 10036, sells cameras and photographic supplies at what they claim are free-port prices. Send for their free brochures and judge for yourself.

B. HI-FI AND ELECTRONICS

Hong Kong is also a prime source for bargains in hi-fi and stereo equipment. Again, I remind you to check local stores before you invest in anything expensive. Sometimes—probably through bulk buying—they'll be able to beat the Hong Kong prices, especially when you consider shipping costs and customs duties. In addition to the houses already mentioned, there's **UNIVERSAL SUPPLIERS**, WW, P.O. Box 14803, Hong Kong. They put out a catalog of hi fi equipment, radios, tape and cassette recorders, and electronic calculators at prices that are for the most part appreciably lower than those prevailing here. They also have another catalog devoted entirely to SONY

hi fi components and tape recorders. Prices are in American dollars.

In the United States, **DIXIE HI-FIDELITY WHOLESALERS**, WW, 10530 Detrick Ave., Kensington, Md. 20795, claim that they offer brand-name stereo music systems at what they claim are "tremendous savings." The catalog is free, so you can check them out. And **CHINAPIG AUDIO ELECTRONICS**, WW, 67 Parker Ave., Maplewood, N.J. 07040, says it doesn't have a catalog yet, but will send you discount quotations on any kind of hi-fi equipment in which you're interested. The **OLSON ELECTRONICS CO.**, WW, 260 South Forge St., Akron, Ohio 44327, puts out a big free catalog of brand-name electronics equipment at what they claim are low prices. They also carry lots of things that the Hong Kong houses don't offer, like closed-circuit TV cameras, alarms of various kinds, radiotelephones, and so on.

If you like to build your own TV and stereo sets, calculators, radios, test equipment, etc., you can buy kits from the **HEATH CO.**, WW, Benton Harbor, Mich. 49022; the **SOUTHWEST TECHNICAL PRODUCTS CORP.**, WW, 219 West Rhapsody, San Antonio, Tex.; and the **RADIO SHACK**, WW, 2725 West 7 St., Fort Worth, Tex. 76107. All the catalogs are free. Southwest even sells kits so you can make your own music synthesizers. Most of them sell specialized electronics equipment, and you'll find more described in Chapter 19 (Workshop).

PLAYTRADE, INC., WW, P.O. Box 5562, Toledo, Ohio 43613, sells unrecorded 8-track Ampex cartridges at prices starting from slightly under $1.00 for the 30-minute variety . . . which, they say, is less than 50 percent of the list prices of comparable tapes. They also offer custom-length cartridges and do-it-yourself supplies and equipment. Price lists are free.

C. WEATHER INSTRUMENTS

Along with their growing interest in the environment, people seem to be taking more and more interest in the weather. Unfortunately, the instruments that the three following firms sell won't help you change the weather; all you'll be able to do with them is watch it. If that's enough for you, write to **DON KENT AS-**

SOCIATES, INC., WW, Civilian Terminal, Hanscom Field, Bedford, Mass. 01730; the AIRGUIDE INSTRUMENT CO., WW, 2210 Wabansia Ave., Chicago, Ill. 60647; and WARD BROOK, WW, East Candia, N.H. 03040. Prices range from $5.00 for a rain gauge to over $420.00 for a complete weather station. Brochures are free.

D. MECHANICAL AND SCIENTIFIC HOBBIES

CALDWELL INDUSTRIES, WW, P.O. Box 170, Luling, Tex. 78648 are, they say, "in the sophisticated mechanical hobby business. We offer machine tools designed for the hobbyist and things for him to do with them." In addition to the machinery (expensive) there are castings for all kinds of steam engines and tractors, gasoline engines, and locomotives (castings for these can run well over $100.00). Also on hand are clock kits—from a paper clock that's guaranteed to work but not to keep accurate time, at $4.00, to the Synchronome, used for time systems, at $327.00 (it's only $122.00 if you buy it in kit form). Catalog is $2.00.

The EDMUND SCIENTIFIC CO., WW, 300 Edscorp Bldg., Barrington, N.J. 08007, puts out a fascinating catalog with more than 4000 items for hobbyists and scientists on all levels, from the sophisticated down to the out-and-out naive. There's a Wankel engine for around $7.00; a portable solar cooker that they say you can use for backyard barbecues on sunny days, $11.00; surplus aerial camera lenses, $500.00 the set; toy parachutes at $1.00 apiece; an ESP kit at $3.00; a dry ice maker, $42.00; a package of mixed transistors, $2.50; a mercury detection kit for $20.00; etc. They have sections on chemistry, electronics, optics, ecology, lasers, light, etc. Catalog is free.

EDUQUIP, INC., WW, 1220 Adams St., Boston, Mass. 02124, puts out biology and chemistry kits for schools; however, nowadays, some of its offerings, like the Water Pollution Test kits, may have a more general interest. The Bacterial Test kit is $32.00; the Chemical Pollution, $29.00; the Nitrate, only $13.00. There are Particle and Gas Samplers (for observing atmosphere pollution) at $17.00. They offer a long list of pollution accessories (but I don't think they mean that the way it sounds), and many other things. I got the catalog free; if you're interested you can but try.

I've already described NASCO, WW, Fort Atkinson, Wis. 53538, in Chapter 14,B.1; however, because the applications there are limited to a use the manufacturer may not have intended, I'd like to repeat that they offer singularly lifelike anatomical replicas, cost-

ing from around $10.00 for a 7-8 week fetus to $400.00 for a human torso with removable viscera.

E. CLOCK MAKING

SELVA TECHNIK, WW, Karl Christian Schlenker KG, Postfach 1260, 7220 Dickenhardtstrasse 57, 7220 Schwenningen am Neckar, West Germany, puts out a wonderful color catalog of clock parts—battery movements (with and without pendulums), hands, faces, ornaments, and so on. They also have barometers, thermometers, hygrometers, etc.—and some fascinating reproduction clocks, including one that seems to use stones for weights, in both kit and assembled form, from around $30.00 up. Also on hand are lots of nice old-fashioned clocks, some electrified (I think I saw an electric cuckoo clock, but I won't swear to it), and some very modern ones. There are also some gorgeous pocket watches, including hunters, starting at less than $30.00. If I seem a little vague, it's because the catalogs are in German. They're free.

In the United States you can get clock kit catalogs from the CRAFT PRODUCTS CO., WW, Elmhurst, Ill. 60126; the MASON AND SULLIVAN CO., WW, 39 Blossom Ave., Osterville, Mass. 02655; NEWPORT ENTERPRISES, WW, 2309 West Burbank Blvd., Burbank, Cal. 91505; and the HOUSE OF CLERMONT, WW, 2282 Woodville Pike, Goshen, Ohio 45122. They have clock kits and cases and hardware, clock movements (plain and electric), barometer and thermometer kits, and all kinds of accessories (hands, dials), and a few music boxes. Craft Products' catalog is 50¢, Mason and Sullivan's and Newport's are 25¢ each, Clermont's is free. KILB & CO., WW, 623 North Second St., Milwaukee, Wis. 53203, puts out a free catalog of clock material and supplies.

F. MODEL BUILDING

The traditionally European hobby of building scale models out of cardboard has been brought to this country by JOHN HATHAWAY, WW, Box 1287, San Pedro, Cal. 90731, who offers an extensive catalog of models from various European countries. There are castles, airplanes, ships, villages, trains, space craft, crèches—everything you can think of that could be reproduced in cardboard, and not a few that are seemingly impossible. The models, all in color, are designed as printed sheets, with directions for cuts, folds, and part location indicated by coded lines. Since instructions are usually in the language of the country of manufacture, supplemental method sheets in English are provided where necessary. Mr. Hathaway has requested me to emphasize the fact that, except for a few items clearly noted as such, these are too difficult for young children to set up, although they will undoubtedly wish to participate in any such undertaking. Prices range from around 50¢ for a small castle or family fortress to around $11.00 for the U.S. carrier *Forrestal* (over 4' long), with the majority of items under $3.00. Even the working clock, labeled "not for the faint-hearted," is $2.00. And to see the catalog (a bargain at 25¢) is to want everything included madly. (What I can't understand, though, is how somebody with the wit and perception to assemble all these fine things can sink so low as to label a fetching Bavarian family room "girl stuff"!)

POLK'S HOBBY DEPARTMENT STORE, WW, 314 Fifth Ave., New York, N.Y. 10001, puts out a bluebook of wooden ship models, which not only shows ships and kits, but gives you all kinds of information, like a list of marine museums of the world. The tiny, inexpensive fittings for the ships (like the wee buckets for 5¢ each and the binnacles, 10¢ to 15¢) will interest miniaturists generally. There are also miniature cannon of all kinds. The catalog is $1.00; Polk's also has catalogs of model airplanes, $1.50, and collectors' miniatures, $1.50.

AMERICA'S HOBBY CENTER, INC., WW, 146 West 22 St., New York, N.Y. 10011, offers a model airplane and boat bulletin for 10¢, plus an all-airplane catalog for 50¢—from which, they say, they supply model builders all over the world. The bulletin has the bargains; the catalog, the items of interest to really serious model builders. They also have catalogs in other areas—including model ships and railroads.

BLUEJACKET SHIP CRAFTERS, WW, 145 Water St., South Norwalk, Conn. 06854, is run by a family of six seafarers who make kits for scale model ships. Prices start at $15.00. They also sell scale model ship fittings cast in Britannia metal. Many of these will be of interest to miniature collectors—like tiny brass bells (35¢), capstans (15¢ to 50¢), binnacles (30¢ to 35¢), boats (40¢ to $3.00), figureheads ($1.25). Deadeyes range from 60¢ to $1.00 a dozen. Also marine gifts. Catalog is 50¢.

PRESTON'S, WW, Main St., Wharf, Greenport, N.Y. 11944, offers ship models in its catalog (25¢). Kits start at $12.00 for the New York pilot boat *Phantom*, 13½ inches long, and go up to $65.00 for a 39-inch model of the *Great Republic*. The same, as finished models, go up to $195.00. They also have ship-in-the-bottle and whittling kits.

You'll also find that many of the models listed in Chapters 15 and 22 also come in unfinished or kit form.

G. MENTAL AND SPIRITUAL DEVELOPMENT

THE SLEEP-LEARNING RESEARCH ASSOCIATION, WW, P.O. Box 24, Olympia, Wash. 98501, will present you with a free catalog offering a whole set of devices for enabling you to acquire information while you slumber—ranging from the $45.00 adapter to convert your own cassette player to a "sleep-study device" up to the "completely assembled stereophonic 3-speed device for sleep study" at $240.00, with several intermediate models. You can also buy such accessories as the "special slumber speaker," ($11.00); the "whisper pillow speaker," ($8.00); or telephone pickups that record both sides of any phone conversation ($6.00). (It isn't clear whether this is supposed to happen while you're sleeping, or whether you do it while you're awake and then play it back to yourself later when you're asleep.) In addition, there are hypnotic aids, plus numerous taped courses like "The Power of Praise and Appreciation," "Dynamic Leadership," "Affirm That You Can Sing," "How to Satisfy Your Wife," "Karma and What It Means to You," "Controlled Concentration," "Deep Meditation," "Will Power," "Hypnosis for Weight Reduction," "Smoke No More," "Self Control," and, in case none of these work, "Affirm Your Power of Applying Sleep Therapy."

BIOFEEDBACK INSTRUMENTS, INC., WW, 213 West Plain St., Wayland, Mass. 01778, says it offers "tools for self-development: devices, processes, ideas, techniques." There is a Biofeedback Trainer and an Alpha Sensor, not to mention an Audible Psychogalvanometer, a Relaxometer, a Psychophysics Meter, a Biosensor, an Illusionator . . . and parts thereof, all grouped under "hardware." "Software" includes such books as *Psychic Discoveries behind the Iron Curtain, Maps of Consciousness, How to Win Games and Influence Destiny,* and so on. **AQUARIUS ELECTRONICS**, WW, P.O. Box 627, Mendocino, Cal. 95460, manufactures and sells Alphaphone headsets, and other biofeedback equipment, priced from $140.00 up. Both catalogs are free.

UNIQUITY, WW, 2035 Glyndon Ave., Venice, Cal. 90291, sells Batacas—cloth-covered foam bats with which you're supposed to get the hostility out of your system. There's the junior economy model for light use, at $10.00 the pair, and the Olympic model, for heavy use, $16.00 per pair. Also available are washable encounter dolls with detachable private parts. They suggest that you cement a photograph of a face to the head for added realism, and you can also attach some hair and fingernails for added effectiveness. They cost about $7.00 to $12.00, not including extras. The catalog is free and so are the catalogs in Chapter 20 listing tomahawks and boomerangs. Real ones.

In the gentler vein, **ALAYA STITCHERY,** WW, 283 Connecticut St., San Francisco, Cal. 94107, sells cushions and mats for meditation. There are stuffed zafus (round cushions), $9.50 to $16.00; stuff-it-yourself zafus, $5.00; and zabutons (flat floor cushions), $9.50 to $14.00, including waterproofed zabutons for outdoor meditating. They come in profound colors—black, olive green, purple, maroon, etc. The futons—sleeping and yoga mats—come in the same range of colors and cost from $20.00 to $30.00. Catalog is free.

You'll find other sources for mental expansion in Chapter 22 (Playthings and Diversions).

H. HOME OFFICE

If you need office supplies to further your hobby, whatever it may be, New York's famous **GOLD-SMITH BROS.,** WW, P.O. Box 833, New York, N.Y. 10038, now offers its office supplies by mail order. The catalog is free, and although some of the items are more expensive than they are elsewhere, you'll find that Goldsmith's has a more complete selection of stationery and related items than you'll be able to get practically anywhere else. You can get office furniture there, too. **SEARS** (Chapter 2,A) also puts out an office furniture catalog, as does **EPHRAIM MARSH,** and several of the other firms in Chapter 9. If you happen to need a Chinese typewriter, the **CHINESE MERCHANDISE EMPORIUM** (Chapter 7, A.1) is the place to find it.

Remember: *Write for the catalog first*. All prices given were valid only at the time of writing and probably have been changed.

Chapter 17

ARTS AND CRAFTS

Since crafts are so very popular these days, I've tried to bring you as many good catalog sources as I could find. Unfortunately, there is such an abundance and diversity of material that it's impossible for me to describe or even list everything that is in every catalog. All I can do is give a general idea of what they have to sell, and leave it to you to ferret out exactly what it is you're after. Unless your needs are very esoteric, I'm sure you'll be able to find them at one or another of the firms in this chapter—and very often at prices much lower than in your local stores.

A. GENERAL

There are several firms that have catalogs so thick and comprehensive that they all really deserve the title that **CCM** gives its catalog: "an encyclopedia of creative art materials." They have fine art supplies for the painter, printmaker, and sculptor. They have supplies for ceramics, leathercraft, mosaics, metalcraft, weaving, plastics and resin, candlemaking, macramé, textiles, beadwork and jewelrymaking, raffia and reedwork, carving, découpage, and so on and so forth. What's more, as seemingly complete as each one is, every one of them has things the others don't. Three of the biggest and fullest catalogs are offered by **CCM ARTS AND CRAFTS, INC.**, WW, 9520 Baltimore Ave., College Park, Md. 20740 (50¢); The **AMERICAN REEDCRAFT CORP.**, WW, 729 Cranbury Rd., East Brunswick, N.J. 08816 ($2.50); and **DICK BLICK**, WW, P.O. Box 1287, Galesburg, Ill. 61401 (free). **SKIL-CRAFTS**, WW, 305 Virginia, P.O. Box 105, Joplin, Mo. 64801, puts out a big all-round catalog with special emphasis on leather supplies ($1.00).

ARTHUR BROWN AND BROTHER, INC., WW, 2 West 46 St., New York, N.Y. 10036, puts out a big catalog of materials mainly for the commercial artist and draftsperson; it's 50¢. The **BONA VENTURE SUPPLY CO.**, WW, 17 Village Sq., Hazelwood, Mo. 63042, issues a drafting catalog for $1.00.

For fine artists, **AIKO'S ART MATERIALS IMPORT**, WW, 714 North Wabash Ave., Chicago, Ill. 60611, puts out a beautiful set of brochures of their artists' supplies imported from Japan. One brochure covers woodcutting tools, brushes of all kinds, paints and

sets (including sumi painting sets), ink-grinding stones and rubbing sets, scrolls for painting or calligraphy, and wood blocks. There is another brochure of batik dyes; another of stationery (with samples); one on books; and so on. The whole job is 50¢. Paper fanciers will find that **PAPERCHASE**, WW, 216 Tottenham Court Rd., London W.1, England, has an amazing selection of papers of all kinds (some of it also Japanese). Prices are extremely reasonable, but shipping costs might make the price prohibitive, unless there's something you absolutely must have! The catalog is free.

Other firms put out large catalogs that are limited more to crafts, although they generally do include some fine and commercial art materials. **VANGUARD CRAFTS**, WW, 2915 Avenue J., Brooklyn, N.Y. 11210, puts out a free catalog of the more popular crafts, with lots of kits, including some for hand puppets and some for marquetry. **CRAFTSMAN SUPPLY HOUSE**, WW, 35 Brown Ave., Scottsville, N.Y. 14546; and **CAVALIER HANDICRAFTS**, WW, P.O. Box 5098, Richmond, Va. 23220, also show lots of basic crafts, and their catalogs cost 50¢ each. Cavalier's is particularly good for leather; it also has some nice miniatures. **NATIONAL ARTCRAFT SUPPLY CO.**, WW, 12217 Euclid Ave., Cleveland, Ohio 44106, puts out a big catalog for $1.00, and they have clocks and music boxes in addition to everything else

HOLIDAY HANDICRAFTS, INC., WW, Winsted, Conn. 06098, issues a cheerful free catalog devoted mainly to seasonal and boutique items, in and out of kits. Lots of craft fabrics—burlap, nylon net, lamé and starched lace; plus sequins, braids, ribbons, trims of all kinds. There are also loads of miniatures; all kinds of things to do with candles; and so much styrofoam that the mind boggles. Then there are music boxes and handcrafted reproductions of Early American tinware ready to decorate or (my suggestion) use as is.

In the same genre is the charming free catalog with delightful color illustrations put out by **LEWIS-CRAFT**, WW, 284-286 King St. West., Toronto, 23, Canada. In addition to the bazaar and boutique crafts, as outlined above, they have a section on lamp and lampshade making; and their own "boss gloss" for enameling and glazing without a kiln. There's a line of standard crafts, a great variety of papers, and toy-making accessories (you have a choice of three colors of glass eyes instead of the more usual two). Prices are very reasonable.

KIT KRAFT, WW, 12109 Ventura Pl., Studio City, Cal. 91604, has lots of beads, jewelry parts, copper enameling, wood boxes, and boutique crafts (spangles and styrofoam, etc.). Most of the other craft firms offer books, but Kit Kraft offers a lot (in proportion to the catalog's size, anyhow; it's small but it's only 10¢).
ASTROCRAFT, WW, P.O. Box 817, Merritt Island, Florida 32952, stocks inexpensive craft kits—"Puff-Pics" (multicolored pictures on linen), burlap flowers, patchwork pillows, gemstone trees, plus lots of shell crafts. **ZIM'S**, WW, P.O. Box 7620, Salt Lake City, Utah 84107, has lots of boutique crafts, but specializes in charming stuffed animals—a 30-inch long antique velvet alligator kit is a modest $2.00 without stuffing; a giant mouse is $1.90.

NORTHWEST HANDCRAFT HOUSE, LTD., WW, 110 West Esplanade, North Vancouver, B.C., Canada, puts out a catalog mainly for candlemakers, weavers, and potters, though they do have some other items as well. It's 50¢.

B. SCULPTURE AND CERAMICS

ART CONSULTANTS, WW, 97 Saint Mark's Pl., New York, N.Y. 10009; **SCULPTURE ASSOCIATES**, WW, 114 East 25 St., New York, N.Y. 10010; and **SCULPTURE HOUSE**, WW, 38 East 30 St., New York, N.Y. 10016, all put out catalogs of supplies for sculptors, ceramicists, and potters. Art Consultants' and Sculpture Associates' are free. Sculpture House's is $1.00.

The **AMERICAN ART CLAY CO., INC.**, WW, 4717 West 16 St., Indianapolis, Ind. 46222, features the company's own products—Sculptamold, Sculpture tape, clays both for modelling and for hardening without firing, paint, etc. Ask for their free catalog of AMACO products, which will give you instructions as well as price listings. Also offering some special products of its own (Monzini and Foamart), the **ADHESIVE PRODUCTS CORP.**, WW, 1660 Boone Ave., The Bronx, N.Y. 10460, specializes in mould-making and casting materials. They also have polyester resins, latex, etc., as well as thinning, coloring, and finishing products. Price lists, descriptive brochures, and instructions are all available free.

KEMPER MANUFACTURING, INC., WW, P.O. Box 545, Chino, Cal. 91710, sells tools for the potter and sculptor. The detailed catalog is free.

After long deliberation, I decided to put woodcarving tools in Section D (Wood and Metal). Look for them there.

C. INDIAN CRAFT SUPPLIES

Most of the houses in this group seem to cater to real Indians, although a few are clearly aimed at children involved in Indian projects, as well as at those strange middle-aged middle-American gentlemen who like to get themselves up as Indians at parades or on lodge nights. However, I'm sure all of them will gladly trade with anybody (a few are a little apprehensive about the misuse of ceremonial attire). Craft supplies carried here generally include beads of all kinds, bone, hides, feathers, bells, fringe, shells, German silver, cloth, ribbon, porcupine quills, and so on. I don't think that there's anything Indian that you won't be able to get from one of the following; in most cases, if they don't have an item in stock they'll try to get it for you, or tell you where you can get it.

Catalogs from the **OZARK TRADING POST**, WW, Box 2564, Oklahoma City, Okla. 73125; and the **BUFFALO ROBE INDIAN TRADING POST**, WW, 18555 Sherman Way, Reseda, Cal. 91335, are 50¢ each. The Buffalo Robe seems to offer mostly supplies for hobbyists, and says austerely, "Oddball items not usually carried in stock."

The catalogs from **DEL TRADING POST**, WW, Mission, S.D. 57555; **GREY OWL INDIAN CRAFT MANUFACTURING CO.**, WW, 150-01 Beaver Rd., Jamaica, N.Y. 11433 (mostly for hobbyists); the **OKLAHOMA INDIAN MARKETING AGENCY, INC.**, WW, P.O. Box 4204, Tulsa, Okla. 74104; **PEYE'SHA TRADERS**, WW, P.O. Box 765, Painesville, Ohio 44077; **TREATY OAK TRADING POST**, WW, 5241 Lexington Ave., Jacksonville, Fla.; **WA KE'DA TRADING POST**, WW, P.O. Box 19146, Sacramento, Cal. 95819; **SUPERNAW'S OKLAHOMA INDIAN SUPPLY**, WW, 301 East W. C. Rogers Blvd., Skiatook, Okla. 74070; **PLUME TRADING AND SALES CO., INC.**, WW, Box 585, Monroe, N.Y. 10950; and **TEPEE ANTIQUES**, WW, P.O. Box 103K, Wentzville, Md. 63385 are 25¢ each. Despite its name, Tepee is an Indian craft supply house, specializing in beads; however, many of the beads are antique.

ROBERTS' INDIAN CRAFTS AND SUPPLIES, WW, 211 West Broadway St., P.O. Box 98, Andarko, Okla. 73005, will send you one of its catalogs in return for a stamp. Free, so far as I can determine, are the catalogs from the **BLACK MOUNTAIN TRADING POST**, WW, Box 19035, Navajo Station, San Diego, Cal. 92119; the **CHEYENNE LODGE**, WW, Box 717, El Reno, Okla. 73036; and the **LONE BEAR INDIAN**

CRAFT CO., WW, 5 Beekman St., New York, N.Y. 10038.

D. WOOD AND METAL

Although you will, of course, find wood and metal items for decorating at almost all of the firms in Section A, there are some firms devoted entirely to that interesting specialty. For instance, the O-P CRAFT CO., INC., WW, 415 Warren St., Sandusky, Ohio 44870; and the DEK-CO MANUFACTURING CO., WW, Box 1314, Amarillo, Tex. 79105, both have large lines of all kinds of wooden items that await your finishing touches. There are boxes—small and large, plain and fancy—shadow boxes, lap desks, desk sets, plaques, buttons, candlesticks, and small plain pieces of wood (for large pieces of wood, see Chapter 19,B). Both catalogs are 50¢.

The WESTON BOWL MILL, WW, Weston, Vt. 05161, which specializes in wooden things for the home, offers a lot of them unfinished, at prices that generally run lower than the craft houses'. There are boxes and boards and buckets and bowls and lots of things that don't begin with a *b,* all for you to turn into the objects of your dreams. (For really large unfinished pieces, see the furniture section of Chapter 9.) The price of Weston's catalog is 25¢.

THE COUNTRY PEDDLER, WW, P.O. Box 742, High Point, N.C. 27261, also sells wooden items to be refinished, including some things I didn't see in the other catalogs, like umbrella stands and miniature chests. In addition, they also have lots of metal objects for tole painting (or whatever you want to do with them). In addition to the usual silent butlers and trays, their collection includes a replica of an old-fashioned lunch bucket, a gypsy milk strainer, an antique deed box, and a colonial butter can, at what seem like quite moderate prices. The catalog appears to be free.

BAXWOOD CRAFTERS, WW, 1171 Commercial Dr., Lexington, Ky. 40505, puts out a free brochure showing the unfinished wooden lamps they sell, ready for you to paint, stain, or découpage. And from Canada comes an interesting new craft, rather, a new interpretation of a centuries-old one. The HANDY WOOD CRAFT CO., WW, 977 Sierra Blvd., Mississauga, Ontario, Canada, has developed wood turning blanks made of different woods in their natural colors laminated together, for a number of different projects. Prices range from around $4.00 for a powder bowl to $10.00 for a lamp—not expensive, when you consider, for example, that the powder bowl, their smallest wood turning blank, contains 105 linear inches of

exotic wood, not counting the central block, with 35 glued surfaces. The illustrated brochure is free.

DAIRY SERVICE, INC., WW, P.O. Box 253, Bluffton, Ind. 46714, offers old milk cans with lids for decorative purposes. Cans are in 3 to 10 gallon sizes and cost $6.00 to $11.00 (depending more on where you live and less on the size of the can). They also have oak barrels and kegs, both old and new, plus old milk bottles in clear and amber glass. Lists are 25¢.

You'll find tools for woodcarvers listed in the catalogs of many of the firms in the first section of this chapter, as well as in Chapter 19. A couple of overseas firms specialize in them. CARL HEIDTMANN, WW, Postfach 14039, 563 Remscheid 14 (Hastens), West Germany, puts out a catalog listing a great variety of tools—which can be delivered without handles, or with loose or fitted hornbeam handles. The catalog is mostly in German but there is enough explanatory material in English to make ordering possible for the non-German speaker. Send 2 IRCs to pay for the postage. ASHLEY ILES, LTD., WW, Woodcarver Works, Spilsby, Lincs., England, also sells hand-forged woodcarving tools. The brochure is accompanied by a price list in American dollars, and it's free.

E. BEADS, NECK ORNAMENTS, AND MACRAMÉ

Beads seem to be as popular as ever, and you'll find lots and lots of nice ones here—perhaps enough to tempt you to make yourself a necklace even if you aren't essentially a craft person (on the other hand, if you aren't, you're not likely to be reading this chapter). You'll find standard beads here, as well as a lot of unusual items, both domestic and imported.

Although many of the firms in this section do list real gemstone beads, in most cases you'll get a better buy if you get them from the East Indian Houses in Section F (prices at the domestic houses listed in that section are apt to be about the same as at the bead houses here). You'll also find large selections of beads of all kinds, many of them antiques, at all of the Indian craft supply houses in Section C.

THE BEAD GAME, WW, 505 North Fairfax Ave., Los Angeles, Cal. 90036, not only offers lots and lots of beads in their catalog, but from time to time, they offer such interesting things to hang on your neck as masks, handcarved by headhunting tribesmen in New Guinea ($4.00); Burma bone stashes (you conceal things like saccharin, talcum powder, or whatever, in them—60¢); Balinese barongs carved out of coconut shells (40¢ to $2.00); desert clay pendants (50¢ up); etc. There are also larger masks, for collectors of primitive art; antique Chinese coins for casting the

I Ching; ancient Phoenician beads; and all kinds of things for averting the evil eye. Catalog is 25¢.

GLORIA'S GLASS GARDEN, WW, Box 1990, Beverly Hills, Cal. 90213, offers an equally large collection of beads, at moderate prices, including some very unusual types. Giant donkey beads from Iran cost 75¢ for 10; handmade ceramic beads cost from 20¢ to 60¢ each; glass ovals from India are a mere 2¢. They also have all kinds of bells, including tiny beaded ones (6 for 50¢). Brochures are 25¢.

Not only Canadians will be interested in the **HOUSE OF ORANGE**, WW, 3621 West Broadway, Vancouver 8, British Colombia, Canada, which puts out a large mimeographed list of beads (all inexpensive and some types I haven't seen elsewhere), bells, and macramé cord. They also have some interesting mosaic pendants from Italy and some antique Indian beads (as well as very inexpensive aromatic oils and sandalwood soap from China, plus incense of their own making). And **LEMCO**, WW, P.O. Box 40545, San Francisco, Cal. 94140, has a huge selection of beads, clasps, rings, buckles, and books in its free price list; as well as lots of macramé, including all kinds of twine, braid, cord, and thread. [The other bead houses have some macramé supplies, and you'll find more at the general supply houses in Chapter 18 (Needle and Loom).]

The two preceding catalogs are all free; however, **ALOHALEI HAWAII**, WW, P.O. Box 10-E, Honolulu, Hawaii 96816, puts out a catalog for 25¢ (ref.). It shows kits of very attractive pearl necklaces, chokers, and collars, which they call "leis." Some of them look intricate, but the firm claims they are all quite simple to put together. All kits are $5.00 each, including shipping. Alohalei also sells beads and patterns separately.

F. GEMS

1. Gemstones

Since most of the gemstones you buy are imported, it pays to get your stones directly from the source, wherever possible. **UNIVERSAL GEMS CORP.**, WW, 61, 10th Khetwadi, Bombay 4, India, sells precious and semiprecious cabochons and faceted gemstones, at prices far below those obtained here. Beads are a particularly good buy. You can get necklaces of such stones as garnet, amethyst, and topaz, from around $5.00 to $12.00. (Unless you're getting them for someone with a very slender neck, or are planning to add spacers, better order some extra beads, as they run about 16" long). You can also get beggar beads at 5¢ per inch, bloodstone, carnelian, and various agates for slightly more. Always order necklaces temporarily

strung; otherwise the duty will be higher and you may get fewer beads, because they put little felt spacers in between them. Loose beads cost from $1.00 to $10.00 per 100; some of the more expensive types are priced per gram. Also on hand are gemstone snuff bottles, animals, and ashtrays—all very inexpensive. The catalog (free) includes listings of several associated firms and is so complicated (even though it's in perfect English) that it's hard to read. Prices are in American dollars.

SHANI JEWELLERS, WW, 61/63 Rajwadekar St., Colaba, Bombay 5, India; and **SAMARTH GEM STONES**, WW, P.O. Box 6057, Colaba, Bombay 5, India, offer similar lines at prices (given in dollars) that seem slightly higher; however, because there are such variations among gemstones, it's difficult to say. All three firms are very inexpensive compared to what you'd have to pay for the same thing here. All three houses also offer cutting rough, but watch out for this; if you order an appreciable quantity, you're likely to need the services of a customs broker. Shani's and Samarth's price lists are also free.

Taiwan is noted for its jade, and you can get some real bargains there from the **LEE SAN LAPIDARY INDUSTRIAL CO., LTD.**, WW, 153 Chung Cheng Rd., Taipei, Taiwan. Dome or flat top cabochons of green jade start at around 20¢ apiece (that's for a C quality 13 x 18 mm oval; a first quality would be $1.20). They have all the standard shapes and sizes, and can get you practically anything you need. They have jade band rings in all sizes, at around 50¢ and $1.00.

If you're interested in Australian gemstones, the **AUSTRALIAN GEM TRADING CO.**, WW, 294 Little Collins St., Melbourne, Australia 30000, puts out a free catalog aimed directly at the U.S. trade, so prices are given in American dollars. Opal is the big feature here—cutting rough is offered in many grades. They also sell cut Coober Pedy and Andamooka opals ($1.00 to $50.00), black opal doublets and black opals themselves ($3.00 to $150.00 per carat). On hand also are Australian sapphires—blue, green, yellow, parti-colored, and black star. **M & B GIFTS OF AUSTRALIA**, WW, P.O. Box 17, The Basin 3154, Victoria, Australia, also sells rough opal (and probably cut stones too, if you ask). **HETTIE'S ROCK SHOP**, WW, 110 Birdwood Ave., Christchurch 2, New Zealand, sells New Zealand gemstone rough and mineral specimens. Brochures are free.

The **CROWN CULTURED PEARL CORP.**, WW, 589 Eighth Ave., New York, N.Y. 10018, is actually the New York office of a Japanese firm, which might be why they appear to offer such very good buys in pearls, jade cabochons, and other items of interest to jewelry craftsmen. Lists are free.

You can get a free catalog of Mexican minerals from **BELTRAVI S.A.**, WW, Saltillo 1281 Sur., Cd. Juarez, Chih., Mexico, which offers Mexican minerals for cutting and tumbling as well as cut stones—agate, jasper, amethyst, sodalite, chrysocolla, opal, etc. They also have chrysocolla and sodalite eggs. Some of their prices seem rather high, and you might do better at the **HOUSE OF ONYX**, WW, Greenville, Ky. 42345, which specializes in Mexican imports, including minerals and inexpensive cut stones (13 x 18 mm jasper, lace agate, rose quartz, and tigereye cabochons cost around 50¢). They also have green and black Oriental jade cabochons, and Australian opal. Price lists are free.

Another good U.S. source of cut stones from all around the world is the **INTERNATIONAL IMPORT CO.**, WW, P.O. Box 727, Stone Mountain, Ga. 30083, which puts out a big yearly free list of gemstones in all price ranges, from 50¢ up into thousands of dollars. There are plenty of inexpensive materials for the craftsperson, however, as you can tell from the fact that their minimum order is only $4.00.

There are so many gemstone firms in the United States that feature local stones that I can't begin to list them. However, there are two that you might find of special interest. The **JADE PLACE**, WW, 1765 West 15 St., Casper, Wyo. 82601, deals mainly in Wyoming nephrite jade—not only the well-known dark green, but apple green, translucent light olive, and apple green snowflake and dark olive snowflake. There is also blue jade from California and thulite, or pink jade. Mostly these are offered in the rough or slabbed, but there's a small collection of cabochons. **RON'S GEM SHOP**, WW, P.O. Box 927, McCall, Idaho 83638, will supply you with the hard-to-get Idaho blue opal, both cut stones and rough. Lists are free.

For other sources of gemstones, see Chapter 15,D (Collections), which deals chiefly with mineral specimens; however, just as most of the firms I have described here also carry mineral specimens, so most of the firms listed there also offer some cut stones. In addition, you will find many cut stones purveyed by the houses that follow.

2. Lapidary Supplies

GRIEGER'S, WW, 900 S. Arroyo Pkwy., Pasadena, Cal. 91109, will send you upon request, free of charge, a big colorful catalog, with all kinds of jewelry mountings, lapidary equipment, gemstones, gem rough (plus a few fossils). I don't think there is any one lapidary

house that offers a greater diversity of material, although some have broader ranges in some areas. Prices are not high (although you'll find gemstones cheaper elsewhere), and they have all kinds of zodiac jewelry. The **GEMEX CO.**, WW, 900 West Los Vallecitos Blvd., San Marcos, Ca. 92069, puts out a similar catalog, also free. They also have zodiac stones and some nice porcelains (some have cats, dogs, or horses on them). There are real gemstone stars, gemstone animals, and cabochons—all priced rather high, but I haven't seen black onyx bats or obsidian cats elsewhere. (**GEMEX** also puts out a big general crafts catalog, which is free, too.)

JEWELART, WW, 7753 Densmore Ave., Van Nuys, Cal. 91406, issues a "Boutique Catalogue" (25¢) of jewelry parts. It has a large collection of fake jewelry stones, including (in addition to straight phony rubies, emeralds, etc.) some really lovely painted porcelains, cameos, and glass intaglios, plus the ubiquitous signs of the zodiac. There's a huge variety of beads, lots of jewelry settings (not the usual ones you see repeated in catalog after catalog), and many other interesting things.

LIBERTY GEM AND SUPPLY, WW, Box 127, Liberty, Ill. 62347; and **LAPIDABRADE, INC.**, WW, 8 East Eagle Rd., Havertown, Pa. 19083, confine themselves to mountings and stones. **UNITED ABRASIVE, INC.**, WW, Norway, Mich. 49870, has only mountings and lapidary supplies. **BASKIN AND SONS, INC.**, WW, 732 Union Ave., Middlesex, N.J. 08846; **BOURGET BROTHERS**, WW, 1011 Olympic Blvd., Santa Monica, Cal. 90404; **GILMAN'S**, WW, Hellertown, Pa. 18055; **WEIDINGER**, WW, 4404 Del Prado Pkwy., P.O. Box 5, Cape Coral, Fla. 33904; and **EBERSOLE LAPIDARY SUPPLY INC.**, WW, 11417 West Highway 54, RR 8, Wichita, Kan. 67209, all put out catalogs of stones, mountings, and equipment. Ebersole's is 30¢; all the others are free.

C. W. SOMERS AND CO., WW, 387 Washington St., Boston, Mass. 02108, has a free catalog of tools for jewelers and silversmiths.

G. SHELLCRAFT

There are several firms that specialize in shellcraft. The **DERBY LANE SHELL CENTER**, WW, 10515 Gandy Blvd., St. Petersburg, Fla. 33702, has a nice plump catalog containing shells both for the shellcrafter and the collector. Many of the jewelry findings they offer are much less expensive than those you'll find in the firms listed in Section F. They show some interesting mother-of-pearl and plastic doodads that seem peculiar to the shell houses, although they have little or no connection with shells per se. (I suppose mother-of-pearl is made out of shell, now that I think about it, but it isn't usually sold in connection with shells.) Their catalog is 25¢. The catalog that's put out by the **FLORIDA SUPPLY HOUSE, INC.**, WW, P.O. Box 845, Bradenton, Fla. 33505, is free. They also have shells, shellcraft kits, jewelry findings, plus some other crafts. Some glass jewel dangles look worthy of notice. They also sell three different types of canned Florida weather at 50¢ per can. The **SHELL LAND NOVELTY CO., INC.**, WW, 14788 U.S. Highway 19, Clearwater, Fla. 33516, offers only shellcraft kits, and their catalog is free.

H. LEATHER

Many of the firms in Section A offer large lines of supplies for leathercrafters. In addition, you can get leather from many of the firms in Chapter 4,B. **BERMAN BUCKSKINS** sells leather by the skin, from $6.00 up; and **ALVORD'S** offers a 2-lb. bag of assorted leather scraps for 75¢, or a 1-lb. bag of cowhide leather strips for $1.75.

THE GIFT HORSE, WW, P.O. Box 226, Penngrove, Cal. 94951, specializes in leather kits for do-it-yourself projects (shown in its free brochure). **BRADFORD SUEDES**, WW, Box 264, Bradford, Mass. 01830, sells suede skins from around $4.00 to $5.00, plus odd-shaped suede pieces at 30¢ per square foot. They also have kits—a patchwork suede skirt is $11.00. Brochure and swatch card are free.

The **JRM LEATHER AND CANDLE CO.**, WW, 26563 Hawkhurst Dr., Palos Verdes, Cal. 90274, sells latago (they don't explain this) leather straps, also latago leather at $1.50 per square foot; and suede at $1.00 per square foot. A 1-lb. bag of miscellaneous leather scraps is $1.00. There's also leather dyes and finishes as well as tools and hardware. (As you can tell from their name, they have candlemaking supplies, which I haven't categorized separately because practically everybody in Section A carries them, as well as all kinds of other firms scattered throughout the book.) Catalog is free.

The **CREATIVE LEATHER WORKSHOP**, WW, 12 Bow St., Cambridge, Mass. 02138, sells kits for making leather garments. Prices range from $19.00 for a woman's suede waistcoat embroidered with multicolored suede stripping to $70.00 for a whipstitched coat. Also on hand are some rather unusual items out of crocheted leather, and leather by the skin, square, or scrap. Catalog is free.

If you'd like to make your own gloves, the **J. P. FLIEGEL CO.**, WW, P.O. Box 505, Gloversville, N.Y. 12078, will sell you leather glove kits at $5.00 to $6.00 per pair, or fabric glove kits, $2.00 each. Or

you can buy the leather or doubleknit cotton and nylon fabric, plus patterns and accessories (including glove stretchers), suitable needles and threads, and so on. The 25¢ you pay for the catalog includes samples of the leathers and the fabrics.

I. SPECIALTIES

IMPACT ENTERPRISES, WW, White Horse Yard, North St., Ripon, Yorkshire, England, specializes in precision moulds, which can be used for casting in polyester resin, plaster, or wax. Most noteworthy is the set of seven rubber moulds for making an exact replica of the British Museum's famous twelfth-century Isle of Lewis chess set. That costs less than $6.00. (Reproduction sets usually cost around $50.00.) For $6.00 you can also get four soldiers in historical uniform or a set of the Queen's Beasts (two sets, each with five moulds). There are also characters from Dickens and Shakespeare, plus some moulds for garden ornaments, featuring the popular British garden gnomes. Send them an IRC to help pay for postage.

The proprietor of **SAND CATS**, WW, P.O. Box 15084, Lakewood, Colo. 80215, has been a sandpainter and a student of sand for several years, and he has now made his materials available commercially. There are kits for sandpainting (the Japanese rather than the American Indian kind), starting at $3.00; a brochure on sandpainting for 50¢; and individual sands from 15¢ to 35¢ per oz. He also has 250 different types of sands for sand collectors. Price list is free.

SITKA SPECIALTIES, WW, Box 1145, Sitka, Alaska 99835, offers a rather curious art medium—bear bread, which is a type of fungus native to Southeastern Alaska. (The brochure tells us that it is similar to the red belt conk, if that conveys anything to you.) It is not edible; even the bears' alleged fondness for it, the proprietors admit, is dubious. They suggest that you use the bread as a base for decorative displays of artificial plants, etc., or as the setting for a miniature scene. For the artist, they say, the smooth side lends itself to oils or acrylics. It's offered in kits. Brochure is free.

A lot of people seem to be going in for eggcraft. In a traditional vein, **SURMA**, WW, 11 East 7 St., New York, N.Y. 10003, sells supplies and kits for making your own Ukrainian decorated Easter eggs or *pysanky*. In case you've never decorated eggs, you might consider taking up the craft. Perhaps you didn't know that, as the catalog informs you, the world will continue to exist only as long as people continue to decorate eggs. Should they stop, an ancient vicious monster will break the chains that bind him to a huge cliff and destroy the world. The kits are $6.00, the catalog is 25¢, and hurry!

In another vein, **NATALIE ORIGINALS STUDIOS**, WW, 4271 Dewey Ave., Rochester, N.Y. 14616, sells a catalog of egg supplies (50¢). There are decorations —gilt and jewels and spangles and such—to put *on* the eggs; and things to put *inside* the eggs—like tiny music boxes at $3.00 (which are described as fitting goose eggs); and imported miniatures of all kinds (to fit both chicken and goose eggs). They also sell blue mallard, Guinea hen, Araucara chicken, East Indian duck, and other kinds of eggs with doors and other apertures already cut in them. For the really lavish egger, there are ostrich, emu, and rhea eggs—prices available only upon request. Egg bases are also available.

There seems to be a number of hobbies involving miniatures, not only in eggs, but decorating all kinds of things. You will find some miniatures listed in this chapter, but the bulk of them got into Chapter 22 (Playthings and Diversions), so be sure to check there.

Something you can't find everywhere is the gravestone rubbing kit put out by **THE PAINT SHOP, INC.**, WW, 59 Main St., Old Saybrook, Conn. 06475. Their brochure, listing this and other art supplies, is probably free. Be sure to specify that you're interested in gravestone rubbing.

HARVEST STUDIO, WW, 906 North 28 St., Morningside Heights, Bismarck, N.D. 58501, specializes in decorations "from the world of ecology"—i.e., cones, pods, seeds, lichens, dried flowers and leaves, and other plant parts. These range from spruce cones at 50¢ a dozen to sugar pine cones at $1.35 each. They also have kits you can make up into wreaths and such, from $24.00. The mimeographed leaflet costs $1.00.

BOYCAN'S FLORAL ARTS, WW, State at Flowera Ave., Sharon, Pa. 16146, puts out a thick catalog that features all sorts of material for making flowers, out of both artificial and dried natural materials, but is not devoted entirely to that craft. They have a large assemblage of extremely inexpensive miniatures in wood and metal, découpage supplies, beads, and boutique-type trimmings. Prices seem unusually low. Catalog is 50¢. **MERRIMACK** (see Chapter 12,D) sells hardwood presses for dried flowers at $5.50 each.

The **ART GLASS AND CRAFT STUDIO**, WW, 401 Bloomfield Ave., Verona, N.J. 07044, will send you free listings of their stained glass "Doo Dad Beginner Kits." Prices range from $1.00 for a mushroom to $5.00 for a rather elaborate set of wind chimes (most prices are in the $2.00 or less area). There are also stained glass lamp kits, starting at $60.00. Catalog is

free, as are the lists put out by the **WHITTEMORE-DURGIN GLASS CO.**, WW, Box 2065, Hanover, Mass. 02339. They specialize in stained glass supplies, and you'll get lots of offerings along that line when you write for their miscellaneous lists, which also include items that might appeal to craftsmen, as well as magpies. From time to time their lists have included such goodies as old cannery labels (50¢), Victorian stickpin heads (15¢), inkwells (75¢), small black glass noses for fur pieces (20¢), and all kinds of things that even they can't identify.

The **BASIC CRAFTS CO.**, WW, 312 East 23 St., New York, N.Y. 10010, specializes in supplying tools, materials, and equipment for the bookbinding craftsman and the librarian. "For those who cherish and love books and are anxious to preserve them," Basic Crafts has assembled from all corners of the globe, the proper equipment, materials and tools to do the job, both in initial bookbinding and in the restoration of books. In addition to listing and picturing supplies, the free catalog tells you how to clean and mend your books and gives directions for simple bookbinding.

HAWTHORNE HOUSE, INC., WW, 1700 West Washington St., Bloomington, Ill. 61701, sells soapmaking sets, at around $9.00, as well as individual supplies. They also sell candlemaking materials and their brochure is free.

HOBBI-ART, INC., WW, 4712 Kirkwood Hwy., Midway Shopping Center, Wilmington, Del. 19808, is devoted to the art of lampshade making, and their 10¢ brochure gives a complete selection of supplies, plus instruction books for novices and those interested in blazing new trails.

LOUIS HERMAN AND ASSOCIATES, INC., WW, 8227 Ridgeway Ave., Skokie, Ill. 60076, vend handcarved picture frames imported from Mexico and Taiwan. There are 25 styles in 5 finishes (brown, green, blue, metallic gold leaf, and antique gold leaf) and in 20 sizes. Also on hand are velvet miniature frames. Prices range from less than $1.00 to around $26.00. Minimum order is $35.00 (or you pay a $2.50 packing charge). Brochures are free, as are the ones offered by the **F. C. ZIEGLER CO.**, WW, 415 East 12 St., Tulsa, Okla. 74120, which sells miniature easels and miniature frames starting at less than $2.00.

R-O-Z CRAFT SUPPLY CO., WW, 9 Laurel St., Hicksville, N.Y. 11801, puts out a brochure of those small hardware items so indispensable for craft work and so hard to find in variety. There are all kinds of ring hangers, miniature latches, knobs, hinges, and fancy nails, as well as pursemaking accessories and ornamental hooks. Brochure is free.

J. PUBLICATIONS

Almost all of the catalogs in Section A, as well as in some of the other sections, feature long lists of arts and crafts books. However, there are certain firms devoted to the subject. **K. R. DRUMMOND,** WW, 30 Hart Grove, Ealing Common, London W.5, England, puts out price lists of books, both new and used, dealing with various crafts and art. Categories include fine art, basketry, bookbinding, calligraphy, ceramics, costume, dolls, dyeing (textiles), embroidery, fabric, printing, leatherwork, metalwork, puppetry, spinning, toys, weaving, etc. Send an IRC for each one of these you want (you'll get the complete list of categories with any of them). Locally, the **UNICORN,** WW, Box 645, Rockville, Md. 20851, has a catalog of books for craftspeople, which it will part with for 25¢.

The **VICTORIA AND ALBERT MUSEUM,** WW, South Kensington, London, S.W.7, England, includes in its list of publications (free), a number of pamphlets of especial interest to craftspeople. They deal with such subjects as embroidery, textiles, patchwork, costume, dolls, furniture, and so on, at prices starting under 50¢.

Remember: *Write for the catalog first.* All prices given were valid only at the time of writing and probably have been changed.

Chapter 18

NEEDLE AND LOOM

A. GENERAL

Naturally there will be some overlapping between the firms in this chapter and the one before. You'll find some needlework and weaving supplies included under *Arts and Crafts,* and you'll find some extraneous crafts listed in a number of the catalogs in this chapter. As for macramé, you'll find it listed in both, because it seems to resist simple classification.

There are several large needlework firms that have been in the business a long time (Herrschner's since 1899), and sell approximately the same kinds of things—all kinds of kits; supplies for sewing, crocheting, knitting, embroidering; and so on. All of them offer big free color catalogs. They are the **FREDERICK HERRSCHNER CO.**, WW, Stevens Point, Wis. 54481; **MARY MAXIM**, WW, 2001 Holland Ave., Port Huron, Mich. 48060; **LEE WARD'S**, WW, 1200 St. Charles St., Elgin, Ill. 60120; and the **MERRIBEE CO.**, WW, 2904 West Lancaster, P.O. Box 9680, Fort Worth, Tex. 76107.

On a somewhat "artier" level, England has some good sources, but they'll cost you money. The **NEEDLE-WOMAN SHOP**, WW, 146-148 Regent St., London W1R 6BA, England, shows a line of needlework kits from all over the world, in their beautiful color catalog, which costs 60¢. There are embroidery, knitting and crochet, rugmaking, needlepoint, and tapestry projects, plus all the supplies necessary for those who start from scratch. Also sold are gifts for the needlewoman, and kits for other popular crafts.

For $2.50, **ART NEEDLEWORK INDUSTRIES, LTD. (A.N.I.)**, WW, 7 St. Michael's Mansions, Ship St., Oxford OX1 3DG, England, will send you a thick package of brochures covering projects in folk knitting of various kinds, and crocheting, together with samples of wool and yarn for those who prefer not to work with the kits that are offered in such profusion here. For the same price, the firm also offers a batch of brochures for tapestry embroidery, rug designs, and kits, mostly based on traditional patterns. Be sure you indicate which set you want. Prices are given in American dollars and they include shipping.

B. SEWING

1. Supplies and Kits

HOME-SEW, INC., WW, Bethlehem, Pa. 18018, has a large array of inexpensive sewing supplies and trimmings—lace, braid, ribbons, thread, fringe, zippers, frogs, sequins, and lots of things you may have been searching for. The catalog is 25¢ (ref.).

For those who'd like to make their own lingerie but don't know where to get the supplies, **KIEFFER'S**, WW, 1625 Hennepin Ave., Minneapolis, Minn. 55403; **KNIT-KITS**, WW, 216 Third Ave., Minneapolis, Minn. 55401; and the **SEWING BEE**, WW, 261 East 7 St., St. Paul, Minn. 55101, are just the places. They sell bra and girdle supplies, fabrics of all suitable kinds—mostly single and double knits in a fascinating range of colors (some prints)—ribbons, and straps. (You'll find them good sources of supply for repair work, too.) Also on hand are materials for making bathing suits, nightgear, and children's things. In case you wonder where you can get the patterns for these, you need look no further; they carry them in abundance. Kieffer's catalog is free; Knit-Kits costs $1.00, but with it you get swatches, plus 25 yds. of assorted laces. The Sewing Bee's is also $1.00, of which 50¢ is refundable.

The **SEWING CORNER, INC.**, WW, P.O. Box 412, Whitestone, N.Y. 11357, puts out a catalog of all kinds of gifts and gadgets for both the dedicated and the frivolous sewer. They have a pleasing selection of handmade sterling silver thimbles, from around $6.00 to $10.00; a portable sewing corner (a little under $25.00) that should be of great assistance to the disorganized needlewoman; and all kinds of other useful things. They also have a catalog of precut kits for what they call "couture fashions," offered at prices ranging from around $15.00 to $35.00. Each kit comes with all necessary supplies and instructions. Both catalogs are 25¢.

HERTER'S, INC., WW, Waseca, Minn. 56093, has handcarved Circassian walnut buttons and buckles, and silk fabrics from India and Thailand, at prices low enough so that it might pay you to make comparisons before you order from abroad. Price of their big catalog is $1.00.

You'll find a vast and engaging collection of buttons from all over the world at the **HOUSE OF YORK,** WW, 63 Oakleaf Dr., Doylestown, Pa. 18901. For 25¢, there's a metal squirrel from Germany; for 30¢, a metal edelweiss from Austria, a glass cat from Germany, or a pewter hare of unspecified origin; 35¢, a German lady bug; 40¢, a glass mushroom; 50¢, a clockface (nonoperating); 55¢, a teddy bear from Sweden; 60¢, a Dresden flower; 85¢, an Irish shamrock from Austria, or signs of the zodiac from Bucks County; $1.10, a Venetian glass kaleidoscope; $1.40, a Navajo squash blossom; and dozens more. There are also buckles, zipper pulls, sweater clasps, dirndl lacers, thimbles, and all kinds of unusual and good things for the sewer. The brochure is 15¢.

HUSFLIDEN, WW, Grunnlagt 1895, 5000 Bergen, Norway, offers those attractive handmade pewter buttons and buckles that you seem to see all over the place these days—you know, the ones with reindeer, Viking ships, and snowflakes, as well as traditional designs. Prices range from about $1.50 to $3.50 per dozen; buckles are higher. Be sure to ask specifically for the button brochure when you write for the set of brochures, which is free.

For an exotic touch, you can get reproduction Colonial uniform buttons at 50¢ each from **K. EWER, PEWTERER,** WW, 1282 Lafayette St., Cape May, N.J. 08204. The free brochure is called "Museum Miniatures."

SURMA, WW, 11 East 7 St., New York, N.Y. 10003, has a brochure (25¢) with samples of their lovely washable embroidered ribbons, from $1.00 to $2.50 per yd. They also sell brass-plated rings for ribbon belts.

2. Fabrics

Many of the firms I described in Chapter 2 sell fabrics by the yard, as well as finished clothes. Most of the Scottish houses—The **ST. ANDREWS WOOLLEN MILL, EDINBURGH TARTANS** (Chapter 2,C.1), **WILLIAM ANDERSON** (Chapter 2,D.1), **HUGH MacPHERSON** (Chapter 3,C)—sell tweeds and tartans by the yard, at prices starting in the neighborhood of $5.00. **MacGILLIVRAY** (Chapter 2,C.1) also offers handwoven Harris tweeds from the Outer Hebrides at around $3.00 per yd., but they're only 28" wide. On request, the proprietors say, they can smoke the fabric over peat, "which we think gives it a distinctive odour and personality of its own." They also have double-width tweed, suiting, and tartans, starting at a dollar or two more per yd.

From Ireland, **O'BEIRNE AND FITZGIBBON** will send you a set of swatches of their lovely 56-inch wide, handwoven Donegal tweeds (from $8.00 to $9.00 per yd.). See Chapter 2,F.1 for details. **JACOBS** (Chapter 2,D.2) also offers handwoven tweeds 56" to 60" wide, from $8.00 to $12.00 per yd. **BROWN-THOMAS** (Chapter 2,D.2) is the place to go to for linens by the yard.

In England, **W. BILL, LTD.** (Chapter 2,E.1), which has specialized in woollen cloth for over 125 years, will send you a little catalog showing 28-inch wide Harris and Irish tweeds, from around $4.50; 58-inch wide cheviot tweeds from $11.00; and other fabrics, including cashmeres and worsteds. Welsh tapestry cloth by the yard is available from **LLYSWEN** (Chapter 2,D.1). Although **LIBERTY AND CO., LTD.**, WW, Regent St., London W.1, England, are noted for their silks and their prints, they actually sell all sorts of fabrics. Cottons start at around $2.00 to $3.00; silks, $5.00 to $6.00; wools at $6.00 to $7.00. Most distinctive of all are their own printed wools, 36" wide, at $6.00 to $7.00 per yd. They'll send you swatches, if you tell them what you want. And you don't have to be bound by what I've written here; they have practically everything. (Liberty also puts out a small brochure of its own scarves, but **SHANNON** seems to have about the same selection in its catalog, at the same prices—or even a little lower.)

For German and Swiss fabrics you may have to fall back on the big mail-order houses (Chapter 2,A). If the catalogs don't show fabrics, ask about them; there may be separate brochures. Ask about Norwegian fabrics at **HUSFLIDEN** (this chapter, B.1) and about Finnish at **STOCKMANN** (Chapter 5,A.1); among the multitude of brochures they have on hand there are bound to be some on fabric.

India, of course, has always been noted for its lovely silks. The **KAVERI MYSORE STATE HANDICRAFTS DEVELOPMENT CORPORATION, LTD.,** WW, 26/45 Mahatma Gandhi Rd., Bangalore-1, India, in its free list, mentions printed raw silk dress material (around $3.00 to $5.00 per meter), silk shirting ($1.50 to $3.00), silk suiting ($4.00 to $6.00), plus other fabrics that are even lower in price. They also sell saris and scarves at very low prices, bedspreads, table linens, and—something you can't find everywhere—jug covers (about 50¢). The **BENGAL HOME INDUSTRIES ASSOCIATION,** WW, 57 Chowringhee Rd., Calcutta 16, India; and the **LEPAKSHI HANDICRAFTS EMPORIUM,** WW, Gunfoundry, Hyderabad, India, both also offer fabrics starting at even lower prices; they also have saris, bedspreads, wall hangings, and so on. The trouble is that all three catalogs, which are free, are extremely vague, and it looks as if you will have to enter into prolonged correspondence after you get them. (It might help if along with your catalog request you mentioned that you were particularly interested in fabrics, though I can't give you any guarantees.)

In Sri Lanka (which is what you must remember to call Ceylon from now on; although you'd better put "Ceylon" in parentheses, since our Post Office isn't always quick on the uptake), the **SERENDIB GALLERY,** WW, Galle Rd., Colombo 4, Sri Lanka, offers batik dress and sarong lengths from around $5.00. **LAKLOOMS,** WW, 72 Chatham St., Colombo 1, Sri Lanka, sells batik dress, suit, and blouse lengths from around $2.00 to $4.00. They also have batik sarongs and saris and wall hangings. In addition there are dress fabrics, starting at less than $1.00 per yd., and bedspreads under $4.00. Seamail shipping is included, and price lists are free. The catch is that the "minimum trade order" must be around $120.00; and I don't know whether you can get away with such sophistry as, "this isn't a trade order, so I don't have to observe the minimums." But they do have a lot of things I haven't had space to mention, and, if you and your friends could get an order of that size together, I think you could have yourselves a good buy. (If you can't, it's possible that you can arrange to pay a surcharge, as many of the wholesale firms permit for orders under their minima.)

Moving on to Thailand, I confidently offer you the **THAI SILK CO., LTD.,** WW, Box 906, G.P.O., Bangkok, Thailand. They'll send you free swatches of their lovely silks (prices start at about $4.00 for the 40-inch width). The firm is American-run, and, so, very definite about prices and such. They also have scarves, stoles, neckties, and so forth, and their price lists are free. **SILK OF SIAM,** WW, 297 Suriwongse Rd., G.P.O. Box 182, Bangkok, Thailand, is also American-run and they'll send you a free catalog, which includes pictures of silks. Don't forget to check America's own **THAI SILKS** (Chapter 2) and **HERTER'S,** to see if it's actually worth your while ordering the fabrics from abroad.

THE CHINESE MERCHANDISE EMPORIUM, WW, 92-104 Queen's Rd. Central, Hong Kong, which has been described in more detail earlier in this book, offers silk and all kinds of other fabrics from mainland China. Their catalog is free, but it's vaguer than most, so tell them when you write that you're interested in fabrics from China and maybe they'll send you swatches or at least a definite price list.

The **TATSUMURA SILK MANSION,** WW, Shmogawara-cho, Nanzenji, Sakyo-ku, Kyoto, Japan, does not have a catalog, but they might send you swatches of their delectable silks, together with a price list, as they did for me. They didn't respond to my request

that they make a token charge to avoid freeloading swatch collectors, so the swatches are presumably free, if you can get them. The bright, lush silks—brocades, printed pongees, chiffons, habutae, and crêpes de chine—run from around $7.00 to $14.00 per meter, and I assume shipping would be extra.

STUDIO ARTS 68, WW, Standard St., Box 47904, Nairobi, Kenya, East Africa, offers fabrics hand-screened and tie-dyed by African people. Prices start from around $3.50 per yd., and, again, price lists are free but vague, so write and tell them that you're interested primarily in fabrics.

In Mexico, **TEXTILES HERNANZ** (Chapter 3,A.2), offer cotton and mixed cotton and woollen fabrics in what seem extraordinarily wide widths (from 2 to 3 yds.) at prices that seem very low. However, unless you speak Spanish, you will have some difficulty in getting full details. The price list is free.

In the United States, **NIZHONIE, INC.,** WW, 810½ Broadway, Box 729, Cortez, Colo. 81321, is an Indian-owned enterprise producing authentic original Indian handprinted textiles, with motifs derived from traditional Indian symbols. Overall prints, 45 inches wide, are priced from $3.50 to around $10.00 per yd., depending on the fabric; 58-inch wide border prints, $3.00 to $8.00. They also offer tea towels, hangings, placemats, etc. Catalog is free.

The **MILL STORE,** WW, Homestead Woolen Mills, Inc., West Swanzey, N.H. 03467, is a Yankee enterprise, selling woollen and wool blend fabrics, 55 inches wide, from less than $3.00 per yd. to about $4.00. They'll send swatches. You'll find other American fabrics scattered through many of the other catalogs. The **VERMONT COUNTRY STORE** (Chapter 8,A.1), for example, has calicoes; **WATUMULL BROTHERS** (Chapter 2,B) carries those wild Hawaiian prints.

If you're looking for leather, it has a little section all to itself in Chapter 17(H).

C. YARN CRAFTS

1. Spinning and Weaving

ASHFORD HANDICRAFTS, LTD., WW, P.O. Box 12, Rakaia, Canterbury, New Zealand, sells spinning wheels from around $45.00 to $55.00 postpaid. They also sell spinning yarns from New Zealand Romney sheep in "the natural color of the sheep." Some samples were attached to the free brochure, and one of the sheep seems to have been purple. (It must be the Romney in him.) Also in New Zealand, **CAMBRIDGE WOOLS, LTD.,** WW, 16-22 Anzac Ave., Auckland 1, New Zealand, offers a free price list of New Zealand weaving and knitting wools, together with samples.

Spinning wheel kits are available from $2.00 postpaid. They also sell 54-inch wool fabric for from $4.00 to $5.00 per yd., and dressed lambskin.

ST. AUBYN, WW, 15 Button St., Bankstown, N.S.W. 2000, Australia, offers genuine Australian natural dyestuffs plus stud fleece wools and Queensland silk (I haven't seen that anywhere else) for spinning and weaving. The price list is free, but samples of the fleece will cost $4.00 seamail, $5.00 airmail. The firm also sells merino lambskin rugs, approximately 9' square in the natural off white, for $20.00 postpaid.

TEXERE YARNS, WW, 9 Peckover St., Bradford BD1 5BD, England, will send you a thick bundle of sample cards of all their yarns for handloom weaving, in the most delightful shades and textures, and with the loveliest names (Glenlyon, Plevel, Tolblac) for three IRCs or 50¢. The **MULTIPLE FABRIC CO., LTD.,** WW, Bradford BD4 9PD, England, offers some very unusual yarns for handweaving—mohair, horse hair, and camel hair, in addition to regular sheep's wool. **J. HYSLOP BATHGATE AND CO.,** WW, Galashiels, Scotland, has Scottish wools for handloom weaving. The latter two will send you free sample cards.

You can get Mexican woollen yarn for weaving, quite inexpensively, from **REY-COSIJOEZA,** WW, Av. Morelos 17, Mitla, Oaxaca, Mexico. All they put out is a typewritten list mentioning that the wool is available, so, again, you'd better mention when you write for it—it's free—that you're interested in yarn. Although, as I have mentioned, there is a member of the firm who can write English, you'll find things much simpler if you're able to communicate in Spanish. If you're interested in Colombian handspun wool yarn, in natural colors only, write to the **WIESENFELDS,** WW, Apartado Aereo 22456, Bogotá, Colombia. Descriptive price list is free, but samples will cost you $1.00.

WILLIAM CONDON AND SONS, LTD., WW, P.O. Box 129, Charlottetown, Prince Edward Island, Canada, sells pure wool yarns for knitting and weaving, plus rug hooking supplies and hairpin lace looms. (They also sell modestly priced blankets and robes, which I assume they manufacture in their own woollen mills.) **BRIGGS AND LITTLE'S WOOLEN MILL, LTD.,** WW, York Mills, Harvey Sta., York Co., New Brunswick, Canada, offers knitting and weaving yarns, plus rug hooking equipment. In addition, they sell blankets of their own manufacture at what seem like very reasonable prices. Both sets of brochures and sample cards are free.

THE SCHOOL PRODUCTS CO., INC., WW, 312 East 23 St., New York, N.Y. 10010, will send you free of charge what they call "the most comprehensive of any catalog on looms and accessories anywhere." They feel sure you will be gratified by the knowledge that they have "new simple tie-ups on all of our LeClerc floor looms." They have spinning wheels, too. You can get a catalog of the celebrated LeClerc looms directly from **NILUS LeCLERC, INC.,** WW, C.P. 69, L'Islet, Québec, Canada—though they might insist on referring you to one of their U.S. offices should you wish to buy a loom.

ROBIN AND RUSS HANDWEAVERS, WW, 533 North Adams St., McMinnville, Ore. 97128, offer a comprehensive-looking catalog (free) for handweavers called "Warp and Weft." There are looms and accessories, spinning wheels (either assembled or in kit form), and lots of books. For some reason, they carry a large selection of sew-on handbag frames. Further south, **STRAW INTO GOLD,** WW, 5550 College Ave., Oakland, Cal. 94618, offers a free catalog of tools and supplies for the handspinner, weaver, and dyer. They have fibers from all over the world, including wool, alpaca, flax, and silk. (For 50¢ they'll send you samples of all their fibers, and, if you include four SAEs along with your 50¢, they'll send you samples of other new fibers as they come in.) There are spinning wheels, several kinds of spindles, niddy-noddies (skein makers), etc., and you may have distaffs made to order. They also offer natural dyestuffs and mordants and stock yarns (for $1.25 they'll send you a sample card of various handspun yarns dyed in 12 different colors).

The **ARACHNE WEBWORKS,** WW, 1227 SW Morrison, Portland, Ore. 97205, has fashioned a little verse out of the things they sell: "Yarns and dyes / spinning supplies / twines and strings / handmade things." In addition, they have needlework supplies; in subtraction, I didn't see any handmade things listed. The rather hairy catalog (yarn samples are attached at unexpected intervals) is free if you send an SAE.

For $1.00, **TAHKI IMPORTS,** WW, 336 West End Ave., New York, N.Y. 10023, will send you a folder of thick Greek handspun sheepswool and goatshair and thin Donnegal homespun sheepswool (they have heavyweight, too) for weaving, knotting, knitting, and hooking. **TINKLER AND COMPANY, INC.,** WW, 237 Chestnut St., Philadelphia, Pa. 19106, offers yarns and other supplies for weavers. They'll send a price list and samples on request. **FREDERICK J. FAWCETT, INC.,** WW, 129 South St., Boston, Mass. 02111, offers a variety of yarns—wool worsted and linen—for handweaving; rope and twine and leather laces—for macramé. They'll send you lots of cards, showing their full line, if you'll send them $1.00. (Brochures are free.) And the **MILL ENDS STORE,** WW, P.O. Box 14505, Portland, Ore. 97214, has a free color card of their numerous yarns.

2. Knitting and Crocheting

A lot of knitting and crocheting wools are inextricably entwined with the aforegoing, but here are some firms that (as far as I know) deal only in yarns intended for knitting and crocheting.

HALL GREEN WOOLS, WW, Hall Green, Wakefield, Yorkshire WF4 3JT, England, sends out the fattest catalog of knitting wools I've ever seen, containing dozens and dozens of samples of yarns of all kinds (including some synthetics and mixtures) in a fascinating variety of colors. It's free, as is the shade card put out by **ST. JOHN'S KNITTING WOOL CO., LTD.,** WW, P.O. Box 55, 39 Well St., Bradford BD5 8D2, England, which sells all kinds of knitting wools, including some synthetics. I was taken by the double knitting crepe which looks like little braids (but, then, I don't knit). They have buttons dyed to match. **SHEEPSPUN YARNS, LTD.,** WW, P.O. Box No. 4, Parkgate, Wirral, Cheshire L64 6TG, England, will send you a shade card of their English knitting yarns—wool, synthetics, and blends—for $1.00.

RAMMAGERÐIN, LTD., WW, 19 Hafnarstraet, Reykjavik, Iceland, offers free samples of Icelandic knitting and crochet wool, available only in the natural wool colors—black, brown, dark grey, light grey, and off-white. Prices are in American dollars.

CLIVEDEN YARNS, WW, 711 Arch St., Philadelphia, Pa. 19106, will send you a price list of their knitting yarns. And **W. B. RODDEY,** WW, Richburg, S.C., 29729, will not only send you a free brochure of their traditional cotton crochet thread (in the natural off-white as well as white), but samples, too.

Most of the Scottish firms mentioned in Section B.2 also offer knitting wools. In addition, **GLEN LOCK-HART** and **WILSON OF HAWICK** (both in Chapter 2,C.1) sell make-it-yourself sweater and sweater-and-skirt kits. **ICEMART** (Chapter 2,C.3), too, has do-it-yourself kits (sweaters are $11.00, ponchos $12.00).

Then there's a fine source in Norway. **SNOWFLAKE KIT,** WW, N-1315, Nesøya, Norway, sells kits of beautiful patterned Norwegian sweaters—in much greater variety than the ready-to-wear firms seem to offer. Each kit contains wool, knitting needles, pewter buttons or clasps, and English instructions. Some have patterns that are both embroidered and woven (the firm says they're easier to follow than they look). Prices for adult sweater kits range from around $13.00 to $25.00. There's an accessories kit ($11.00), which has sufficient materials for you to knit up to four caps or four pairs of mittens. Snowflake also puts out a colorful brochure of Norwegian embroidery kits at prices that seem far below those prevailing locally. They also sell yarn by the skein. If you order a Snowflake kit, you'll be glad to know that it may be taken to the post office by the firm's sled dog Jåmpa. (They sent me a picture of her—him?—reclining on a sweater.) The catalog and price list are free, but they prefer to offer them together with their booklet, "Introduction to Norwegian Knitting" for $1.00.

3. Embroidery and Rugmaking

THE STITCHERY, WW, 204 Worcester Turnpike, Wellesley Hills, Mass. 02181, has something new (to me, at least)—needlepoint "career plaques"—which you work for "the very special people in your life," like your doctor, your accountant, your stockbroker, and so on. They're $16.00. There are also needlepoint and crewel kits, and kits for the popular embroidery pictures (from $6.00); plus some other embroidery ideas, like bargello director's chair covers, Jacobean tree tote bags, calendars, and needlepoint coat hangers.

THE COUNTRY HOUSE OF YARN, WW, R.D. 1, Box 268, Dover, Del. 19901, puts out a folder of embroidery, crewel, and needlework projects, mostly to be used either as pictures or pillows. There's a tree of life, $6.00; a frog toadstool pincushion, $1.50; an abstract, $11.00. The folder costs 25¢. **HARMONY ACRES STUDIO,** WW, RR 1, G. 9, B 7, St. Norbert Manitoba R0G 2H0, Canada, sells embroidery fabrics, yarns, and such. Price list and samples are free.

KARLA STITCHERIES, WW, P.O. Box 255, Sherwood, Ore. 97140, offers "a new approach to the old art of embroidery, using and misusing regulation embroidery stitches to achieve special effect." Gaily colored brochures show a sleeping lion, a perky mouse, lots of flowers, and so on. Kits are priced from around $6.00 to $16.00, and there are also rug kits to match.

JANE SNEAD SAMPLERS, WW, Box 4909, Philadelphia, Pa. 19119, sells, as you might imagine, sampler kits (starting at less than $1.00). The cost of the catalog is 20¢ coin. **FASHIONS IN WOOL,** WW, 305 White Plains Rd., Eastchester, N.Y. 10707, sells needlework kits. Catalog is free.

SUDBERRY HOUSE, WW, Wesley Ave., Westbrook, Conn. 06498, sells kits for making your own needlepoint bag ($23.00), or suede shoulder bag ($10.00 to $11.00). **TUXEDO YARN AND NEEDLEWORK,** WW, 36-35 Main St., Flushing, N.Y. 11354, sells crewel and needlepoint kits, knitting yarn, and other needlecraft supplies. The **MILL STORE,** Dorr Woolen

Co., WW, Guild, N.H. 03754, puts out a mimeo-graphed list of braiding and hooking accessories. All three brochures are free.

I wrote to **FRIENDS OF FINNISH HANDICRAFT** and got back a reply from **SUOMEN KÄSITYÖN YSTÄ VÄT**, WW, Yrjönkatu 13, Helsinki 12, Finland, so I imagine that must be what the name means. The free brochures depict some marvellous looking rya (or *ryijy* in Finnish) rugs in full color. Even the do-it-yourself kits are rather expensive, from around $85.00 to $110.00 for scatter rugs (the complete rugs come to almost three times the amount), and there's an extra charge for shipping . . . but you might just fall in love with them.

SCANDINAVIAN RYA RUGS, WW, P.O. Box 447, Bloomfield Hills, Mich. 48013, offers several catalogs of C.U.M. Swedish embroidery at 50¢ each, and of rya rugs at $1.00. **SKÖN**, WW, 53 Lambert Lane, New Rochelle, N.Y. 10804, has catalogs of Nordiska rya rugs and wall hangings, and another of Nordiska embroideries. The big colorful rug catalog costs $1.00, and the embroidery is $2.00 (both ref.).

BERRY'S OF MAINE, WW, 20-22 Main St., Yar-mouth, Me. 04096, specializes in rug braiding and hooking supplies. Available are braiders, frames clamps, stripping and slitting machines, needles, thread, eyes—even fabric if you don't have a supply of your own. Also on hand are needlework and crewel kits. Catalog is 10¢.

Remember: *Write for the catalog first.* All prices given were valid only at the time of writing and probably have been changed.

Chapter 19

WORKSHOP

This, like all the chapters in this book, is a somewhat arbitrary division of the subject. You'll find a considerable amount of workshop equipment offered by the firms described in Chapters 16 (Hobbies) and 17 (Arts and Crafts). In Chapter 9 (Around the House) there is a lot of knocked-down furniture; in many cases, the same firm that sells the furniture will also sell finishing supplies and, sometimes, tools. Similarly, in Chapter 13 (Music and the Theater), the firms that have materials for building or repairing musical instruments will also sell the requisite tools and finishing supplies.

A. GENERAL

Surplus stores are excellent sources of supply for the craftsperson, because they not only have a good deal of standard workshop equipment (often, if they are to be believed, at considerable discounts), they often offer strange things to challenge his or her ingenuity. The **AIRBORNE SALES CO.**, WW, P.O. Box 2727, Culver City, Cal. 90230, sells things for hobbyists, sportsmen, machinists, boatmen, and so on, including much government surplus. They say they have one of the largest pressure switch inventories in the world, and the illustrations of "only a few of the many we have" are mind boggling. The catalog is 35¢ and, if you need a pressure switch, or a screw jack activator, or a worm drive handwinch, this is the place to find them. Not to forget Airborne's famous mixes—2 lbs. of assorted grommets are less than $3.00, 1 lb. of grease fittings is $2.50; and, if you're tired of it all, you can get the 1 lb. terminal mix for $2.50.

The **U.S. GENERAL SUPPLY CORP.**, WW, 100 General Pl., Jericho, N.Y. 11753, seems to supply everything for the workshop at considerable discounts for the dealer, who is, so far as I can tell, everyone who shells out a buck (ref.) for the catalogs. All merchandise is new and guaranteed. In addition to tools, there's hardware, sports equipment, and appliances. The **SURPLUS CENTER**, WW, P.O. Box 82209, Lincoln, Neb. 68501, sells surplus motors, tools, automotive supplies, electrical and telephone equipment, and so on, at what they claim are great savings. Catalog is 25¢.

In Canada, **SABRE INDUSTRIES, LTD.**, WW, 1370 Sargent Ave., Winnepeg, Manitoba, offers a lot of electronic shop and test equipment, machinery, marine and hydraulic supplies, tools, and outdoor clothing and gear. They also offer a lot of unusually diversified surplus—office machines, ammo boxes, Canadian government surplus, military gear, generators, and some things that even they can't identify. The catalog is free.

You'll find other surplus stores (those devoted mainly to sports equipment and clothes) in the next chapter.

B. WOOD AND METAL

There are several firms that, although they specialize and are best known for wood, plywood, and veneers, also offer other workshop supplies—tools, hardware, machinery, adhesives, lamp and clock parts, kits, patterns, and so on. **ALBERT CONSTANTINE AND SON, INC.**, WW, 2050 Eastchester Rd., The Bronx, New York 10461, which has been selling woods and craft supplies ever since 1812, is one of the largest and best known if not *the* largest and best known. Others are the **CRAFTSMAN WOOD SERVICE CO.**, WW, 2727 South Mary St., Chicago, Ill. 60608; and the **MINNESOTA WOODWORKERS SUPPLY CO.**, WW, 925 Winnetka Ave. North, Minneapolis, Minn. 55427. All three catalogs are 50¢. A somewhat smaller catalog is offered free by **BARAP SPECIALTIES**, WW, 407 South Monroe, Sturgis, Mich. 42091.

The **EDUCATIONAL LUMBER CO., INC.**, WW, P.O. Box 5373, Asheville, N.C. 28803, owes its somewhat curious name to the fact that it's set up to deal primarily with school shop classes, although it will sell to everybody, and the catalog is free. They sell nothing but wood, and quote you delivered prices on orders over $80.00, so you won't have to guess what your bill will total. In addition to regular wood by the board foot, they have veneers, dowels, turning squares, baseball bat billets, plywood, hardboard, and the currently popular log slices. Prices seem extremely reasonable.

NELCRAFT, WW, Box 66, Cortaro, Ariz. 85230, sells desert-weathered wood to craftspeople who would like to work in something different. Cholla, iron, and jaguaro wood are included. Brochure is free.

BIRCHWOOD CASEY, WW, 7900 Fuller Rd., Eden Prairie, Minn. 55343, has a handbook of wood and metal finishing products they'll send you without charge, if you write and ask for it.

Although **FINNYSPORTS**, WW, 2910 Glanzman Rd., Toledo, Ohio 43614, specializes in outdoor equipment, it also carries an assortment of interesting woods—some old chestnut boards, timbers, and fence rails; holly wood; sassafras (smells like rootbeer); claro walnut; Port Orford cedar; greenheart; persimmon wood; madrone wood, etc.—as well as blocks, turning squares, etc. Catalog is free. The **MIDLAND LUMBER CO.**, WW, Savannah, Mo. 64485, specializes in walnut and cherry lumber, squares, legs, and frame moulding. List is free.

C. PLASTICS

MAIL ORDER PLASTICS, WW, 56 Lispenard St., New York, N.Y. 10013, puts out a nice catalog dealing with all kinds of plastics—acrylic, vinyl, polyethylene, mylar, acetate—plus plastic things to put other things into—lots of little drawers, boxes, vials, etc. Also on hand are covers for boats, cars, airconditioners, bicycles, motorcycles, and outdoor furniture. **COPE PLASTICS, INC.**, WW, 1111 West Dalmar Ave., Godfrey, Ill. 62035, also puts out a complete-looking catalog of various plastics, with more emphasis on the arts and crafts angle. It includes gift items and plain polished shapes for carving. Available here is machinery for cutting, carving, and molding plastics. The **U.S. PLASTIC CORP.**, WW, 1550 Elida Rd., Lima, Ohio 45805, features industrial plastics. All three catalogs are free.

D. TOOLS AND HARDWARE

The **BROOKSTONE CO.**, WW, 13 Brookstone Bldg., Peterborough, N.H. 03458, has been a favorite source for amateurs, professionals, and hobbyists for years. Its catalog (25¢) of "Hard-to-Find Tools" offers all kinds of blades, rasps, vises, clamps, files, trammels, spray guns, chisels, and what not; plus screws, nuts, bolts, and washers in sizes you can't get easily elsewhere. There are vacuum tweezers to pick up lenses and coins, a set of miniature nut drivers, and a glass cutter that not only cuts circles or straight but is, as they say, "a very pretty tool." For some reason, they also have plastic snowshoes.

The **WOODCRAFT SUPPLY CORP.**, WW, 313 Montvale Ave., Woburn, Mass. 01801, offers a catalog of fine woodworking tools (many of them imported from overseas) for the cabinetmaker and carpenter,

as well as the woodcarver. Also available here is Solingen steel cutlery by Dreizack. The catalog is 50¢.

The **TASHIRO HARDWARE CO.**, WW, 109 Prefontaine Pl., Seattle, Wash. 98104, was founded in 1885 to supply professional tools to Japanese craftsmen. Today they also offer handforged cutlery, and warn you that "these tools are sharp; buyer assumes all responsibility for their safe use." The **JAPAN WOODWORKER**, WW, 1701 Grove St., Berkeley, Cal. 94709, also carries fine tools imported from Japan for the handcrafter. Both brochures are free.

JENSEN TOOLS AND ALLOYS, WW, 4117 North 44 St., Phoenix, Ariz. 85018, specializes in tools for electronic assembly and precision mechanics. Their microminiature tools, with active working elements as small as 1/1000 of an inch in size are nothing short of amazing. Their catalog is free, and it's a fat one. The **CAMPBELL TOOLS CO.**, WW, 1424 Barclay Rd., Springfield, Ohio 45505, offers precision machinist tools and small shop supplies. A partial catalog is free, a complete one is 50¢.

Although **NATIONAL CAMERA, INC.**, WW, Englewood, Colo. 80110, does sell cameras, if you insist, it is actually a workshop supply house, featuring tools and equipment. They have, for example, a bellows lug lifter to be used with any self-adjusting screwdriver handle; solder removers; and a hand knurler; as well as pliers, screwdrivers, ratchets, and stuff like that. **SMALL PARTS, INC.**, WW, 6901 N.E. Third Ave., Miami, Fla. 33138, stocks "a variety of small mechanical parts necessary in the creation of prototypes and useful in many research and production operations." Both catalogs are free.

PENNSYLVANIA CRAFTSMEN, WW, P.O. Box 14, Johnstown, Pa. 15907, sells porcelain knobs in various sizes, plain and decorated, from around 35¢ up; and casters with porcelain wheels (and brass ones as well) in many different sizes. Brochure is free.

The **NUTTY CO.**, WW, P.O. Box 1576, Fairfield, Conn. 06430, sells nuts, bolts, screws, and washers of all shapes and sizes. They're sold by the box of a hundred, although you can buy as little as a quarter of a box, and assortments are also available. Catalog is 25¢. Even more specialized is the **HARDWARE PRODUCTS CO.**, WW, 84 Fulton St., Box 97, Boston, Mass. 02113, which offers a catalog containing nothing but springs, both compression and expansion types, together with their prices, and all kinds of technical information about pounds per inch and maximum deflection—which is almost embarrassing for a product that begins at 6¢ "per each." But spring lovers will undoubtedly be enthralled.

E. SPECIALTIES

The **GENERAL SUPPLIES CO.**, WW, Fallbrook, Cal. 92028, puts out an upholsterers' catalog, containing tools, fabrics, and supplies at what they say are discount prices. Catalog is 50¢ and fabric swatch books are $3.00 (ref.).

The **FOUNDRYMEN**, WW, P.O. Box 5123, Garden Grove, Cal. 92645, offers a service to craftspeople and hobbyists who have the need for a cast metal shape that is not on the market, no longer manufactured, or an entirely new idea. By using a form of the lost wax process, they are, they say, "able to supply you with the widest range of cast shapes possible at the lowest cost to you, since we eliminate the cost of expensive tooling, patterns, and dies." Casting may be made in ferrous or nonferrous metal, in a choice of alloys. Brochure is free.

JACOBY APPLIANCE PARTS, INC., WW, 57 Albany St., New Brunswick, N.J. 08901, don't have a catalog, but they say they can get you replacement parts for almost any old appliance in all the well-known brands, and some less well-known ones also. Write and tell them what you're looking for.

Everybody who really knows about cars knows **J. C. WHITNEY AND CO.**, WW, 1917-19 Archer Ave., P.O. Box 8410, Chicago, Ill. 60680, who call themselves, with some justification, the "world's largest automotive department store." They sell parts and accessories, not only for most cars, but for campers, trailers, and mobile homes as well. On hand is an attractive assortment of the hood ornaments that are coming back into popularity (there's an illuminated owl whose eyes light up). And there are horns, which explains some of those strange sounds I've been hearing in the street—horns that go hee-haw, beep-beep, or ah-oo-gah; horns that whinny, yelp, give wolf whistles, or play tunes (like *La Cucaracha*); etc.

Remember: *Write for the catalog first.* All prices given were valid only at the time of writing and probably have been changed.

Chapter 20

OUTDOORS AND SPORTS

A. CLOTHING

Most of the firms in this chapter sell clothes appropriate to the activities featured in their catalogs. However, there are some firms that make a specialty of sports clothing, and, since I mentioned early on in the book that the type of clothing that seems to be most popular in America would be found here, I'm starting off with it. Of course not all of the firms written up here are American, and much of the merchandise offered by the American firms is imported, but if you look hard you'll find lots of authentic American clothing.

For instance, there's **SHEPLER'S**, WW, 6501 West Kellogg, P.O. Box 9021, Wichita, Kan. 67207, which calls itself the world's largest Western store, and its big free color catalog is full of all sorts of rugged outdoor wear. There are boots, from $20.00 to $135.00; leather coats; widebrimmed hats; and real chaps! There aren't too many things for women, but lots of items for the well-dressed horse—saddles, blankets, spurs (I don't suppose those are exactly for the horse), and so on. (For more riding and equine wear, see **KAUFFMAN** and **MOSS** in Section F.)

The **SIOUX FALLS ARMY STORE**, WW, 124 North Phillips Ave., Sioux Falls, S.D. 57102, offers mostly surplus outdoor-type clothes, which will, of course, change from catalog to catalog. The last one I saw had Viet Nam combat jackets for around $3.00; government surplus ponchos, from $3.50; Air Force flight trousers, from $4.00 to $13.00; British Royal Lorry vests, $11.00; combat boots, $10.00; and World War I helmets, $3.00. There are lots of Western items and camping equipment. Catalog is free.

The **VISTA SALES CO.**, WW, 654 Broadway, New York, N.Y. 10012, occasionally puts out free catalogs of government surplus clothing. They have offered such items as U.S. Army steel helmets (around $3.00), U.S. Army barracks bags ($2.00 up), U.S. Army fatigues ($4.00 up), bush jackets from Tunisia ($7.00), Canadian Navy shorts ($6.00), British tank tops ($4.00), Royal Air Force mittens ($6.00), plus tents and things for the camper and backpacker. They also have some military relics for collectors.

I got a form letter from the **HUDSON'S BAY CO.**, WW, Hudson's Bay House, 37 Stevenson Rd., Winnipeg R3H OJ1, Manitoba, Canada, saying that they do not publish a catalog; and along with it they sent a pretty, color brochure of their famous Hudson's Bay blankets ($22.00 up), as well as their attractive and unusual sportswear, made for the most part out of either Hudson's Bay "duffel cloth," or the actual blanketing material. They are not inexpensive, but I haven't seen anything like them elsewhere. If the company admits to having a brochure, it's free.

J. BARBOUR AND SONS, LTD., WW, Simonside, South Shields, Co. Durham NE34 9PD, England, has been manufacturing and selling waterproof and protective clothing for nearly a century. Even though many of the items have been approved by the London Council of Industrial Design, these are made for utility rather than glamour—for working men (no women here) or men who take their sports seriously (like the Duke of Edinburgh from whom they have a royal warrant). The firm's Beacon Thornproof Waterproof garments are made out of specially coated woven Egyptian cotton guaranteed to be "wind, rot, and mildew proof." Prices are quite reasonable. A three-quarters hooded coat, partly lined in nylon, is less than $30.00. For extra warmth, you add their independently buttoning fleece lining, which costs around $10.00. They also have overalls, boiler suits, casual jackets, hats, and boots of all kinds (including Wellingtons). My favorites are the hats. There are deerstalkers (in three different kinds of fabrics), Cotswold sports caps, Trilbys, and many others with less nostalgia-evoking names. The very well-designed catalog is free.

HUSKY OF TOSTOCK, LTD., WW, 115 Bury St., Stowmarket, Suffolk, England, puts out a catalog (35¢) of thermo-insulated clothing for hunting and shooting and other outdoor activities. Although the proprietor is an American, he boasts that "peers, baronets, wealthy business people, local landowners . . . figure prominently on Husky's client list." The clothes don't seem to be expensive, however, starting at under $20.00 for a quilted car coat. (Almost everything is quilted, except for their line of custom-made insulated tweeds.)

London's famous sports shop **LILLYWHITES, LTD.,** WW, Piccadilly Circus, London SW1Y 4QFM, England, puts out a catalog of very good-looking ski and general sports clothes. Most striking here are the colorful "boiler suits," from about $100.00. There are more modestly priced items, but, as you can see, this is not an inexpensive place. The pretty, colorful catalog is free, and, although I'm sure this offer applies only to natives of the United Kingdom, you might be interested to know that Lillywhites will insure skiers against accidents or illness on their holidays.

Other firms in this chapter that are especially good sources of sports clothing are **ABERCROMBIE AND FITCH,** for those who are not on a budget (they have lots of clothes for elegant spectators, too); **L. L. BEAN,** which offers practical clothes for the outdoorsperson; and **HUDSON'S,** which has a lot of rugged inexpensive clothing. In addition to those mentioned, most of the camping firms in Section C offer down-filled jackets and suits and warm woolies.

B. GENERAL

L. L. BEAN, INC., WW, Freeport, Me. 04032, is one of the nicest sporting goods stores, with its service as attractive as its merchandise (much of which it manufactures itself). There are lots of good sturdy sports clothes for both men and women, made more with an eye to practicality than beauty, though most have a functional attractiveness. You'll find many useful things for camp, cabin, and boat here, as well as for backpackers and fishermen; and a lot of the things would be useful around the house as well. Their cutting blocks and cutlery would be welcome in even the best-equipped kitchen, and they have stunning saddletan leather carryall bags, which would invest even a trip to the supermarket with an aura of chic. (They cost from $12.50 to $16.50.) Catalog is free.

FORESTRY SUPPLIERS, INC., WW, Box 8397, 205 West Rankin St., Jackson, Miss. 39204, has something different in the way of outdoors catalogs. It specializes in "quality forestry, engineering, and environmental equipment" and it has the biggest outdoor catalog I've seen; in fact, outside of the giant mail-order houses, it puts out one of the biggest catalogs in the book. It begins with some items of general interest—backpacking equipment, with bags and frames arranged according to the length of the trip; day bags for short trips; bags and frames for 2 or 3 day trips and for trips of over 3 days. There are sleeping bags and snowshoes, too. After these conventional offerings, the catalog goes off into things like sound pressure level integrators (which automatically signal when permissible daily noise exposure

is reached), pocket transits, snakeproof leggings (and snakebite kits in case the snake makes for your arm instead), directional dustfall samplers, pyranometers (used to obtain a continuous record of the intensity of direct and scattered solar radiation), 17 different kinds of hard hats, brush chippers, vapor decreasers, forest starter tablets (which apparently are used to start forests), and all kinds of things like that. These items are not, as you can see, for the casual camper, but for strong, silent he-men (not a woman in the catalog) who spend their lives doing important things in the great outdoors. It's free.

For $1.00, **HERTER'S, INC.,** WW, Waseca, Minn. 56093, will send you their huge catalog containing everything the outdoorsperson could possibly need—at prices that seem substantially lower than those of many of the other houses. (They also have nonoutdoors things, which have been described elsewhere in this book.)

LeBARON, WW, 742 Notre Dame St. West, Montreal, Québec, Canada, offers a complete supply of sporting goods—or *equipement sportif,* since the catalog is in both English and French—at what they claim are wholesale prices. I've never seen *sacs de couchage* offered more cheaply (of course they come in different qualities and types). There are marine and underwater gear, camping supplies, and, as might be expected from a Canadian firm, hockey equipment and English dart boards, as well as other sports equipment. The catalog costs a quarter and American money seems to be acceptable.

ABERCROMBIE AND FITCH, WW, Madison Avenue at 45 St., New York, N.Y. 10017, were supposed to write to tell me whether or not they decided to make their catalogs available to the general public or not. I haven't heard from them, but that doesn't mean you won't if you write asking for a catalog—that is, if you're interested in elegant but expensive sportswear and sports equipment.

Other firms that offer free outdoor catalogs are **PARKER DISTRIBUTORS,** WW, 40 Industrial Pl., New Rochelle, N.Y. 10805; **GANDER MOUNTAIN, INC.,** WW, P.O. Box 248, Wilmot, Wis. 53192; **CABELA'S,** WW, P.O. Box 199, 812 Thirteenth Ave., Sidney, Nebr. 69166; **SPORTS LIQUIDATORS,** WW, P.O. Box E, Sun Valley, Cal. 91352 (mostly fishing); and **TIGHT LINES, INC.,** WW, 220 South Main St., West Bridgewater, Mass. 02379.

C. CLIMBING, CAMPING, BACKPACKING, SKIING

ARTHUR ELLIS AND CO., LTD., WW, Dunedin, New Zealand, offers to its U.S. customers a color catalog of its "Fairy Down" sleeping bags, which were the kind used on Sir Edmund Hillary's ascent of Mount Everest, as well as on numerous expeditions to the Arctic. In addition, there are all kinds of cold-weather clothes, including polar down jackets, hoods, trousers, even gloves and slippers. They're very gay, in the bright colors that are standard for mountain wear, but they're not for the fashion-conscious, unless you *want* to look like a teddy bear from outer space. (All the down clothes make you look like that; I don't mean to pick on Ellis'.) Prices seem very reasonable for equipment that will keep you from freezing at 40 below. The sleeping bags cost from about $16.00 to $60.00, and the down jackets start at around $50.00. Another New Zealand firm, **ANT-ARCTIC PRODUCTS CO., LTD.,** WW, P.O. Box 223, Nelson, New Zealand, offers mountaineering specialties—mainly sleeping bags and clothing. They also have quilted down blankets, which should appeal to stay-at-home sleepers, too, at prices beginning at $55.00. Prices are given in New Zealand dollars, which, at the time of writing, were worth over a third more than the American. Both catalogs are free.

FROSTLINE, INC., WW, P.O. Box 2150, Boulder, Colo. 80302, deals exclusively in do-it-yourself kits for campers, supplying materials so you can make your own down-filled sleeping bags, jackets, coats, parkas, trousers, ponchos; plus packs and tents (which are not down-filled) all in the same selection of five pretty colors. There are also down comforters and pillows (which come ready-made covered in a white liner; you just make the cover); and you can get the raw materials, too, if you want them—cloth, down, thread, grommet setters, etc. Frostline says you can save yourself at least 50 percent by buying the kits (jackets start as low as $15.00, sleeping bags at $45.00); but it's hard for me to believe that even a beginner can whiz these numbers up on his or her little portable sewing machine, the way the catalog (free) says.

HOLUBAR, WW, Box 7, Boulder, Colo. 80302; and **LAACKE AND JOYS CO.,** WW, 1432 North Water St., Milwaukee, Wis. 53202, both offer sleeping bags and tents that they make themselves, as well as down and woollen clothing. Laacke and Joys also puts out a nice line of portable camp furniture. **MARTIN'S,** WW, P.O. Box 141, Fremont, Cal. 94537, makes "Pak-Tents," which weigh only 2 lbs. and cost only $9.00 postpaid. They're opaque for privacy, and orange so you won't be mistaken for an abominable snowperson. All three catalogs are free.

STOW-A-WAY SPORTS INDUSTRIES, WW, 166 Cushing Hwy., Cohasset, Mass. 02025, sells lightweight equipment for hikers, campers, and backpackers, but what they're best known for is the large line of freeze-dried food that they manufacture. They give the calories on each item, so you won't come down the mountain heavier than you went up (or bring the mountain down with you). Catalog is free. Many of the other firms included in this chapter also offer freeze-dried foods for the camper, both Stow-a-Way's brand and others.

YETI ENTERPRISES, WW, Box 617, Topanga, Cal. 90290, is a one-man cottage industry. The proprietor, Mr. John Williams, makes white goosedown sleeping bags made to fit not only your individual measurements but your concepts as well. Prices range from $80.00 up, depending on how many of you plan to share the bag and how low a temperature you expect to be hit by. With each sleeping bag you get a free "stuff bag" (I'm not sure whether you stuff the sleeping bag into it, or just carry stuff in it), with Mr. Williams' idea of a Yeti's face on it. He declares belligerently that you get the face whether you want it or not. He also makes down jackets for a modest $40.00 or so, and down blankets at what he admits is an outrageous $100.00. He says they're worth it, though. Everything is offered in a choice of colors—light blue, dark blue, green, red, orange, and aqua. Yellow used to be on the list, too, but he crossed it out, and such is the aura of the catalog (free) that you find yourself wondering why.

Other firms that offer free catalogs of lightweight camping and backpacking equipment are **THE TRAIL HAUS,** WW, 1031 San Mateo S.E., Albuquerque, N.M. 87108; **MOOR AND MOUNTAIN,** WW, Concord, Mass. 01742; **OREGON RECREATIONAL ENTERPRISES, INC.,** WW, 8103 North Denver Ave., Portland, Ore. 97217; **GABRIEL'S,** WW, 1436 Easton Ave., Madison, Ohio 44057; **BLACK'S,** WW, 930 Ford St., Ogdensburg, N.Y. 13669 (they're the U.S. branch of the famous Scottish firm); and **RECREATIONAL EQUIPMENT, INC.,** WW, 1525 Eleventh Ave., Seattle, Wash. 98122 (emphasis on skiing here).

In case you want to build yourself a tipi, **WA'KE DA** (Chapter 3,A) offers do-it-yourself tipi kits from around $40.00 to $300.00. Poles are extra ($40.00 to $75.00). In addition, there are liners, floors ("not Indian at all but nice to have"), and other optional accessories, including door covers, tie ropes, and painted designs. Instructions for measuring yourself for your tipi are carefully given.

DICK CEPEK, INC., WW, 9201 California Ave., South Gate, Cal. 90280, specializes in flotation tires and wheels, as well as off-road and camping equipment. They seem to have a lot of usual things at what look to me like very reasonable prices, as well as some interesting things. I particularly liked the campfire skillets that come without handles—you cut your own in the woods at the proper length to suit your inclinations. Also on hand is some surplus. Catalog is free.

HUDSON'S, WW, 105 Third Ave., New York, N.Y. 10003, offers a free catalog of all kinds of camping supplies at what they say are discount prices. They also carry modestly priced work clothes, levis and levi stretch dungarees from $7.00; chinos, $7.00 up; overalls, from $9.00; and so on. They, too, offer some surplus, and their catalog is also free.

D. BOATING

JAMES BLISS & CO., INC., WW, Rte. 128, Dedham, Mass. 02026, have been catering to yachtsmen since 1832, and their fat catalog ($1.00) seems to contain everything the luxury-loving mariner could possibly want. There's even a comprehensive navigational starter kit for the tyro, which includes the booklet "How to Fix Your Position with a Sextant" (it's $40.00). There are bilge pumps, swaging eye terminals, adjustable brass through-transom boat bailer plugs, jibfurl and mainfurl spinnaker cleats, and life preservers of all kinds, including doggie vests (no, that's not a nautical term; it's a life-preserving vest for your doggie). Also on hand are nautical gifts, many of them decorated with code flag signals—such as a coaster with a flag saying, "I am on fire in the hold."

CHRIS-CRAFT MARINE ACCESSORIES DIV., WW, Algonac, Mich. 48001, sells all kinds of things for boats and boatpeople, including a bicycle you can fold up and take aboard. The clothes will probably appeal to landlubbers—the sneakers and pullovers could be worn anywhere, and the hats, while definitely nautical, probably will be worn everywhere. One particularly useful jacket ($43.00) becomes a life preserver should you find yourself in the drink. Here, too, are all kinds of things for the sybaritic sailor. I like the Chris-Craft "Uni-berth" comforter, which is a blanket, sheets, and colorful spread rolled into one. (You get into it like a sleeping bag, but they say it definitely isn't one.) It's machine washable, $24.00 for single, $38.00 for double. The colorful catalog is free.

Other nautical gifts are available from the **MYSTIC SEAPORT STORES, INC.,** WW, Mystic, Conn. 06355, which puts out a free catalog. See also **PRESTON'S** (Chapter 15,E) and the **ANCIENT MARINER** (Chapter 15,A.8).

GOLDBERG'S, WW, 202 Market St., Philadelphia, Pa. 19106, issues a big catalog ($1.00) of boating supplies. (They also offer a free camping catalog.)

The **SHIP'S STORE,** WW, 2031 Boston Post Rd., Larchmont, N.Y. 10538; and **STOKES MARINE INDUSTRIES,** WW, Coldwater, Mich. 49036, both specialize in marine equipment and gear and both offer free catalogs.

The **HANS KLEPPER CORP.,** WW, 35 Union Sq. W., New York, N.Y. 10003, both manufactures and sells folding boats and kayaks. The **TAFT MARINE CORP.,** WW, 636 39 Ave. N.E., Minneapolis, Minn. 55421, sells boat kits. The **FOLBOT CORP.,** WW, Stark Industrial Park, Charleston, S.C. 29405, sells folding boats that you may, they say, "store in odd corners around the house, garage, office, closet, under bed, or in car trunk." They're available only factory finished, but there are also rigid boats that the firm makes available in kit form. All three catalogs are free.

E. FISHING

MILES AND CARLAW DUTY FREE SHOP, WW, Auckland International Airport, Auckland, New Zealand, offers a selection of fishing and other sports equipment in their free catalog (which has many other things; unfortunately, none of them apparently of New Zealand provenance). Prices are in New Zealand dollars.

The **LIMIT MANUFACTURING CORP.,** WW, 515 Melody Lane, Richardson, Tex. 75080, produces a complete line of products for the manufacture of plastic lures for the fisherman. Along with their free catalog, they sent me a lovely pink plastic worm; and maybe they'll send you one, too, although I'm not promising anything. They also sell all kinds of fishing equipment.

Other free catalogs for the fisherman are available from **FINNYSPORTS,** WW, 2910 Glanzman Rd., Toledo, Ohio 43614; the **ORCHARD TRADING CO.,** WW, Box 241, Hastings, Mich. 49058; The **ORVIS COMPANY, INC.,** WW, Manchester, Vt. 05254; **SPIN-LINE,** WW, 11 Thomas St., Kingston, N.Y. 12401; and the **NETCRAFT CO.,** WW, 3101 Sylvania Ave., Toledo, Ohio 43613.

F. SPECIALTIES

1. Riding

In England, **MOSS BROTHERS,** WW, Bedford St., London W.C.2E 8JB, puts out an attractive "Riding and Saddling" catalog that includes everything both horse and rider could possibly need. It's free, but the catalog put out by **H. KAUFFMAN AND SONS,** WW, 141 East 24 St., New York, N.Y. 10010, is 50¢. Kauffman sells equipment, saddles, and riding clothes for both English- and Western-style riders.

2. Exotic Weapons

BEE-JAY'S, WW, P.O. Box 8711, Canton, Ohio 44711, offers genuine tomahawks, handforged by Amish blacksmiths in the Ohio Valley, with heads guaranteed against breakage. Eight different models are offered, from the tiny Mouse Hawk to the mighty Iroquois, and prices range from $10.00 to $30.00. In case you wondered why they were recreated, it was for match throwing—not to go on the warpath with. Catalog is free. If you're interested in boomerangs, you can get them from **QUEENSLAND** and **THE DEPARTMENT FOR COMMUNITY WELFARE** in Chapter 11,C.9 (and you'll find lots of other exotic weapons in that chapter too). More conventional weapons will be found at the general sporting goods houses, but I hope you won't use them.

3. Golf and Tennis

If you have trouble getting Slazenger golf and tennis balls, you can buy them directly from **SLAZENGER,** WW, 850 Pennsylvania Blvd., Feasterville, Pa. 19047. Also available there are tennis rackets, squash rackets, some tennis dresses (pretty expensive, considering that panties are not included), and other sports equipment. **STEPHEN J. FERON, INC.,** WW, 55 East 44 St., New York, N.Y. 10017, has everything for the well-heeled tennis player—clothes, equipment, tennis gifts. Both catalogs are free. For discount golf balls, send for the catalog from **SHANNON** (Chapter 2,D.2).

4. Acrobatics

KAY-LARKS ACROBATIC SUPPLY, WW, 2035 Fremont Ave., Casper, Wyo. 82601, sells gym mats (from $35.00), as well as the more expensive acrobatic and tumbling training mat; plus acrobatic safety belts, and all kinds of allied equipment. Catalog is free. You'll find other acrobatic equipment at some of the ballet supply houses described in Chapter 2.

5. Doomsday

If you're looking forward to your outdoor vacation, maybe you'd better not send to **NORTHWEST OUTFITTERS,** WW, Rte. 5, Box 97, Camano Island, Wash. 98292, for their free catalog, because what they specialize in is survival equipment. "Each year," they say cheerfully, "we read of how casual strollers, campers, vacationers, and a surprising proportion of this country's hunters and fishermen become lost. The papers also carry article after article about plane crashes, water craft both large and small being wrecked, while automobiles and entire trains are stalled with alarming persistency by accident, storm, and disaster. . . . It costs very little time, money, and effort to be ready for an emergency. If you are not ready, it may cost you your life." Now that they've got you in the right frame of mind, they really sock it to you with such wares as surplus U.S. Navy water distillation kits ($12.00), discount surplus army field rations (with slight dents in the cans), combat knives, signal flare kits ($7.00), tear gas kits ($9.00), "Chemical Billies" (from $6.00), and, a real budget item, a "survival combination matchbox-compass with built-in whistle, flint striker, and signal mirror" ($1.50)—everything you need to make your vacation complete. Or maybe you'd rather stay home.

Remember: *Write for the catalog first.* All prices given were valid only at the time of writing and probably have been changed.

Chapter 21
ANIMALS

There was a time when it was difficult in many areas of the country to outfit your animal associates properly. You might have been able to go into a pet shop and find a sweater in your dog's size, but you'd be very lucky if you could get it in his favorite color; while if you asked to have him fitted with a fake fur coat complete with rhinestone buttons and matching beret, you were likely to be asked to leave the store. If it was your cat you wanted to buy a little something for, you could choose between a small catnip mouse and a large one, and that was it.

Things are different now. As you can tell from the pet food commercials on TV, animals have at long last come into their own. Even supermarkets have corners full of nice things to please your furry, feathered, or finny friends. However, now that there are so many things available for pets, no pet shop can carry them all. What's more, a lot of pet shops tend to be outrageously overpriced, and so, for one reason or another, I think animal lovers may find the firms described in the following pages very useful.

A. GENERAL

ANIMAL SPECIALTIES, INC., WW, P.O. Box 531, Camden, N.J. 08101, puts out a thorough catalog (free) devoted to cat and dog needs. Mostly it's devoted to basics, like combs, clippers, health products, leads and collars, and feeding dishes. However, for your proteges' lighter moments, there are some attractive toys, many at lower prices than I've seen anywhere else recently. There are also some lovely posters for $1.50. Some horse supplies are also offered, but there are no toys for horses.

EVE'S PET BOUTIQUE, WW, P.O. Box 30, Chicago, Ill. 60650, will send you, on request, a free folder of nice things for cats and dogs—toys, scratching posts, beds, grooming aids, vitamins, carrying cases, etc. Their sale prices are often below the standard prices you find in the pet stores, and I've never received a brochure from them that wasn't a sale catalog.

R. D. SYMONDS, WW, Essex, Conn. 06426, sells the firm's own line of Safeguard Accessories for dogs and cats. There are nylon handy harnesses (which combine harness and lead) for small dogs and cats, as well

as, the brochure says, skunks, raccoons, and monkeys, priced from $1.25. They're especially good for growing animals, because they're continually adjustable. (I must tell you, however, that I tried to equip my cats with those harnesses when they were kittens and they ate them.) There are also harnesses for large animals at $3.50; some very superior cat exercisers, at $1.50 the pair; fuzzy mice (made out of solid felt), $1.25 for 3; stripping brushes; nail clippers; and so on. Postage is included. Brochure is free.

G. & H. PET SUPPLY, WW, P.O. Box 4474, Panorama City, Cal. 91472, sells grooming slings for dogs, which, the free brochure notes, "facilitate grooming of the more sensitive parts of the animal." Also offered are other animal grooming products, plus dog and cat doors, and nice cardboard dog or cat houses with carpeted floors. (They're $6.00, knocked down and postpaid.) And **TUREN, INC.**, WW, Danvers, Mass. 01923, sells different types of Flexport pet door installations, so that your cat or dog can exit and enter without disturbing the family; as well as some grooming, feeding, and recreational equipment. Free brochure.

The **HYDROPONIC CHEMICAL CO.**, WW, Copley, Ohio 44321, has added some items for dogs and cats to its free garden supply brochure. There's a heavy duty tie-out stake for $2.20, and a 50-ft. dog run line with accessories is a little under $5.00. Also on hand are inexpensive bird feeders. **I LOVE PETS**, WW, P.O. Box 23876, Fort Lauderdale, Fla. 33307, specializes in health products for pets. Send SAE for list.

PETS-U-LOVE, WW, 120 West 44 St. (Suite 617-8), New York, N.Y. 10036, is planning, the free catalog says, to offer the latest thing in pet products. They have automatic feeders for water and dry food, no-splash drink dishes (for motoring trips), exercise pens, and barriers to partition off a station wagon or car and keep your pets from leaping upon the driver. That's $35.00. There's also a shoulder bag that's intended as a small pet carrier. It's called (I'm sorry) a "puppoose," and it's $6.00. Catalog is free.

There are times when, for purposes of security or transportation, your pet will need to be confined elegantly yet inexpensively, if possible. If you have a cat or small dog (or a raccoon or a monkey or a small wallaby), you'll be interested in **ALCO CARRYING CASES, INC.**, WW, 601 West 26 St., New York, N.Y. 10001. Lots of pet shops carry them, but you're not likely to see the full line (in avocado green, skyflower blue, charcoal gray, and slate) unless you send away for their brochures, which are free. A retail price list comes along, so you can order directly.

COLLAPSIBLE WIRE PRODUCTS, WW, P.O. Box 691, Butter, Wis. 53007, sells collapsible travel cages for dogs and cats (as well as live-in cages for various small animals and birds) at prices lower than I've seen anywhere else—from around $3.00 to $5.00. Postage is included but not floors (you have to pay extra for them). The **KEIPPER COOPING CO.**, WW, 3235 West Burnham St., Milwaukee, Wis. 53215, will also furnish you with modestly priced cages for your pets, should they need transporting or secluding. Both brochures are free.

If you need to pen in your loved ones, the **BRINKMAN MANUFACTURING AND FENCE CO., INC.**, WW, Rte. 8, Huntoon and Auburn Rds., Topeka, Kans. 66604, offers portable residential runs, "for dogs, cats, and primates." They're flexible so you can order an arrangement to suit your particular needs (and rearrange it should your needs or your desires change). They also sell fiberglass igloos for animals that need to be sheltered rather than confined. Catalog is free.

B. MOSTLY DOGS

DU-SAY'S, WW, P.O. Box 24407, New Orleans, La. 70124, offers "everything for pampered pets," chiefly dogs. There are utility coats, "designed for maximum cold weather, protection, and durability" (but fashionable, they hasten to add), from $10.00 to $13.00; and glamour coats, "handtailored for a superior fit, custom designed in the most gorgeous fabrics," from $9.00 to $14.00. All are available with caps or berets to match. There's also a line of foul-weather gear, beginning at $5.00; the red snowsuit at $11.00 to $13.00 is especially fetching (unless you have a dachshund, for which it is not recommended). They also have car seats, bike baskets, and life jackets 'for pets on the go." All the usual beauty and health supplies, and a vast array of toys and boudoir accessories are on hand. (There's a small selection of things—mostly toys—for cats, including a rugged kitty gym at $25.00, and all sorts of catnip confections, starting at less than $1.00.) Catalog is 25¢.

The **DOG COLLAR WORKS**, WW, Maysville, Ga. 30558, offers the largest catalog I've ever seen that is devoted entirely to dog collars, harnesses, and leashes; in fact, it's the only brochure I've ever seen devoted entirely to those canine necessities. Prices range from less than $1.00 to $7.50 for a fancy jeweled number for very large dogs. Harnesses cost from $3.50 to $6.00 (some of these are jewelled also). Collar prices include inscribed nameplates. If you'd like just the nameplate alone, it's yours for 30¢ to 35¢ (or you can get 4-5 for $1.00, depending on size), with not only the lettering of your choice, but rivets. Shipping seems to be included, catalog is free, and it looks as if you could get some good bargains here.

What the **UNITED GUITAR CORP.**, WW, 278 Johnston Ave., Jersey City, N.J. 07304, has to sell is, curiously, do-it-yourself dog house kits, from $20.00 to $45.00. (Maybe the dog lies on the roof and plays the guitar.) Data sheet is free.

C. MOSTLY FOR CATS

CADRIN'S, WW, 22 Main St., South Grafton, Mass. 01560, offers a folder (15¢ ref.) containing a selection of items designed to please your cat. There are, among others, catnip bean bags (2 for $1.00); a cat scratching bar stool with retractable mouse ($3.00); and, for the Early American cat, a Colonial kitten playmate ($2.00). The **KATNIP TREE CO.**, WW, 416 Smith St., Seattle, Wash. 98109, puts out a catalog (15¢) containing everything for the well-rounded cat— including scratching posts and climbers, travel cases, grooming aids, toys, and many other things of feline interest.

WEN-RUB PRODUCTS, WW, 8921 National Blvd., Los Angeles, Cal. 90034, offers a selection of absolutely inspired furniture for cats. A carpet-covered pole goes from floor to ceiling, with a carpet covered tree house halfway up and an extra perch above that. It's a little over $40.00. A modified version, consisting only of a tree house on a pole, the whole thing 33" high, is about $25.00. Then there's the cat hassock, which is also a house; your cat (or small dog) can repose inside, while your feet repose on top (which is covered with nice scratchy carpet, so watch out for your feet when the inhabitant emerges); it's $20.00. Shipping is extra. Brochures are free. A word of warning: they offer a small selection of colors. A relative of mine and I each ordered two in gold, because we wanted the pairs to match. They came in four different colors. I suppose Wen-Rub would have exchanged them, but, seeing that we were a continent apart, I felt it was too much trouble.

D. BIRDS AND FISH

DUNCRAFT, WW, 25 South Main St., Penacook, N.H. 03301, offers everything for the outdoor bird. There are feeders for general birds and feeders for specific birds, and feeders designed to exclude specific birds. These begin as low as $2.50 and go up to $23.00 for the impressive Yankee Superfeeder (a smaller Yankee Feeder is a mere $12.00), and $50.00 for the Manorial Estate Feeder—without suet holder. There are birdbaths and devices to keep the water in them warm, miniature weathervanes for birdhouses ($2.50), owls to frighten away birds you don't like, replacement parts for feeders you already have, and wild bird seed. There are also bird books, bird gifts, glasses for spying on birds, bird calls to arouse false hopes in bird breasts, and records of bird songs. Everything except the birdseed is postpaid, and the catalog is 25¢.

FOREST INDUSTRIES, WW, P.O. Box 597, Hyannis, Mass. 02601 has a free brochure of bird supplies, with their patented automatic small bird feeder, which keeps out jays, grackles, and larger birds. It's $10.00, but they have feeders that start as low as $1.00. In addition, there are bird baths and squirrel baffles.

In their free seed catalog, **GEORGE TAIT AND SONS, INC.,** WW, 900 Tidewater Dr., Norfolk, Va. 23504, show a large collection of bird feeders and birdhouses, from a modest suet holder at less than $2.00 to a palatial martin residence at a bit under $25.00; also bird seed, suet seed cake, and, for your hummingbird feeder, instant nectar (I swear it!). Most of the other garden supply houses (Chapter 10) offer bird things.

The **LOG CABIN,** WW, Rte. 30, Newfane, Vt. 05345, sells New England Village birdhouses—church, schoolhouse, town hall, and library, at $5.00 each, or you can get the whole town for $18.00. Catalog is free.

If you need an outfit for your falcon, **NORTHWEST FARMS, INC.,** WW, P.O. Box 3003, Portland, Ore. 97208, sells hoods, jesses, bewits, bells, gauntlets—in short, everything the most demanding bird could possibly need. Although I hadn't wanted to include live animals, as I disapprove of most shipping practices, I must point out that, if you should happen to have a falcon outfit and no falcon, Northwest can supply the birds, from $70.00. They also sell all kinds of other birds, from chickens (starting at 40¢), ducks (60¢), and geese ($1.75) to emus ($950.00), bustards ($660.00), and cassowaries ($875.00). Some kinds of birds may even be bought in egg form, which is much less unnerving—and you will feel even closer to them if you hatch them yourself. Although Northwest are primarily bird people, they also sell lions ($500.00),

wolves ($400.00), bears ($75.00 to $325.00), and the like, all bred in captivity so it's legal. Cougars are $400.00 and pumas $900.00, which baffles me because I thought they were the same animal. . . . But please, if you do decide to buy a leopard ($300.00) or a flying squirrel ($25.00), or whatever, don't have it sent. Go to Oregon and bring it back yourself; you'll both enjoy the trip. Catalog is free.

AQUA ENGINEERS, WW, Box 1, Ortonville, Mich. 48462, sells all kinds of aquarium equipment, including automatic fish feeders, senior water polishers, and, of course, tanks, plus an unusual variety of fishfood. They also sell fish, and snails ("the cleanest pets in the world") to keep them company. Catalog is 25¢. You'll also find a lot of fish equipment at the houses in Chapter 10 that sell water plants.

The **BAY RIDGE MARINE WORLD,** WW, 6809 Eleventh Ave., Brooklyn, N.Y., offers everything for the well-equipped fish and other aquarium denizens. Catalog is free.

E. GIFTS AND BOOKS

LARKLAIN PRODUCTS, LTD., WW, 3700 South Garrison St., Denver, Colo. 80235, sell self-stick weatherproof decalomanias of practically every breed of dog there is, plus some cats and horses. There are also dog ashtrays, stationery, buttons, and iron-on transfers. You may even have a rug handhooked with the pooch of your choice ($30.00 to $35.00). Brochure is free.

The **ARK,** WW, Marshalls Creek, Pa. 18335, puts out a catalog of animal gifts, not for animals, but with animal motifs, such as the handsome lion apron ($4.00), the ceramic coati box ($15.00), the walrus pendant ($4.50) . . . and all kinds of toys and prints. The delightful catalog is free. The **KREBS,** WW, Dunns Corners, Westerly, R.I. 02891, and **ROMBINS' NEST,** WW, Fairfield, Pa. 17320, also show lots of items with animal designs. Rombins' catalog is 25¢; The Krebs is free.

The **LEANIN' TREE PUBLISHING CO.,** WW, Box 1500, Boulder, Colo. 80302, sells Western greeting cards and stationery, featuring horses and cows and loads of wildlife.

For books about cats send for free lists to the **CAT BOOK CENTER,** WW, P.O. Box 172, Wykagyl Station, New Rochelle, N.Y. 10804, and the **LITTLE BOOK SHOP,** WW, Farnham Common, Bucks, England.

Chapter 22

PLAYTHINGS AND DIVERSIONS

There are many things in this chapter that some of my readers will probably feel should have been placed in other chapters, just as they may feel there are things in other chapters that really belong in this one. For example, except for passing references, I have listed all dolls here. Doll collectors who might be inclined to take umbrage should realize that it is almost impossible to separate collectors' dolls from children's dolls, because most shops deal in both. Similarly, as I can't feasibly separate miniatures from dollhouse furniture . . . or collectors' miniatures from dollhouse or craft miniatures, they are all grouped together here; you can simply assume that the expensive ones are meant for collectors or very rich kids.

On the other hand, some items that you might expect to find here are included in other chapters. Models—ships, airplanes, etc.—for the most part have been put in Chapter 16, and those offered in kit form, in Chapter 15. Tin soldiers are mainly in Chapter 15; wooden soldiers, mainly in this chapter. Although you will find some craft kits for children here, the bulk of them are in Chapter 17.

A. GENERAL

1. All-Around Establishments

Probably the largest and best-known toy shop in the United States is **F. A. O. SCHWARZ,** WW, Fifth Ave. at 58 St., New York, N.Y. 10022, and it seems to carry practically every kind of plaything you can think of. You'll rarely find any bargains here; on the other hand, when you find the same items in most other stateside catalogs, they will generally cost about the same. Schwarz just seems to carry more expensive items than others—and that's probably what makes their catalog (50¢) so fascinating.

And probably the largest and best-known toy shop in England is **HAMLEY'S OF REGENT STREET, LTD.,** WW, 200-202 Regent St., London W1R 5DF, England, which puts out a free yearly catalog showing some of their attractive stock. There are model trains from many countries; Meccano (the British version of Erector) sets; build-it-yourself castles, beginning at $10.00; the celebrated Pelham puppets, starting at around $4.00 (and other puppets beginning at even lower prices); Peggy Nisbet character dolls, with

$9.00 the lowest price of those shown; plus dolls of all kinds.

Three good sources for German and Austrian toys are **JOSEF KOBER,** WW, Graben 14-15, Vienna 1, Austria; **OBLETTER SPIELWAREN,** WW, Industriestrasse 20, 8034 Germering, West Germany; and **SPIELZEUG RASCH,** WW, Gerhart-Hauptmann Platz 1, 2 Hamburg 1, West Germany. Available there are the delightful Steiff animals, at prices much lower than they are here; as well as construction sets, trains, toys and games, and models. All three catalogs are in German and are free.

The **FEDERAL SMALLWARES CORP.,** WW, 85 Fifth Ave., New York, N.Y. 10003, puts out a charming catalog (25¢) of toys and games. Since Federal is one of the retail branches of Shackmann's, well-known wholesaler of imported playthings, you'll see here a lot of the small toys shown in many of the general mail-order catalogs (sometimes at the same price, sometimes cheaper). Included in the current catalog are lucite flower eggs with dried flowers embedded in them (under $2.50); old fashioned jigsaws (from 75¢ up); reproduction antique dolls (from $2.50); puppets and puppet theatres; nests of wooden soldiers and clowns (around $4.00); plastic nesting soldiers and penguins ($1.00); mechanical toys; and lots of puzzles. Their book branch, the **MERRIMACK PUBLISHING CORP.,** at the same address, sometimes offers a catalog at erratic intervals (when it's available, it, too, is 25¢). When last seen it was showing old-fashioned paper dolls; reproductions of the French Pellerin Imagerie d'Épinal construction color prints, including a Harlequin jump doll set and a circus construction set ($1.00 each); antique stuff-'em-yourself dolls ($3.50); old-fashioned puzzles; old-fashioned card games; and tiny newspapers and magazines for your doll house.

There are several smaller shops that specialize in well-thought-out selections of toys from around the world. One is **ASK YOUR FATHER,** WW, 120 South St., Pittsfield, Mass. 01201, which has a 20-piece construction set from Holland, with bright-colored plastic baseboards, building squares, roofs, etc., that slide together. "Voor Kleine Architecten" is $10.00. Then there's the castle kit of Camberwick Green Pippin, which consists of a fort and seven soldiers in full-color fiberboard (you slot them together), for $6.00. Lots of miniatures are available too. Another such store is the **GINGERBREAD HOUSE**, WW, 9 Christopher St., New York, N.Y. 10014, which carries a very nice assortment of toys. And the **TOY SHOP OF HAPPY THINGS**, WW, 7 Spring St., Eureka Springs, Ark. 72632, calls itself "an old-fashioned toy shop." All their toys, they say, "are designed to stimulate young imaginations and they do it without batteries . . . or delicate moving parts." They have reproduction iron toys and banks, Speel Goed wooden toys from Holland, doll houses, dolls, and so on. All three catalogs are free.

2. Specialty Shops

PAPERCHASE, WW, 216 Tottenham Court Rd., London W.1, England, has a fascinating array of paper products. There are simple-to-construct (or so they say) doll houses, complete with furniture, for about $7.00; mobiles at less than $2.00; easy-to-assemble (again, their claim, not mine) model buildings, including Elizabethan cottages, Regency shops, a country church, and so on, starting at less than $1.00 and going up to about $2.00. (You'll find similar items offered by **HATHAWAY'S** in Chapter 16, but most of their constructions are more elaborate.) Catalog is free.

Also from England comes the fetching little hand-drawn catalog put out by **HAPPY THINGS**, WW, 4 Babbington Village, nr. Eastwood, Nottingham, England, which shows three different Amara rag dolls, a girl, a clown, and Queen Victoria—all carefully handmade and selling for about $7.00 each. They're each 18 inches tall; a winsome 36-inch caterpillar made with equally loving care is $10.00. Also on hand are the celebrated Cuckoobags, pocket tidies for stowing things. Models include a fine regal British lion, a London bus, and other subjects of appeal to both children and light-hearted adults. Prices average about $5.00. Cuckoo Washpacks (packs of washmitt and handtowels) in the same prints cost around $2.50. All kinds of stocking stuffers are available, too. Send 1 IRC for the catalog (3, if you want it by airmail, and so specify).

The **VICTORIA AND ALBERT MUSEUM**, WW, South Kensington, London, S.W.7, England, although you wouldn't exactly call it a toy shop, does include, in its free price lists, several sets of cut-out fashion dolls in eighteenth- and nineteenth-century costume, at prices starting at less than 10¢ per set. In addition, there are jigsaw puzzles based on famous paintings, for around $1.00 or so, and cut-out-and-stuff rag dolls, for the incredibly low price of 50¢.

KLODS HANS, WW, 34 Hans Jensenstraede DK-5000, Odense, Denmark, is located right across the street from Hans Christian Andersen's house, and offers a Hans Christian Andersen doll (with wee carpet bag) for around $7.00. There are also gnomes and elves of all shapes and sizes (a 4½-inch elf house for a little over $5.00); loads of miniatures, and other knicknacks. Catalog is 35¢. And here in the United States, **TRE KRONOR**, WW, 248 Main St., Farmington, Conn. 06032, has trolls from Norway ($10.00), straw animals and ornaments ($1.00 to $4.00), and all kinds of figures. Catalog is free. (If you crave Icelandic trolls, you can get them from **ICEMART**, Chapter 2,C.3).

SPIELWAREN-SCHMIDT, WW, 20 Neuhauser Strasse 20, Münich, 2, West Germany, will send you a free catalog (in German) of Märklin trains.

DICK SCHNACKE, WW, Mountain Craft Shop, Rte. 1, Proctor, W. Va. 26055, calls his firm the largest producer of authentic folk toys. It actually is a cottage industry, because the dozen or so craftspeople who produce these toys work out of their own homes. Featured in the line are gooneyweights (handpainted stones), whimmydiddles (identified as bullroarers, "a legendary toy"), and corncob pigs, all under $2.00. They also have corncob dolls, flipper-dingers (unidentified), and bean bag girls, under $3.00. Catalog is free.

Some of the firms already described include noteworthy toy collections. **APPALACHIAN SPRING**, WW, 1655 Wisconsin Ave. N.W., Washington, D.C. 20007, has a thoroughly huggable fat 24-inch patchwork hippo, for $16.00; and a plump 15-inch pig covered in a neat floral design, for $7.00. In addition to other stuffed toys, there are handmade wooden toys and games, plus cornhusk dolls ($2.50 to $6.00). The catalog is $1.00. **ROMBINS' NEST FARMS**, WW, Fairfield, Pa. 17320, has a nice group of reproduction cast iron antique banks in its catalog (25¢), from around $2.50 to $12.00. There are cats, pigs, dogs, a Liberty Bell, a buffalo, an elephant, George Washington, and a cute little miniature treasury. They also sell replicas of old cast iron toys—a trolley, an ice wagon, a fire engine, etc.

Although **QUEENSLAND ABORIGINAL CREATIONS**, WW, 135-147 George St., Brisbane, Queensland, Australia, doesn't have a line of toys as such, they do offer aboriginal-made Koala bears, costing from around $2.00 for the 3-inch size up to $20.00 for the 18-incher. And the **SOURDOUGH TRADING POST**, WW, Box 40175, Anchorage, Alaska, has a very specialized item indeed—Eskimo yoyos covered in sealskin, at $5.00 each.

3. Educational Wooden Toys

CREATIVE PLAYTHINGS, WW, Princeton, N.J. 08540, puts out the type of catalog that tells you children need "different kinds of toys for different experiences: physical, sensorial, mental, emotional and social," and goes on like that for pages. There are the sturdy wooden educational toys they have been showing for years, and that everybody else now shows, too; some particularly attractive stuffed animals covered in unusual fabrics; and other things. **CHILDCRAFT,** WW, 52 Hook Rd., Bayonne, N.J. 07002, also offers educational toys, both domestic and imported—the expected wooden and an ever-increasing line of plastic.

JAMES GALT AND CO., INC., WW, Brookfield Rd., Cheadle, Cheshire SK8 2PF, England, puts out two catalogs, a small one which is, apparently, free, and a large one, "Early Stages," which they said, the last time I could induce them to communicate, was $2.00. They specialize in the kind of educational toys Childcraft and Creative feature, at prices that are, in many cases, lower than here.

Another English firm, **GOOD-WOOD PLAYTHINGS, LTD.,** WW, Lavant, Chichester, Sussex, England, describe themselves as "manufacturers of high quality wooden toys of imaginative design." They put out a lot of the usual wooden toys, plus some charming specialties, like the peep-hole puzzles, which are jigsaw puzzles with little doors that open to reveal further secrets. They're less than $2.00. An unusual line of "jacks" in sturdy wooden boxes include a bear in a box "with growl," for around $3.00. Hexbrix, which are like no blocks I've ever seen (they're patterned), cost from around $3.00 to $6.00. Catalog is free.

CONSTRUCTIVE PLAYTHINGS, WW, 1040 East 85 St., Kansas City, Mo. 64131, puts out a big catalog of this kind of toy for the preschool child. However, it seems to be aimed at teachers and may not be available to the general public, at least not free. It's marked $1.00. I got it for nothing, but they might have thought I was a teacher.

COMMUNITY PLAYTHINGS, WW, Rifton, N.Y. 12471, is run by the Society of Brothers, a religious community founded in Germany in 1920, and forced to flee to England during the Nazi regime. When England went to war with Germany, they moved to Paraguay; after the end of the war they came to the United States and established themselves as toymakers. Naturally they make educational wooden toys. A 22-inch "toddler tractor" is about $16.00; and there are some attractive animal puppets (8 for $19.00); and some handy storage units. Catalog is free.

EVERDALE TOYS, WW, Box 29, Hillsburg, Ont., Canada, is a residential school-community formed, they say, for the purpose of giving students and teachers an alternative way of learning, teaching, and living. In order to help meet the operating costs of the school, they have started a toy business, beginning with big, simple wooden trucks, handcrafted out of hard maple and priced from $17.00 up to around $23.00 (some are over 2' long). They're planning to branch out into other lines of playthings and perhaps, by the time you send for their free catalog, they will have included those as well.

MY UNCLE, WW, 133 Main St., Payeburg, Me. 04037, puts out handcrafted wooden toys that would please collectors as much as children. Both can enjoy them, for they're tough enough to be played with from generation to generation. A really terrific Noah's Ark, constructed according to the directions in the Bible, is 30" from stem to stern, and costs $40.00 empty. It can be outfitted with miniature Steiff animals, which are available (in pairs, of course) from the shop, although it would probably pay you to order them from Germany or Austria. There's an old-fashioned wooden circus train, 50" long, at $30.00. The most fascinating thing here is an eight-room Victorian doll house, 46½" long, 29" wide, 44½" high, meticulously constructed on a one inch to one foot scale, and opening up in all directions (not just the usual one opening you'll find in the ordinary dollhouse). It has one bay window and five dormers and costs $400.00. (It weighs 180 lbs.) If you want one, you have to wait 4 weeks, because it's all handmade. Brochure is free.

The **VERMONT WOODEN TOY CO.,** WW, Old High School Bldg., Whitsfield, Vt. 05673, says it is "engaged in designing and building safe and beautiful toys for children that will last." They're made of wood held together by pegs and dowels, and have no paint or artificial finish. Here, too, they declare proudly, "All of our toys operate on child-power—there are no lights, batteries, or extra gimmicks." In other words, they are educational wooden toys—priced from around $7.00 for a small stylized bus, to $60.00 for a "Green Mountain Choo Choo," which is actually a whole train, 53" long. There's a Brooklyn trolley of yesteryear (though it is never explained why a New England firm should choose a Brooklyn prototype) for $20.00, and a Vermont farm truck for $10.00. Catalog is free, and so is the brochure put out by **COUNTRYCRAFT WOODEN TOYS,** WW, 4 White Birch Ct., Smithtown, N.Y. 11787, which sells unpainted pine playthings handcrafted in the firm's own workshop. The line includes a 7-inch steamroller for a little over $9.00, and an 11-inch racing car for $4.00 plus.

The **WESTON BOWL MILL,** WW, Weston, Vt. 05161, has a miniature spinning wheel for $1.25, plus a few other wooden miniatures and some wooden toys that seem to be more reasonably priced than at most other places. A big red trailer truck is $3.00; and a sea-worthy Maine coastal skiff is $4.00. Catalog is 25¢.

For the parent who wants to build his or her child a "high-quality wooden toy," and doesn't have a "fully equipped workshop or special skills," the **PAUL J. GRUEN STUDIOS, INC.,** WW, Ash St., West New-bury, Mass. 01985, puts out four kits—a racer and three different kinds of truck—which have no nails, screws, or plastic parts; they're glued and pegged to-gether in the old-time way. Costs run from $9.00 to $15.00. The catalog is free.

The **WORKSHOP FOR LEARNING THINGS, INC.,** WW, 5 Bridge St., Watertown, Mass. 02173, specializes in cardboard carpentry for children's furniture. Used to be they offered the cardboard items themselves (and they still do offer some), but now they want to sell you kits and tools for making the things yourself. It's mostly aimed at schools and such, but there are some things that might interest enterprising parents as well. The catalog is 50¢.

B. DOLLS

1. General

The **MARK FARMER CO., INC.,** WW, El Cerrito, Cal. 94530, have been dollmakers for 37 years and sell all kinds of dolls—old-fashioned and contempo-rary—dressed, undressed, or in kit form. A china head Civil War doll 18" tall is a little over $9.00 in kit form, with dress pattern; $15.00 assembled but undressed, with pattern; $21.00 assembled and completely dressed. Available, too, are lots of doll parts and pat-terns, and a line of doll house furniture. Catalog is 25¢.

The **ENCHANTED DOLL HOUSE,** WW, Manchester Center, Vt. 05255, puts out an attractive doll cata-log, with special emphasis on Mme. Alexander's crea-tions, from $8.00. There are also doll houses ($22.00 to $150.00), and the wherewithal to furnish them. Tatalog is 50¢.

The **DOLLSPART SUPPLY CO., INC.,** WW, 5-06 51 Ave., Long Island City, N.Y. 11101, offers what the name implies: doll parts, including not only limbs and wigs, but also stuffed muslin bodies, unstuffed leather bodies, etc.—for both antique and contemporary dolls of all sizes. They also carry complete dolls, ranging from "Barbie" types for less than $2.00 to reproduc-tions of rare French dolls, going up to $80.00. Also on hand are tools, books, and doll house furniture. Catalog is free.

Many of the general catalogs offer dolls. **HERTER'S** features some particularly inexpensive stuff-and-sew dolls imported from England. There's a clown, a harlequin, a Coldstream guard, Raggedy Ann and Andy, a teddy bear, a rainbow trout (after all, it is primarily a sporting goods house), and a "Very Eager Beaver," from around 70¢ to $1.70.

ANTIQUE DOLL REPRODUCTIONS, WW, Box 103, Montevallo Rte., Milo, Mo. 64767, puts out an illus-trated price list showing the wares they have to sell. It's rather shocking at first, because one page shows rows and rows of dismembered limbs, but, if your treasured period puppet lacks a leg, this is the place to find it. You can buy complete dolls, or the parts to put one together yourself, or individual replacement parts (arms and legs start from around $1.00 per pair). Prices are not high, considering that the pro-prietor of the shop makes all the dolls (and parts) her-self. **YESTERYEAR DOLLS,** WW, Rte. 2, Box 195, Parker, Colo. 80134, will send you a list of reproduc-tion old-fashioned china dolls if you will send them two stamps.

For a stamp, **KIMPORT DOLLS,** WW, Box 495, In-dependence, Mo. 64051, will send you a complimen-tary copy of their magazine "Doll Talk," which de-scribes the antique dolls they have for sale (starting at around $12.00 and going up to $1000.00), as well as contemporary offerings (which start at a modest $4.00). These are mostly imports, and include a Greek evzone, an Irish leprechaun, Javanese shadow puppets, and carved driftwood dolls made on Pit-cairn Island by descendants of the *Bounty* mutineers. Another stamp will bring you a list from **BLUE BARN ANTIQUES,** WW, P.O. Box 295, Mount Airy, N.C. 27030, describing the antique dolls they have for sale, and illustrating a few. The ones I saw started from $4.00 for a 2¾-inch "Frozen Charlotte" boy to $495.00 for a 21-inch bisque socket head doll with a French body. Most of the dolls offered are less than $100.00, however.

2. Regional

All of the preceding sell imported dolls, and most of the regional and foreign firms described in Chapters 2, 3, and 11 sell dolls, for the most part at extremely reasonable prices. You can get Mexican dolls from **SANBORN'S,** Ecuadorian dolls from **AKIOS.** Virtu-ally all of the American Indian houses sell dolls for both children and collectors; note **CHEROKEE ARTS AND CRAFTS, SEMINOLE OKALEE, QUALLA,** and **IROQRAFTS** in particular.

For non-Indian American dolls, write to **OZARK OPPORTUNITIES, INC.,** WW, 707 North Vine, Box 400, Harrison, Ark. 72601, which sells wooden dolls that walk and dance, from around $2.00 to $4.00; corn shuck dolls, around $2.00; and stuffed dolls and toys, $2.00 up. The **PIKE COUNTY CITIZENS' ASSOCIATION**, WW, c/o Sue Ramsay, 1917 North Oakland, Milwaukee, Wis., sells clothespin dolls from $1.00 to $3.00; cornshuck and rag dolls, $3.00; and small dolls stuffed with beans, for $2.00. I believe both catalogs are free.

The **YESTERYEAR TOY CO., INC.**, WW, P.O. Box 4383, Charleston, W.Va. 25304, which is the sole industry of Davis Creek, West Virginia, manufactures and sells handmade handpainted toys of the 1875 to 1900 era. Their chief product is the original West Virginia stomper doll, which sells for $10.00, complete with dancing platform and antique support. (The dolls actually do a clog dance with a bit of assistance from you.) There are also the Davis Grenadiers (classical red-coated toy wooden soldiers), which the firm chauvinistically recommends "for a little boy's most treasured and long-remembered possession," but girls will like them as well. They're $2.50 each ($15.00 per dozen, if you're planning an army). They also have lots of nice Christmas ornaments—fish, angels, and birds, at the same prices as the soldiers. Catalog is 25¢.

SWITZER'S has some Irish dolls. **SHANNON** offers the Peggy Nisbet dolls at prices lower than I've seen them anywhere else. The **SCOTTISH SHOP**, WW, P.O. Box N-422, Nassau, Bahamas, puts out the longest list of Nisbet dolls I've seen, at prices that are higher than Shannon's, lower than they would be here. **EGERTON'S** also carries the Nisbet dolls, plus the cuddly Tolli-Dolls, which include the rather ferocious Kitty-Cat (a little over $3.00 to $12.00, for the two-foot high feline), the wistful Tolli-Dog ($3.50 to $5.00), and the Tolli-Pixie, who looks like a troll to me, (slightly over $2.00). You can get Scottish dolls from the **EDINBURGH TARTAN GIFT SHOP. KILKENNY** has a sew-and-stuff doll of an Irish peasant lass, which could also be used as a dish cloth or a wall hanging, at around $1.25.

Belgian dolls are available from the **LACE PALACE**; Dutch dolls from **CHOCOLATERIE DAUPHINE**. **OBÉRON** offers a group of dolls in various French provincial costumes. Dolls in regional Austrian costumes may be purchased from **TIROLER HEIMATWORK**; Portuguese dolls from **MADEIRA SUPERBIA** and **JABARA'S** (which also has handmade sailboats); Greek dolls from **ATTIKA**.

CHARLOTTE WEIBULL, WW, Box 43, 230 47 Åkarp, Sweden, specializes in dolls dressed in accurate depictions of the various Swedish national costumes, faithful down to the last tiny button. Fabrics are handwoven according to traditional designs; caps and sweaters are knitted; wooden shoes are carved by hand; jewelry is made by a silversmith. Prices range from $4.00 for the smallest doll, up to around $14.00 for the elaborate collectors' dolls. Prices are in American dollars; catalog (in English) is free.

ANDRZEJ SZCZEPKA, WW, Ul. Pulawska 132-12, Warsaw, Poland, sells wooden dolls handmade by Polish folk artists, from around $4.00 to $10.00. He also has historic Polish dolls; paper dolls in Polish national costume; and dolls from Bulgaria, Russia, and Hungary. Also on hand are those popular nesting dolls, both Russian and Polish, from around $4.00 up; plus an interesting-sounding selection of miniatures. There's a reproduction of a nineteenth-century Polish mountain room setting—7 pieces of furniture in natural wood pokerwork decoration costs a little over $15.00. All prices are in American dollars and include airmail postage. The one-page typewritten price list is in English and costs 50¢ (I sent 3 IRCs, which seemed to be satisfactory). I'm a little dubious about this place, because he requests payment in "banknotes only" in a registered letter. (Maybe he'll change his mind now that the dollar has been devalued.)

For those seeking Middle Eastern dolls, **CHILINGURIAN** sells an assortment in traditional Lebanese costume at what seem like incredibly low prices. If you want Ceylonese dolls, try the **DEPARTMENT OF SMALL INDUSTRIES** (Bangkok); Indian dolls from **BENGAL HOME INDUSTRIES, KAVERI**, and **LEPAKSHI. HARPENG LIANG** offers 11 different silk dolls in Thai national costume, and most of the other Thai houses also sell dolls.

Dolls from mainland China may be bought at the **CHINESE MERCHANDISE EMPORIUM**; Hong Kong dolls from **WELFARE HANDICRAFTS**. For Formosan dolls, try the **TAIWAN VARIETY AND NOVELTY CO.**, which sells them very inexpensively (except that you have to buy them by the dozen). They also sell colored wooden eggs, bamboo junks, T-stone touchstones, shell whistles, furry animals, and so on. In Japan, the **UCHIDA ART COMPANY** sells Kabuki dolls.

Particularly noteworthy are the African dolls from **STUDIO ARTS 68**, WW, P.O. Box 7904, Nairobi, Kenya. There are handcarved wooden Masai dolls (old ones are a little under $5.00, modern ones half that), and traditional Sambun clay dolls, which they warn you are not for playing with, because they break easily (around $15.00). Both of these are primarily collectors' dolls; however, Studio does have inexpensive (around $2.50) plastic dolls, dressed in tribal costume, which are also easy to pack and send. Also suitable for children are the rope and rag dolls ($3.00 to $4.00) and pajama case dolls ($7.00). Handscreened tribal dolls (Kikuyu, Turkana, and Masai) are available stuffed or unstuffed, from $4.00 up. Prices are in American dollars. Lists are free.

C. MINIATURES

Many of the firms in Section B.1 also offer doll house furniture. A firm that specializes in this area is **CHESTNUT HILL STUDIO, LTD.**, WW, Box 38, Churchville, N.Y. 14428, which offers miniature doll house furniture, faithfully reproduced from museum originals and private collections on a scale of one inch to the foot, and with miniscule accessories to complete the decor. They're expensive—a winged fireside chair costs $65.00, a tiny Aubusson rug, $70.00—but they're meant for collectors, not children. Some of the accessories might interest miniature collectors; there are tiny sterling silver reproductions of antique pieces—Queen Anne candlesticks are $13.50, a seventeenth-century porriger is $7.50—plus other exquisite little things. The catalog is $1.50 (50¢ ref.).

On a more modest level is the doll house furniture catalog (25¢) available from **FEDERAL SMALL-WARES** (see Section A). Most of the furniture is handmade of cherry wood. A Boston rocker is $3.00; a highboy with eleven drawers that open is $12.00. Also sold are tiny accessories, such as oil lamps from 85¢ to $1.15; bedwarmers, $3.00; a spinning wheel, $1.60; and a miniature tea set, under $1.50.

MILES KIMBALL, WW, 41 West Eighth Ave., Oshkosh, Wis. 54901, puts out a free catalog devoted entirely to miniatures, mainly furniture. The cast iron Duncan Phyfe living and dining room furniture—the table is about $3.20—and the petit point Victorian furniture—the rocker is $9.00—are especially interesting. Other items include handcarved ivory miniatures from Spain (though why anybody, even in Spain, should choose to carve a mouse sitting on a Swiss cheese out of ivory, beats me; it's $5.00); little animals (for 75¢ you can get a ceramic teddy bear, snail, snow owl, or baby rabbit); general store appliances; and a really lovely Limoges mortar and pestle and samovar ($5.00 to $6.00) from France.

Among the firms already mentioned, **YIELD HOUSE** has some attractive antique reproduction doll furniture and doll houses. A tiny coat tree is $1.50, a bench-table is $3.50. A knocked-down New England saltbox doll house is $40.00

K. EWER, PEWTERER, WW, 1282 Lafayette St., Cape May, N.J. 08204, issues a free brochure of "Museum Miniatures," delightfully illustrated with line drawings. Among the tiny reproductions of antiques, made on a scale of an inch to a foot, are a 1¾-inch Victorian mirror at $1.50; a 5/8-inch 1790 Revere teapot, $2.50, and a 5-piece set of fireplace accessories, $4.00. Also on hand are period toy soldiers, with the original lead reproduced in pewter.

The **COLONEL'S HOBBY**, WW, 8 Shawnee Trail, Harrison, N.Y. 10528, sells delightful miniature reproductions of antique silver museum pieces, authentic in every detail, in silver—made to the apparently customary scale of one inch to one foot. A copy of the inkstand used to sign the Declaration of Independence is $12.50; a teapot based on a Peter van Dyck (1684-1751) original, $12.50; a 1768 Revere salt cellar, $7.25. The brochure is free.

DOROTHY HESNER, WW, 5064 West 31 St., Cicero, Ill. 60650, puts out a mimeographed price list containing a huge assortment of modestly priced miniatures, many of them handmade by Ms. Hesner herself. Among items you're not likely to see in too many other places are miniature clothes hangers (35¢), miniature clipboards and dust mops (50¢ each), and ½-inch tomato pincushions complete with 3/8-inch pins (75¢). She also sells 8½ x 11-inch sheets of paper with miniature allover patterns, suitable for doll house decor or découpage (6 for $1.00). Send an SAE with double postage, because sometimes her lists are thick, and be prepared to wait for a reply, as this is a one-woman operation.

MAID OF SCANDINAVIA (see Chapter 8,A.3) has miniatures meant mostiy to decorate cakes, place cards, and such, but there's nothing to stop your using them however you like. There are tiny wooden animals as well as a Holy Family, 85¢ to $1.65 per set; tiny tools; miniature bowling alleys; miniature skeletons (35¢ each); gavels, steins; bone china costume dolls; angels; tiny sewing machines (25¢); working windmills; space capsules; and spacesuits. The other cake decorating firms also offer miniatures, but Maid seems to offer the most.

The **HOBBYIST HOUSE OF TREASURES**, WW, P.O. Box 6778, Fort Meyers, Fla. 33901, puts out a free mimeographed catalog that lists a huge number of miniatures at very low prices.

D. THEATERS AND PUPPETS

POLLOCKS TOY MUSEUM, WW, 1 Scala St., London W.1, England, offer a little brochure (free) describing their toy theaters. Prices are a lot higher than penny plain and tuppence colored these days, but much lower than they are here, run from a little under $2.00 apiece for the theater sheets (you cut out and set them up yourself), with plays about $1.00 to $1.50. Also on hand are some old German toy theater sheets. You can also get estimates for large wooden stages, which will, of course, cost considerably more to ship.

PRIORS DUKKE THEATRE, WW, Købmagergade 52, II Copenhagen K, Denmark, sells model theaters, either set up in cardboard on a folding wooden frame, or, like Pollock's, in sheets that you can build into a theater yourself—obviously more practical when you order from overseas. One of the theaters represents the Royal Theatre in Copenhagen; another is the pantomime theater in Tivoli Gardens. Lithographic sheets for the Pantomime Theater, accompanied by the play *Harlequin and Columbine,* complete with cut-out characters and scenery and an English book, are around $5.00 (set up it comes to around $20.00, and would probably be much more difficult to ship). Plays are available in English for both theaters, but most of the offerings are in Danish. Brochures are free, and in English, but the price lists are in Danish.

The **STORYTELLER TOY CO.,** WW, 5918 Ibbetson, Lakewood, Cal. 90713, puts out what they call the "world's largest selection" of hand puppets, at $3.50 each postpaid. Catalog is 25¢. You'll also find puppets sold by several of the other firms already mentioned, notably Hamley's, Federal Smallwares, and many of the doll houses.

E. GAMES AND PUZZLES

WORLD WIDE GAMES, INC., WW, Box 450, Delaware, Ohio 43015, offers an interesting collection of games from all over the world (although most of them are actually made here, many by World Wide itself), at prices ranging from less than $5.00 to over $60.00. Included are the English "Nine Men's Morris," the German "Mensch Argere Dich Nicht" (also known here as "Wahoo"), The Ghanaian Adi board, Korean Yoot, Kenyan Shisima, and the American Indian Pommawonga. Most of these are $10.00 or less. Table games such as skittles, hockey, and shuffleboard are at the higher end of the price range. Catalog is free.

BEREA COLLEGE, WW, Berea, Ky. 40403, has a catalog of gifts handcrafted by Appalachian students earning their way through the college. There are intriguing wooden games fashioned out of walnut or cherry woods, beginning as low as $2.25, and including such old favorites as Fox and Geese ($6.50). There are lovely maple and walnut chessboards ($22.00), and big wooden games, such as skittles and hockey (from $35.00). There are also stuffed animals, including a fetching series of bean bags, from $2.00 up. Catalog is 25¢.

The **HASSETTS,** WW, 3 Hilltop Dr., Cherry Hill, N.J. 08034, have a collection of adult jigsaw puzzles, both domestic and imported. Of particular interest here is a group of puzzles printed on basswood, priced from $9.00 to $20.00. (The others are much less expensive.) Catalog is free.

You'll find chess sets of various kinds available from many of the firms already described in this chapter and in Chapter 11,C. In this chapter, Hamley's (A.1) has a wide selection, beginning at $3.50 for a standard Staunton set and going up to around $75.00 for a reproduction eighteenth-century set made of reconstituted stone and complete with a board made of walnut and sycamore squares. Federal Smallwares (section A.1) sells a small wooden box that opens up to become the board of the miniature wooden chess set inside. (It's $2.25, and there's an even tinier set in their doll house catalog.) From Chapter 11 . . . the **HOUSE OF ONYX** (C.2) sells Mexican Onyx chess sets as cheaply as you can get them from many Mexican firms. Aztec design chess sets cost from $4.00 to $6.00 per set (Staunton chessmen run a few dollars higher). Boards, also in onyx, are extra, and cost more than the sets, starting at $11.00. **AKIOS** has Ecuadorian chess sets handcarved out of ivory nuts with painted faces, for $10.00 ($15.00 with a box that opens out into a board); there are also chess sets handmade from cedar and orangewood in the shape of Inca idols, from $7.00 to $20.00 without board, $12.00 to $30.00 with board. **KOREAN HANDICRAFTS** sells some beautiful Oriental style stone chess sets from $4.00 to $60.00; Gothic styles from $17.00 to $40.00 (in some the kings are as tall as 7"). Chess board-boxes begin from $4.50 for a plain box, $10.00 for a carved one, $20.00 for a chess table with folding legs (and go up to a top of over $40.00). The **HAKUSUI IVORY CO.** in Japan offers handmade ivory chess sets, with Staunton sets running from around $25.00 to $150.00, the more intricate Japanese types from $110.00 to over $320.00. Prices include boards. The **TSANG KING KEE IVORY FACTORY** in Hong Kong offers a much larger selection of Ivory chessmen (also handmade). Staunton sets cost from about $12.00 to $100.00, but it's the exquisite, complicated traditional Chinese sets that really take the eye here; they're offered in various sizes, beginning at less than $20.00, and going up to over $400.00 for the kind that I've only seen in museums. All prices include boards. (You can also get Mah-Jongg sets here.) **INKENTAN** sells African chess sets.

There's one firm that's devoted entirely to chess. **G. HENKE AND CO.,** WW, 3522 Karlshafen/Weser, West Germany, is a wholesale supplier of chess sets. There's a minimum requirement of around $75.00 but they'll sell you less if you pay a surcharge. Anyhow, the most attractive sets cost more than that, but still much less (about half the price of those I could check) than they cost here. Elaborate ivory chessmen carved in the Oriental style cost from around $70.00 to $600.00. They also have handcarved wooden sets—Gothic and mediaeval heroes, crusaders, animals, and so on—in the same price range. But there are much less expensive sets available as well, with men in the form of gypsies, Viennese, farmers, and traditional old German models, also handcarved of wood (from $10.00 to $80.00). In addition there are traditional chessmen, very modern chessmen, and figurine chessmen . . . even some nice plastic chessmen starting at only a few dollars. Chessboards and tables and clocks are also sold here. The catalog, so far as I can determine, is free.

F. NOVELTIES

The **JOHNSON SMITH CO.**, WW, 35075 Automation Dr., Mount Clemens, Mich. 48043, well-beloved by children and young-at-heart adults puts out a catalog full of, in the firm's own words, "novelties and unusual items." For 50¢ you can get selfadhering fuzzy hot lips or plastic ice cubes with real bugs in them; for 60¢, fake Confederate money or glow-in-the-dark bloodshot eyes; 70¢ to 75¢, exploding fountain pens, corn cob pipes, or Jew's harps; $1.00, hot foot warmer, mobile love balls, or lifesize monster ghosts; $1.50, double barreled yoyos, or ant farms; $2.00, spy pen radios, fake Croix de Guerre, fake chest hair, gory horror rubber feet, and so on. There are also more expensive items like a giant Bombay taxi horn for $9.00. How could anyone bear to be without a catalog that offers such fine things? Send for it now; it's free.

FABULOUS MAGIC, WW, 3319 East Charleston Blvd., Las Vegas, Nev. 89104, will send you a catalog (50¢) of magic supplies and accessories. Johnson-Smith has many of the same tricks, but Fabulous has many, many more—all the familiar oldies plus some new wrinkles in the art of prestidigitation.

The **MAHER SCHOOL OF VENTRILOQUISM**, WW, Box 9037, Denver, Colo. 80209, sells "ventriloquial figures," from less than $10.00 for a puppet with mouth movement up to over $300.00 for puppets with moving eyes and eyebrows, eyes that wink separately, and stick-out tongue. When you become the owner of one of these figures, the catalog (25¢) says, "You'll find you've acquired not only a prized possession but a pal."

LONG GROVE TOWN AND COUNTRY DISTRIBUTORS, WW, P.O. Box 194, Lake Zurich, Ill. 60047, sells strictly adult toys like one-armed bandits (slot machines), which are, of course, to be used as banks (though they do pay off), at $35.00. You'll also find two-headed coins ($2.50 to $3.00), creeping golf balls ($1.50), and some table games—electric baseball, football, manual hockey, etc., from $8.00 through $20.00. Catalog is free.

Since, as I said in the Introduction, I hope to have something in this book for everyone, my adult and/or degenerate readers will be pleased to know that the **TALK OF THE TOWN BOOKSTORE**, WW, 2232 East Charleston Blvd., Las Vegas, Nev. 89104, offers a guide to the local sporting houses (perfectly legal), as well as a selection of gadgets (for ladies as well as gentlemen—no chauvinism here) that might well be sold in the gift shops of these establishments. The catalog is free, but don't write for it unless you're broad-minded, sick, or have a perverted sense of humor.

Remember: *Write for the catalog first.* All prices given were valid only at the time of writing and probably have been changed.

Chapter 23

SMOKING AND RELATED VICES

I'm putting this chapter in the book out of sheer nobility of character, because I disapprove strongly of tobacco smoking, not so much because of what you smokers are doing to yourselves (serves you right, actually), but because of what you do to me; I'm violently allergic to tobacco smoke. At least I can take my revenge on you cigar smokers. Practically all of the overseas firms in this section offer Havana cigars, and you (unless you're living outside the United States) are *not* allowed to buy them. If you try, I believe the U.S. government does something awful to you.

All the catalogs in this chapter are free.

A. GENERAL

FRIBOURG AND TREYER, WW, 34 Haymarket, London SW1, England, which has been catering to the smoker (and snuffer) since 1720, has a good-looking catalog offering all the appurtenances of this vice. In addition to cigars, cigarettes, pipe tobacco, and all kinds of snuff, they also sell their own pipes, starting at around $9.00, with pipes for the connoisseur starting at approximately $38.00. On hand also are tobacco pouches and, particularly fetching, a set of brass pipe stoppers in the shape of characters from the *Pickwick Papers,* at about $1.00 each. Another English firm, even better known here, is **ALFRED DUNHILL, LTD.,** WW, 30 Duke St., Saint James's, London SW1, England. They call themselves suppliers of smokers' requisites to her majesty the Queen (I didn't know she smoked) and put out a handsome color catalog—all very expensive and elegant (they also show some jewelry and accessories).

In Holland, **P. G. C. HAJENUIS,** WW, Rokin 92-96, Amsterdam-C, issues a little brochure of smokers' supplies, including tobacco, cigars, and pipes (among them meerschaums and waterpipes). The catalog is in Dutch and the prices are in guilders; however, somebody typed in the American prices on the one I got. In addition, they wrote me a letter explaining the various Dutch terms. Since they probably are not going to go to the same trouble if a lot of you write in, here are some of the most pertinent: *merken,* brands; *aantal stuks per verpakking,* contents per box; *in blikverpakking,* in flat or round tins; *knakmodel,*

perfecto shape; *kist,* box; *afmetingen,* measures. Prices seem reasonable.

Another Dutch firm, **ROOYMANS MULLER,** WW, Demer 5, Postbus 352, Eindhoven, Holland, puts out an attractive catalog of cigars and pipes that isn't too helpful unless you can read Dutch. There aren't any prices, either, but I'm sure they will supply them on request.

The **PIPE OF PEACE,** WW, Nassau, Bahamas, calls itself the "world's most complete tobacconist." There are pipes of all kinds, including hookahs and some unusual numbers, including one shaped like a woman's leg, and others covered in leather; plus all kinds of tobaccos and smokers' accessories.

If you're interested in something different in the tobacco line, the **WA'KE DA TRADING POST,** WW, P.O. Box 19146, Sacramento, Cal. 95819, offers six different kinds of Kinnikinnick American Indian tobacco, at 90¢ for a 2-oz. package.

B. PIPES AND HOLDERS

ASTLEY'S, LTD., WW, 109 Jermyn St., London SW1Y 6HB, England, specializes in pipes of all kinds, beginning at around $5.00 for Atlantic briars and going up to over $70.00. The antique carved meerschaums are even higher. There are also modern meerschaums and the briars for which Astley is celebrated, in all sorts of interesting shapes, among which the calabashes are the most attention-provoking. Naturally there are tobaccos and all kinds of smokers' accessories as well.

J. A. KENNETT, LTD., WW, 9-11 Tottenham St., London W1P DEY, England, started making briar pipes back in 1862 and the present-day firm will send you a brochure showing eight of its most popular models. Prices seem quite moderate compared to some other briars I've seen—mostly under $8.00. Two of the models have special mouthpieces for denture wearers.

SWITZER AND CO., LTD., WW, Grafton and Wicklow Sts., Dublin 2, Ireland, sells Peterson pipes, from less than $3.00 for a typical Irish clay pipe, to around

$12.00 for their deluxe version or the handcarved meerschaum. Irish tobacco is available, too.

NURHAN CEVAHIR, WW, Istiklâl Caddesi Bekar Sokak No. 12/4, Beyoglu, Istanbul, Turkey, offers an attractive little pack of brochures showing the meerschaum pipes they sell, starting at $4.00, with a tops of $18.00 for their most elaborate model. There are pipes in the shape of a tulip, Cleopatra's head, a mermaid, a lion, a dragon's head, and Abraham Lincoln. Also available are plain and fancy cigarette holders.

Many of the firms described in Chapter 11 sell pipes and cigarette holders as part of their handicrafts line. You can get ivory ones from **HAKUSUI** and **TSANG KING KEE,** and bone cigarette holders from **ORIENTAL HANDICRAFTS. SERENDIB** has ironwood and ebony pipes with bowls in the shape of elephant, lion, and monkey heads. They're around $3.00, but I'm not sure they're actually smokable. The same goes for the ebony lion-headed cigarette holder, but what do you want for less than a buck?

Many of the American Indian firms sell Indian Pipes. Among them are the **PIPESTONE INDIAN SHRINE ASSOCIATION,** WW, Pipestone National Monument, Pipestone, Minn. 56164, which sells 20 different types of Indian pipes, which I assume are practical as well as authentic. Prices range from $5.00 to $100.00, and the descriptive brochure gives a history for each. Pipestone also sells beaded pipe bags at $35.00. **PEYE'SHA TRADERS** and the **BLACK MOUNTAIN TRADING POST** (see Chapters 3, 17) sell pipes made of red pipestone (also known as catlinite) at prices ranging from $10.00 to $50.00. Black Mountain sells seventeenth-century style tomahawks that may also be smoked.

C. SNUFF AND ALTERNATIVES

G. SMITH AND SONS, WW, 74 Charing Cross Rd., London WC2H OBG, England, sell over four different types of snuff, available in miniature bottles and pocket tins at around 30¢ to 50¢, or by the oz., from around $2.50 up. They have names like *Town Clerk* ("a subtle blend of floral and aromatic oils") and *Consort* ("a rich dark snuff fairly coarse milled and slightly scented"). They also sell tobacco and snuffboxes.

DEAN SWIFT, LTD., WW, Box 2009, San Francisco, Cal. 94126, offers fancy snuffs at prices that look good to me—small dispenser tins at 35¢ each, ½-oz. tins are $1.00 each, 1-oz. tins $1.75. There are a dozen varieties with such alluring names and descriptions as *Boswell's Best* ("a delicate though masculine snuff laced with Attar of Rose"). Also purveyed are "Snuffboxes—Chaste and Ornate," from $5.00 up. The brochures not only give prices, but such information and advice as: "A switch to snuff is the easiest way to quit smoking and certainly the most elegant, attractive, and attention-getting way of quitting an offensive, unattractive, unmannerly, and noisome habit."

For something different, **ARTIKRAFTS,** WW, P.O. Box 1944, Bombay 1 BR, India, offers Indian snuff for around $9.00 per kilogram.

If you prefer to chew your tobacco, **JOLLEY FARMS,** WW, Dresden, Tenn. 38225, sells several varieties of chewing tobacco from $4.50 to $11.00 for 5 lbs. postpaid. They also have sweet, mild, and regular snuff, at $2.50 per lb. for the #1 grade; and smoking tobacco.

Remember: *Write for the catalog first.* All prices given were valid only at the time of writing and probably have been changed.

INDEX

INDEX